From original oil painting by Jennie Huls Lilyquist.

Jennie Huls Lilyquist

BITTER ROOT TRAILS III

Produced by the
Bitter Root Valley Historical Society
with the help of many volunteers

While being as accurate as possible,
we adhered to the following policy:

"I CANNOT TELL HOW THE TRUTH MAY BE,
I SAY THE TALE AS 'TWAS TOLD TO ME"

— Quote from "The Crutchfields of Montana" Story

Bitter Root Trails III

ISBN No. 0-912299-79-7 (Softcover)
ISBN No. 0-912299-80-0 (Hardcover)

Library of Congress Catalog Card Number 98-61500

Publishing Consultant: STONEYDALE PRESS, 523 Main Street, Stevensville, Montana 59870

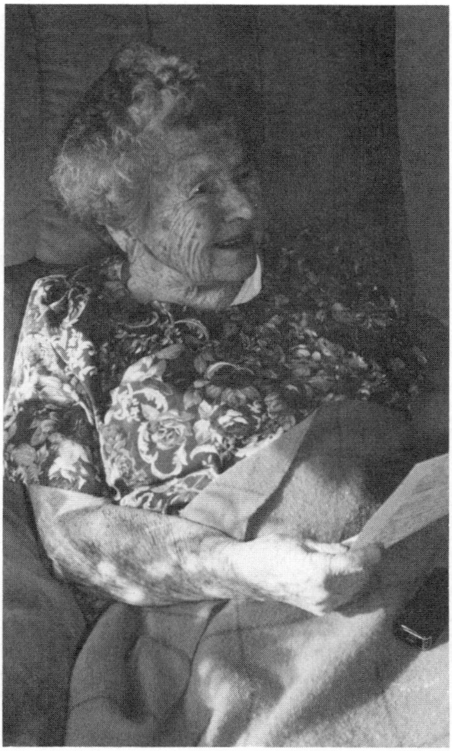

TRIBUTE

Even before the publication of Volume I and II, May Vallance was gathering stories, many of which are contained in this volume, for Volume III of Bitter Root Trails.

The vision and idea that a Volume III to cover Hamilton, Corvallis and Woodside could be possible can be attributed to May Vallance.

Her efforts and her dedication to the project are herewith acknowledged by the Bitter Root Historical Society.

* * * * * * *

The late Clarence Popham aided her efforts, and we add our appreciation for his time and historical perspective which led to a completion of this volume.

ACKNOWLEDGEMENT:

This Volume III of the Bitter Root Trails is the result of many hours of combined effort by a group of volunteers interested in preserving the personal history of the Bitter Root.

These "Bitter Rooters" include Roscoe Hall, Clarence Popham, Robert Talbot, Wilma Allen, Astrid Morris, Billie Linkletter and Dr. Donald Maclean.

They have encouraged old-timers and their descendants to write their family histories.

These stories and articles pertaining to the period from the mid-1880's to about 1920 have been typed, editing and compiled into this book as a continuation of Bitter Root Trails, Volume I and II. The area covered is from south of Hamilton to north of Corvallis, east and west sides of the River.

Special acknowledgement is made to Jennie Huls Lilyquest for the paintings of the Bitter Root flowers.

1906 Indian encampment.

1905. Haying the Bitter Root Valley. The Elihue Hall family.

Off to the Ravalli County Fair! Sign points to Marcus Avenue east of Hamilton.

Emil LeChambre's blacksmith shop, Hamilton. Now Cybernet Computers, North Second.

H. H. Spaulding Grocery on North Second under the I.O.O.F. Hall. Now Red's Office Supply.

Valley Mercantile. Burned in 1937. Now Bowser Building, southwest corner of Second and Main.

Hamilton City Hall, Built in 1906. Now Hamilton Fire Hall.

Table of Contents

Chapter One

About Ravalli County

EDWIN C. SMALLEY

Early day druggist. Father of Ravalli County.

Edwin C. Smalley was born in Ohio, in 1846, and was the sixth child of a family of eight. He started in the drug business at the age of 22, and had various Drug Stores in the east,before coming west to Montana in 1880, and starting a Drug Store in Stevensville.

Mr. Smalley was elected in 1892 as one of the Missoula County Representatives to the Montana State Legislature. He was Chairman of the Committee on Towns, Counties, and Highways in the State Legislature when he introduced a bill to establish the County of Bitter Root on January 11, 1893. The bill received its first two readings on January 13, 1893, and was ordered printed, according to the House Journal of the third Legislative Assembly of Montana. However, after passing through many sets of official hands and being read for a third time, Judge T. D. Fitzgerald of Anaconda moved that the name be changed to Ravalli. The amended bill was passed unanimously the next day. "The legislators rendered a graceful tribute to a worthy man when, on motion of Judge Fitzgerald, they changed the name of the new Bitter Root County to Ravalli" stated the Anaconda Standard on February 7, 1893.

The path to the division of Missoula county had not been without potholes. First there was the matter of the boundary. According to published accounts in the Western News, there was a "little mistake" in the original bill by which about 18 miles of the Northern Pacific Railroad near Bonita were erroneously included within the proposed new county. Evidentially, members of the Missoula legislative delegation discovered the blunder and had an amendment written, not only reclaiming the strip in question, but lopping five or six miles off the north end of the new county! Although the significance of the boundary change was called to the attention of valley representatives, G. W. Ward and E. C. Smalley, Bitterrooters felt the change was rammed through by Missoula interests before opposition could be mounted. "There is every probability that in the near future a railroad will go through the Lolo Pass, and this latest action will deprive Ravalli County of the taxes on many miles of the roadbed," the Western News reported.

"It is said that the Missoula schemers, when the first error was noticed, saw an opportunity to benefit themselves in the future, at our expense, and that the amended bill was framed by one of their smart lawyers with this object in view, and assisted by a select body of Missoula rustlers, was hastened through the Senate before its real significance became known here...Missoula took an underhanded advantage of the situation and the late hour, to rob us of our just rights. Let our people remember this," the newspaper said.

Stevensville was named as the provisional seat of the new county, a proposition which was to be reviewed in two years. The Western News, published then in Stevensville, sounded confident that the town would grow and become the permanent county seat. Stevites were less than thrilled when Hamilton received the coveted designation as county seat. While no concrete evidence was ever introduced, rumor had it that some of the county records were "lost" in the transfer from Stevensville to Hamilton.

THE BILL THAT CREATED RAVALLI COUNTY CONTAINED THE NAMES OF THE FIRST OFFICERS AND THEIR ANNUAL SALARIES:

Thomas Irvin,	Sheriff	$2,700
John A. Landrum	Treasurer	$2,200
Charles Johnson	County Clerk	$2,200
J. H. Simpson	Assessor	$1,800
R. Gwinn	Clerk of Court	$1,500
K. L. Knapp	County Attorney	$1,200
J. J. Bond	County Supt. of Schools	$1,000

NO SALARIES WERE GIVEN FOR THESE OFFICERS:

County Commissioners,	J. M. Johnson, B. S. Chaffin, and Abe Mittower
Coroner	T. B. Owens
Surveyor	G. T. Jones
Public Administrator	J. W. Lancaster

RAVALLI COUNTY

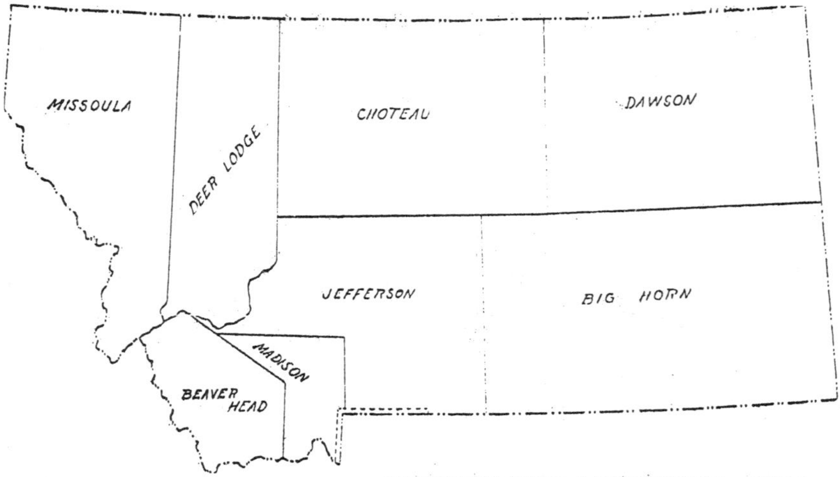

FIRST IDAHO ASSEMBLY – 1864

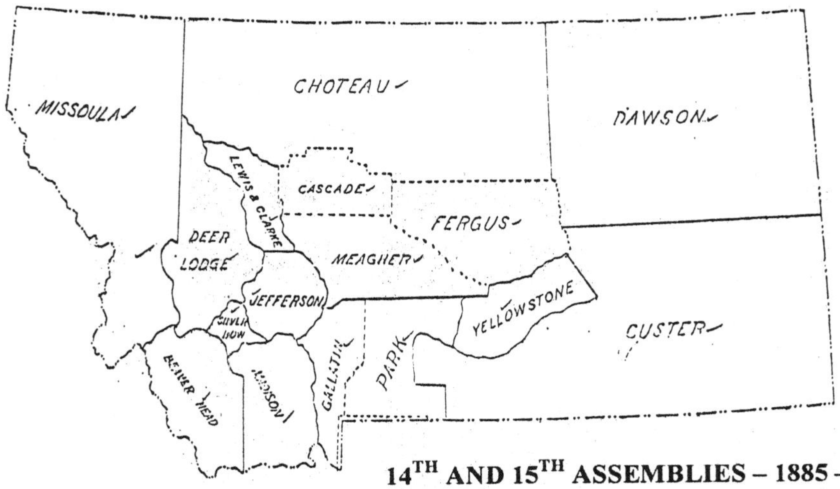

14TH AND 15TH ASSEMBLIES – 1885 – 1887

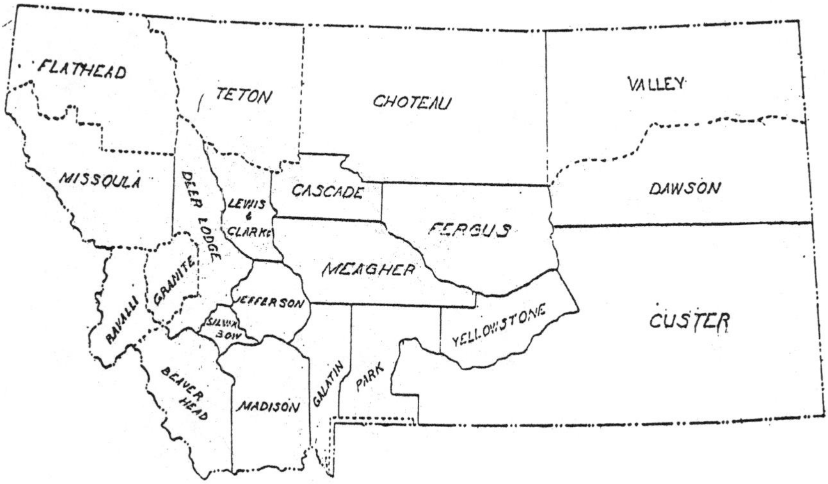

1ST AND 2ND MONTANA STATE ASSEMBLIES
1889 - 1893

PRICES PAID FOR COMMODITIES:

APRIL 1888

1 SACK FLOUR	$1.50
29# PORK	$4.35
4# RICE	$0.50
8# SUGAR	$1.00
30# POTATOES	$0.60
1 PKG BAKING SODA	$0.25
2 ½ # BUTTER	$1.25
15 # CABBAGE	$0.30
1 PAIR OVERALLS	$1.00
1 PR BOYS BOOTS	$3.75
2 DOZ. EGGS	$0.50
½ GAL SYRUP	$0.75
3 BARS SOAP	$0.30
8 # PARSNIPS	$0.36
1 TIN TOMATOES	$0.35
1 TIN MILK	$0.35
1 CASE TOMATOES	$3.75
60# LARD	$6.60

Early Day display of fruits and vegetables.

May 23, 1891, Statement from **O. C. Cooper and Company, Grantsdale, Montana, General Merchandise**

June 9, 1891		1893	
15 # beans	$0.75	70 # beef	$3.50
5 # coffee	$1.50	1 hind qtr, 84 # @.06	$5.04
25 # bacon	$3.13	1 front qtr 90 # @ .05	$4.50
8 # rolled oats	$0.50		
5 boxes bluing	$0.25		
1 whip	$1.25		

BITTER ROOT VALLEY STAGE COACH ROAD OF 1867

A petition signed by residents of the Bitter Root Valley was filed with the Missoula County Commissioners on May 6, 1867, for a road to be established and laid out from Missoula to Skalkaho. The petition was approved; Thomas Harris, John Slack, and George Wentworth were appointed to locate the road, the first for the area — other than Indian trails.

The road started in Missoula, and extended south through the Miller ranch on lower Miller Creek, and from there climbed the steep hill to the bench lands east of the Bitter Root River. Dropping down to Davis Creek, the route followed the creek to its junction with the river, crossing the latter at a ford about one and one-half miles northeast of Lolo. From Lolo it followed much the same route as the present U. S. Highway 93 south, to the Robert Carlton ranch. The ranch was located in what became the center of the little town of Carlton a few years later, in the area surrounding the present Florence-Carlton Community Church. A big red barn across the road from the Carlton farmhouse served as the stage coach stop. Here the freighters horses were rested, fed, and sheltered for the night when necessary. Traveler's bedrolls could be rolled out under the wagons, or in the barn itself, in severe weather. Both the barn and farmhouse are still standing.

The stage coach route continued south across the William Gleason farm and the A. B. Boltz farm and then across the land that later became the ranch of James Luby, Sr. The latter built his house on the east and his barns on the west sides of this road. The road crossed the Bitter Root River at the McKeen Ford, named for the ranch where it was located, approximately east of the present Bass Creek road. It then followed the eastside of the river through the Chatfield ranch, on past the Hangman's Tree where in January of 1864, the Virginia City Vigilantes had hanged "Whisky Bill Graves", and on south along the Francois (Fransway) Slough. Here stood the sweathouses and small huts of the Salish, built on the bank conveniently for plunging their hot, sweating bodies into the cold water. Just south of the slough, the road passed the Salish ceremonial grounds, where the young Indian men were taught the many tribal dances for different occasions. All this latter part of the stage coach route ran through land now part of the Ravalli (Lee Metcalf) National Wildlife Refuge.

The road continued south to the Fort Owen Trading Post and to Stevensville, which latter had been laid out in 1864; it then went south some ten miles to the settlement of Chaffinsville. It reached the present site of Corvallis at the John Slack ranch, and the area east of Hamilton at the Gird Creek settlement. (Hamilton was not established by Marcus Daly for another 25 years.) The road finally ended at the Skalkaho area on the flats at the mouth of Skalkaho Valley on the spot where H. H. Grant founded the community of Grantsdale a few years later.

Researched by: Luther Stanley, December 1969

RAILS INTO THE BITTER ROOT VALLEY

By Scott Nicholson, February 28, 1998

When the Northern Pacific Railroad (NPR) tracks reached Missoula in June of 1883, talk began immediately of many branch lines radiating out of Missoula. The most promising of these proposed branches was south to the Bitter Root Valley with its rich farm ground, rudimentary mining activity, and easily accessible timber. Charter prohibited the Northern Pacific from building any branch line, but there was nothing stopping them from purchasing lines, after they had been built. Over the next two years, several half-hearted attempts were made to construct a branch south, but most lacked the necessary capital or the means to secure it.

In the summer of 1886, Samuel T. Hauser, A. B. Hammond, R. A. Eddy, E. L. Bonner, and other investors from Missoula and the Bitter Root Valley formed the Missoula & Bitter Root Valley Railroad Company. The project was to be partially financed by the Northern Pacific and would be sold to NPR upon completion.

Serious survey work was started in August of 1886. The NPR survey team favored a route along the eastside of the Valley, through the existing communities of Stevensville and Corvallis. (This route was also the route surveyed by the Missoula & Bitter Root Electric Railway in 1907.) Hauser and Hammond's interests in the mining activity at Victor and available timber moved the route to the West Side of the Valley, through Tyler, Victor, and

Mill Creek.

The Missoula and Bitter Root Valley Railroad was incorporated in January of 1887, with construction starting on May 17, 1887. By October 1887, the bridge over the Bitter Root River was completed. The rails reached Victor in December of 1887, and the line was opened for limited business. The line made it to Mill Creek by January 1888. In February 1888, work began on the river bridge at Sanders Ford, which is just north of today's Silver Bridge north of Hamilton. **On June 9, 1888, the Missoula & Bitter Root Railroad reached Grantsdale, and was declared completed**.

By Deed dated September 7, 1888, the Missoula & Bitter Root Railroad Company conveyed all its property to Northern Pacific and Montana Railroad Company. Then, April 21, 1898, Northern Pacific and Montana Railroad Company conveyed all its property to the Northern Pacific Railway Company.

The Northern Pacific extended the branch six miles beyond Grantsdale to Judds Hill (Charlos Heights) in 1900.

In 1904, the newspapers were abuzz with the news that the Bitter Root Branch was soon to become the **new NP mainline, with a direct line linking Missoula to Portland, Oregon.** As the excitement built among the Valley residents, the NP officials admitted that the expansion was going to happen, but they had only contracted a 14-mile extension to Darby. This is the furthest south that the NP rails were ever built.

By the early 1920's, the easy timber supply was dwindling and a new cash crop, sugar beets, was catching on. This change prompted the Northern Pacific to move the branch to the East Side of the Valley, to be closer to the growing area. This line was completed on September 2, 1928, just in time for the beet harvest. The eastside line was built on the right-of-way secured by the aborted Missoula & Bitter Root Electric Railway. The re-alignment swung east at Kenspur (south of Florence) across to the East Side of the Bitter Root River, and rejoined the old main at Riverside (north of Hamilton).

By 1935, the NP moved its passenger and mail traffic from the rails to its bus line, ending 48 years of passenger trains on the Bitter Root Branch. By 1959, the NP had closed the depots at Post (Fort Missoula), Carlton (Florence), Corvallis, and Charlos Heights.

Throughout the 1950's, 60's, and 70's, the traffic on the branch continued to decline. In 1971, the Northern Pacific, Great Northern, Burlington, and the Spokane, Portland & Seattle merged to create the Burlington Northern, shortly after the last sugar beets were shipped out of the Valley.

By the 1980's, the traffic had diminished to one train a week and from all appearances the branch had outlived its usefulness. Burlington Northern was making plans to abandon all trackage south of Missoula. But, in 1987, shortly after receiving a new lease on life from a new owner, Montana Rail Link, and a national re-birth, the Bitter Root Branch quietly turned 100 years old.

MISSOULA & BITTER ROOT VALLEY ELECTRIC RAILWAY

In late 1906, rumors began floating about the greater Missoula & Bitter Root Valley areas about a new electric railroad being proposed. As per the community based rumor mill, the new railroad was going to be a fast link connecting Hamilton to Spokane, via Kalispell. Residents of the communities served by the Bitter Root Branch of the Northern Pacific were elated with the prospect of having an alternative to the poor service and high rates charged by the NP. No "official" news of a new railroad was published until February 27, 1907. The headline in The Western News read: "ELECTRIC Line — Plan is presented to the Missoula Chamber of Commerce by John Magee — Committee Appointed to Investigate."

Mr. Magee proposed that stock would be sold locally to fund the preliminary work needed to secure the funding from the east to build the 47 mile between Hamilton and Missoula (note, no mention of Kalispell or Spokane), at an estimated cost of $600,000.00. He also proposed to run the rails along the East Side of the Valley, serving Corvallis and Stevensville, which were bypassed by the NP. The roadbed would be built to handle both

Northern Pacific Locomotive 764 wrecked near Florence in 1899. Engineer Beebe was killed. The ancient wrecking crane is one of the first used by the railroad.

passenger and freight traffic. The alignment would also be built to permit a 75 mile–per–hour time schedule.

By March 6, 1907, The Western News headlines now proclaimed, "THE ELECTRIC RAILROAD WILL BE BUILT FOR SURE — The Mass Meeting Held Last Friday Night was Enthusiastic Affair — Over Seven Thousand Dollars has Been Raised." At this meeting, Mayor McCracken of Hamilton appointed a committee not to investigate, but to solicit subscriptions to fund the preliminary work.

The March 27, 1907, The Western News read "THE ELECTRIC RAILWAY IS INCORPORATED — Board of Directors Chosen and Promoters are Now Busy Securing Contracts — Plenty of Money for Preliminary Work". The article stated that there should not be any difficulty in securing necessary freight contracts and right-of-way as electric rates for both freight and passenger is guaranteed to be twenty-five per cent lower than that of steam. (An NP ticket to Missoula at this time is a whopping $.35 cents.)

April 10, 1907, The Western News stated, "GOOD PROGRESS MADE ON THE ELECTRIC ROAD — The Surveys are About Completed — Freight contract and Right-of-Way in Sight — Magee Goes East to Finance the Road." The article goes on to say that eleven miles of right-of-way had been secured without any opposition and that Mrs. Daly would donate a right-of-way across her property. This is the last news article concerning the Electric Railway to be found in The Western News files. Although the right-of-way was secured most of the way to Stevensville, there is no record of any construction taking place. This right-of-way was the basis of the route the NP used in relocating their line to the Eastside of the Bitter Root River in 1928.

Chapter Two

Towns, Schools and Villages

CORVALLIS

Excerpts from The Western News, Hamilton, Montana, Tuesday, December 19, 1911

Corvallis is Backed by an Incredibly Productive District

Nature gave to the present site of Corvallis a charm that, half a century ago, allured the first comers to the Bitter Root valley. To the travel-weary pioneers who had crossed the plains, it beamed like an oasis in the desert. There were grass-covered levels, land that could be converted easily into growing fields, great trees that invited with their shade—it seemed altogether a place suited admirably to their needs.

For the men and women that first peopled the Bitter Root valley, settling at Corvallis and Stevensville, were not gold-seekers. They were not of that great, picturesque horde of argonauts that, more than ten years before had rushed madly across the desert in a promiscuous scramble for the treasures of the Sierras. Some of these, it is true, stopped at the breakwater, turned their faces eastward and disappointed, sought solace in the soil; but few found their way into the Bitter Root.

Not so romantic as these, perhaps, but steadier and more easy to please, the pioneers who halted in the neighborhood of Corvallis in the early 1860s, were in quest of land. Inherent restlessness had sent them west. They were in search of room, freedom—in which the West abounded.

They were headed for Oregon, most of them, or there were other settlements which beckoned them. The Bitter Root was, metaphorically, a halfway house. Many stopped here and went on later to Oregon, only to come back. They could find no other place so favored.

And the judgment of the old-timers has been vindicated. Well did they choose. The land they selected near Corvallis was, for the purpose's sought, the best to be obtained. There is no disputing that the land between Corvallis and Victor is, for agricultural crops, the best in the Bitter Root valley. Its yields of grain and hay have been enormous, almost incredible.

Behind Corvallis, the thing that gives the business of the town firmness and stability, is a great body of agricultural land that, for sheer productivity, is scarcely equaled in the world. This has been its life-spring in the past and is to be the reliance of the future.

The development of the east bench, as a result of the building of the big canal of the Bitter Root Valley Irrigation Company, has given the town a new source of support that will, in a few years, immensely swell the volume of its business. Hundreds of acres of new orchards have been planted in this district, which is destined to be one of the most important fruit growing sections of the whole valley.

Corvallis was a settlement before it was a village. The area was favored by both Indians and early settlers (see Mose Chaffin story). Cantonment Stevens was perhaps the first, as John Mullan established and maintained winter quarters in 1853 and 1854, from which to make certain observations and explorations to find an overland route to the Columbia River. The party headed by Lt. Mullan erected four cabins at a big spring on the Willow Creek.

In 1864, the Slack, Mitchell, and Chaffin families formed an area known as Chaffinville. In 1865, Willow Creek Town Company was formed and the town of Willow Creek was surveyed into lots, blocks, and squares, with water rights from Willow Creek and Gird Creek.

Apparently, the people moving into the area rejected the different names, and when Thomas Rollin established a store in 1869, the name Corvallis was given to the village. The name was a "coined" name meaning "Heart of the Valley", and was given to the town by a Frenchman named Herron. This name was accepted by the people.

THE OLD FORT

One of the distinctive landmarks of Corvallis in early days was a large fort built as a refuge for the citizens against the Nez Perce Indians, who, under Chief Joseph, swept through the valley in 1877. The fort was built of turf and was strongly constructed. It was so arranged that a man on the inside could shoot along the sides or ends. On the outside, a stockage of sharp-pointed fence rails was placed, the spear-like ends pointing outward, to ward off an attack by horse. This made the fortification almost impregnable. The enclosure was used as a refuge for but a short time, the citizens and their families camping inside in tents. When the Nez Perce passed through the valley, there were but ten men inside to protect the women and children, the others being away fighting the Indians, but the fort was not attacked. The redskins sized it up as they passed through and let it alone.

Editors' Note: Fort Corvallis was located in the general neighborhood of the present location of the Ravalli County Electric Cooperative building on the north side of Corvallis alongside the east side of Corvallis County highway. Some years ago, the site was marked at a point about 25 yards north of the present REA structure, with a granite rock, upon which was placed a copper plaque which was inscribed with the following wording: "This monument marks the site of Fort Corvallis, erected July 1877, by the early settlers of Corvallis community for protection from the Indians." This stone was placed by the Corvallis Women's Federated Club on December 1, 1928. It was generally agreed by old-timers that the actual site of the fort could not be pinpointed, but was somewhere thereabout. Originally, it was believed to have been farther north of the building; then, the spot where the marker had been placed in 1928 was determined as the proper location. The monument is now located on REA property in front of the building and probably as close to the actual site as is possible. It was moved to the present location in 1954, when the REA building was constructed.

THE FIRST STORE

Thomas Rollins, in 1869, opened the first store in Corvallis, a primitive mercantile institute. He was not in business long before competition threatened. The late J. W. Winslett, afterward of Stevensville, had lumber hauled for the purpose of constructing a store building. This action so enraged Rollins that he hunted up Winslett, "licked" him, as history records, and kept control of the field. This was the first instance of restraint of trade practiced in the valley. Winslett was compelled to move his lumber to a site in what was afterward the old Wehr field. The structure he reared at this point served as the first schoolhouse in Corvallis.

Although, enjoying an unrestricted monopoly, Rollins went broke and was succeeded by William McWhirk, who moved from Missoula, at that time a straggling village at the mouth of Hellgate Canyon. One Blake established the first blacksmith shop and "Doc" Tibbey ran the first saloon. A legend, which few are living to refute, is to the effect that this first rum shop was liberally patronized. The only trading point south of Stevensville, Corvallis grew and was at one time, the largest town in the valley.

Looking south on Second Street, Corvallis, Montana.

It was in 1885, that the Eddy-Hammond Company, now Missoula Mercantile Company, entered the merchandise field in Corvallis by taking over the business of William McWhirk. Dan Ross, now postmaster of Missoula, was placed in the store as manager. He later was succeeded by George W. Dougherty, who, after managing the business for a number of years, gave way to John Price. Dougherty started a store of his own, which he afterward sold to T. J. Hefling, and Price went to victor and later to Missoula, where he now resides. Joseph Bowden succeeded Price, managing the store for five years and then taking it over on his own account.
(His story is told elsewhere in this book). One of the pioneer mercantile firms of the town was that of Cowan & Young and another was that of Bishop & Fowler. Many different merchants have operated in Corvallis. (His story is told elsewhere in this book).

CHANGE AND IMPROVEMENT

By 1911, Corvallis itself, as well as the surrounding country, had made material advances toward those appearances and conveniences that go to make up a town's outward aspect. Its business houses, homes, and many of the farmhouses in the immediate country were supplied with electric lights, telephone, and other modern appliances and creature comforts. New buildings, notably the structure built by Dr. C. R. Thorton and Guy

Blacksmith shop in Corvallis.

Cochrane to house the Corvallis Drug store and the post office, were evidence that growth was slow but substantial. The census of its business houses included a bank, three general stores, a drug store, a hotel, a restaurant, two barbershops, two blacksmith shops, a millinery, a pool hall and two saloons.

HISTORY OF SCHOOLS IN CORVALLIS

By Edna Johnson Thomas in 1975-1976

Longtime resident and school teacher for whom The Edna Thomas School is named.

My information about schools in Corvallis has been gleaned from three sources which are newspaper articles, a booklet put out by the 8th grade students of Russell Bay in 1952, and from my own experiences.

In 1867, the first school was kept by a man named Wood, it being the first school in Missoula County (there was no Ravalli County at this time) becoming District # 1, as it is now. The first Community Schoolhouse stood a mile north and slightly west of the present townsite. In the early 1870's the

Corvallis baseball town team, 1908. Top Row, Rube Millian, Joe Bowden, Dudley Bowden; Midle row, Carl Magni, Irwin Green, Jamie "Curly" Lear, Fred Reilly, Ole Simmons. Bottom row, Charley (?), Lee Simmons, Artie Holt, Mark Hall.

Former teacher, EDNA THOMAS, stands in front of the school building named for her, THE EDNA THOMAS MIDDLE SCHOOL. This structure was built in 1972 and dedicated to Mrs. Thomas in appreciation for the 28 years she taught Corvallis first graders (1943-1971).

school was moved to the site of the former Charles G. Johnson home, which is near the high school.

The next schoolhouse was built where the present Primary Building now stands. I could not find the exact date, but it must have been in the early 1880's, because the younger members of my mother's family attended school there. Later, there were more rooms added to the south side. I do not have information concerning the first graduation class. There were only 3 or 4 members in that class.

In 1914, the Corvallis Consolidated School was created by uniting Mountain View (near the present Swanson home), Willow Creek School, and Woodside School (Fairplay, of the Dutch Hill area). Later the Hamilton Heights, Birch Creek and Dominic schools also consolidated with Corvallis.

A new brick school was built which was occupied in 1915-1916, giving Corvallis an accredited High School. This building had a gymnasium on the top floor (third story). There are pictures owned by some families in the community showing the move from the old school to the new. I went to school in first and second grades in 1916-1917, in the old school. The schoolyard was fenced and many trees bordered the grounds. In the early 1950's, many of these trees were chopped down, and the fence taken out. There was a stile instead of a gate at the front entrance to the playground. There was a pump outside where we got our drinking water. We each carried our own cup with us. There were swings and teeter-totters. The grounds were used all the year around for play and picnics as it still is. At that time there were no school buses. Wagons drawn by horses brought the children in. I remember that sometime in the 1920's school trucks were used, then we became really modern sometime later with blue school buses, until state law required yellow, as this color was easier to see.

When I was in the third grade, we went to the brick building until I finished high school in 1927. At one time we had a hot lunch program in the basement.

During my high school days, there was a girl's basketball team. The first football team was organized in that time, too. Once a week, we had movies in the evening. There were four high school teachers and eight grade school teachers.

In 1930, on January 14th, the brick school at the end of Main Street burned to the ground. It was below zero weather. Many children lost their coats and boots. There was no fire fighting equipment at that time. I was teaching my first year at the Hamilton Heights country school and about noon, a lady came to the schoolhouse to tell me about the fire. I was worried about our home which was next door to the school, and found out later that a bucket brigade had been used to save it. People in town gathered up extra coats and boots in their homes to take care of the children who had lost theirs.

As a result of this disaster, every available place in town was used for classrooms; the old frame schoolhouse, Masonic building, Methodist Church annex, and the Community House. No lives were lost in the fire, and the

January, 1915. Students moving into the new school building. This building burned in 1930.

class of 1930 graduated without a schoolhouse. My sister, Irene Johnson Hickey, was in this class.

In May (1930), the $55,000.00 school bonds were sold at 5% interest. The bonds were voted on by freeholders of the district, 135 for and 8 against. The insurance on the building, $25,000.00, was used toward equipping the new building. By September the new school, which is the present High School, was ready for occupancy.

In 1940, the old frame building was torn down and at the same site the Primary Building was built and again some of the grades had to occupy available places in town. By fall, the building was ready for the first four grades with a playroom downstairs which was the entire south side, and another room on the north where the Women's Club met. It wasn't long until a hot lunch program was set up in the north part of the basement and the south part was used for high school shop.

In 1948-1949, the present dining room, Home Economics, Shop, and classrooms were built. This was called the Vo-Ag Building.

The basement in the Primary building was divided into three classrooms. At one time one of them was a library which is now true in 1975-1976.

Finally, because of new standards, the first six grades were divided into two classes each, making a need for twelve classrooms where only six

Corvallis High School burns, January 14, 1930, leaving many students without precious clothing they had just received as Christmas presents. No lives were lost, and the building was re-built.

were needed before, and also a need for more teachers. Instead of forty to fifty students in a classroom, there were twenty to twenty-five.

In 1943, I started teaching in Corvallis. There were fifty-three first graders in my class that year. In 1944, I had forty-seven pupils. In 1945, there was the beginning of combination rooms in the Primary grades. For twenty-eight years, I taught first grade in Corvallis.

During the years from 1915-1948, four schoolhouses were built. The original 1915-1916 school, rebuilt when destroyed by fire, old frame school torn down and replaced by Primary Building, and the Vo-Ag Building. These years included the bleak 1920's, when banks went broke, Depression years of the 1930's, and World War II.

In 1971-1972, a new Elementary Building was built. In 1976, plans were made for a new gym, music, and science complex. The bond issue for that was defeated at the June 1, 1976, election. State law standards are bringing pressure on schools.

At the present time, the Primary Building has two first grades, and two second grades on the first floor; a library, a storeroom, a supply room, and also a room where movies and strip films are shown. It can be used for P. E. in inclement weather.

In September 1976, a kindergarten will be added to the system. There are now eight school buses.

There have been many changes. Twice as many teachers, also a part-time speech therapist, part-time Psychologist, a full-time Special Education teacher, and several tutors. There are four custodians. The school board having foresight, bought land in prior years. There are twenty acres of lawn, a track, and several ball diamonds.

HISTORY OF SCHOOLS IN CORVALLIS

Information received from Ed Gibbons about 1952.

The first Corvallis school was a log cabin with one small room. Carl Jones (or Garl Jones), an old man with white whiskers, was the teacher. When this building became too small for the number of pupils attending, the farmers bought a building which Joe Blodgett (great uncle of high school principal and Coach Max Blodgett) had started to build for a store but had never finished. This store was to be located on the site of the present R. D. Geisy home. About the time that Mr. Blodgett started it, the townsite of Corvallis was plotted. He learned that the store would be out of town, so abandoned the partly built structure and sold it for a school. It took 12 pair of Cayuses to move it to the location of the Bob Johnson (son of Charles G. Johnson) residence about the year 1878. It is believed this was when the school district was formed. The building consisted of one large room with homemade desks, which seated two students, seats for the boys on one side of the room and for the girls on the other. The teacher's desk was also homemade.

About 20 students attended. The teacher was Miss Sue Asmouth, later Mrs. Jimmy Jones.

The next building, built in 1886, was located at the present College Avenue school site. The land was donated to the district by Emma and Naamen Johnson. The building consisted of 2 stories with one room upstairs and two downstairs. The schoolhouse was built by Tom Gibbons, Jim Barr, Jim Jones and Bob Martin.

DOMINIC SCHOOL

Excerpts from Bitterroot News article, 6-9-82, by Pat Perry

East and north of Corvallis, above the Big Ditch, in the dry, rolling foothills where nothing much seems to grow except rocks, sagebrush and winter wheat, there is a fairly new housing development.
This is north of Chaffin or Bald Butte. There are even a couple of houses up there. One might wonder who in the world would want to live up there. One might even get the idea that living up in that area is a new idea. It's not.

In the early 1900's, there were a number of families who lived north of Bald Butte. There was even a school for the children — **Dominic School.**

First Dominic School, about 1910.

Zola Treece, who was a long-time and well-known Corvallis resident, grew up around the Dominic area and says that life in those days was very good.

Zola's father, Charles Edson Smith, was a teacher who migrated with his family from Kansas to Montana about 1900. They settled in the valley and for a time he taught school. However, they later moved up to the Dominic area where there was land to be homesteaded. This area also had several good springs, which they would use for water.

The family made its living by growing wheat. Charles Edson Smith farmed about 200 acres and later owned more, his land extending to Birch Creek. The family raised a large garden and several patches of strawberries. These were irrigated with water from a spring and from a reservoir, which Smith built farther up the mountain. Zola believes that the produce was larger and tastier than that which is grown in the valley. Water from the spring was used to keep butter, milk, and other foods cold. The family also kept cows, chickens and pigs. Flour came from their own wheat. Zola's father would haul the wheat to Hamilton to the flourmill. Later on, Haufs ran a mill in Corvallis where Smith would have his flour made.

Every couple of weeks, a trip would be made by buggy to Corvallis to get other supplies that the family needed. Seven miles one way, the road used was the Soft Rock Creek Road. Less frequent trips were made to Hamilton, perhaps for some business at the courthouse, and every fall, wheat grown on the farm was exhibited at the Ravalli County Fair.

The Smith children walked the three-quarters of a mile to school, even when the snow got deep. Zola remembers once in March when the snow was three feet deep she was going with her future husband to a birthday party for his mother. He had to carry her through the snow.

One winter game that children of Dominic School loved to play was "Fox and Geese". A large circled was made by tramping around and around until the snow was packed down. Next, cross lines were made to dissect the circle so that the pattern tromped in the snow looked like a large wagon wheel. The person who was the "fox" had to catch all the "geese" and put them into the center of the circle. A player was caught if he was tagged. Players could only run in the tramped lines. Stepping out of the lines put a player **out,** and he had to get in the middle with the rest of the caught geese. One year the children played this game so much that they wore the snow off in the running lines completely down to the ground. The ground became so packed that the lines were still visible after the snow had all melted off and the children continued to play what was normally thought of as a winter-only game.

There were dances at the schoolhouse every two weeks, and, of course, school programs. Charles E. Smith was one of the school trustees for eight years. At a school board meeting during this period, there was an argument over the election. It became very heated, and a fellow by the name of Gerry pulled a knife and stabbed Mr. Smith several times in the back. Nothing legally was ever done about this assault.

Besides the 12 Smith children who went to the Dominic School, there were the Jenkins, White, Ward, LaFrance, Mace, and Wickham families. Some lived farther away than did the Smiths — and rode to school on horseback. One teacher was Mrs. Dorman, who had a daughter Katherine, and another teacher was Rose Cutler.

The little community in the hills eventually disappeared due to drought. After several years without enough rain to grow wheat, people left the area. Today, nothing much is left of the Dominic School or the Smith families log house and barn. Recently, a new interest in the area has begun, and new families are settling into this same area.

MOUNTAIN VIEW SCHOOL

Article in the Corvallis Echo, January 22, 1960
Information furnished by Mr. and Mrs. C. J. Swanson

Another of the predecessors of the Corvallis School District # 1, was the Mountain View School.

Construction of the Mountain View School was under the direction of Mr. Snyder, a Hamilton Heights contractor, and was started in the early fall of 1911. Unlike some of the early schools in our community, much of the equipment was bought with tax money from the newly formed district.

Mountain View School, 1914. Now Swanson's apple houses.

For a short period before the opening of the Mountain View School, some youngsters in the area went to a school held in a building known as "Cook's Shack", located on the present Joe Sutherland land. The Mountain View School, which still stands on its original location 5 miles north east of Corvallis, replaced this one. It was also attended by students who previously traveled to one of the other schools in the community.

The 28-foot by 34-foot structure included one main room and two cloakrooms. The first teacher was Louis Nelson, who still resides in the Corvallis community. (Note: in the spring of 1961, Mr. Nelson moved to Wisconsin.) His tenure was followed by that of Miss Neil and Miss Owing. Among the early students were representatives of the Snow, White, Holloron, Erickson, Nimerick, Huls, Jackman, and Wilcox families. Early school board members were H. K. White, Mr. Fisher, and Mr. Wilcox.

After consolidation with the Corvallis School district, the Mountain View school building served as a church. It was purchased by C. J. Swanson in 1919, and has been used as a storehouse since that time.

WILLOW CREEK SCHOOL

From article in the Corvallis Echo on December 1959
Information furnished by Boss Lockwood.

The first Willow Creek schoolhouse was built in about 1890 by the parents of the children who would attend the school.

William Humble donated the land, the northeast corner of present Vern Gardner pasture on Willow Creek. The seats, desks, teacher's table and chair were all handmade. The blackboard was painted lumber.

The first teacher was Ann Johnson of Corvallis. The pupils were Alice and Boss Lockwood; Maud and Ida Burch; Mary, Sarah, Tom, Maudie, and Henry Randolph; Maudy and Maggie Humble; Mattie Forsyth; Anna and Ella Strange; Burch Swaggart; Mattie and John Cavis; Clyde Whitesitt; and likely many others.

An addition was added a few years later. M. N. Whitesitt was the first clerk and G. G. Lockwood was one of the trustees.

Inez Whitesitt Hull and Frances Boyer Lockwood were the first eighth grade graduates from the school in 1904. A. B. Hoblitt was the teacher. The old school house was moved to the present Hansen home on Willow Creek, and a new one built in about 1905 or 1906. This building was used until consolidation with Corvallis.

Mr. and Mrs. Rissler (Ann Rissler Thomas) used the lumber from the building to rebuild their store in Corvallis which had burned down.

FAIRPLAY SCHOOL

From article in Western News, July 26, 1961

FAIRPLAY SCHOOL was situated up on "Dutch Hill", which is about two miles almost directly west from Woodside, Montana. The people, in that area in 1896, determined to have a school for their children and organized School District # 11 of Ravalli County under the laws of Montana. One acre of land was donated by John Hauf with the understanding that it would revert again to him should the district ever cease to operate the school. This acre was situated in the northeast corner of his ranch.

Shortly after the land was acquired, a one-room schoolhouse of good construction was built, and school started that autumn. The school was operated until March 20, 1914, when this school consolidated with Corvallis School District # 1 by a vote of the people. After that time the children attended school in the town of Corvallis.

As the school was used, it became too small to accommodate the growing number of children in the community which reached as far east as Woodside. There was no transportation of school children in those days so the children had to walk, in some cases several miles, to school. When the school became too small, another room was added and when it was determined to provide two years of high school studies, another room was added as well as a partial basement.

During these years, the building was far from being a school alone. It served as a community center for dances, polling place for school elections and for meetings of the Mill Creek Irrigation district, for basket socials and amateur theatricals and for church services.

After consolidation of the two school districts, the acre with the structure reverted to the former owner, John Hauf, and he used the building for a packinghouse during his apple harvest and as a storehouse for apples and most everything else.

As the years passed, vandals broke the windows and tore up property stored in the structure, until the Hauf heirs decided to sell the property. The building was acquired by John Maydole in 1947, who took it apart board by board and built a machine shop in Hamilton on River Street between North First and North Second Street. Later Russell Unrue operated a machine shop there. The building in 1961, is remodeled and used for church purposes by the Christ Bible church.

During the years of operation of the Fairplay school the following persons served as teachers: Frank Clifton; Minnie Whitticer; Della Keeling; Jason Jones; George B. Wold; Ruth Remington (now Wilcox); Minnie Bailey (now Law); Janet Walls; Essie Whitsitt; Nora Smithey; Carrie Iddings; Frances Higgins; Betty Johnson (now of Darby); Susie Sherwin; M. O. Mull; Clara Kramer; Bernice Jackson; Dixie Willson; Harvey Cope; Hazel

FORMER FAIR PLAY SCHOOL STUDENTS GATHER AT WOODSIDE GRANGE HALL.

(From a newspaper clipping)

At the July 22-23, 1961, initial meeting the committee in charge of the annual Fair Play picnic was Mrs. Louis (Ruth) Wolfe, Mrs. Frank (Nina) Rummel, Mr. and Mrs. Jay (Fern) Severns, Mr. and Mrs. Earl (Mima) Malone, Mr. and Mrs. Otis (Virginia) Talbot, Mrs. Mary Reynolds, Mrs. Hazel Young, Mrs. Ella Hall, Mrs. Vista Aishe. Thre were about 150 in attendance.

*In the 1904 picture students are identified as follows: bottom row, right to left, Lola Wing, *Hazel Blodgett, Hazel Severns, Myrtle Smith, Chrissy Wolff, Orvie Mace, Frank Rummel, George Garrard, *Dot McCloud, *Clinty Boughman, *Lloyd Lockwood, George Smith.*

*Second row, left to right: *Elmer Talbot, *Leonard Allnutt, *Feek Gunter, Otis Talbot, Ellen Popham, *Howard Moore, *Stacey Thompson, *George Rummel, Arthur Lyall, Jay Severns, Arthur Hauf, Claud Allnutt, William Garrard, *Arthur Popham.*

*Third Row, right to left: *Roy Mace, Charley Mace, *Theo Lockwood, *Henry Wolff, Edith Malone, Ada Johnson, Nina Malone, Ruth Moore, Mary Rummel, *Hazel Elliott, Laura Allnutt, Carrie Rummel, *Tim Garrard, *Alfred Kenny, Fred Luderman, *John Lockwood.*

*Sitting on porch rail: Frank Remington, *Tom Popham, *Henry Kares, *Rufus Johnson, Dave Popham.*

*Fourth row, right to left: *Clara Blodgett, Jane Hauf, Myrtle Miller, Cassie Turnage, May Talbot, Annie Aichele.*

*Back row, staggered: George Wold, teacher; Mollie Remington, *Clara Boughman, *Maud Miller, *Christine Kares, *Muriel Gunter, Ruth Remington, teacher; Elsie Rummel, Phyllis Johnson, Effie Blodgett, *Theresa Hauf, Lucinda Miller, Ethel Johnson. *Deceased.*

Herman; Clifton Jackson; Clare Gleason; Olive Waddell; Bethel Irwin.

DURING THE YEARS OF OPERATION AN ESTIMATED 300 PUPILS ATTENDED THE FAIRPLAY SCHOOL. A reunion occurred on July 22nd & July 23rd, 1961, held on the Corvallis School grounds with 132 registered former students, spouses, family and guests.

EARLY CORVALLIS CHURCHES

by Reverend Roger Robison

Many of the families who came from eastern and southern states to settle in the Bitter Root Valley were churchgoing folk who welcomed the efforts of traveling preachers to plant churches in the valley. But, the church was not an easy crop to cultivate.

The first attempt was made in 1871, when there were only a scattered few ranch families in the Willow Creek area and the first store had been opened by Thomas Rollins just two years earlier. It was the Southern Methodists who, under the leadership of Reverend L. B. Stateler, brought in half a dozen missionary preachers from Missouri, Illinois, and Kentucky. One of them, George O. Hilton, was assigned to "The Bitter Root Valley". A man in his thirties, he left his wife and children in Illinois and traveled by train to Corrine, Utah, then by coach to Montana Territory. He hoped to establish a congregation, to build a house for his family and enable them to join him. On December 22, 1871, he was cutting trees with Mr. Joseph Hull, with whom he was staying (the Hulls lived on Willow Creek road) and with others. A tree, which had lodged in another the day before, slipped and fell with great force, "striking him in different parts of the body," according to a report written later in the Journal of the Montana Conference. "He was immediately taken to the residence of Mr. Hull, where everything that kind friends could do for his relief was done. He gradually grew worse until five o'clock in the morning, when death released him from his sufferings. He was a plain, kind-hearted man, who had won his way into the hearts of the people". His remains were later moved into the present Corvallis cemetery, where his grave is marked by a "properly engraved and polished native stone placed there by the Montana Conference." After a lapse of several months, other Southern Methodist preachers were appointed to follow Hilton, but their charge also included Missoula, so there probably were no resident Methodist preachers for some time.

Methodist in the United States became divided over the slavery question in the 1840's, so there were two Methodist denominations. The northern branch, The Methodist Episcopal Church, was at work in Missoula. Thomas C. Iliff, the preacher who supervised the construction of a church building in Missoula in 1872 (at the time, the only Protestant Church building between Walla Walla and Helena), made some preaching tours in building between Walla Walla and Helena), made some preaching tours in the Bitter Root, gave the first "M.E." sermon in the Etna schoolhouse in 1871, and preached also in the schoolhouse at Corvallis, but it was the Southerners who persisted in trying to establish Bitter Root churches. Outside financial help was non-existent. The records of the 1884 session of the Montana annual Conference reflect the struggle.

"In February, 1874, there was a remarkable religious awakening at a meeting held in Corvallis by Revs. S. J. Catlin and C. W. Sanford. It was a sweeping revival, resulting in scores of conversions. . . A church building was commenced, but sad to relate, was never completed."

"In 1877, the Presiding Elder begged for permission to use $250.00 of missionary money then in his hands to complete a church building at Corvallis, but it was refused. The money was returned to the Board, the building blew down, and a grand opportunity for securing a house and establishing our church in that place was lost."

"In 1875, Rev. S. J. Catlin, Presiding Elder, received an appointment in Colorado and left the Territory soon after Conference. Also, R. M. Craven, pastor at Corvallis and Missoula, left his work to go with Catlin, which resulted in serious damage to the church."

"In 1877, E. J. Stanley, then the only Presiding Elder in the Territory, spent from one to two weeks on every charge. Through the united efforts of the Presiding Elder and the pastor, T. W. Flowers, (visiting from house to house and laboring earnestly day and night) the downward tendency of the church in the Bitter Root Valley was arrested and confidence revived."

CORVALLIS CHRISTIAN CHURCH. Built in 1883. Later called the "Community House." First church to be built south of Stevensville.

Methodist and Protestant-Episcopal leaders as they met on a hot, sultry day in the 1880's, as depicted by artist E. S. Paxson.

Reverend William D. Lear was the key figure in starting the Christian Church. In 1880, he came west from Iowa to Montana with a group that arrived in the Beaverhead Valley with four feet of snow and no shelter. For a time, he served the First Christian Church of Helena, but moved out to establish churches in Missoula, Florence, Stevensville, and Corvallis. In 1883, he returned to Iowa to bring his wife and son, Jamie, back to Montana. They came into Missoula on the first train to make it beyond Deer Lodge. He was a schoolteacher in Corvallis while he organized the church and helped to build the building (1883) which was then the only church building south of Stevensville. The Christian church building, later called the Community House, stands on the north east corner of the block which faces the elementary school.

The second church building in Corvallis was the Presbyterian, built in 1894, presently serving as the Corvallis Community Church. The founding pastor was Reverend Edwin H. Ellis. Finances were scarce, and the minister's salary was often paid "in kind," meaning wood, chickens, lard, beef, or labor. The Presbyterian Church sometimes exercised rather strict discipline. Records show, in one case, "Rev. Edwin Ellis, moderator, met with elders W. J. Popham and W. W. Lockwood. It was reported that Mr. W. had been repeatedly engaged in dancing. The members present were appointed to talk with Mr. W. and report at the next meeting. Mr. W. did not intend to abandon the dancing. He was not present to answer the charge. He was to be excluded from communion of the church for his continuance until he would repent."

The Methodist Episcopal Church, South, finally completed a building in 1894, a third church building for Corvallis. A key figure was Reverend E. J. Stanley. One of Bertie Lord's finest photos in the Ravalli County Museum collection shows Rev. Stanley and family in front of their tent, vacationing at Medicine Hot Springs in the 1890's. He had supervised the new building at Stevensville earlier, in 1882, then raised the necessary funds for the building in Corvallis.

E. S. Paxson, western artist, illustrated an incident in the 1880's, while Methodist services in Corvallis were conducted in the schoolhouse. Rev. E. J. Stanley's book, LIFE OF REV. L. B. STATELER, describes the incident. (pg. 280)

The Protestant Episcopal Church in Montana was under the leadership of Bishop D. S. Tuttle of Virginia City. . .He was one of the most energetic and popular men in the country. . . .For a long time it was common for other ministers to dismiss their services in honor of the bishop's visits. On one occasion, the bishop was in the Bitter Root Valley at the same time as some Methodist preachers were visiting. The Methodists held forth at Corvallis and the Episcopalians at Stevensville at 11 AM on Sunday, and were to exchange places at 4 PM. The two parties of preachers met about midway on this hot, sultry afternoon. Two of the Methodist preachers were riding in a brand-new top buggy drawn by two horses. The Bishop, accompanied by two other clergy, and a boy, was in an open, two-seated vehicle being drawn by one horse that sweated profusely. As they reined in for a moment of pleasant chat, the Bishop called out, "Oh, you rich Methodist parson, rushing along here in your two-horse buggy, while we poor Episcopalians have to go plodding along with one horse! How it that?" "Perhaps, you are one horse preachers," rejoined one of the parsons. "A-a-ah, that is it," responded the Bishop, and this was followed by a roar of laughter from his companions.

Head carpenter for the erection of the Methodist buildings was Thomas Gibbons. Construction had to be halted for several months when he fell from the top of the building frame and broke his leg. But, it was completed in time to house the Annual Conference session of the Methodist Church, South, in August of 1894.

John Edward (Ed) Gibbons was one of the five children of Thomas Gibbons. Ed lived almost all of his ninety-some years in Corvallis, starting on the homestead ranch a few miles east of Corvallis. Ed helped haul rock from the Soft Rock area for the Corvallis Drugstore and other buildings in town. He used four white horses to pull the rock wagon. For many years, Ed worked on the county road crew. After retiring, he operated a small gas station on the corner just across from the Methodist Church. We once asked Ed if he remembered the session of the Methodist Conference in 1894, when the building was dedicated. He responded, "I'll never forget it! That was the summer Mr. Humble raised an exceptionally good crop of watermelons. When he invited a group of his daughter's friends for a watermelon social, it seemed as though all the teenagers were invited except one other lad and myself. We made up our minds that they would be sorry to have slighted us! We rounded up eight horses and a bunch of gunnysacks, and late one night got into the watermelon patch from the back. What an uproar the next day! The party was called off and a $50.00 reward offered for the apprehension of the thieves! Some people suspected us, but they had no evidence. The next week was the Conference, and my parents had invited eleven visitors to stay at our ranch. On Sunday afternoon, Dad was showing them around. They congratulated him on his turkeys, calves, and other stock around the place. Suddenly, one of the preachers appeared from out of the fruit cellar with a huge melon in his hands. "Why Brother Gibbons, you've been holding out on us! Such a look as my father gave me, and such a tongue-lashing the next day! I'll say I remember that Conference!!"

In 1915, representatives of three congregations with buildings in Corvallis, along with some Baptists and Lutherans, decided to pool their resources to form a Federated Church. R. H. Farris, pastor of the Methodist Church, was chosen as pastor and served about six months. The Montana

Conference of the Methodist Episcopal Church, South, did not approve and threatened to dismiss him from the Methodist ministry. He reluctantly resigned, and along with most of the Methodist lay people, continued to worship and serve the community in the Methodist building on the east side highway. The others continued to meet together, first as the United Church, and later as the Corvallis Community Church. There were similar movements to form federations at Victor, Florence and Hamilton. The Corvallis Community Church decided to dissolve their denominational ties, but another plan was followed in the other places. The present Hamilton Church continues active involvement with the American Baptist and United Methodist denominations, alternating between the two when there is a change of pastors.

HAMILTON HISTORY IS LIKE AN OLD MENU MADE UP OF MANY UNFORGETTABLE DISHES

by Miles Romney for the Banque Club, Revised April 1976

The site which Marcus Daly picked for his town was not chosen carelessly. Daly acquired large acreage extending eastward from the Northern Pacific right-of-way in the area now known as Hamilton, which he consolidated into his Bitter Root Stock Farm. He erected Tammany Castle on one of the hills east of Hamilton, where a residence was erected for his ranch superintendents. It became known as Shannon Hill. Tammany Castle still stands, a little east of the residences of Mrs. Margit Bessenyey and Mrs. Theodore Fullerton.

On the other hill to the south, Daly had constructed a large barn-like building which was the horse hospital. It no longer stands. That hill now has a growing number of modern residences whose inhabitants possess a marvelous view of the Bitter Root mountain range which looks down upon Hamilton from the west.

Daly's stock farm was primarily the home of his racing stock. During his lifetime the racing stable he accumulated through purchases, both in this country and abroad, as well as thoroughbreeding upon the farm, became one of the foremost in the world. His horses Hamburg, Ogden, Tammany, and others won many of the principal stakes and sired race horses whose progeny are today winning laurels on the race tracks.

Daly, as a mining magnate in Butte and Anaconda, director of the Amalgamated Copper Co. operations in Montana, needed timber for the mines. He likewise needed a functioning community for his ranching and racing operations. The Hamilton site in proximity to his ranch, near the forests he and his company had acquired, was ideal for his purposes. He

Hamilton, Montana. Main Street 1893-1895, looking west. Hamilton Hotel on the southwest corner of Main Street and Highway 93. (Showell Photo)

acquired the four ranches which lay on the big flat between the river and the foothills to the east, had it platted Sept. 4, 1890, and incorporated in 1893. Daly named his town after one of his lieutenants, James W. Hamilton, not after Alexander Hamilton. Hamilton had acquired, for Daly, the farms of John M. Eastland, James B. Stevens, Samuel Hall and Tillman L. Adair. The land embraced within Hamilton's original boundaries comprised about 160 acres, 49 city blocks, and about 1032 lots.

The Hamilton site was located north and adjacent to the "Big Corral" which was an enclosure of land which fenced land belonging to John B. Catlin, D. C. Elliott, Pope Catlin, R. W. Nicol, L. E. Elliott, and Alex Nicol, embracing 1,100 acres. It included part of the present Hamilton townsite and land lying south of town. The Pine Grove, Hart, and Nicol additions were in the Big Corral. So was the Toole-Jones-Efteland View Acres — Moen property. The present Floyd Bailey residence is about the only structure still standing that existed in "Big Corral" days. It was the Elliott-Hart residence. The pioneers formed a sort of co-operative which they fenced with a "snake pole" fence, which made it possible for them to handle their herds of livestock together, to better advantage. The "Big Corral" was fenced in 1871, and thus long antedated Hamilton. When it was discarded, the Doran, Hart, and Nicol additions provided small acreages which provided homes for families, many of whom worked at the ACM sawmill and planer which Daly built north of the pond which resulted when his dam backed up the Bitter Root river, west of Hamilton.

Large crews of "river pigs", "lumberjacks", and "timber beasts" — all men — cut the timber along the river throughout the year and then ran it down the river, to the sawmill at Hamilton during high water. The "river runs" in a few seasons exhausted the timber adjacent to the river so the Northern Pacific, working with the Amalgamated Co., built railroad spurs into the timbered areas, mostly west and south of Hamilton, up the valley, and hauled the logs to Hamilton. A railroad spur led from the main line to the sawmill and pond down what is now Desta Street. Another spur went to the planer mill down River Street. Its vestigial remnants still persist.

The big mill operated most of the winter, six to seven months most years, providing work for about 200 men, who enjoyed long vacations the rest of the year, fished, maintained gardens and went into debt at the "company store" which carried them until the next pay day.

Daly had new buildings erected for his various enterprises. The Ravalli Hotel, a three story brick edifice was the center of the social life of the community, with huge lobby, large dining room, bar, billiard room, and office on the first floor and rooms on the two upper floors. The hotel was consumed by flames September 22, 1919. Daly also built a flour mill. It was operated at first by water power provided by a flume from the mill pond. The flour mill was located on land adjacent to the residence of Mr. and Mrs. John Parker, northwest of Hamilton. Their remodeled home was originally the residence of the manager of the mill. The flour mill burned to the ground on May 8, 1917.

Daly also needed a bank. For this, he built the structure which is the present home of The Banque. This building was erected in 1895. Until 1962, the building was the home of the Ravalli County Bank.

In the early days of Hamilton with the large population of workers in the woods, at the mill, the jockeys, trainers and camp followers of the racing stable, the large transient population, with a preponderance of males, it was inevitable that life would be rather turbulent. To provide entertainment and solace to the rough and tough population of cosmopolitan makeup, the town offered the hospitality of 23 saloons, a number of "parlor houses", and no less than three rows of cribs, where the "soiled doves" endeavored to calm the fevers of their patrons. Life was cheap and crime was common but never rampant, because justice proved stern.

Just what would have happened to Hamilton, had Daly lived, is an enigma which though fruitless to contemplate, is intriguing. But the father of the town died, a little after seven o'clock, at the New Netherlands Hotel in New York City, on Monday, November 12, 1900.

Following the founder's death, his widow almost immediately began liquidating her husband's racing stables. The running horses were shipped to

New York for sale the year following his death, the harness horses the next year, until there were soon only a handful of horses remaining. With the horses went the jockeys, trainers, and handlers. This brought to an end much of the high life of the community and the lights of the Red Light district went out one, by one until, after migrations to Venus Alley in Butte, to West Front street in Missoula, and other like areas, after mergers and closeouts, there finally remained in Hamilton only the red brick emporium operated for years by Mammy Smith. For some reason, the officials of the community and the bloodhounds of the law rarely discovered that this enterprise was operative, as it languished into oblivion after the death of Clara. Then for years the building stood almost vacated until the haunting memory was forever removed when it was razed.

During the years 1894-1898, there was much commotion in the Bitter Root over the location of the county seat. In the 1894 election Stevensville won over Corvallis by a vote of 953 to 727. Mr. Daly shrewdly kept Hamilton out of the initial race and had given ostensible support to Corvallis. As a consequence, when the next county election was held in 1898, Hamilton won handily, 1,119 to 616, and strange to note, Corvallis favored Hamilton 166 to 47 for Stevensville.

During the 1905-1911 years, Hamilton was the center of the so-called "Big Ditch Boom" days, as a group of Chicago financiers built the dam which impounded water in Lake Como, to provide irrigation water for their long canal which furnished water for lands they had acquired on the Bitter Root's east bench lands. Offices of the B. R. Irrigation Co., and its successors were located in Hamilton in the former Daly-built residence, now the Dowling Funeral Home. Hundreds of investors from the Midwest and other parts of the nation acquired orchard lands under the Big Ditch project. They came with funds expecting to make more from the production of McIntosh Red apples, and the Ravalli Hotel was busy. Business was good in Hamilton, prosperity was widespread, everything was merry. This story is long and runs from happy notes to sadness. But eventually the "Big Ditch" through funds provided by the U. S. Bureau of Reclamation and by operation as a farmer owned cooperative, has found stability. As the project flourished or faded, Hamilton felt the condition.

Beyond doubt the most important addition to Hamilton was the laboratory originally erected by the State of Montana and later taken over and expanded by the federal government. This multi-million dollar undertaking provided employment for approximately 170 workers, and brings scientists here from numerous foreign countries. It is not only the largest employer in Hamilton but one of the most important in Montana and its efforts have nation and world-wide significance. During World War II, all of the yellow fever vaccine used by American service forces was manufactured at this laboratory. It has conquered a number of vexing maladies including Rocky Mountain spotted fever and its possibilities of similar conquests over ailments of mankind continue great.

Hamilton is a city of wide streets, with trees of numerous varieties standing as sentinels along them. Main Street was paved with cement in 1927, and additions in 1928. Most of the remainder of the streets are oiled, and nearly all are lighted.

The first sewers in town were laid back of Main street in 1909-1910. Since then a city-wide sewer has been constructed with a disposal plant which protects the river from pollution.

The city is served by an excellent school system, embracing six modern schools, with an exceptional staff of 87 instructors and an enrollment of 1,608 this year of whom 568 are high school.

The elevation of Hamilton is 3,572 feet above sea level.

The yearly average mean temperature over the last 39 years has been 45.31 degrees, and the average precipitation for the same period has been 12.08 inches per year.

Some years the temperature never drops below zero, but in January 1931, and February 1934, the mercury sank to minus 36 degrees. Warmest reading recorded in Hamilton was in July 1931, with a 103 temperature recorded.

Always Hamilton has found an interest in good living. The old Ravalli

The Ravalli Hotel. Photo taken in 1910. The hotel burned in 1919.

Hotel provided culinary offerings which won wide recognition. Then there were the groaning tables at the establishment of Aunt Tish Nevins which brought gourmets to Hamilton from far places. Now there is The Banque, which herewith offers its guests the best of fine foods, expertly prepared in sumptuous quarters, with gentle reminders of the days that used to be.

In the "Good old days", woods workers and the boys from the race tracks invaded the city to find the red eye liquors vended in the numerous moist spots then extant. Times are different today although during 1975, the Montana Liquor Control Store sold $507,090.95 worth of alcoholic beverages. Now discriminating users of beverages can find them at our bar or tables served just as they like them, very dry, or very wet, and always the best.

THE TOWN OF RIVERSIDE

Ravalli County Museum Archives

When Riverside became a place, there was no Hamilton nor Ravalli County. It was a part of Missoula County and at that time, it was called Sanders Crossing. There was no post office and residents either called for their mail at Corvallis or at "Skalkaho", a post office operated at the Robert Nicol and Henry Chambers ranches south of the present site of Hamilton.

"Red Bridge" at the end of Adirondac Avenue, with mill in background.

Percy Edward's Meat Market. At left of Ed Wakeham, butcher, at right is John Russell, butcher.

Brunswick Pool Hall. Located on what is now the western half of Citizen's State Bank.

This was also prior to the establishment of a post office at Grantsdale.

George F. Brooks surveyed the area in December, 1888, and platted it into 15 blocks known as the town of Riverside for Benjamin F. Sanders, owner of the land. It became a booming hamlet because it was the site of the sawmill operated by James Hedge and was the terminus of the Northern Pacific branch from Missoula. Hedge operated the sawmill using logs brought down the Bitter Root River during the high water period each spring. Hedge was a businessman who homesteaded atop the hill formerly known as the Shannon Hill or Crawford Hill east of Hamilton.

He started construction of the irrigation canal, known as the Hedge Ditch, which took water from the River at the Rennaker bend east of Charlos, crossed Sleeping Child and irrigated for miles northerly down the valley. Marcus Daly bought the canal, enlarged it, and used it on his big ranch. It is still in use as part of the Daly Ditches system.

Riverside had a siding where Daly's horses were unloaded before being taken to the Home Ranch. The famed Tammany was unloaded here. Hedge erected and lived in the big two-story white house on the Eastside Highway south of the Brooks Hotel. While Riverside was "booming", it had a hotel owned by Civil War Veteran, Henry Page, who later moved it and expanded it in Hamilton as the Hamilton Hotel on the corner of Main and First Street. When the hotel was dismantled, the City Center Chevron was located there. The town also had a Chinese operated restaurant and a

Riverside, Montana. The White-Taber Sawmill, 1955.

boarding house for mill workers, as well as saloons and an implement store.

The town hall of Riverside was moved to Hamilton, on May 27, 1893 by Jack Leonard. It was placed on a lot on second street next to the office of the Bitter Root Times (an early newspaper). The structure was brought up in two sections each being loaded on four sets of wagon wheels, two in a set, and pulled by about 20 horses. On December 8, 1893, Leonard's Saloon and hotel buildings and P. W. Quickborner's residence at Riverside burned to the ground. The saloon and hotel were two-story buildings valued at $2,500. The residence was a one-story dwelling valued at $500.

The landmark smoke stack dates back prior to World War I, 1917, when a Utah Sugar company began construction of a sugar factory. The awakening was short-lived. Opposition by "Sugar Trust" forces in Missoula caused them to discontinue the idea.

The building which now houses Montana Westgate Realty began life as a "convenience" store atop Skalkaho Pass when the Skalkaho road was opened in 1924. Charles Hardy, a linotype operator, having decided upon a life in the open for his health, felt a "half way" service store would be the answer. He established Stoney Lake camp and he and his family lived for several summers in a cabin and in tents upon frame bases. He sold gasoline, oil, and supplies to passing motorists.

In 1929, Charles and Walter Neaves acquired the establishment and set out to expand it. They built a large log structure as a base for their service operation, which included a stop station for the Intermountain Transportation Company daily bus which ran from Hamilton to Anaconda. The Neaves constructed three tourist cabins on the North side of the road to add to the one built by Hardy. Due to lack of use of the road, the business didn't thrive. They decided to move the log building to Riverside and place it on land obtained from John Donovan. The site was that of the former Blindauer Saloon. The building was dismantled with logs being marked as to position, and hauled to Riverside by truck and reassembled.

In December of 1933, they opened for business as a road house under the name, Riverside Bar, which name it retained for many years under such owners as Ole Landers, Dick and Eula Lakenan, John Wickman, O.B. Collins, and Harley Perrin, as partners. When Perrin and Collins established the Old Turf in the building in Hamilton later used as Tom's Home Bakery, they sold the Riverside property to Jackie and Ray Blume.

Two main occurrences contributed to the demise of Riverside as a town. One was the illness and death of James Hedge, and, secondly, was the establishment of the town of Hamilton by Marcus Daly. The Hedge Mill shut down and the Pages, Lancasters, Howleys, Adairs, Nobles, and others moved to Hamilton and either sold or abandoned their previous properties. The depot was closed and Mrs. Palmer lost her job. Matt Blindauer's saloon was closed and he moved to Hamilton, his wife having died in Riverside.

Riverside, at one time a flourishing sawmill town, died officially at a meeting of the Ravalli County Commissioners in November, 1935, when the land became acreage by their order.

RIVERSIDE SUGAR FACTORY

The stack at Riverside was to have been used by the Montana-Utah Sugar Company. They were supposed to build a factory, but it never got beyond the foundation and stack.

From the meager information available it is hard to determine what took place. It may have been an honest effort that failed because of financial problems, or it may have been a "stock sales deal" to make money. Stock sales were a common practice at this time. Whatever, nothing was ever completed.

Apparently, it was first talked about in 1901, but nothing was done until February of 1917, when construction was started. The beet seed was supposedly in a warehouse in Oregon, and machinery was on order from Chicago. The beets were to be planted beginning April 15, 1917, and the factory was to be ready for operation and would process the beets that fall.

Apparently the beets were never planted, even though in February they were busy having meetings with the growers.

One account says the project was short-lived because of opposition by "Sugar Trust" forces in Missoula.

Part of the foundation was taken out in the 1980's, and in 1997 only the stack remains as a landmark.

THOUSAND ACRES

by Louis Nelson in 1957

I was one of the first foremen on the Thousand Acres, out to the East and North of Corvallis. I had a degree in Horticulture. When I came to the Thousand Acre Ranch in May of 1911, this was the set up:

CAMP I.

1. About 500 acres of young apple orchard which had been planted about 2 years.
2. A new barn with 12 work horses, one road horse and a saddle pony.
3. A new bunk house with double tier bunks along both walls in the sleeping room, an ante room and a front office where the foreman slept.
4. A cook house made from two homestead houses put together.
5. A large root cellar with a dirt roof and walls.

The crew consisted of: the lady cook, Mrs. White, and two daughters;

the foreman, Mr. Phillips, a little runt of a man, 65 years old; an elderly barn man, Mr. Kitt; and the crew of four young men from Julietta, Idaho

Our neighbors were:

North on top of the hill, Marcus Budan, bachelor.
On the Northeast, Mr. and Mrs. C. Wilcox, daughter and son (Zacha place).
Mr. and Mrs. Roy Fisher and 2 children; the ranch manage.
Mr. and Mrs. H. K. White and twin sons, (Jimeno place).
Mr. Grove and his housekeeper, (Raudabaugh place).
Mr. and Mrs. Spencer Huls and 3 children; Mallory, Connie and A. Spencer Huls.
Across the gulch to the South:
Mr. Gastfield, a bachelor.
Mr. and Mrs. C. J. Swanson, and daughter Helen.
Hugh Simpson, a bachelor.
Mrs. Bigelow, a retired lady doctor.
Mr. and Mrs. Peter Erickson.
Zarbell sisters.

At camp the men worked four horses abreast, pulling four sections of spring tooth harrow up and down the orchards, ten hours a day at $40.00 a month and board. And good board it was.

I was to look after the young trees and do most of the irrigating. We had to furnish our own bedding and the bunks were crawling with bed bugs. One man sifted a powder into his bed every night. The rest of us just took it until one day, Mr. Fisher hired a man from Hamilton who had been night clerk at the Ravalli Hotel named Fred Manke. He spent the first day getting his bunk in shape, tore out the lower bunk to make room for his trunk and other stuff, and spread white sheets on his bed. Bedtime and lights out. In about an hour, Fred hit the floor, lit the lamp and examined the bed. His cursing woke the rest of us. He pulled his bedding out and made a bed on the table in the ante room.

Just about that time a violent thunder storm occurred and as there was a stove pipe for a chimney, every once in awhile the room was lit up as the lightening played around the stove. That was the only time I ever saw that happen. Between the devil and the deep blue sea, Fred was awake the rest of the night! Next morning, right after breakfast Fred went to see Mr. Fisher. How could any man keep his crew in a bunkhouse like that? That forenoon, Fred and Mr. Fisher went to Hamilton and just before supper the Valley Mercantile drove out with a load of iron (single) cots and new mattresses. We all slept out of doors for several nights while the men tore out all the bunks, washed and disinfected the room. Then, we moved back in again.

The horses were turned loose on the sage brush every Saturday night and rounded up on Sunday. It was often my duty to get them in. This was, for me, sometimes quite a job, especially if our work horses got mixed with a lot of range horses that were always hanging around. The cow pony knew more about that than I did, so I just held onto the saddle horn while he cut them out, always on the dead run, right and left and around! The horses generally fed on open ground where Richard's house now is. But one night, just as they were turned loose, they headed south and I thought it odd. Sunday night, we couldn't find them anywhere. They had all been purchased in the Ross Hole country, so Mr. Fisher telephoned to Darby. Yes, they had just gone through town! That was the only time they did it and they seemed to have all talked it over!

A man by the name of John Bauer had leased the south 80, and planted a large part of it to potatoes and carrots, and other vegetables for which the camp was to get part of the crop. He had his own team. They were pretty handy with their heels, and as they occupied the first two stalls, you had to be on guard when going behind them. We tried to get John to move them farther back, but he wouldn't.

The first years crew were a fairly good bunch, but the fellow that bunked next to me slept with an iron bar under his pillow. I was kind of uncertain about him and was glad when, later on in the summer, he suddenly left camp. The next years crew was made up of young boys fresh from old Missouri. I learned a new language and heard words I didn't know were in the English language. They were a good bunch and I liked them very much. One young fellow at once proceeded to fall in love with the cook's older daughter and the foreman, Mr. Phillips, who had married the cook by this time, objected very much to having Dan Watts hanging around the cook house. So much so, in fact, that one Saturday night one of the men brought him a bottle of whiskey from Victor and on Sunday morning Mr. Phillips was dead drunk. When Dan came down to the cookhouse to gas with Josephine, Mr. Phillips met him with a gun! The cook came running out of the house and threw herself upon Mr. Phillips and knocked him to the ground. And, dear Josephine came screaming up to me. Dan had disappeared. I took the gun away from Mr. Phillips and called Mr. Fisher. He came down, got the gun, and took Mr. Phillips up to his house. That was on Sunday, and on Monday morning, I told Mr. Fisher that after what had happened I didn't think we could work together anymore, and that I had better be going. "Don't be in a hurry" he said. That afternoon Mr. Fisher took Mr. Phillips to the Victor depot. Poor guy. The cook left a few days later, and we were sorry to see her go. She was a Missourian, and a very good cook.

She stayed and worked in Missoula, and Mr. Phillips went to his home town in Idaho.

The crew always left in the fall, and I and one man batched during the winter. We had five cows to milk and a few hogs. The horses were turned out on the big flat on the Victor Crossing as no hay was raised on the ranch. If the snow got too deep down there, we bought hay wherever we could get it and had it hauled down there.

One day, Mr. Grove wanted to go to Victor and climbed upon one of the hay loads. The water was a little high and as we crossed one stream the hay was washed off the rack with Mr. Grove on it. He was washed down stream a way and finally landed on a sand bar.

When Mr. Phillip left, I became foreman and moved into his quarters. I was a little sore at him as he was always telling Mr. Fisher that the men working with me were always loafing on the job.

On the first of March, every year, we began cleaning out the bunkhouse and soon the new crew would be arriving with their bed rolls on their backs and soon we would have an entirely new crew of mostly young fellows fresh from Missouri.

It was a real treat on Saturday nights to take a team that had not been working that afternoon, and drive to Victor. If you didn't get there before 8 o'clock, there was no place to tie up and there was a long tie rack at the depot and another near the M. M. store. The stores were crowded and we didn't get back to camp 'till way after midnight. A haircut after 12 o'clock was $1.00.

Going back to John Bauer and his crop. The camp put their share in the big cellar. As there was no sale for the spuds, we cooked them with wheat and fed the hogs we had on hand. Toward spring quite a few of them got sick and died. The vet said it was cholera, and to burn the carcasses. Have you ever tried to burn a big fat hog? That is something!

Up to now the orchards had been clean cultivated except where Jim Hill Mustard had taken part possession. You never saw anything grow like that mustard! There was no other weed then. These big mustard plants would break off in the winter wind and roll back and forth across the orchards, filling the gulches. Up against the fences and over seeding the ground everywhere they rolled. When the apple trees were small we often couldn't find them.

We picked rock early spring and late fall after cultivation was over using a "dumpola" as we called it — a large box on a roller fixed on wagon gear to dump sideways. We could drive to the side of the gulch as far out as the team could go, unhook the chain on the upperside and let her dump. We picked all winter if there wasn't snow and the rocks thawed loose by ten o'clock.

As the company felt the need of some income, we planted Canadian field peas between the tree rows and cultivated a narrow strip close to the trees. We did that for a couple of years and then tried potatoes once more. The big potato crop of 1910 had been harvested and pitted in the field — no sale for these most beautiful spuds and the pits were never opened — car loads. As the pits rotted down we gradually cultivated over them. Now the market seemed good enough so in goes 200 acres in the tree rows. Worked long and late in the fall. The ground froze and still we dug and picked spuds. I became quite rheumatic from crawling on the frozen ground. We filled the big cellar full and shut the door, awaiting a market. No market! Spring, no market! Early summer, no market, and spuds sprouting. Offer them to farmers for hog feed — no call. Mr. Kimberly drove over from Summerdale and took two sacks! The ground around the cellar had been planted to oats and on the first irrigation waste water filled the cellar to the roof, and no drain. First, to dig a drain ditch to let the water out. When that was finished the spuds had begun to rot somewhat. Now to get a man and team with a slip to drag them out. Jud Treece volunteered but before he was thru he had to eat alone and be alone much of the time. The odor was something to be remembered. He finished the job.

The next year after that we seeded all the orchards to alfalfa using wheat as a nurse crop. That fall of 1914, Mr. Fisher was let out and Mr. Thatcher came as ranch manager. Mr. Blissing and Mr. Shirley were also discharged from Camp II. I stayed on. I don't know why he didn't fire me too.

We had a lot of snow that winter, and Earl Watts and I were batching in the cookhouse. Mr. Gastfield was taken sick and as he was alone, I drove over one day, brought him to camp and kept him there the rest of the winter. He was good company, but demanded a lot of waiting on, which we didn't mind.

Early in the winter before Mr. Fisher left, he came to camp one day at noon and on leaving the bunkhouse, he lit a cigarette and flipped the match into a box of kindling standing near the stove. He went on home and we went to the barn to hook up a team. When we came out of the barn, smoke was coming out of the shingles all along the roof. Dan was using the ante room and I, the office. I ran into my room and threw my bedding out onto the snow and ran back to Dan. That forenoon, we had just hauled up a barrel of water and it stood right in front of the bunkhouse door. We both began throwing water into the room which was all ablaze from the pitch which had oozed out of the boards. We finally got it out but it had ruined the walls in my room which I had recently painted at my own expense. I prevailed on Mr. Fisher to put us in a brick chimney which was done. Mr. Gastfield did it, and I papered my room with a heavy grey felt paper, at my own expense of course, — and a new floor too. We thought we were lucky, to get a brick chimney. When Mr. Thatcher came we were in pretty good shape. A granary full of wheat and a nice bunch of hogs, mostly sows. Mr. Thatcher decided to go in for hogs in a big way, so we kept and bred all the sows. I don't remember how many, but a lot of them. We were to build individual hog houses and the lumber ordered from a Mr. Latham of Darby.

The spring roads were so bad up there they couldn't get the lumber out. The sows began farrowing under the apple trees in the orchard. Finally, the lumber came and Mr. Cole from Hamilton, began building houses. As soon as a house was done, to get a sow and her young out of the orchard and into the house was, to me, a dangerous undertaking. I was to drive the sow off to a safe distance and the other man was to scoop the little pigs into a box, and beat it! When those little pigs began squealing the old sow took after him, and I had to run for my life! After all was finished we had quite a hog colony.

Mr. Thatcher hired John Morton, a hog expert from Kentucky, to have charge of the hogs. He wanted to send back to Kentucky for a cheap Negro to do the hog house cleaning, and when he found he had to do it himself, it didn't set so good! He wanted mostly to fit hogs for Fairs and travel with them, and Thatcher wanted to feed hogs for pork.

We kept a team on the road most of the time looking for wheat. The company bought the Fisk place and planted it to wheat. They shipped car lots to the Spokane market, but it was a losing game and in 1918, Morton went into the Army and I left thousand Acres and went to Michigan for a little over three years.

Our 1916 and 1917 hay crop was very good. The hay was baled out of the stack during the winter, and we hauled it to Victor and loaded out about a car a day.

Going back to John Bauer's stay at camp. As he was getting along in years he wanted to get married, and answered a Heart and Hand ad to a woman with five children in Malden, Missouri. John asked me to write his love letters, which I foolishly did, as he said he wasn't up to it. After three or four letters, John sent her the money and John met her in Missoula and they were married. When I saw her and the children, I felt badly — real bad, as she was a fine person and her children also fine, and John was such a pig of a man. They lived in two little houses up by the red barn which had been used in 1910 by the barn man and road man who waited on the punks who lived in the Club House. They were subject to call night or day to take these guys to Hamilton or anyplace else. George Thatcher, Hamilton Thatcher, R. H. Daniels, a Mr. Starr, and a couple other stockholders sons sent out to sow their wild oats, and get out of the old folks way. They had their own cook.

That fall (1912), John bought some land in the Flathead and moved his family there. Early in the summer, his wife and her children were back in Victor, having run out on John while he was out in the field. He didn't come after her and she continued to live in Victor and raised her family here. Two of the boys were old enough to work a little and did chore jobs for Albert Wood. One of them still lives in Victor, two more near Hamilton.

After John left, I tore down one of those houses and built a couple hog houses and a sleeping room for myself on my end of the bunkhouse. As it had been, everybody who came into my room sat on my bed, and by bedtime my bed looked like a rats nest or worse.

After I left Thousand Acres, Jim Meason of Camp II looked after both places. Bill Grey of Hamilton was hired for a short time as foreman. During the last few years of camp activity, Earl Redding, had charge of things. The orchards were about gone. The big apple house stood empty except for one year. Ed O'Hare stored his crop of potatoes in the basement.

After Mrs. White left camp, Mrs. Cantelon came from Darby and cooked for several years. Then Mrs. Sawner from Missoula, one year. They were both very good cooks and then bum days ahead. Mrs. Hartley, drunk now and then; Mrs. Cunningham from Missouri, a good cook but when anything was put on the table it stayed there until you ate it! She put a cloth over it until the next meal. Then came two women from Darby — Satterlee and Mrs. Inman — not too bad and not too good. Then, Mrs. Miller, the wife of the barn man. She had it in for some of the men and tried, and about succeeded, in driving them away by her cooking. Then to cap them all, Mrs. Kupke, whom Mr. Groff recommended to Mr. Thatcher. I can hardly forgive him for that ! About that time I left Camp I.

When Mr. Thatcher took over the camp, he began a vigorous campaign of pruning. He hired a crew from Stevensville with Ralph Robinson as head man. We had about two feet of snow and a very bad winter. The men froze their feet and suffered from snow blindness. They finished Camp II first and then came to Camp I. Ralph and his wife lived in the club house. The men stayed at Camp I. They brought a cook with them. Earl and I were batching.

When I came back from Michigan, the apples were going strong. At Camp they built a new $25,000.00 apple house with a full basement over the old root cellar. John Peterson built it. They had installed a Delco light plant for light and power and a new apple grader. Apples were wrapped, packed and shipped to the New York market. I had purchased an apple orchard and a 10 acre sage tract across the road from the apple house.

Mr. and Mrs. Crerar had run the cookhouse while I was in Michigan. Mr. Owings and Mr. Steele were running the cookhouse, boarding Thatcher's men and they had also taken over the hay land. Mr. Thatcher now had only the apple trees. He later acquired a band of sheep, sold off the hog houses and built long sheep sheds. He ran the sheep above Darby during the summer and fed his share of the hay during the fall and winter. Mr. Gardner and then Mr. Jesse Mickens had charge of the sheep.

During the depression, apples were so hard to sell and the New York market had been entirely lost. Quite a few of the valley apple growers brought in an apple salesman from Idaho, I think. He told them he could sell all they had if they would put them up in small fancy boxes with paper trim.

This they did and shipped the entire lot to St. Louis. That was the last they heard about them as far as I know. Mr. Parker in Hamilton had furnished much of the material used in packing. He died of a heart attack. I don't know if it was from that or not, but there was talk Mr. Thatcher had to sell all his sheep and we thought for awhile he was going to lose his mind. Mr. Bartley just moved off his place in Hamilton Heights and he and his wife went to live in some lodge home in Illinois. Loren Gander was one of them too, but he took it in stride.

The people who have lived at Camp as far as I know:

After Owings and Steele left (Steele lived in the Club House when he worked the camp acreage and Owings lived in the cookhouse). Claude Allnut moved over from Camp II, and lived there a couple of years; then George King, Mrs. Crerar's son, and his wife. Then Mr. and Mrs. Higgins; next Mr. and Mrs. Odell; then Mr. and Mrs. Blen Hinton (Note: Hinton's were before Odell's); Mr. Bill Richards lived there also, but I'm not sure if it was before or after the Woodwards. I think it was after. Anyway, he was the one who tore down the old barn which was now about to fall down, and converted the once famous bunk-house into a cow stable with stanchions and all. He made some hog sheds out of the lumber from the barn. He stayed only one year.

Meanwhile the apple business had gone from bad to worse. In 1923, they had so many apples culled out for pin point scab to keep a truck running from the apple house to the dump in Birch Creek, and there the pile of rotting apples killed all the cottonwoods. Mr. Thatcher had a picture taken of the pile but wouldn't let anyone have a copy, but sent it in to the company headquarters.

In the latter years of Camp existence, Mr. Thatcher had to take his wages in company stock and such money he could make on the farm. Toward the last, he just about owned it I believe. He began selling parts of it to get money for taxes and water. More and more of the apple trees were taken out every year and now just a few remain on an abandoned tract up near the Big Ditch.

As originally planted at Camp I:

Mostly MacIntosh, some Rome Beauty, Delicious, Jonathan, Gano and Transcendent and Hyslop crabs. Sweet cherries and pears. The pears on the flats along Birch Creek killed out the first year but 10 acres grew to bearing near H.K. White's place, now owned by Jimeno. Blight took these after two crops. Sweet cherries were planted in the "triangle" and at Jimeno's. They bore two good crops and winter killed.

Our first crab apple crop (beautiful apples) was shipped on a box car to Billings. The weather was warm and they arrived too ripe and were not accepted. The car was then sent on to Minneapolis where they arrived rotting. The company received a bill for freight and I don't know if they paid it.

During the winter of '16 and '17, we had a lot of pea straw and Thatcher sold it to a stock man on the Flathead who shipped his cattle here to feed for the winter. As they were all bred cows and had put in such a hard winter, although Mr. Thatcher had agreed to build shelter for them, the spring calf crop was so poor and most of the calves died. He was threatened with a law suit. I don't know how it came out.

I must tell you about the greyhounds. We had wonderful dogs! A white female was bred in Boston and shipped out here and she had three pups — two males and a female. By inbreeding, we soon had a pack; eight at Camp I, and some at Camp II. They were used to hunt jack rabbits which killed thousands of small trees every winter. While the entire place was fenced with supposedly rabbit proof fencing, we had weeks of replanting to do every spring. When Mr. Measom came to Camp II, he crossed the hounds with Shepherd, and raised a bunch of outlaws that roamed the hills and killed young stock belonging to dryland farmers. On several occasions, we had to take our young stock from Camp I to give to these farmers to make up for their loss. He made me mad. While I was in Michigan, Thatcher killed off the Camp I hounds, leaving only two who came to stay with me as soon as they found out where I was. I was then living at H. K. White's.

Just a few more notes in passing; Our cow pony, Bobby, was the grandest little horse. A few days after I came to Camp, Mr. Fisher sent me to his house for a transit. "Take the horse", he said, as it was some distance. I took the horse — or rather it took me! I was no sooner on his back, than down the hill by the barn he went, jumped across Birch Creek, across irrigation ditches and thru the orchard just as fast as he could go. I got the transit but walked back leading the horse. Mr. Fisher said "He always runs away the first time a stranger rides him". When I rode him after that, I could hardly make him go as he had to sample every tuft of green along the road.

We went for the mail down the main valley road at the end of Wood's lane. We cut directly across the sagebrush north of Camp. That was our road to Victor. Our road to Corvallis skirted the south fence below the cookhouse to White's, down the sand hill to Huls', through Fate Humble's lane to the main road. It was good of old Fate to let us go that way, as the road led right close to his house — between the house and barn and I know coming home late we kept him awake nights, often.

In the "south 80", we had 18 acres of Alexanders. In about 1913, blight showed up in them. It had evidently been carried from a large crab apple orchard that stood where Bailey's house now stands. I called Mr. Fisher on the camp phone, and he called the inspector, Mr. Shirley. He came right out and I think that was the first blight on the Bench. It soon showed up in a lot of places and the farmers got together and hired a man, Lawrence

Watters, to patrol all the orchards and to cut it out where ever found. Each agreed to pay according to the time spent on each place, and Thousand Acres would use the rest of his time.

The more they cut, the worse it got. The next spring we dehorned all the Alexanders and top grafted to Delicious. Later on as apple trees were being taken this piece of ground was planted to pie cherries and now (1957) they are being taken out. "Man proposes, the Lord disposes".

To help pass the long evenings at camp after the horse talk had been finished, I bought an Edison phonograph that played blue amberol wax records. Everyone bought records and we soon had about a hundred on hand. They were good, too. As this crew had gone when I left camp, I gave the whole outfit to Swanson's, who still have it.

The ranch was officially called Bitter Root Valley Orchards, Inc. (B. R. V. O., INC.), but locally known as Thousand Acres.

The other little house that stood near the red barn was moved to camp as a bunk house for the women apple graders, and later moved up to Crerar's where it now stands. Ruth and Jesse Mickens lived in it one year.

The company paid a bounty of $.25 on all jack rabbits killed in the orchards, and the men made good money. But, after one year, it was discontinued as there were too many run-aways. If a rabbit was scared up, the man would stop their horses and all take after the rabbit and in the following confusion the horses would become frightened and run wildly across the orchard, dragging the harrows over the apple trees and all!

The funniest run-away we had, of the many, was when four horses hitched to four sections of spring tooth started running at the top of the hill where Riley's live now. Down the hill they came, the harrows bouncing from rock to rock, knocked over a little oil house that stood on the bank of the creek, and all piled up in the creek bed with most of the harrows on top of them. We all ran over, got the harrows off, untangled the harnesses, got the horses up one at a time and not one of them were hurt!

The man who homesteaded the Camp I land had dug and cribbed up a well at the northwest corner of the cookhouse. The Company didn't use this, but piped water to all the buildings from a cistern on top of the hill near Wilcox's, using ditch water and when thirsty lay down on your belly and drank out of the nearest ditch. Good healthy stuff. This well was covered with loose boards and as Fisher's and the cook had children playing around there, I thought I had better fill it in, and did so with the rock and stuff we picked from the garden.

WOODSIDE MEMORIES

By Tom Dunbar, written in 1993
1920-1950

First of all, I will tell you how Woodside got its name. Woods siding was a lumber loading side track of the Northern Pacific railroad. It was located one mile north of the present site of Woodside. The railroad decided to build some side tracks at the Corvallis crossing of the Bitter Root River. They built a depot and stockyards and called it Woodside. This occurred about 1900.

I came to Woodside in 1918, when I was almost two years old. So my memories are from 1923 on, as a small boy.

I remember two stores, one blacksmith shop, a livery barn, several warehouses, a creamery, and one elevator. The big store was owned by William Thrailkill, and later by William Pierce, and then by Dewey Reimel, and into the early thirties by the Tilton family. The smaller store was owned by John David and was located in the Popham building. The blacksmith shop was an add-on to the Popham building, owned by Jim Popham. The livery barn was just west of the Popham building. The meat market was on the corner, just west of the railroad tracks, and was owned by Russell Iman. They also ran the post office for many years. A large ice house was located just north of the meat market. It held ice for the meat market.

The post office was later moved to the big store which also had the only gas pump in town. Woodside store was a busy place in those days. Besides the gas pump, they had a commercial scales to weigh the wagons that were hauling grain, hay, potatoes, onions, cabbage, carrots, and sugar beets that were to be loaded on the rail cars. At one time Woodside was the largest shipping station in the Bitter Root. I remember seeing many wagons and trucks lined up waiting to go across the scales.

In the fall there were two apple packing warehouses. The apples came from the orchards and were sorted, packed, and loaded into the refrigerated cars and shipped to eastern markets. The cull apples were made into cider in the big press in the south end of the creamery building. The refrigerated cars that carried the fruits and vegetables were cooled by ice. Each car had a place at each end of it that was filled with ice, and the doors were only opened when they were loading the car. It was nice to run into one of these cool cars on a warm day!

On any given day, they might be loading apples, and on up the siding be loading grain, potatoes, or possibly loading a couple of carloads of cattle at the stockyards.

On the west side of the main line there was a conveyor to load sugar beets. Just south of that was a lumber loading dock.

There were several mills west of Woodside that loaded lumber and mine timbers onto the railroad cars. I was always fascinated by the old solid tire trucks that hauled lumber from the mills to the siding.

Another thing that created a great deal of excitement was the arrival of the freight train with the big steam engines. They would pull the cars out and spot the empty cars back to be loaded.

The passenger train came up the valley to Darby. The big event of the day was to meet this train, seeing the people getting on and off the train, watching them unload the baggage. They also loaded at this time, the crates of eggs and the berries (in season) to be sent to Butte. It was a big thrill when Mr. McGee would let me glue the shipping tickets on the ends of the berry crates. Sometimes it was worth a dime for a bottle of pop!

The depot had a wide plank platform clear around the building. Between trains, Mr. McGee would let us kids run our coaster wagons around the platform. This was a great treat as there were no sidewalks or pavement in the town of Woodside. Sometimes we got slivers in our bare feet from the rough planking, but that didn't slow down our enthusiasm. It always amazed me how the agent could listen to that clicking noise on the telegraph and know when the train was coming.

The railroad had a four wheel trailer they pulled behind the speeder that Mr. McGee would let us put on the track when he knew that there were no trains coming. It was slightly uphill to the south, so we would push it up about one half mile and then coast back down to the station — great fun, and lots of exercise!

The old Woodside store was a very interesting place. It was a general store with groceries, hardware, and clothing. You would find mostly men's work clothes, gloves, kerosene lanterns, army blankets, tobacco, and candy. It was a neat old store with only one gas pump, and a kerosene pump out in front. There was also a card table just back of a large heating stove, where older citizens from around town would come and play Rummy almost every day. I've heard some great stories there! I remember that one day a bunch of Gypsies stopped at the store. Mr. Pierce was the owner at that time. He said, "Everybody get behind the counters and be sales clerks, and keep an eye on this bunch or they will steal me blind!" They didn't stay long. I guess they thought they had been outfoxed.

In the summer evenings, the boys from the neighborhood would gather in the empty lot just north of the meat market (now Skip's Garage) and play baseball. They would later go over to the store and play hide-and-seek, and someone would win big in the card game and stand some treats — such as pop, or maybe bring out a watermelon and cut in on the store porch.

Another one of my favorite memories takes me to the old swimming hole in the Woodside canal. It was located just south of the Dunbar Sawmill. Many afternoons were spent there. My two brothers and I all learned to swim there. Other regulars found there on a hot afternoon were Byron and

Bill Thrailkill, Ralph Miller, and the McGee kids. We built a dressing shack out of boards scrounged from Dunbar's and the Thrailkill boys found a large tin sign that we used for a roof. On a hot day, it was like an oven in there! Those were worry free days. The only problem was with the ditch-rider. We would put more boards in the headgate to make the water deeper for diving. We had some conversations with him over that, but we continued the practice.

Cattle loading was another highlight. With all the noise of the cattle and the whips snapping (no electric prods in those days) we boys were drawn there like a magnet. We probably learned a few swear words there, too. We would peek through the bars and watch them kick those cattle into the cars.

Woodside had some spectacular fires. The first I can remember was the livery barn. It had a loft full of hay, and burned for several days. There was no fire protection in those days. The only fire engine was in Hamilton, and it didn't carry any amount of water so it was not very effective. It had only a small tank and some soda extinguishers.

The Equity apple house burned a year or so later. It was also full of baled hay. The only fire protection available was a garden hose from the McCrae house, mainly used to hold down the sparks after the building burned.

One fire I remember well was a grass fire that started in dry June grass just north of town. It was caused by a spark from the engine on a freight train. It came quite fast across an empty lot north of the meat market. There were quite a few men loading cars, and also the train crew was available. They all got gunnysacks and were beating out the fire. They packed buckets of water from the depot pump to wet the sacks. They got it under control just before it got to the Popham place and the back fence of the meat market. It was a very exciting afternoon!

In the early 1930's the meat market was rented to a company that was making bone meal and dried meat for dog food. One morning I was milking a cow in the field and I saw a fire start in the cedar shingles around the chimney of the meat market. They were firing up their wood burning boiler and a spark flew onto the roof. When I spotted the blaze, I hung my bucket on the wall of an old barn and ran about a block to tell them their roof was on fire. By the time I got there the roof was in flames. They had a well pump, but by the time they got their garden hose hooked up — the fire was out of control! Hamilton had a better fire engine by now, but by the time they arrived and got some water from a nearby irrigation ditch, the whole building and the big icehouse were burning out of control. A small house just west of the market burned also, meaning the whole corner was burned to the ground. The fire boys saved the Popham building.

The next big fire was the Popham building. It occurred about 1932 or 1933. The building belonged to "Old Unc", Howard Moreland. There was a dance hall upstairs and two families lived downstairs. The families saved most of their belongings, but the building burned clear to the ground. The last big fire was Dunbar Sawmill in the spring of 1946. It began in the boiler room, and spread fast! The alarm was given by Melvin Hess, about 4 a.m., and the Corvallis Fire Department came, but there was little they could do except to keep the fire from spreading to the lumber and sawdust piles. The sawmill was rebuilt that same year, and is still in operation in 1993.

In 1928, the railroad was moved across the river to better serve Stevensville and Corvallis. The apple boom had pretty well gone by the wayside, and sugar beets and farm produce were taking its place. The apple buildings were torn down as were the elevator and the depot. For the next few years, Woodside was just a nice, quiet, small village. Highway 93 was built on the old railroad right of way. Then, Woodside began to grow again with first a small country store owned by Roy Busenbark, and next a service station and repair shop owned by Chet Parks, (This is now Skip's Repair). The Dunbar Sawmill continued in operation.

WOODSIDE WAS A GREAT PLACE FOR A BOY TO GROW UP.

Chapter Three

Early Business And Industry

THE BEE INDUSTRY IN THE BITTER ROOT VALLEY

by Mrs. David Pile in 1955

Sometime before the year of nineteen hundred, Marcus Daly must have felt the need of pollination of his orchards. There were, no doubt, German Black Bees or Wild Bees in the Bitter Root Valley at this time, but these had their homes mostly in the trees along the Bitter Root River. For this reason, and the fact that he wanted a little of everything on his many ranches, he was the first to import to the valley a pure stock of Italian three-banded bees. He purchased three hundred colonies and had them shipped from Italy. They were shipped in double walled hives, and a great deal of money was spent for them.

These bees were all put in an orchard on what is known as the Hamilton Ranch near the Daly Mansion. Mr. Frank Meeks, one of Daly's hired men who had worked for him for many years, was put in charge of the apiary until his death. Mr. P. M. Shannon was in charge of the Stock Farm interests at that time.

When Mr. Meeks died, Mr. Crawford was manager of the Stock Farm, and was at a loss to know what to do with the bees. He hit upon the plan of renting the bees. For two years the bees were rented to Frank Morgan, a bee keeper from Minnesota, living in Corvallis. After that two year period, they were again rented, this time to David Pile, brother in law of Mr. Morgan, who was also a bee-keeper from Minnesota. After he purchased them from the Daly Estate, part of the bees were moved to his home at Corvallis and part to various out yards.

Mr. Morgan and Mr. Pile were the first commercial bee-keepers in the Bitter Root Valley. For many years, Mr. Pile reported for the "American Bee Journal" column, "Weather and Crop Prospects," while Mr. Morgan wrote for the magazine, "Gleanings in Bee Culture".

The bee-keeping industry began to grow as other early day apiarists such as Adolf Renn, Oliver Blood of Hamilton, and Ralph Keays of Corvallis, and Albert Heath of Stevensville, bought the Italian strain of bees from California and the southern states. These bees were purchased in three pound packages to replace colonies that had died from winter loss and disease and to build up the apiaries.

During World War I, a government man called on the commercial bee-keepers of the valley and persuaded them to change from producing comb, to extracting honey. The reason for this was that the bees can produce two pounds of extracted honey in the same time it takes them to make one of comb. Most of the bee-keepers changed over and at a considerable amount of expense to each of them. The extracting of honey was done with an electric extractor. Hand extractors were used by those keeping bees on a smaller scale. The large extracting combs used in the process could be put back on the hives and used over and over.

During the war years, large crops of honey were produced and much honey was used as a substitute for sugar. During the year 1928, Mr. Pile produced his largest crop — 86,000 pounds of honey.

Honey was shipped in large, tin, sixty-pound cans. These cans of honey were repackaged into five and ten pound pails and various glass containers, similar to those seen in stores today. Buyers were anxious to purchase Montana honey, and train carloads were sent as far east as New York, and to California, and many other states. The reason for the desires for Montana honey, and especially Western Montana honey, was that the higher the altitude, the better the grade of honey is from the same flowers.

Most pure honey granulates, or sugars, in time. The honey produced in the Bitter Root Valley contains a high percent of dextrose and makes it granulate sooner than honey produced in some places.

Weather conditions govern the honey crop as much or perhaps more than any other crop produced in the valley. Some beekeepers keep a hive on a scale and weighed it at the end of the day. On a good day, as high as eighteen pounds of honey has been known to have been made by a single hive. The ideal weather for honey gathering is still, warm, days.

The Bitter Root Valley has never known a complete honey crop failure, but the shortest crops were had during the very dry years, because flowers do not secrete honey during a too dry season.

The first flowers the bees work on in the spring are the apple blossoms and the dandelions. Apple blossom honey is of the most delicate flavor, but it cannot be kept separate as the apple blossoms and dandelion are in bloom at the same time. Other of the honey producing plants in the valley are sweet clover, both yellow and white; small Dutch clover; alsike; and alfalfa. The knapweed seen along the highways and road sides produces a higher grade of honey than dandelions, however, it is not as high as that from clover and alfalfa.

It is interesting to note that bees prefer a blue flower to work on, in preference to any other color. Another interesting thing about bees is that if necessary, a bee will travel as far as three miles for pollen.

There are two diseases which affect the bees, the American and European foulbrood. It has played a part in the history and development of beekeeping. However, the bee diseases in no way affect the honey produced.

Pollen from flowers has been known to be carried by the bees from willows and alders along the river as early as February. This is fed to the young bees. Royal jelly is made by the bees to feed their larva and to produce queen bees. It is a wonderful food for young bees. Pollen is known to carry almost every known vitamin. Scientists are experimenting with royal jelly as a medicine food supplement. The bee larva grows so rapidly that it fills the cells in one week from the time the egg hatches. This is an increase of six hundred volumes in one week.

In the early days in the valley before so many orchards were done away with, the orchard owners would pay the beekeepers to move their hives into their orchards for pollination. The beekeepers would also be benefitted by the early honey flow while the apple blossoms were blooming. This was fed to the young bees and helped build the colony stronger and get it ready for the main honey season which began about the middle of June and ended about September First.

During these years, the beekeepers would hold their annual picnic, and whole families would participate. When the outdoor picnics were held at an apiarists home, hot biscuits and honey, of course, were one of the main courses!!

The prominent names among the apiarists during this period in the Bitter Root Valley were Parson Pile, Dale Felix, Ray Goodman, George Hudson, and Robert Keays, all of Corvallis, and Snowden Reynolds of Hamilton. Prominent beekeepers of later years were James Pile, Delbert Pile, Howard Marsh, and George Handley of Corvallis, Wendell Simonsen and Glen Winship of Victor, William Hetterick of Hamilton, and Frank Jacquette of Darby. Most of these men owned from one hundred to one thousand colonies of bees at one time. There were also a great number of others up and down the valley that owned fewer colonies.

Through the years, many prizes have been awarded at the Ravalli County Fair for bees, honey, beeswax, and food cooked with honey. A bee and honey exhibit can be seen each year at the fair and never seems to grow old.

Thus, the beekeeping industry was born and still grows. Little did Marcus Daly think, when he brought the first Italian bees to the Bitter Root Valley so many years ago, that his few bees would grow into the thriving bee industry in the Bitter Root Valley today.

BITTER ROOT IRRIGATION COMPANY

Sidelights to the building of the "Big Ditch"

by Luther Stanley

In 1905, some of the personnel of an Eastern Syndicate came to this valley to give an on the ground check on the proposed irrigation canal starting at Lake Como, and following some eighty miles to the north to the Eight Mile country just east of Florence. A man by the name of W. I. Moody, in representing a big money syndicate, approved the project and gave the go ahead to begin this huge proposition, costing some 3 1/2 million dollars. It was finished in 1911. This huge canal was to carry, at full capacity, a head of water 25 feet wide and 6 feet deep at the head, and was siphoned across the river, flumed across three canyons and then was siphoned across the Sleeping Child valley. The steam shovel was powered by a steam boiler which was fired by cord wood and coal.

It was a slow building process and encountered many obstacles. Much hard luck was to accompany this tremendous digging job of building the largest canal for irrigation in the world at that time. They had many set backs over the years as the canal progressed. After they got as far as the Birch Creek country northeast of Corvallis, the steam shovel was abandoned and teams with fresnos and scrapers were used the rest of the way to Eight Mile.

There were many flumes and siphons along the way in crossing the Burnt Fork valley. There was a flume 11/4 miles long, which was the longest on the entire canal.

There were some 45 thousand acres of orchards planted in this valley with the largest portions on the north bench of the Burnt Fork, across Ambrose through the Three Mile country, across Dry Gulch and on to the Eight Mile area. Some 700 men were employed. The orchard sprouts were raised in an orchard nursery on the Harold Hagen land where several acres of sprouts were sorted on a long table in a warehouse at Camp One (where Roland Clevidence lives today). They worked some 90 teams and 120 men in this one camp, but there were several other smaller camps from Eight

THE BIG DITCH. The Big Ditch is being dug, in 1907-08, by a steam shovel which runs on railroad tracks.

Mile to Corvallis.

The "Big Ditch" was completed to the Burnt Fork by the spring of 1909, and as they were about finished, others planted 35 thousand acres of trees. The new small town of "Bitter Root" was laid out with streets and alleys with a water system to use in case of fire. The Bitter Root Inn was built in 1909, and in 1910, where the company housed their offices after a move from Hamilton in February of 1911. Several residences were built, all designed by the famous architect, Frank Lloyd Wright. He also designed the Bitter Root Inn and a Lutheran church established there.

These acreages were bought from the farmer for as little as $ 2.50 to $15.00 per acre, but after planted to fruit trees, sold to the buyers for as much as $400.00 to $1,000.00 per acre! Millions of dollars were invested here. Just a few of the buyers stayed to become good citizens, while many others, after building beautiful new homes, left for their previous home before paying off their land. The county was owed delinquent taxes, and had to step in and sell these homes to recover the taxes. This happened in the late 1910's and the early 1920's.

This "Big Ditch" irrigation canal was what made parts of the Bitter Root valley what it is today. Before this canal was put in some of these areas would not raise anything but fall rye and not over 10 to 12 bushels to the acre. Now, with the modern sprinkler systems for irrigation, some of these farms raise a comfortable living.

THE CATASTROPHE OF JUNE 1908

In June of 1908, as the Bitter Root Valley Irrigation Company was in the process of digging the "Big Ditch" along the foothills east of Victor, they had two work camps. On Willoughby Gulch, an Italian labor camp where forty men were employed in the advance work that went on before the actual digging began, and a camp on Spooner Gulch some two miles south, where a crew of men and teams with scrapers were digging the Big Ditch. In the middle of the night, while everyone was sleeping, a wall of water some twenty feet deep came down Willoughby with no warning, to the men sleeping in their tents. Only the roaring of the water awakened some of them, and they warned others, as they all tried to get dressed and make it to safety. But, all did not make it. Three who were too slow dressing lost their lives when this twenty foot wall of water hit and demolished their camp. The next morning, two bodies were found not far below. A third body was found in the afternoon by a farmer, (Doc) Frank Williamson, on his father's farm, some four miles down below the destroyed camp, on the valley floor one mile from the mouth of Willoughby Valley.

This same storm brought a twelve foot wall of water down on Spooner Gulch, which is located some two miles south. Several teams were tied for the night to the feeders, and when hit by this wall of water had no chance to save their own lives — drowning several horses. Some of the men losing animals were; Martin Rowan, two mares and their colts; brothers Tom and Bill Collins lost some horses; and Emmett and Bill Black also lost some horses. There were no human lives lost here as the sleeping men were well above the flood level.

HISTORY OF THE "BIG DITCH"

Although many people visualized the east bench land of the Bitter Root as an ideal area for development for agriculture and orchards, only small areas near the eastside creeks were developed.

Marcus Daly is credited with the vision and capital to start the development of the area. He purchased, enlarged and extended the Hedge Ditch, and built the Republican Ditch. He originally planned to extend the system to cover the bench lands that skirt the eastside of the valley for a distance of 60 miles. These plans were abandoned after his death and it wasn't until about 1900 that Samuel Dinsmore had promoted a small project near Missoula, and could see the potential for the eastside of the Bitter Root Valley.

Dinsmore organized a company known as the Dinsmore Irrigation Company and surveyed a ditch out of the West Fork of the Bitter Root River down to a point opposite Lake Como. In 1906, Dinsmore's group was running out of money, so they went back East to Chicago to interest more capital. W. I. Moody became interested and with the assistance of F. D. Nichols, F. H. Bailey, S. H. Lord, A. C. Walbridge and W. M. Noble re-organized and renamed the company to be the Bitter Root Valley Irrigation Company. They were able to raise the money and within three years had completed the Lake Como Reservoir, as conceived by Moody, and completed 56 miles of canal. The first water was turned in in April 1909.

The dam at Lake Como was built under the supervision of engineers from the State of Montana and the Interior department of the Federal Government. Four steam shovels, several small trains with steam locomotives and dump cars were called into service. A standard gauge railroad was built to carry supplies from the Northern Pacific at Darby which was a spur from the main line at Missoula. Tons of explosives were used and millions of feet of forest cleared. Eight hundred thousand (800,000) yards of earth were put in place. By 1909, the dam, rising 50 feet above the former surface of the lake, was completed. The lake was increased to four times its former size. As the rivers and streams diminished in size in the summer months, the impounded waters of Lake Como were available. The Company also obtained rights on Lost Horse, Skalkaho, Willow, Three Mile, Ambrose, and Burnt Fork Creeks.

DEVELOPMENT OF THE LAND

During the years of 1908 and 1909, over 15,000 acres of land were purchased by investors and newcomers. The average tracts were in size from 10 to 20 acres, and one was up to 1,400 acres. As many of the purchasers were university people, the development lacked the pioneering spirit. The area was made up into divisions known as University Heights, Sunny Side, Mountain View Orchards, Summerdale, Home Acres, Thousand Acres, Hamilton Heights, and East Side Addition. Large Inns were built on each division with servants in attendance, and golf courses were laid out. Special trains were run from the East, and met with automobiles bright red in color), to take the prospective buyers from Missoula to the Bitter Root. Thousands of acres of orchards were planted with the MacIntosh apple trees.

The advertising to attract people was fantastic! With land selling from $200.00 to $300.00 per acre, net returns of $5,000.00 per ten (10) acre plot was assured. There was to be constantly increased production with increased returns. While the trees were growing to maturity, diversified crops were recommended with returns of $1,000.00 per acre for celery, and $250.00 per acre for strawberries. The rocks were said to attract the sun and then in reflecting it to make the apples redder, the temperature warmer. The rocks were said to retain the moisture in the ground so that the rockier the place, the more moisture, the more the asking price!! Irrigation water was promised at $1.25 per acre, unrestricted use, and for the first five years all water charges and taxes were to be included in the down payment. "It is the land of homes, where people breathe pure air and imbibe the spirit of the Mountains. The nerve-racking struggle of existence of the cities is not to be found in these everlasting hills."

Undeveloped land sold for $300.00 per acre. The Company featured a development plan whereby they would plant and care for an orchard for five years, after which it was represented to be self supporting, and the buyer could either settle on it or have the Company continue to take care of it for a stipulated sum. This land was then to be worth $500.00 per acre.

BANKRUPTCY — 1916. Alas and alack for the plans of man. On January 3, 1916, the Bitter Root Irrigation Company filed a petition of bankruptcy. Litigations in the courts to adjust the financial losses of the company lasted several years, but the country's need of farm products in World War I made it imperative to keep the project in operation. From 1916 to 1920, the project was operated by the landowners under court jurisdiction. When the Company's indebtedness was settled, the original investor's loss was about 4 1/2 million dollars. The project was sold to private interests.

RAVALLI WATER COMPANY

The private interests organized a company known as the Ravalli Water Company. They petitioned the court for the creation of a district. Francis Powell was chairman and executive officer of the committee in charge of organization. The original petition carried the signatures of 594 owners representing 17,389 acres of land, and was filed January 7, 1920. This company too, was unable to meet its financial obligations. Thus it was that the farmers themselves took over the project.

BITTER ROOT IRRIGATION DISTRICT

The Bitter Root Irrigation District was formed as a municipal corporation under Montana law in December of 1920. During the years of 1923-1924 a $600,000.00 bond issue was sold under Sections 7166 and 7346, — 1921 codes of the State Irrigation Law. The bonded debt was estimated at $23.85 per acre or $31.44 per irrigable acre. The assessed valuation was three times the bonded debt. The charge for interest and retirement of principal for the years 1924-1927 was set at $1.89 per acre, and for the years 1928-1952, at $2.44 per acre. To this was added the cost of operation and maintenance, estimated at $1.00 per acre.

The $600,000.00 bond issue was used to make payment for the canal system and for the replacement of about half the wooden flumes. The water rights of the district and the plans and specifications for improvement to the system were approved by Mr. A. J. Wiley, consulting hydraulic engineer of Boise, Idaho, a nationally recognized authority in this type of work.

The reconstruction work consisted of the most permanent type, concrete and steel and earth fills. About 32 of the original 76 flumes were replaced by earth fills. The remaining flumes were repaired. At all pipe lines, reinforced concrete intakes and outlets were constructed and a modern spillway installed at Lake Como. Concrete wasteways and siphons were constructed at the East Side Crossings and new concrete and steel turnouts for the main canal. The lateral system was also overhauled.

As the district was organized in 1920, there were 25,067 acres gross, of which 18,240 acres were classified as irrigable agricultural lands. The actual irrigated acres was 16,095, and the cropped area was 15,309 acres. There were 256 farm families following diversified farming practices.

The flood water season usually ended about July 1, after which the Lake Como Reservoir storage and runoff of about 40,0000 acre feet was available until October 15, the end of the irrigation season. The requirements to properly irrigate the lands for maximum crop production was estimated to be 50,000 acre feet of water.

LAKE COMO RESERVOIR

Lake Como Reservoir was formed by a dam across the outlet of a natural lake which had an area of 250 acres at the outlet level. The dam was an earthen embankment, 2,500 feet in length with a maximum height of 65 feet above the original creek bed, and 50 feet in height above the original lake level. The top width was 30 feet and the slopes 3 to 1. It was composed of sand, clay, gravel, and granite boulders. In the original ground under a portion of the highest part there was a double row of sheet piling. At the northern end was a reinforced steel concrete spillway 75 feet wide and 11 feet deep. The opening was spanned by a 75 foot flat girded steel bridge with ends fixed to the abutments of the spillway. Fifteen steel gate frames were pivoted at their tops to the bridge and at the bottom fixed to low sills on the floor and arranged with trips so that part or the entire spillway could be cleaned. The original spillway capacity was 2,400 cfs., emergency capacity 8,400cfs.

The conduit under the dam was a 74-inch-diameter circular reinforced concrete tube 526 feet long. The outlet gates were tandem, two 66 inch diameter coffin valves set in steel casing. The conduit was designed to permit raising the dam 20 feet.

The Lake Como Reservoir storage water is turned back into Rock Creek. It is then diverted by Rock Creek Diversion Dam into the main canal about 1 mile below the reservoir. Como Dam was rehabilitated in 1954.

BITTER ROOT OIL COMPANY

1923.

The Bitter Root Valley has an oil well!!! Oil was struck on the Stondall-Toftoy ranch, four and one-half miles northeast of Hamilton, Saturday afternoon at about 5 O'clock.

The news reached Hamilton, and the office of the Bitter Root Oil company was the most popular place in Ravalli County that evening. The locating of oil came so soon, at a depth less than 1000 feet, that drillers and officers of the company were surprised. Residents hurried to the company's office on State Street to verify the report, and to hear first hand how the strike was made.

During the day, the bit was lost in the hole and it was necessary to drill around it. While working around the bit in an effort to bring it to the surface, oil was struck! The tools of the drilling outfit were covered with dark brown oil, which the drillers instantly recognized as petroleum or crude oil. At the same time, it is said, gas issued out of the hole carrying particles

INCORPORATED UNDER THE LAWS OF THE STATE OF MONTANA

NUMBER

SHARES 96

BITTER ROOT OIL COMPANY

CAPITAL STOCK [illegible] SHARES
PAR VALUE $1.00—NON-ASSESSABLE

This Certifies that Miles Romney
is the owner of Ninety Six Shares of the Capital Stock of
BITTER ROOT OIL COMPANY
transferable only on the books of this Corporation in person or by Attorney upon surrender of this Certificate properly endorsed.
IN WITNESS WHEREOF, the said Corporation has caused this Certificate to be signed by its duly authorized officers and its Corporate Seal to be hereunto affixed
this 29 day of June A.D.

Secretary

President

SHARES $1.00 EACH

Photos show shares of stock in the Bitterroot Oil Company owned by Miles P. Romney, Sr., plus view of the Bitterroot Oil Well.

of oil. Work was immediately suspended, and will not be resumed until provision is made to take care of the oil. Should there be a large supply of oil at the present depth it would be wasted by removing the bit, in case it is plugging the outlet to the source of supply.

The oil well was spudded in November with a barbecue. Almost 400 people were present to witness the beginning of the first test oil well in western Montana. Drilling did not progress as favorably or rapidly as was hoped at the time. Once the cable broke and then the bit was lost. There was delay in receiving the casing. But the operators were never discouraged, and kept at their work just like the old-time Montana miner.

As to the quantity of oil in the well, they were not prepared to say yesterday. They believe in playing safe and will not resume operations until in a position to take care of the oil if it should prove to be a gusher. The finding of oil does not make a paying well, but this well shows that there is oil in the Bitter Root Valley.

Western News, Hamilton, Montana, Thursday, November 15, 1923:

MUNGEN IS OUT SPIRLIN COMING TO FINISH WELL

MUNGEN GIVES UP AND CHAS. SPIRLIN COMING FROM CANADA TO COMPLETE BITTERROOT OIL WELL"

"Chas. C. Mungen, contracting driller, who has been fishing for tools in the Bitter Root oil well near Corvallis, ever since he cut the cable last July, gave it up this week and effected a settlement with the company. Accompanied by Mrs. Mungen he left this morning for Butte via Big Hole.

The board of directors has engaged Chas. D. Spirlin, an experienced driller. He is en route here from Alberta, Canada, and wired yesterday that he would arrive here this week.

The showing was excellent when drilling was suspended, the drill penetrating an oil sand at 1,200 feet. It became necessary to raise the casing and the tools were lost and the drillers have been 'fishing' ever since."

The Western News
Hamilton, Montana
Thursday, November 15, 1923

"Chas C. Mungen, contracting driller, who has been fishing for tools in the Bitter Root oil well near Corvallis, ever since he cut the cable last July, gave it up this week and effected a settlement with the company. Accompanied by Mrs. Mungen, he left this morning for Butte — via the Big Hole.

The board of directors has engaged Chas D. Spirlin, an experienced driller. He is en route here from Alberta, Canada, and wired yesterday that he would arrive here this week.

The showing was excellent when drilling was suspended, the drill penetrating an oil sand at 1,200 feet. It became necessary to raise the casing and the tools were lost and the drillers have been "fishing" ever since.

Shown in the photo is a paper representing 95 shares of the Bitter Root Oil Company, owned by Miles Romney, owner and publisher of The Western News. Apparently the well had been "salted", and no real oil existed. The shares were only worth the paper they were written on.

In 1997, the north-south road in this Corvallis area carries the name "Oil Well Road".

CHEESE DAY PICNIC IN CORVALLIS

From the Darby Dispatch, August 4, 1927

People from all parts of the Bitter Root Valley and from many points outside the county, flocked to the second annual Cheese Day celebration at Corvallis last Thursday to picnic, greet friends, and find enjoyment in the various entertainment features.

The picnic was held on the old school grounds with ideal weather conditions prevailing. The program started at 10 o'clock with a musical program. Those who took part included Mrs. H. Toftoy, Mrs. R. P. Wilson, Miss Kathryn Bailey, Miss Ruth Bailey, Miss Winifred Frogge, Miss Frances Myers Elliott, Arthur Dowse, D. O. Cobb. J. G. Leibel, J. W. Rockafellow and R. B. Myers entertained in a fiddler's contest.

The speaker of the day was Senator W. J. Paul, of Deer Lodge, who was introduced by Senator Tom Kane of Corvallis. Senator Paul complimented the audience upon their homeland and its accomplishments in agricultural and manufacturing endeavors. **He brought out the fact that Corvallis had the largest cheese factory in the world.**

During the morning hour one of the trucks from the cheese plant circled the grounds and cheese sandwiches were dispensed to the throng.

In the afternoon Stevensville won a baseball game from the Corvallis team, 14–2.

Afternoon sports results follow:

Horseshoe pitching — won by J. C. Howe, Jr. and H. Fehrenkamp. Carl Printz won the battle royal.

Jigging — Mrs. A. Glehan; Others entered were Thomas Kane, Charles Wolfe and H. Hilder.

Rope climbing — Russell Geisy, first.

Boxing Contest, boys under 8 years — Carl Hoblitt Jr., winner; Under 12 years, Carl Yadon, winner; Over 12 years, Carl Printz, winner

Egg smashing contest — Douglas Hoblitt, first.

Nail driving contest for women — Mrs. Frank Printz, first

Gooseberry pie eating — Henry Moore, first.

Race — girls under 12, Margaret Pile, first.

Women's race — Mabel Baumgartner, first

Boy's race 50 yds — under 12 years, Arthur Overturf, first; over 12 years, Clarence Popham, first.

Fat man's race — V. Yadon, first.

Young man's race — 180 yards, Clarence Popham, first.
Boy's race — 100 yards, 12 to 14 years old, LeRoy Cobb, first.

The selling of milk for use in the making of butter, cheese, curds, and other dairy products was a very viable endeavor in the early years in Ravalli County. Collection depots sprang up in almost every little town. Milk and cream delivered to these depots gave the small farmer an immediate "cash crop". They used their "cream check" to purchase the daily necessities of life or to save toward a large purchase. The value of the milk or cream was determined by measuring the butter-fat content, so not only was the liquid amount important, but also the richness of the product.

HAIGH'S

You know of Haigh's Bar, recently Staver's and most recently the Spice of Life restaurant. Perhaps you have even been there in the '60s and '70s when it still was Haigh's Bar with the card room in back and the pool table in front and the long bar and back bar with its great collection of beer cans. Even if you did not go inside you could stay on the sidewalk and order through an outside window popcorn or a soft drink. Did you know that the building at one time was the First National Bank?

Here is how it all came about.

Joseph Haigh was born at Alma, Wisconsin Feb. 22 1877. He was one of 18 children (nine boys and nine girls) of John and Mary Haigh. He came to the Bitterroot March 17, 1899, to work at the Daly racing stable until it was disbanded after the death of Marcus Daly. He then worked for Swan Johnson in Florence and came with him when the latter gentleman took charge of a portion of the Daly Stock Farm, which was later named the Johnson Ranch. Joe became foreman, but in 1903 returned to Wisconsin and married Emma Koepp, his former sweetheart, on Jan. 5, 1904. They returned to the Johnson ranch, had three children, Irene and Ruth born there and Herb born on the Shulund place on the Skalkaho.

In 1907 Joe and Emma returned to Wisconsin, but soon came back to the Bitterroot and he became foreman on a crew building the 'Big Ditch". When that was completed he bought a ranch on the Skalkaho between Shuland's and Hauswirth's. He sold that place and moved to the Doran addition and worked at the ACM mill on the river west of town.

In 1915 he bought a cigar store from M.L. Kelly on north second where the Rainbow Bar is now located. He operated that until 1922 when he sold it and went back to farming again on the Skalkaho for three years. Three years later he then bought another cigar store from "Bill" Frogge where the Signal Bar is now located, ran it for a number of years and then moved it to the former First National Bank building. This was built in 1910, the first hospital had formerly been located here. He bought the north half of the building in 1935 and the rest of it in 1950. He had retired from active proprietorship of the business on Jan 1, 1946, and sold it to his son, Herb, and son-in-law, Lawrence H. Applebury, the husband of Irene, March 25, 1952. He passed away Nov. 2, 1959.

The building has changed hands a few times and is now the Spice of Life restaurant.

INDEPENDENT DITCH

The first irrigation ditch to divert water from the Bitter Root River in Ravalli County was what was known as the Independent Ditch, and delivered water to the Chaffins, Popham, Humble and Parkhurst ranches. This did not cover all of those places, so as the Surprise ditch that was taken out of the river at Hamilton, and was gradually extended northward, the ranches under the Independent decided to join the Surprise and become part of that company, moving the priority date back to January 1, 1871, for the Surprise Ditch — which today is known as the Corvallis Canal and Water Company.

THE CORVALLIS CANAL AND WATER COMPANY

History:

This ditch was first incorporated under the name of the "Surprise Ditch Company," on June 31, 1884, for a period of twenty years. Under the Surprise ditch the first water users were John F. Allen, William D. Lear, Nana Johnson, Ferdinand Wehr, and B. F. Sanders.

Before the twenty year period of existence expired for the Surprise ditch Company, Reincorporation Articles were filed on February 27, 1897, and the name changed to "The Corvallis Canal and Water Company," with the term of existence twenty years.

The last incorporation of The Corvallis Canal and Water Company took place on February 17, 1917, with the period of existence forty years. However, the Corporation Articles were not recorded until January 22, 1922, and therefore will not expire until January 22, 1962. An amendment to the Articles of Incorporation of The Corvallis Canal and Water company occurred on March 4, 1933, with the amount of capital stock increased from $4,250.00 divided into 85 shares at $50.00 per share to a capital stock of $17,000.00 and 85 shares of a par value of $200.00 each.

Present Statistics:

Location: The canal diverts water from the right bank of the Bitterroot River, west of Hamilton in NW 1/4 NW 1/4 of sec. 25, T. 6 N., R. 21 W. and follows a generally northeasterly direction, for the irrigation of lands in

State of Montana

-ss-

County of Ravalli

Matt I. Vaughan being first duly sworn deposes and says:

That he is 93 years of age, and lives at 423 No. 4th Street, Hamilton, Montana.

That he moved to Ravalli County in 1888 from Missouri, and has lived in Ravalli County ever since that time.

That in 1888 the Surprise Ditch, now known as the Corvallis Canal, ended at what was then the Elijah Chaffin Ranch, now owned by Mrs. Ethel Fierce. That thereafter, between the years 1900 and 1903 said ditch was extended so that it crossed the East Side Highway where it runs east and west.

It then emptied into a small waste water ditch known then as the Parkhurst Ditch. The Surprise Ditch was extended to the Parkhurst Ditch at the request of the owner and owners of the Parkhurst Ditch, and the waste water from the Surprise Ditch was delivered to the Parkhurst Ditch at the request of the owners of the Parkhurst Ditch and by arrangements and agreements made between the then owners of the Surprise and Parkhurst Ditches.

Thereafter the owners of the Parkhurst Ditch enlarged said ditch so as to take care of the waste water delivered to it from the Surprise Ditch. The Parkhurst Ditch later became known as the Supply Ditch.

The undersigned was married in 1890 to Patsy Popham, daughter of J. W. Popham. In many of the years during the period between 1891 and 1912 the undersigned farmed the land through which the Surprise Ditch was extended between 1900 and 1903, sometimes self-employed, sometimes working with or for said J. W. Popham who then owned said land. The undersigned help build the extension to said Surprise Ditch between 1900 and 1903, and worked on said Ditch in following years, and is well acquainted with the facts as are herein set forth.

Matt I. Vaughan

On this 7th day of November in the year 1957, before me, Charles H. James, a Notary Public for the State of Montana, personally appeared Matt I. Vaughan, known to me to be the person whose name is subscribed to the within instrument, and acknowledged to me that he executed the same.

IN WITNESS WHEREOF, I have hereunto set my hand and affixed my official seal this 7th day of November, 1957.

Charles H. James
Notary Public for the State of Montana,
residing at Hamilton, Montana.
My commission expires Feb. 21, 1960.

sections, 13, and 24, T. 6 N., R. 21 W.; sections, 4, 5, 6, 7, 8, and 18, T.6 N., R. 20 W. and sections, 9, 10, 15, 16, 20, 21, 22, 28, 29, 31, 32, and 33, T. 7 N., R. 20 W.

Length and capacity of canal: The main canal of the Corvallis canal and Water Company is approximately 9.5 miles long and has a carrying capacity in excess of 125 cubic feet/sec. An upper lateral of the canal system starts from a point on the main canal in the NW 1/4 NW 1/4 of sec. 33, T. 7 N., R. 20 W., and continues in a northeasterly direction for a distance of 4.5 miles where it ends in the NE 1/4 /SW 1/4 of sec. 10, T. 7N., R. 20 W.

Operation and Maintenance: In 1956 each share of stock in the canal company was assessed $29.41, with the cost of operating and maintaining the canal totaling $2,500.00 for the year.

Present Users: With 85 active stock shares in the company, each share is equal to 58.8 miner's inches of water. The 85 shares of stock are divided among 133 water users in the canal system.

Acreage Irrigated: For the year 1957, there were 3,827.5 acres irrigated, and 21 acres potentially irrigatable under the canal.

Water Right Data:

The Corvallis Canal and Water Company has a decreed water right from the Bitterroot River of 5,000 miner's inches with a priority date of January 1, 1871. (Ref. Case No. 1287, Judgment Book 2, Page 481, Ravalli County Courthouse, Hamilton, Montana).

MONTANA CAFE AND THE HOMS

Residents of the valley from the 1950s through the early 1980s will remember the Montana Cafe on Main Street, Hamilton and the Homs: Harry, May, Jimmy and Kim. Let me tell how it all came about.

The original cafe was run by Sherman Lee, beginning in the early 1900s. In 1916, Lee Suey, Harry's foster father, and his brother, Lee Poy, came to Hamilton from Butte and started a laundry on north Second about the 300 block. Sometime thereafter they acquired the cafe from Sherman. Lee Poy, the older, was the chef and Lee Suey the waiter and manager.

Harry came to Hamilton in 1930 at about sixteen years of age and went to school at Jefferson. He would work in the cafe after school, but in 1935 he went to Helena and worked in the White Eagle Cafe. While there he met and married May Wong in 1942 and they returned to Hamilton a year later. Harry worked in the cafe then and acquired the cafe from Lee Suey and Lee Poy in 1951. At first it was located in the building owned by A.P. Nickel, but later moved to a building next-door that Burns built for it.

Jimmy Lee Hom, Harry's cousin, came to Hamilton in 1935 about the same time that Lee Suey's son Bill and Lee Poy's son Howard came.

Jimmy worked in the cafe after school and went into the service during World War II, where he learned to cook. Harry and May acquired the cafe in 1951 and Jimmy helped them. After a while Jimmy went back to China married Kim and brought her back here. The four of them ran the cafe until it closed in 1983.

The cafe was a remarkable place. If you were a good friend of Harry's, your tumbler of water might contain pure gin. If you came in for lunch and ordered a hamburger, you might also get a freshly cooked duck. For many years the time from 9:30 to 10:30 am was taken up by a loosely knit coffee club that played knock poker. Once a year, Harry and Jimmy would invite many of the men of the town to a Duck Dinner on a Monday when the restaurant was usually closed. At these times the food, liquor and gambling was unlimited. I think some of the local bar owners finally put a stop to it as the cafe had neither liquor nor gambling license. Another remarkable feature of the place was that almost all visiting or passing through athletic teams stopped for a meal as the four could feed a team faster and better than any other place. Talk about Fast Food!! I would be remiss if I did not also mention Harry's Chinese arthritis cure of Rattlesnake whiskey. George Beechwood would supply the rattlesnakes and somehow they would stuff a live rattler into a half-gallon jug and then fill it up with whiskey. Tasted terrible, but the Chinese thought it was great. If someone from Hamilton was going to San Francisco, Harry would often have them take a jug to friends or relatives there.

The relations of all these people have done very well. Lee Suey's son, Bill, is a civil engineer. Lee Poy's son, Howard, is a physician connected with a university.

May's dad was a tailor in Butte; he died in 1960, her mother in 1979. She had four brothers and a sister, all scattered over the U.S.

Harry's father ran a laundry in Philipsburg. Harry had a brother and a sister that came to New York city and are still living. His other siblings remained in China, but have since passed on.

Harry and May have a son, Harry, a professor in Missouri; daughters Nancy and Beverly in Oregon, Linda in Missoula (married to Dr. Kress). Harry passed on in 1992.

Jimmy and Kim had two sons, Tom and John, both living in Seattle and a daughter, Fong, in Helena, and Emily in Tucson. A nephew of Kim's, Ed, came here from China in about 1972; he was a brilliant student and now resides in Virginia. Kim died in 1977 and Jimmy in 1988.

EARLY DAY SAWMILLS
IN THE BITTER ROOT VALLEY

by Paul "Roscoe" Hall

At the time the white man came to the Bitter Root Valley, the foothills on the west side, and the canyons just above the foothills on the east side, were covered by large and beautiful yellow pine. After the log cabin era, there was a large demand for lumber to build the houses, barns, and sheds as the population continued to increase.

Thanks to an article written by Frank Rummel, we have some idea of the early day mills located around the Dutch Hill, Mill Creek, and Blodgett Creek areas. They are as follows:

George Mace on Blodgett Creek, Ed Johnson & Dunbar on Henry Oppegard land, Johnson, Dunbar, Tom and John on Churn Creek with a 6 horse and an 8 horse power with a jack shaft hookup, Charley Squires on Mill Creek, Archie March on Tamarack Creek, Sandy Mac Mellon on the John Elliott Ranch, one mill on the Ludeman Ranch, one on the Jerry Earnest Ranch, Jim Horn on the south side of Mill Creek, Joe Blodgett on south side of Mill Creek, Wolf Ranch, Joe Blodgett on the north side of Mill Creek, Keeling Ranch, Joe Blodgett on the south side of Schiffman Creek, Harper & Baird, Largee outfit on Cow Creek, John McClarey on Cow Creek, Baker & Hanson on Tagalder Creek, Hanson on the north side of Mill Creek, Bert Garnett on Schiffman Creek, Tom Dunbar on Churn Creek,

Kress-Brennan Sawmill, 1890.

cutting permit timber, Kern Bros. on Malone Ranch, Tom Dunbar on Elliott Ranch, Lee Shook on Rummel Ranch, L. Huber on Schiffman Creek, Speck on Lucky Bill Gulch, Joe Blodgett 1 1/2 miles north of Woodside, Noon on Blodgett Creek, Walter Tie Mill on Cow Creek, Harold Rose on Tamarack Creek.

These mills were moved from time to time as the timber was too far from the mill. One man did not have two or three mills running at the same time, but relocated to be close to the source of timber.

In 1887, James A. Hedge started a good-sized mill at Riverside. By March, 1888, it was in full production and was sawing 25,000 feet of lumber per day, to supply his contract with the Montana & Bitter Root Valley Railroad with a million feet during the next two months. Some of this was for ties and bridge timbers.

About 50 men were employed at the mill which included a planer mill, a Blacksmith Shop, and shingle mill. About this time, Hedge started a lumber yard in Grantsdale. The M & BRV Railroad was completed to Grantsdale in June of 1888.

Hedge continued a large operation, a siding was built to the mill. It was reported in 1888, that one million feet of lumber was shipped from the Bitter Root each week and 700,000 feet were shipped to Butte, Anaconda, and Helena.

In 1890, Hedge secured a contract with James Hamilton for lumber for improvements on the Daly Ranch.

In April, 1893, Hedge renovated his mill at Riverside and in September,

1910. Jess Smith driving four horses — logging. Others not identified.

sold his Riverside Mill property to the Montana Lumber & Manufacturing Company for $60,000. Hedge remained as manager.

In 1898, the ML & M Company sold out to Daly. It's not known when the mill was dismantled.

In 1889, Brennan & Kress built a mill on the west side of the river across from Skalkaho Creek; this mill was the forerunner of Daly's timber operation in the Bitter Root. It was apparently backed by Daly.

At the same time, Hamilton was secretly acquiring land for the town site of Hamilton and a large sawmill. Kress sold his interest in the mill to Hamilton. Brennan & Company had unlimited backing from Daly. In August, 1890, the Bitter Root Development Company, was incorporated and by the end of the month, the town of Hamilton was taking shape.

They established a pond on the river large enough to hold 40,000,000 feet of logs. In May, 1891, the Brennan Mill was moved to the dam site. Construction was started on a big mill in the fall of 1891. In April, 65 men were working on the new mill. It included a building 60 x 160 to house the mill, planer, and Blacksmith Shop.

In May, 1891, Robert Harper obtained the first of many contracts with the Bitter Root Development Company to haul 500,000 feet of logs. Harper logging remained in business for many years. They were still logging in the Bitter Root until the early 1950s, and possibly later. Granville Shook also started logging for Bitter Root Development in 1891. Shook also remained in business for many years.

Bitter Root Development Company mill and dam at the west end of Main Street in Hamilton.

The log drive from the West Fork employed 100 men and was not completed until mid July. The sawmill was producing 150,000 feet of lumber with 10 hour shifts. The mill closed at the end of November, 1894, and began operating in March 1895, with production of 200,000 feet per day. Thirty-two railroad cars were required per day to keep the yard clear. They had a lath mill which was turning out 25,000 lath per day.

In 1896, the mill opened in March employing 300 men, an increase of 100 over 1895. During the winter of 1897-1898, the A.C.M. established its own logging camp and employed 50 men. By 1899, there were signs that the readily accessible timber was nearing depletion.

In January, 1900, the West Lumberman reported that Daly was possibly the biggest lumber manufacturer in the world. In 1898, his mills were producing 180 million feet of lumber and in logging and lumbering, he was employing 1700 men; and had in the past, year, invested $2 Million in lumber and logs. ACM's principal mills were at Hamilton, Bonner and St. Regis.

In 1903, the Hamilton Mill manufactured 150,000 apple boxes and 52,000 berry crates — five times the amount produced five years earlier. In 1908, the ACM told the Bitter Root Fruit Growers Association it could supply 100,000 apple boxes at 12¢ a box. The mill operated off and on until 1915, when they closed the Hamilton and St. Regis Mills, concentrating their

Anaconda Copper Mines Mill located at the west end of Main Street in Hamilton, about 1910.

operation at Bonner.

In 1900, J. O. Lagerquist and Erick Erickson started a mill on North Fourth in Hamilton. In 1908, Lagerquist bought out Erickson and operated at the North Fourth location until 1914, when it was moved to the ground South of the fairgrounds that is now used as parking during the fair.

At about this time, the name became Lagerquist & Sons. They continued to operate under this name until J.O. Lagerquist retired. The name was again changed to Riverview Mfg. Co., and was operated by sons, George and Victor (Luke) Lagerquist. In 1938, they built a new mill that could produce 15,000 feet of lumber in an 8 hour shift, and were employing 17 men. The new mill was powered by a 100-horse power electric motor. A lot of timber was then made into apple boxes and crates of all types in which Bitter Root apples and produce were shipped to market. The mill operated until the early 70s when it was closed and the property was purchased by the county in 1972.

In the early 1920s, Frank Printz had a mill in Little Willow Creek east of Corvallis.

In the late 1920s, Tom Dunbar moved his mill to Woodside. It was later taken over and operated by Tom Dunbar, Jr. and his brothers. In the early 1960s, Tom, Jr. started a building supply retail store in a building that had been a Northern Pacific warehouse when the railroad went through Woodside. In the late 1940s and early 1950s, a man by the name of Fullerton had a small mill 1/4 west of Woodside and Robinson had one, 1 mile north of Woodside.

In 1925, Willard and Guy Hall had one on the South fork of Birch Creek on their own property. After that property was logged, they moved it to a location on Popham Lane and hauled logs from the north side of Willow Creek.

In the 1950s and 1960s, Bob Carmichael and Loren Kraft had a mill on Tucker Crossing. It was located on the south side of the road between the river and Highway 93.

The early day mills that Frank Rummel writes about were probably powered by horses. John and Tom Dunbar had 6-horse and 8-horse power with a jack shaft hookup. Before gas engines and steam became powerful enough to run sawmills, threshing machines, hay presses, etc., they were powered by horses walking around in circles.

In later years, after the use of gas and steam, the output of a mill was about 1,000 board feet per man per day.

SUGARBEET INDUSTRY

By Pat Rhodes for the Ravalli Republic 10-15-97

A generation ago sugar beets were king in the Bitterroot Valley. And, October was the beet harvest time on the farms of the central part of the county.

Sugar beets, for about 50 years, were a valuable cash crop on irrigated acres, particularly from Corvallis to north of Stevensville. The industry was profitable for many farmers from around World War I until the late 1960's and 1970's. During most of those years, fall harvest dominated the ag scene with long railroad trains of gondolas filled with beets headed for the Great Western Sugar Company factory and then to the American Crystal Sugar Company factory in Missoula.

Early on, the sugar beets were a labor-intensive crop. At harvest time, they were lifted from the earth, hand-topped and tossed into a V-shaped open row between beet rows. Then they were thrown by beet fork into the back of a truck or wagon and taken to a railroad siding where they were weighed, recorded and loaded on a gondola. The dirt knocked from the beets during this process was loaded back into the farmer's truck and then the truck was re-weighed and the weight of the dirt, or tare, was subtracted from the original weight of the beets.

In those years, all beets went to Missoula to be made into sugar. In later years, the Missoula factory closed and fewer and fewer farmers raised sugar beets. The remaining growers shipped their beets to Billings during that time. Although beets are no longer grown here, sugar beets are still an important part of the Ag industry in Montana, particularly in the Yellowstone Valley.

The history of sugar beets in Ravalli County actually dates from about 1917, when the big smokestack on the north side of Hamilton was built to be part of the Montana-Utah Sugar Company's sugar beet processing plant, according to a story in the Ravalli Republic's Centennial special issue printed in 1989. The smokestack represents a failed dream and includes a scar on the company, which promoted the use of child labor in the beet fields. Valley residents were hopeful the plan would work as they watched the smokestack rise at a rate of about 7 feet a day. Farmers had already planted the seed, but labor was scarce so the company appealed for child labor to work in the fields. By July of 1917, a company official was in Hamilton and said: "We are mighty well satisfied with the children's work." The children were paid $1.50 per day for cultivation (hand-hoeing the fields).

By December, the Ravalli Republican reported on the complete failure of the Montana-Utah Sugar Company and said: "The tall and symmetrical concrete stack, which for the past few months has stood

Windrowing the sugar beets.

Sugar beet wagon, with horses pulling a heavy load.

forlornly and alone, a monument to what might have been, is now to become the rallying point for renewed activities, to culminate in a modern, efficient and actual sugar manufacturer for Hamilton and the Bitterroot Valley."

Although the sugar beet industry prospered for many years, the old stack stands today, without its promised factory.

Homer Bailey, whose father raised beets from the earliest days of the industry, followed in his stead and Homer's son, Bob, saw the crop through to end about 50 years later.

Bailey has old records from the sugar beet era and he said at its peak, the processing plant in Missoula processed beets from about 12,000 acres in western Montana. As Homer remembers, about 5,000 of those acres were in the Bitterroot Valley. The peak years for the industry were from about 1931 to 1949, he said, but a significant number of acres remained in the crop into the late 1960's and beets were grown here and shipped to Billings for a time after that.

There was money to be made from sugar beets. Farms were bought and paid for; homes were built and automobiles and equipment were affordable for the farmers who raised the crop in the glory years. Bailey said, according to his old records, the lowest gross was $50.00 per acre in the early '30s and the highest gross was more than $300.00 per acre in the later years. The beets yielded about 10 tons per acre early on and then moved upward to as high as 25 tons per acre on some farms later on.

Originally, the growers had a contract price for their crop based on the tonnage they delivered. Then the company negotiated for a participating contract that depended on what the company could sell the refined sugar for that year. The company would make an early down payment and then final payment came about planting time the following spring.

The company that operated the longest time in western Montana was the American Crystal Sugar Co., which had a factory in Missoula. It was preceded by the Amalgamated Sugar Co., Bailey said. In the final years, the factory in Missoula closed and growers shipped their beets to a Great Western sugar Co., factory in Billings.

During the active sugar beet years, the company supplied migrant workers, seed, fertilizer and by-products to the farmers — all for a price, of course. Raising beets was highly labor-intensive, almost around the clock from spring through harvest and a large number of Mexican and Philippine field workers were a necessary part of the whole economy. Other migrant workers came in to work in the fields, as well, but Mexico and the Philippines had the highest number. Some families of workers stayed and bought their own farms and later generations of those families are here today.

Originally, the company went to Mexico to recruit braceros. They would bring the Mexicans to a labor camp near the Bailey place and then

Sugar beets piled high awaiting hauling to the sugar factory.

divide them among the farmers. Eventually most of the farms provided little help houses to accommodate their own laborers. In the 40's, German prisoners of war were brought to the valley to help with the crops and they were put up in the labor camp north of Corvallis as well. Later, Mexican-Americans organized their own labor crews and would come to Montana for beet thinning and weeding and then go on to work in Minnesota in the cucumber fields. After that, they would return to Texas to work in the cotton. Some ranchers established long-term relationships with their workers and the migrants would return to the same farm year after year.

Throughout most of the years of beet growing in the valley, hand labor was needed for thinning, weeding, and hoeing. In the early days, laborers also had to chop off the beet tops at harvest time. Later, part of the process was mechanized.

There were about 10 beet dumps in the valley, according to Bailey. They were at major railroad crossings and the farmers hauled their beets to the dumps for shipping to Missoula. When there weren't enough train cars or there were too many beets at the height of harvest, the beets were piled high to await shipment.

Once the beets were out of the ground and delivered to the factory, another step of the industry kicked in because the beet tops and by-products from processing had value. Farmers would pick up the tops and make silage out of them for livestock feed or turn the cows right out in the fields to eat the tops. Cows loved beet silage. It was like candy to them. Then, the company would sell beet pulp and beet pellets back to the farmers for livestock feed supplements.

Despite all the work and difficulties, sugar beets were good for the Valley. They constituted a bright spot in the economy for almost half of the 20th century. But it all came to an end. Yields dropped off. They were disease problems and the cost of labor and equipment adversely affected the industry causing its decline and eventual halt here.

HISTORY OF THE WESTERN NEWS

By Clarence Popham, nephew and cousin

The Western News, although it was not the first newspaper in the Bitter Root, nor was it popular with the Republicans, certainly espoused the same message and supported the same causes for more years than any other paper that has served the Bitter Root Valley. Its history and the fact that The Western News and the name of Miles Romney were synonymous for over 80 years, demands that it should be included in Bitter Root Trails.

James T. Farris founded the Western News in Stevensville, Montana, in 1889. Because all the activity was at Stevensville, it having been the first capitol of Washington Territory, home of St. Mary's Mission, Fort Owen, and the first county seat, it was the logical location for a newspaper.

A local paper in those days not only had all the local news such as personal items, church, and lodge news, it would also have state, national, and world news. Politics and advertising demanded most space, but also demanded much time from the editor and staff, so in 1890, R. L. Davis was hired as Associate Editor.

It seems that although Mr. Farris was always involved, you could almost bank on some changes in title or position on a regular basis. By 1891, Mr. Farris was editor and publisher. Then in 1891, or early 1892, he apparently sold, or at least relinquished, the position of editor and publisher to Mr. Weisenflue, who held this position for about six months. At that time, Mr. Farris took back the paper and retained the ownership and position of editor until late 1892. In 1892, the paper was sold to Mr. L. A. Woodward. He became owner, editor and publisher, but Mr. Farris stayed on as city editor.

In August 1893, the paper was moved from Stevensville to Hamilton. Mr. Farris and Mr. Woodward were both involved in the move. However, from then until February of 1894, Mr. Farris was again publisher of The Western News.

Miles Romney, Sr.
Born 1-18-1872
Died 3-31-1943

The Western News

Miles Romney, Jr.
Born 12-6-1900
Died 2-19-1976

It is interesting to note that although Stevensville and Hamilton were some 20 miles apart with horse and buggy transportation, there were two trains a day each way which served the Bitter Root. With the unhurried approach, the two were just as close as they are now.

The paper of August 1, 1893, published in Stevensville, carried the following item, "The Western News will be removed to Hamilton in a few days, but will continue its Stevensville service the same as at present. Owing to the want of time and space, we will give our reasons for moving next week." This writer was unable to find a copy of the next weeks newspaper, for August 9, 1893. So, anything further must be from the references and speculation. An item of September 6, 1893, Hamilton, "The Western News has added 50 new names to its subscription list in a little over three weeks past. Not a bad showing for a period of depressive times like the ones through which the County is passing." The impending move of the county seat to Hamilton shows the move to Hamilton was excellent judgment.

Mr. Woodward continued as owner and editor, and Mr. Farris as city editor, after the move to Hamilton. However, in February of 1894, Mr. Farris announced that he would be leaving The Western News and in March of that same year, he started the Darby Sentinel. Mr. Woodward hired Mr. R. L. Davis, as associate editor to replace Mr. Farris. As of July 1895, the masthead carried the line "Woodward and Davis, publishers." This ended Mr. Farris's involvement with The Western News except that when the Darby Sentinel was discontinued, The Western News bought the machinery and the subscription list.

Although the place of publication was changed a number of times by various accounts, the most authentic references was in the March 1958 issue of "Way Back When" in The Western News. The February 1895 issue is quoted as follows: "But of no less evidence of solid prosperity of this city is the new home for The Western News, which is being constructed on Main Street near Fourth." The writer in the March 1958 issue goes on to explain that in February of 1895, The Western News was printed on the "Second floor of the Swayze's Livery Stable," (later the Harris Garage) which occupied the present site of the Federal Building and Post Office. The building under construction on Main and Fourth was on part of the "lots" where Fullerton Plumbing and Heating built their plant. It goes on to say, "Later The Western News was located in a frame building situated where Haigh and Applebury now maintain their establishment." The March 31, 1976, issue of "Way Back When" was more specific in pinning this location to the back of the Coulter Block to the rear of the Geiman Building (Federal Credit Union building). This is south of the alley in the block between Main and State, and Second and Third. It was during this period The Western News changed hands again.

Miles Romney, Sr., who had come to the Bitter Root Valley with his parents, in the spring of 1881, from Utah, had gone as far as he could in the local schools, then went to Ohio where he trained to be a teacher. After having taught for a couple of years, the first year at Bannack, Montana, he returned to the Valley and became interested in the newspaper business. In 1895, as a young man in his twenties, **Miles Romney purchased The Western News** from Mr. Woodward. He published his first issue on October 2, 1895. Miles' younger brother, Kenneth, was of much assistance to Miles with the paper in the early times.

Not long after the purchase of the paper, **Miles Romney and Elizabeth Robbins were married.** Their early home was the back room of the print shop. **It is entirely hearsay with this writer, but it has been said that Miles Romney, Jr., was born there.** This would add credence to the theory that early surroundings can influence a life.

Apparently, the life of The Western News was stable from 1895 until December of 1900. At that time, not only a son was born to the Romney's, but they purchased the land and building where The Western News was printed from 1902 until 1977. Miles Romney, Sr. purchased the land from John Zilinsky and announced that he would be moving the"shop" directly across the street from R. L. Perkins' store on South Second Street as soon as a building was ready.

The "Rest of the story" about The Western News is that:

•On August 9, 1910, the first edition of a paper set in Ravalli County with a linotype machine instead of hand set was published.

•In 1911, C. B. Cotrell, 2-revolution Flatbed press was installed. This was a hand-fed press and at first was powered by a treadmill with human power. A gasoline engine with a jackshaft was used and finally electric motors were used to run it. This press is now owned by the Historical Society, and is in storage waiting to be set up somewhere.

•Miles Romney, Sr., the first day war was declared, enlisted in the Army, leaving the paper to be operated by his wife. He served all through World War I, becoming a Major in the Quartermaster Corps.

•In 1922, Miles Romney, Jr., graduated from the University of Montana, in Journalism, and after a 2 year period of world travel and education, became the Editor of The Western News for a period of five years.

•In 1929, Miles, Jr., left the paper as it could not support two families, and he was employed in Washington, D. C., later working with the Internal Revenue Service. Miles, Sr., returned to Hamilton and ran the paper while Miles, Jr., was gone.

•In 1937, Miles, Jr., returned to The Western News as Editor, and continued as such until the time of his death.

•In 1938, The Western News was ravaged by fire. The greatest damage was from smoke and water.

•On March 31, 1943, Miles Romney, Sr., passed away and Miles, Jr., became the sole owner, as well as Editor.

•In 1946, the old building built and occupied in 1902 was replaced by a modern cement block building. The new building was not in use long until another fire in 1947, was experienced with the greatest damage from smoke and water being in the office and make-up area that was rented out and required the refurbishing of the complete area, but little damage to the equipment.

•Another fire in 1953 was the most destructive of all the fires. It did a great deal of damage to the linotype and the rollers on the press, besides the damage to the office and stock. Although the paper never missed an issue, it was because of the good graces of the Journalism Department at the University allowing the crew to work there until school started, and then the Northwest Tribune permitting the crew from The Western News to work nights in their shop in Stevensville. When you can't find what you want in the Bitter Root Trails, go to the Museum and look it up in The Western News.

•February 19, 1976, was the greatest tragedy of all when Miles Romney, Jr. passed away, and the Romney tradition was ended for all time.

•March 1976, The Western News was sold to the Southwest Publishing Company, owners of the Ravalli Republic. Publication continued for one year, at which time the name "The Western News" was discontinued.

Perhaps the most fitting tribute that was published at the time of the sale should be repeated at this time. This is a quote in The Western News of March 31, 1976.

"*The paper has been noted throughout Montana for its vigorous editorial stance, its unflinching defense of public rights, and its war on corporate domination and influence in Montana. The Romney's, both father and son, using The Western News, spoke with a strong and independent voice that is now stilled.*"

Miles Romney, Jr., liked to be known as the chronicler of the neglected truth, using this in the masthead of the paper, and on his stationery.

The Bitter Root Drug Store, 1908. Located on the northwest corner of Second and Main Streets.

Chapter Four

Medical Care

MEDICAL CARE OF THE PIONEERS
and
HOSPITALS IN THE BITTER ROOT

The Western News
November 20, 1895

The much talked of hospital is at last a stern reality. It was opened in the upper story of the Johnson building Thursday with Doctors Minshall and McGrath in charge.

Good, well-furnished rooms with accommodations for ten beds have been provided. The beds are comfortable, with clean, warm clothing and cozy home-like surroundings generally. Pipes connected with the water works are being placed in position and soon the clear, pure water from the snow-fed Skalkaho will be on tap. Electric lights and other conveniences will be provided as soon as possible.

Doctors Minshall and McGrath, who are promoters of this praiseworthy undertaking, are too well known to require introductions.

Laurence Sellers of the Cikson's logging camp sustained a serious crushing of the foot and ankle by a log rolling on it the other day, became its first inmate. He is making good progress.

The hospital at present is mainly maintained by subscription. A great many of the large number of men working on the surrounding ranches, at the big mills and up in the woods, who have no homes to go to in case of injury are only too glad to contribute a small monthly sum that insures good medical attendance and all other requisites free in time of need.

The following was written by
MRS. J. B. (KATE) MITCHELL, 1922

When the Pioneers of whom I'm speaking came into the Valley in the fall of 1864, they found a desolate place. There was no irrigation then and as the grasshoppers had visited the country that summer, there were no signs of vegetation, only buffalo grass and wild sage covered the land. There were no bridges, railroads, or good roads then. Autos, telegraphs and telephones were unheard of. The Bitter Root was very sparsely settled and after leaving Bannack, the pioneers did not meet a soul or see a human habitation until they reached Jim Tolen's ranch on the Skalkaho, about a mile from where the town of Grantsdale now stands. A man by the name of Pat Bray lived about a mile north of Tolen. Where the Daly residence now stands was the next place, J. K. Gird, whose wife was the daughter of Uncle Billy Rodgers and afterwards noted for his part in the Indian War of 1877, lived here.

Corvallis was then called Willow Creek, and only a few settlers lived there. From there on the next place was Fort Owen, where the Indians lived.

Stevensville was not named, but comprised of one log shack where Winslett & Houck traded with the Indians. This county was then part of Missoula County, and Missoula was not started at that time, there being only one unfinished house on the Rattlesnake at the crossing of Mullan Road. Father Ravalli had come and gone, and Major Owen was in the East that year.

There was not a doctor, trained nurse, or even a drug store in this part of the state. The only hospital was 500 miles away, and it was not possible to take a patient there from the Valley. It was fortunate that there was little sickness among the pioneers, as anyone who withstood the perils of that long, hard trip in a covered wagon, across the Plains, was naturally possessed of a strong constitution and not susceptible to disease. Every man was his own physician in those days. He made his own diagnosis and prescribed the remedy. . .and if the prescription did not fit the disease, "It was just too bad."

Remedies were naturally simple. A tea made of wild sagebrush was used in cases of mountain fever, and all other fevers. Woe betide any tenderfoot who complained of headache — they were dosed with the bitter stuff! One pioneer woman told me that after drinking the tea, she could never smell sage again without turning deathly sick at her stomach!

A tea made of a vine growing in the woods called larb, was used in kidney troubles. Soda was used for stomach trouble, and a diet of boiled milk was used for intestinal trouble. Whiskey was used by many of the men, and was the cure for snake bites, mostly in the imaginations of some who imbibed too freely.

An oil for Rheumatism and such ailments was rendered out of the wild animals which abounded here. They were bear oil, snake oil, and an oil from a little black and white odorous aruma (was a specific for stiff joints . . as the odor was gone, the remedy was not so bad.)

The pioneer women in those days would leave their own families in care of their husbands and go to a sick neighbor and care for her for days. When she had to go home, another neighbor would take her place. Their lack of training was made up for by their tenderness of heart, and the experience they had gained in caring for their own families in time of illness.

At the end of two years things began to brighten. In 1866, Father Ravalli was returned to the mission at Fort Owen, and on his return brought a stock of drugs. He was a skillful physician and while his duties as Priest kept him from making visits to the homes, he never failed to prescribe for anyone going to him, and furnished them with drugs.

In 1871, Missoula had developed into a village, and Dr. Buker came there. He would come up the valley when called, but as he charged $50.00 for one visit he was not often sent for until it was too late to be of any service. Money was scarce in those days among the pioneers.

In 1869, Major McCormick was Indian Agent on the Jocko, and in the winter of that year he sent to Missoula for lumber to build a large house on the site where St. Patrick's Hospital now stands. Before this building was finished he sold it to the Sisters of Mercy, and they started the first hospital in this part of the country. From then on, anyone in the valley needing an operation was sent to Missoula. There had never been an operation performed in the Bitter Root until then, although there had been need of some. The first patient to be sent to the Missoula hospital was a man from the Burnt Fork by the name of Jim Chapin, whose condition was more mental than physical.

In 1895, the first hospital in the Valley was a private one, operated by Drs. McGrath and Minchell, on 4th street in a house since torn down. Although doing good work, it was not a paying proposition and was discontinued at the end of a year. Then in 1910 (1907?), a hospital was built in Stevensville. It contained fifteen rooms and Dr. W. T. Thornton operated this hospital until 1917 when he moved to Missoula. He performed over 12,000 operations there.

In 1911, Dr. Lillian Miller saw the need for a hospital in Hamilton, and added the annex to the Ladd Flats, now called the LeSuer Flats. This building consisted of four apartments of four rooms each. Three apartments were used as the hospital and the other one was the nurse's quarters. The building was renovated and an operating room installed. The furniture was the simplest, only a few chairs and an operation table. The place was well lighted but all the water used was obtained from the bathroom downstairs and the sink in the kitchen. The doctors furnished their own instruments and the basins they used were kept in the tin tea chests which had been enameled white by the Superintendent. Wood heaters heated the patient's rooms with one heater for two rooms. With no door between, one room was too hot while the other was too cold. The bells were used to call the nurses. Carpentry work went on in the building for a month after the hospital was installed. This hospital lasted only a year when Dr. Miller turned it over to a Board of Directors, and the management and expenses were assumed by the physicians and others of Hamilton. It was then moved to Second Street, upstairs in the building owned by the Dalys and Mrs. William Teit (Teidt?). The Daly rooms were donated, and through the generosity of the doctors, lodges, and others, were adequately furnished. Mr. Teit charged rent for his room. Mrs. Daly furnished a real sterilizer, among many other gifts, to the new hospital.

I cannot finish this without referring to the Emergency Hospital operated by the Red Cross during the flu epidemic. Mrs. Stewart was the President of this county then, and she appointed Mrs. Ralph Crane (formerly Miss Caserly) as Superintendent of the other hospital for years, and as the Superintendent of this hospital. The Dalys donated a building. I think there were fifteen rooms, outside of the kitchen and dining room for nurses. The food was cooked and donated by the citizens of the town and surrounding farms, and it was abundant and the very best. It was served by the teachers who were on enforced vacations. In this place, seventy-five people were cared for and there was a record of only one death from the flu. One man died a victim of alcoholism. Every nurse, with the exception of two, contracted the flu there.

After a few years, all the rooms being needed for patients, the Drinkenberg rooms over Wells Creamery were rented for nurse's quarters. The room number 13 was marked 31. When I asked the Superintendent, she said, "So many are superstitious, so I won't have number 13 here." Number 31 was one of the favorite rooms.

All honor is due to all who helped maintain these hospitals. For years they were a blessing to the sick of the Valley. No one needing care was ever turned from their doors, and many a sufferer went out from them to a new life of health, while the dying ones were soothed into a dreamless sleep with tender care.

All honor is due Mrs. Daly, for had it not been for her financial support the hospital on Second Street would have had to close its doors at one time.

Then, the Hospital Auxiliary deserves praise for the work it has done, keeping the old hospital going until Mrs. Daly and her son came to the rescue by giving us the Memorial Hospital on South Fourth Street. As to this hospital, I know there is no one so capable of speaking of it as Mrs. Stacy, its superintendent. To her, I gladly relinquish that task.

BITTER ROOT PHYSICIANS

Medical care continues to evolve in the Bitter Root Valley. It started with Father Ravalli, our first physician in 1845 at St. Mary's Mission. He stayed five years, then went to California thence returned in 1866. He died in 1884.

James Mullan, brother of Capt. Mullan, practiced in one of the bastions of Fort Owen in the 1850s. No other physician was here until 1868 when J. B. Price came to Stevensville, stayed one winter and then went to Washington. He died there in 1899. Following him, R. A. Wells, a retired physician, came to Stevensville in 1871, did not practice much, but had a drug store. He was a Civil War Veteran, and died in 1892. Next, a Dr. Curtis, who was also a Methodist minister, arrived in Corvallis in 1879. His pay for saving souls was so low he tried to make up for it by charging more for saving bodies and because of this attitude did not last very long. The Todd brothers, one a dentist and the other a physician, set up in Stevensville in 1880. However again his charges were too high, and this forced people to go to Missoula. Consequently, he did not succeed either.

Dr. Joseph T. Coughenour was the first one to actually stay. He came to Montana in 1874, located in Deer Lodge where he also served as clerk of District Court. In 1882 he moved to Corvallis and practiced for 20 years, then retired to his ranch in 1902. He was also a Civil War Veteran. He died in 1915. Thereafter relatively few physicians located in the valley until the 1890s, when there were about nine.

I might just add here that the railroad came to the valley in 1887 and Ravalli County became an entity in 1893.

St. Patrick's Hospital was started April 19, 1873, but there was no hospital here in the valley until Drs. McGrath and Minshall started one on the second floor of the Johnson or DeNayer building. This building has since been demolished and I cannot find out its exact location, but believe it was in a frame building that existed before the First National Bank was built where Haigh's bar or as it is now known, the Spice of Life Café is located. They were able to operate it only for one year, as it was too much of a financial drain on them. A second hospital then briefly existed in what was known as Ravalli House.

Dr. McGrath graduated from Queens University Toronto and came directly to Hamilton. He was also active in commercial affairs having purchased the Bitterroot Drug, which was located on the northwest corner of Second St. and Main, as well as having built the McGrath Block in 1914. He was a director of the Ravalli County bank for 30 years and its vice president when he died in 1939.

Dr. George Washington Monroe was born in Virginia and raised in Alabama. He began the study of medicine in 1856 under another practicing physician in a small Alabama town. After one year, he entered the medical department of Louisiana University, from which he graduated in 1859. He practiced until the Civil War began, at which time he joined the Confederate Army and served throughout the war. He came to Montana in 1872 stayed in Helena a few months and then moved to Bozeman to practice medicine. He also served as superintendent of public instruction, mayor and register of United States land office. Next he moved to Butte and then to Darby in 1904, where he practiced until retirement in 1910. He died in 1912. His first wife died while they were in Butte and he remarried while in Darby. B. K. Monroe was his daughter-in-law. He was one of seven physicians who started the Medical Association of Montana, as it was then known, in 1879. He became president the second year.

There were two Thornton brothers, Dr. Will and Dr. Charles. Dr. Will arrived in Stevensville in 1908. He built a hospital there in 1909 or 1910. In 1916 he went to Missoula with his brother Charles and they built hospitals there which eventually became the Community Hospital. Dr. Charles practiced first in Corvallis beginning in 1909. I don't know how long either brother lived, but I do know Charles acted as pallbearer for Dr. Browning, another Hamilton physician. Dr. Browning's story is rather interesting. He graduated from Rush Medical School in 1892. He practiced first in Illinois, until 1910, when he came to the Bitter Root and operated a ranch northwest of Hamilton. Because of a shortage of physicians during World War I he took some post graduate work and became licensed in 1918 and practiced until seven weeks before his death due to a cerebral hemorrhage in 1941.

A Dr. Elmer Fessler also had a small hospital in along with Dr. Elton Rogers in Stevensville in 1909. He later lived in Superior and Polson, and, finally, Thompson Falls. While there, he was involved in an auto accident, suffering a head injury that caused mental problems for which he was committed to Warm Springs. A week after his release, he committed suicide with a 30-30.

In 1919, Dr. P. S. Rennick purchased the Thornton Hospital in Stevensville. He came to the valley as a boy, lived on the West Side, worked in Robert's Book Store and for the railroad. Following graduation from University of Kentucky Medical College, he served as a major in World War I. After discharge he went to Helmville and operated a drug store there before coming back to the valley about 1919. He continued to practice until his health caused him to quit shortly before his death in 1944.

In 1911, Dr. Lillian Miller started a hospital in the Ladd Flats apartments. The building still stands south across Bedford St. from the Old Marcus Daly Hospital Apartments. She was only able to operate it for one year and had to turn it over to a board to run it. Shortly after, it was moved to the second floor above the old Stock Farm offices on the east side of South Second Street. She continued to practice until her death in 1922.

Another early woman physician was Winifred Reynolds. She and her husband practiced in Stevensville beginning in 1917. He died in 1936. She became city health officer after his death and practiced until she died in 1942. A son, Gordon, was a dentist in Missoula. He had two sons, William A., a physician at the Western Montana Clinic, and Marvin, a dentist practicing in Missoula.

J. F. S. Marshall practiced in Stevensville from 1912 to 1916 when he joined the Canadian Army. After the war, he went to Missoula and was one of the founders of the Western Montana Clinic.

One of the better known valley physicians was Herbert Virgil Hayward. He was born in Leeds, England, in 1882 came to the United States at age 17 first to Pittsburgh then to Milwaukee. He graduated from Marquette in 1908. He arrived in Darby in 1909 and remained until entering service. Following the war, he returned to Darby and later Hamilton until retiring in 1951. He was an accomplished surgeon, but besides medicine he participated in many community activities. He was responsible for building twelve different structures, including his office building on the corner of Third St. and Bedford, the Hayward-Woods cabin on Lake Como. He also renovated the present Bibler Apartments which had been used as a laundry and employees' quarters in connection with the Ravalli Hotel that had stood where the Bedford Building, or present City Hall, now stands. This latter building was built as the Elks Club and he had much to with its development. He also was involved in the development of the first Marcus Daly Memorial Hospital, as well as the original airport. He married Grace Kerlee and so is related to B. K. Monroe, an author and newspaper correspondent. Helen Bibler, director of the Ravalli County Museum, is a granddaughter and Ada Zoske a niece.

Dr. Armon Meis was associated with Dr. Hayward and practiced in that office until he died in 1968. However you might say that practice survives today because Dr. Glenn Mathias had joined him and continued after Dr. Meis died. Dr. Mathias left in 1970, but Dr. Walker J. Ashcraft, (Butch), had joined him and continues today along with his partner Dr. John Moreland. The office has since moved to Physicians Clinic at the new Marcus Daly Memorial Hospital.

The other clinic, Bitterroot Clinic, by stretching a point could be said to have started with Dr. Donald A.Gordon, although it was not called that until 1968 when that building was built. Dr. Gordon's father, Dr.George, came to Hamilton in 1909, practiced until 1936 when he had a stroke. Dr. Donald was brought up in Hamilton. He graduated in 1932 and joined his father, staying until going into the service in 1942. On his return in 1946, he was associated first with Dr. R. L. Peterson. Dr. Eugene Swanzey joined them shortly before Dr. Donald died. Dr. Swanzey left in early 1956. Dr. Donald W. Maclean joined them in late 1955. In 1963, Dr. Charles Russell Petty joined them and in 1968 they built the present clinic building. Dr. Peterson had been president of the Montana Medical Association and, and served on the Board of Medical Examiners. He retired in 1980 and died in 1993. Dr. Maclean retired in 1986. Dr. Petty retired in 1996. The clinic continues with Drs. Randy Stewart, Mike Moran, Lisa Milch, Teresa Borino and Gary Smith. The last three are Internists.

Up to the present almost all physicians have been family practitioners or generalists. There have been a few exceptions. Dr. Steve Ellis does major surgery and some general practice. There have been three orthopedists, but only one remains, namely Dr. James Chandler. There have been three pediatricians, but only two remain, namely Drs. Ellyn Jones and Blaise Favara. There have been three ophthalmologists, but just Dr. John Kupko is still here. Of the obstetricians, two remain, Drs. Marshall White and Roman Malvehy. The radiologists have more or less rotated through here. Dr. William Anderson was the first. He started at the old Marcus Daly Memorial Hospital. Since he left in about 1988, there have been three more. Dr. Steven

Sutherland currently serves. A urologist was here for three years, but left because he was not busy enough. Perhaps the largest group of specialists has been the emergency room physicians. At present there are four. Dr. James Hansen was the first one. He has gradually built the staff up to its present level. Dr. Brett Bender is currently the director.

The role the hospital plays in the medical delivery system has changed over the years. The first hospital started in 1895 by Drs. McGrath and Minshall lasted only a year, as did the second. The third, in 1911, had to be bailed out, so to speak. The fourth, the old Marcus Daly Memorial Hospital on South Fourth Street, built in 1931, did quite well, but was replaced because of a lack of beds at the time. In the 1930s to the early 1970s, the hospitals served primarily in-patients. Thereafter they began to look more toward out-patient services. The old hospital did not have a proper emergency room as the physicians at that time were used to having patients come to their offices even during off hours. When the new one was built in 1975 emergency room services were anticipated, but have since had to be expanded. Presently the hospital has expanded its services to include the ambulance, home health, hospice and home oxygen service.

One last thing I should mention is the role of Dr. W. R. Spencer in Stevensville. He started in 1952 and alone served the area for about 30 years. Since he retired, he has been replaced by seven physicians. I believe this is due not only to the increase in population in that area, but also because of the competition between Community Hospital in Missoula and Marcus Daly Memorial Hospital in Hamilton.

I have mentioned only a small percentage of the physicians that have practiced here over the years. A complete list exists, but does not make for good reading. There have been one hundred and twenty-four physicians practicing here since Father Ravalli. At present, there are twenty-one in Hamilton, including the emergency room physicians. There are four in Stevensville and one in Darby.

BITTER ROOT VALLEY PHYSICIANS IN PRACTICE FROM 1845 TO 1920

Father Ravalli, St.Mary's Mission 1845-1850, thence to California and returned in 1866. He practiced until he died in 1884.

James Mullan, brother of Capt. Mullan, practiced in one of the bastions of Ft. Owen in the 1850s.

J.B.Price, came to Stevensville in 1868, stayed one winter, left and returned in 1873, but did not stay long going on to Washington. Born 1818 in Pennsylvania, graduated Pennsylvania Medical College in 1842, died in Ellensburg, WA 1899.

R. A. Wells, a retired physician, came to Stevensville in 1871, did not practice much, but had a drug store. He died in 1892. He was a Civil War veteran.

Ed Maxwell. The only thing I could find out about him was in Clarence Popham's book "Early Days in the Sagebrush Country" and it stated, according to a newspaper article, he was in practice in Stevensville in 1888 along with Dr. Wells and Dr. Gwinn.

Curtis was also a M.E. minister, came to Corvallis in 1879. His pay for saving souls was so low he tried to make up for it charging more for saving bodies, but was so exorbitant that he did not last long.

Todd, brothers, one a dentist the other a physician, came to Stevensville in 1880, but again his charges were too high and he did not last long, as people would go to Missoula. He would charge $30 to go over 10 miles and once charged $122 for a normal delivery.

Joseph T. Coughenour was born in Pennsylvania in 1844, came to Montana in 1874, located in Deer Lodge where he served as clerk of district court. In 1882 moved to Corvallis and practiced for 20 years, retiring to his ranch in 1902. He was a veteran of the Civil War. He died in 1915.

S. P. Ives practiced in Stevensville in 1888, but I could not determine for how long.

Thomas Benton Owings was born in Indiana in 1847, came to Hamilton and Grantsdale in 1889. He developed tertiary syphilis with tabes dorsalis, or as they called it then locomotor ataxia, and had to retire in 1900. Up to then he had a very successful practice. He died in 1908.

J. B. Harris. Do not know when he started to practice, but moved up from Victor in 1892. He died in 1894.

Thompson settled in Stevensville in 1892, but I could not find out anything more about him.

The following physician's names were on a number of prescriptions in 1899, which Wayne Hedman, the proprietor of Bitter Root Drug, let me study. However, I could find nothing else about them elsewhere.

Raybold-Fox.

C. G. Forrest did list his office location on the prescription blank as South 2nd over Cook's Business College.

Three others had only one or two prescriptions so they may have been called in from elsewhere and written by the pharmacist. They were: Footrix, Ellis, and H. J. Smith.

A. J. Watts was another physician who had written prescriptions in late 1899. I did find an obituary about him. He was born in 1854 in Webster County, Missouri. He began the study of medicine at age 18 and became a skillful surgeon there in Missouri. In 1895, he developed Bright's disease and because of this disease sought a change of climate and came to the Bitter Root in July of 1899 staying with a nephew. He practiced here until

November when he realized he did not have long to live, so returned home to be with his wife. He died five days after his return.

Delos N. Reber came to Hamilton in 1892 and developed a very large practice. He eventually went to New York State and was known to be alive in 1935, according to Dr. McGrath.

T. H. Hanbidge practiced in Victor during the heyday of the Curlew mine in the early 1890s. In 1894, he spent the year in London and became an EENT specialist, and settled in Missoula when he returned, but eventually retired in Darby where he owned a drug store when he died in 1942. He was born in Ontario in 1856.

W. J. Davis was born in Indiana in 1855, graduated from Cincinnati Medical College, apparently had tuberculosis, as the obituary mentions frequent hemorrhages. He was in Government service in Arizona for two years before coming to Stevensville the spring before he died in November 1894.

Gilbert P. Mills, all I could find regarding him was an ad in the paper of his practice as a physician and surgeon in the Gwinn Bldg. in Stevensville in early 1895.

J. G. Smith. The only reference I could find was an advertisement in the Bitterroot Times Aug. 28, 1896, listing his office in the Dunbar & Johnson building on Second Street, Hamilton. This makes me wonder if this could be the same Johnson building that Dr. McGrath and Minshall had their hospital in during 1895.

J. B. DeNayer was born in France, educated as a physician, went to Africa as assistant surgeon in the army, then came to Omaha and Lincoln before coming to Montana in the early 1880s. He practiced a number of years in Missoula before abandoning the profession and turned to sawmilling in Stevensville for 15 years. He moved to Hamilton in 1907 and passed away a year later.

Russell G. Gwinn did general practice in Stevensville in 1890s. Was clerk of the county court from 1893 to 1896. He went to Missoula in 1908 and practiced EENT. I do not know when he died as Dr. McGrath reported him hale and hearty in 1938.

George McGrath, born 1866 died 1939. He graduated from Queen's University Toronto in 1893 and came directly to Hamilton. He and Dr. Minshall were instrumental in founding the first hospital in Hamilton in 1895 in the DeNayer building or the Johnson Building, whichever article you read. They were able to run the hospital for only a year as it took all their money to do so. The building has since been torn down. He was also active in commercial affairs, having purchased the drug store now known as Bitterroot Drug, which at that time was on the northwest corner of Main and Second, as well as having built the McGrath block in 1914 and been a director of the Ravalli County bank for 30 years and its vice president at his death.

S. W. Minshall and Dr. McGrath started the first hospital as stated above. He came to Hamilton from Deer Lodge (how long he stayed I do not know) but left and practiced in Missoula.

J. Theodore Brice practiced in Stevensville in the late 1890s until 1912, when he went to Lewistown and eventually Georgia.

Thomas J. Baird was born on February 17, 1865 in Toronto, Canada and came to Victor in 1897 and practiced until his death in1907.

W. P. Reynolds was born in Canada in 1869, came to Montana in 1900 and Stevensville in 1917. He died in 1936.

Winifred Reynolds, wife of W. P., was born in Canada in 1876, graduated from medical school Dalhouse University, Halifax, Nova Scotia, in 1899, married W. P. in Butte in 1901, came to Stevensville in 1917 after practicing in Alder and Lane, S.D. She was city health officer since her husband's death. A son, Gordon, a dentist in Missoula, had a son, William A., a physician at the Western Montana Clinic, and another son, Marvin, a Missoula dentist. She died in 1942.

J. W. Howard was born in Missouri in 1842, moved to California, then Oregon and graduated in 1871. In 1884, moved to Dillon for a year, then to Butte for ten to twelve years, then to Bozeman for a year, thence to Hamilton about 1896. In 1903 was injured in a runaway and had been in failing health since then and died of a stroke in 1903.

Herbert Brethour was born in Toronto in 1877, graduated from University of Toronto and came to Hamilton in 1901 and practiced until his death in 1911. He died in Butte after an operation for a brain abscess.

Freiherr Frederick Ernst Baron von Buchen, usually known as F.E. Buchen, was born in Germany in 1863, educated at the University of Bonn and also Vanderbilt University. He served as a physician in the Spanish-American War, during which time he contracted malaria and, failing to get relief from it elsewhere, came to Hamilton in 1903 and practiced until his death in 1938. He was vice-president of the Montana Medical Association.

Robert L. Owens was born in Ohio in 1885 and came to Hamilton in 1908, served as a major in WWI, and on his return went to Missoula. While there was a director of the Chamber of Commerce, president of the Western Montana Medical Society, president of the St. Patrick's Hospital staff and was connected with the medical clinic, as well as a surgeon for the Milwaukee RR.

Anna C. Owens. The only thing I could find on her was that she was a subscriber to the hospital that was proposed to replace Dr. Lillian Miller's hospital.

G. W. Monroe was born in Virginia and raised in Alabama. He began the study of medicine in 1856 under another practicing physician in a small Alabama town. After one year, he entered the medical department of

Louisiana University, from which he graduated in 1859. He practiced until the Civil War began, at which time he joined the Confederate Army and served throughout the war. He came to Montana in 1872, stayed in Helena a few months and then moved to Bozeman to practice medicine. He also served as superintendent of public instruction, mayor and register of United States land office. Next he moved to Butte and then to Darby in 1904, where he practiced until retirement in 1910. He died in 1912. His first wife died while they were in Butte and he remarried while in Darby. B. K. Monroe was his daughter-in-law. He was one of seven physicians who started the Medical Association of Montana, as it was then known, in 1879. He became president the second year.

Edgar A. Brooke was born in 1861 in Maryland. His grandfather was a surgeon in the War of 1812, and his great grandfather was a surgeon in the Continental Army. His early education was in Helena. Later he was engaged in stockraising, but in 1884 he decided on medicine as a career. He graduated from the University of Maryland in 1887. He practiced in Helena and Butte until 1893, when he returned to Washington for post graduate work. Following this he returned to Butte in 1896 and two years later moved to Virginia City, until 1902 when he moved to Stevensville. He was a skilled surgeon, having in 1897 relieved the suffering of a youngster by removing a fragment of a depressed skull fracture and inserting a silver plate.

E. C. Anderson. Again, could find little about him except for ads in newspapers in 1908 and 1909.

Karl H. Kellogg, whose father was W. H. Kellogg of cereal fame and who also bought the Bass brothers ranch, practiced in Stevensville during the late 1890s and early 1900s, then retired and raised strawberries until he returned to Michigan about 1915.

W. T. (Will) Thornton was in Stevensville about 1908, built a hospital there in 1909 or 1910 and, along with his brother, Charles, went to Missoula in 1916 and built hospitals there, which eventually became Community Hospital, located where the present Missoula Public Library now sits.

Charles Thornton practiced in Corvallis around 1909 and went to Missoula with his brother, Will, in 1916. I do not know how long either brother lived, but I do know Charles was a pallbearer for Dr. Browning in 1941.

Frank J. Prince was born in 1873 in Ohio, graduated in 1907 from University of Cincinnati Medical School, came to the Bitterroot in 1912, first practiced in Florence, then Dr. Thornton persuaded him to come to Stevensville in 1918 and become an anaesthetist. He continued his practice until he retired 1953. He died in 1957.

Elmer Fessler was born in 1870. In 1909, he and Elton R. Rogers formed a partnership and opened a small hospital in Stevensville. He later lived in Superior and Polson, finally Thompson Falls. While there, he was involved in an auto accident, suffering a head injury which caused mental problems for which he was committed to Warm Springs. A week after his release he committed suicide with a 30-30.

Elton R. Rogers. All I know about him is that he was initially associated with Dr. Fessler.

Louis H. Fales came to the Three-Mile area with tuberculosis, practiced on an emergency basis for neighbors around 1915, eventually moving to California where he became medical director for a VA hospital.

Walter Neil King was born in Pennsylvania in 1878, graduated from the University Medical School at Kansas City, came to Victor in 1912, thence to Corvallis in 1916. In 1917, went in the army for 2 years, then returned to Corvallis until 1923, when he moved to Missoula to practice. He retired in 1935 for health reasons and died in 1946.

Lillian G. Miller was born in 1872, graduated from the Woman's Medical College in Baltimore, took graduate work at Johns Hopkins came to Hamilton in 1910. In 1911, she started the second Hamilton hospital in a large apartment building known as Ladd Flats that still stands south across the street from the Marcus Daly Hospital Apartments. She practiced in Hamilton until her death in 1922.

England-born Dr. Herbert Virgil Hayward first came to the Bitter Root in 1909 and, except for a stint of service in World War I, he practiced in the valley until his retirement in 1951.

P. S. Rennick was born in 1880 in Missouri or Ohio, came to the valley as a boy, lived on the west side, and worked in Roberts Book Store before entering the University in Missoula. He obtained his medical degree at the University of Kentucky. He served as a major in WWI, following which he went to Helmville and operated a drug store before coming back to the valley in about 1919 when he purchased Dr. Thornton's hospital and practice. He continued to practice until his health caused him to be hospitalized in Missoula for several months. He was home a few weeks and then was hospitalized at the VA hospital in Helena, where he died in 1944.

Robert W. Getty was a graduate of the University of Pennsylvania Medical College in 1891, came to Montana in 1895 and lived in Philipsburg, Glasgow and Hamilton before joining the medical staff at the state tuberculosis hospital in Galen in 1920. He practiced in Hamilton according to a newspaper ad in 1910, so perhaps he stayed here until going to Galen. He died 1945.

J. M. Casserly was born in Canada, graduated from the University of Toronto in medicine. He practiced in Hamilton, according to a newspaper ad in 1910, went to Canada before the United States entered the war and served overseas in the Royal Army Medical Corps. Following the war, he practiced in Canada and served on the staff of associated coroners. He died in Canada in 1931.

J. F. S. Marshall practiced in Stevensville from 1912 until 1916, when he joined the Canadian army. After the war, he returned to Missoula and became a co-founder of the Western Montana Clinic.

Sam Simpson took over Dr. Marshall's practice in 1916.

Herbert Virgil Hayward was born in Leeds, England, in 1882 and came to the United States at age 17, first to Pittsburgh, then Milwaukee. He obtained his medical degree from Marquette University in 1908. He arrived in Darby in 1909 and practiced there until he entered service in WWI. Following the war, he returned to practice in Darby and Hamilton until retiring in 1951. Besides medicine, he was also interested in building construction of 12 different structures, including the Medical Arts building at the corner of Bedford and South Third, now an attorney's office, and the Hayward-Woods cabin on Lake Como. He had a lot to do with the decision of Margaret Daly to build the first Marcus Daly Memorial Hospital. He was quite a motorist, built two cabin cruisers and was an airplane pilot, and was instrumental in developing the Hamilton Airport. Another project of his was the Elks building, which is now the city hall. He died in 1954.

George Thompson was born in Illinois in 1870, graduated from University Medical College, Kansas City, in 1897, practiced there until 1903, moved to St. Maries, Idaho, retired from practice in 1918 and came to Hamilton in 1923, where he farmed south of the city. He died in 1954.

H. D. Browning was born in Illinois in 1869, graduated from Rush

Medical School in 1892. He practiced first in Illinois until 1810, when he came to the Bitterroot and operated a ranch northwest of Hamilton. Because of the shortage of physicians during WWI, he took some post graduate work and became licensed in 1918 and practiced until seven weeks before his death due to cerebral hemorrhage, in 1941.

Niels Anderson Kaa was born in Denmark in 1865, came to the United States at age 19 and became a civil engineer, working at that profession for several years. He graduated from University of Illinois College of Physicians in 1902, practiced there until 1916, when he came here and practiced in Victor and Corvallis, and perhaps in Hamilton. He served as county physician and also was the one who vaccinated more people for spotted fever than anyone else. He retired in 1949 and died in 1952.

J. Wilson Reed was mentioned in Jeff Langton's book "The Victor Story" as having practiced in Victor at about this time.

George A. Gordon was born in Canada in 1876, graduated from Detroit Michigan College of Medicine 1904, came to Hamilton to practice in 1909, and did so until 1936 when he suffered a stroke. He died in 1941.

SPOTTED FEVER: A BLIGHT ON THE VALLEY

by Robert N. Philip

An early account of spotted fever in Montana based on contemporary information during the Parker years is that of Price, Esther Gaskins, Fighting Spotted Fever in the Rockies, Naegele Printing Company, Helena, Montana pp269, 1948. A recent very comprehensive report of spotted fever to the present time is that of Harden, Victoria A., Rocky Mountain Spotted Fever; History of a Twentieth-Century Disease. The Johns Hopkins University Press, Baltimore and London, pp375, 1990.

Settlement of the Bitterroot Valley increased sharply during the 20 years, 1890 to 1910. The population increased from 3,950 to nearly 12,000, and surveys of agricultural land were completed by the General Land Office. By 1913, 99% of the unreserved land had been appropriated in parcels of 160 acres or less.

With the arrival of the Missoula and Bitter Root Valley railroad in 1888, many small lumber mills became emplaced on newly settled land to harvest and sell the timber to mining companies of Butte and Anaconda. Proceeds were used by settlers to improve their land holdings.

An oversight of the eastern flanks of the mountain when the Bitter Root Forest Reserve was established in 1898 caused a temporary withdrawal of a 2 to 8 mile strip of unappropriated land along the eastern border of the Reserve. This withdrawal strip included forest and stump-land strewn with logging slash, which became the source of tick and ground squirrel problems. By 1910, most timber had been cut out of the foothills and Valley floor. Land had to be cleared of stumps, brush and rocks before it could be tilled. The unbroken cluttered ground afforded prime habitat for burgeoning small mammal populations which in turn became the hosts of immature wood ticks, Dermacentor andersoni. Large domestic and wild animals provided blood meals for adult ticks and the means for completion of their life-cycle.

Eons ago, the causative agent of Rocky Mountain spotted fever was introduced into the small mammals and ticks that populated the talus slopes and rocky shelves of the Bitter Root Mountain canyons where environmental conditions were especially favorable for the high rodent and tick densities necessary to perpetuate the spotted fever organism indefinitely.

Before the Valley was settled, the disease cycle was largely confined to the mountain canyons. Early settlement established favorable environmental conditions for movement of disease out of the canyons to proximity of human habitation. Although man was not essential to the transmission cycle, he was the unfortunate victim of spotted fever which was a significant health problem in Western Montana from the 1890's to the early 1940's. In retrospect, the first case probably occurred in 1873 and the disease was encountered for a few years thereafter. In 1902, Drs. Russell Gwinn of Stevensville and George McCullough of Missoula described the clinical characteristics of the disease at the annual meeting of the State Medical Association.

Typically, the disease occurred during spring months, beginning with a high fever and followed by a characteristic rash involving the extremities. The rash was measles-like, but shortly became confluent and hemorrhagic. The most alarming feature of spotted fever was the high fatality rate. Death usually occurred during the second week of illness, and no treatment seemed to be effective, although various regimens were tried.

From 1873 to 1980, some 647 cases occurred in western Montana, of these 375 died, a fatality rate of 58%. The epidemic peaked in 1902, coincident with incrimination of the wood tick as the vector of disease. Most early cases occurred among settlers at mouths of canyons and in foothills of western Montana, spreading as far as the West Fork in the upper Valley, and the Big Flat area west of Missoula. Many early cases occurred among mill workers and "hot" foci of disease followed lumbering workers. After 1940, spotted fever was virtually eliminated from the Valley and once again it was confined to the Bitter Root Mountains. Decayed foliage from trees, and even snow fleas were suggested as possible sources of disease, but the role of ticks was not mentioned in local newspapers.

In 1902, Dr. Longeway received permission from Governor Toole to engage an expert pathologist to determine the cause of spotted fever. Dr. Louis B. Wilson and his assistant, Dr. William M. Chowning arrived in mid

May and after performing eight autopsies concerning spotted fever, announced to the local press that they had identified a malaria-like parasite in red blood cells from all their patients, and felt sure that was the cause of spotted fever. Wilson and Chowning were wrong about the cause, but they were right about the mode of disease transmission. Even though the tick theory was not widely accepted, it did focus attention to this arthropod which led to the decline of spotted fever after 1902.

The gopher and the tick were both suspect. The gopher had become such a problem that the territorial legislature in 1887, offered a bounty of $.05 per animal for its elimination. The response was so overwhelming that the biennial appropriation was exhausted in months, and a special session called to solve the financial crisis.

Dr. John F. Anderson attended several cases of spotted fever and agreed with the piroplasma etiology and the role of the tick in disease transmission and in fact advocated treatment with large doses of quinine based on the supposed similarity of spotted fever and malaria parasites. The treatment was ineffective.

Conflicting views from experts left Valley residents confused. Burning the brush, poisoning gophers and treating bites with carbolic acid were all accepted aids. In 1906, the stage was set for a new approach. A young Chicago scientist, Howard Taylor Ricketts, believed the use of experimental animals might provide the clues as to disease causation. Early in May, Ricketts demonstrated that spotted fever could be transmitted to a guinea pig through a successful experiment using the blood of an infected individual. He worked out the tick life cycle and investigated the properties of the bacterium which he visualized microscopically and suspected as being the cause of the disease. He used some serum therapy, but went on in 1909 and 1910 to Mexico City for investigation of typhus and while in haste to complete his studies in Mexico, contracted typhus and died. His short but distinguished career was memorialized in the name of the causative agent of spotted fever, Rickettsia rickettsii, the group of related bacteria, the new science of rickettsiology to which he contributed so greatly

In 1910, Clarence Birdseye conducted a wild animal survey of the Bitter Root Valley to determine tick\host relationships. This work emphasized importance of the gopher as a source of blood meals to immature ticks and domestic stock as hosts for adult ticks. Dr. Ricketts had proposed a scheme for control consisting of livestock dipping during spring months and gopher eradication in areas of high tick activity. These measures were begun west of Florence in 1911. Dipping vats were constructed at Victor, Woodside, and Gold Creek as well as at Stevensville, Florence, and later on O'Brien Creek. Cattle and horses were required to be dipped at specified times during the spring tick season. The formula used in the vats was an arsenical solution and often caused skin irritations, so there was a good deal of resistance to the

Rocky Mountain Laboratory, Building No. 1 on Fourth Street in Hamilton, in 1927.

plan from the settlers. Blooded horses and milk cows were hand sprayed with the dip solution and in 1913, spotted fever occurred in two brothers who were hand spraying. One boy died and the other recovered after a protracted period of convalescence. Shortly thereafter, the vat was dynamited! The culprit was never apprehended. Dipping of stock was eventually accepted and continued in the Bitter Root Valley until 1935.

> *"Dad had some blooded mares he didn't want to go through the vat. My brother and I were to spray them with solution from the vat which was filled with ticks and debris. Both of us came down with spotted fever and were hospitalized under the care of Dr. Will Thornton in Stevensville. My brother died; I spent 54 days packed in ice but still running a fever. Someone blew up the dipping vat with a whole case of dynamite. I never was told who did the deed."*
>
> *Interview with Carl Wemple on 2\20\1986*

Gopher control using strychnine baits was found to be most efficient and economical in rodent control, and considered effective in controlling spotted fever. Reducing the tick population by removing the source of blood meals for adult ticks was another hope. Concentrated efforts to control spotted fever between 1913 and 1917 were at least partly successful, but impending war led to withdrawal of the two federal agencies from the Bitter Root Valley.

Typhoid fever was also a threat to the Board of Entomology and Dr. Ralph R. Parker had been employed to define the role of house flies in transmission of this disease. Dr. Parker headed up the spotted fever control program in the Bitter Root and was credited with establishment of the Rocky Mountain Laboratory in Hamilton. From 1918 to 1920, Parker continued the control program on a reduced scale. Particularly noteworthy during this period were his collaborative investigations with Dr. S. Burt Wolbach of Harvard University. From a human case that occurred in 1917 on O'Brien Creek west of Missoula, Wolbach isolated, characterized and described the causative agent of spotted fever. He named the organism Dermacentroxenus rickettsii (later renamed Rickettsia rickettsii) in honor of Howard Taylor Ricketts.

From 1913 to 1920, cases declined. However, in 1921 there was an upsurge of spotted fever. The deaths of a prominent Lolo couple brought renewed attention at the local and state levels. Several civic organizations, both Montana Senators, and Dr. Cogswell appealed to the Public Health Service for support. The Surgeon General delegated Dr. Thomas Parran to evaluate the spotted fever problem in Montana and to determine need for federal assistance in disease investigations. Dr. Parran recommended the PHS fund and conduct a research program on spotted fever and that Dr. Parker and his assistant, G. Henry Cowan be transferred to the Public Health Service for this purpose. Parker pursued acquiring of equipment and experimental animals and rented the recently vacated Canyon Creek school from the Hamilton School District. Funds for the equipment, animal cages, and transportation for field work were partly donated by local civic groups. In the spring of 1922, Dr. Roscoe R. Spencer was dispatched to take care of the laboratory where he was especially interested in developing a vaccine. Dr. Parker carried out investigations of disease maintenance in nature, and the pair worked well as a team. William Gettinger, who assisted Dr. Spencer, succumbed to the disease on June 30, 1922. Despite this tragic setback, prospects of a vaccine made from infected ticks looked promising. Dr. Spencer returned to Washington that fall to pursue this possibility in experimental animals under more favorable laboratory conditions. Finally in February of 1924, he was successful in immunizing guinea pigs against spotted fever with a vaccine prepared from infected tick tissue inactivated with phenol. The 1924 season was hectic. Numerous ticks had to be collected, and infected preliminary to vaccine preparation. An unknown disease, Tularemia, was introduced into the animal colony during tick feeding, and several employees including Dr. Parker had contracted this protracted but usually nonfatal disease. However, the cruelest of blow came during Dr. Parker's illness — Henry Cowan succumbed on October 29th to spotted fever acquired while feeding ticks in the laboratory!

In 1924, Dr. Spencer himself took the vaccine without harmful effects and the following summer, the staff of the schoolhouse laboratory was vaccinated. Field trials began in 1926-1927 for persons at high risk. Results showed the vaccine to be safe, and it protected sheepmen against the risk of spotted fever during their spring trek to the Sawtooth Mountains, reduced mortality and shortened the course of the disease.

New larger facilities were needed to accommodate the thousands of rabbits and guinea pigs needed to make more vaccine. Finally a site was selected near the Pine Grove Addition in Hamilton. A lawsuit by nearby residents to block construction was unsuccessful, but underscored the need for rigorous containment measures to prevent community exposure. Extreme precautions were taken to preclude escape of ticks; a chain-link fence was erected to keep out animals and small boys; and the grounds were flagged regularly for ticks. Three months before completion of the new laboratory, Albert Leroy Kerlee, a young assistant, died in spite of having received two doses of vaccine five months earlier. This incident caused a despondent Dr. Spencer to ask for re-assignment in the summer of 1928.

Dr. Parker's directorship went into high gear. Vaccine production became the mission of the lab and an increasing demand for it came from other Rocky Mountain states who had the same problem. In 1931, spotted fever was recognized in south Atlantic states, and it was now realized that research and control of spotted fever was a national responsibility rather than a state function, so in February of 1931, a bill was passed that transferred the lab to the U. S. Public Health Service for a purchase price of $68,757.00. The state continued to administer the livestock dipping and rodent control activities.

The vaccine use peaked in 1939 when an estimated 7000 persons were vaccinated in Ravalli County, and 24 liters were used in Missoula County. In 1940, most residents had been vaccinated at least once, and many had received at least one dose per year. During the 1930's, nearly as many cases occurred in Missoula County (33) as in Ravalli County (39). This was due to their recent logging activities in the mountains to the west.

For several years, Dr. Parker hoped to develop a better vaccine and no commercial laboratory would undertake to produce a tick-tissue vaccine as preparation and testing was difficult.

In 1936, Dr. Herald R. Cox was recruited to investigate use of tissue culture to cultivate spotted fever and other rickettsiae. He found he could grow enormous numbers in yolk sacs of embryonated chicken eggs. This revolutionary discovery led in short order to the replacement of the old tick-tissue vaccine. The number of cases dropped noticeably in Western Montana during the 1940's for reasons not entirely understood. In 1949, Lederle Laboratories agreed to manufacture spotted fever vaccine in embryonated eggs, and Dr. Cox left Hamilton to supervise that operation, returning some time later. He retired in Hamilton. For those persons allergic to egg protein, a tick-tissue vaccine was continued.

In 1950, Spotted Fever was no longer a large problem in Montana.

Vaccination clinics sponsored by Parent Teacher Associations continued until the 1960's. Commercial preparation of spotted fever vaccine was discontinued in 1979, as broad spectrum antibiotics were effective treatment, provided they are given early. Thus the blight that hung over the Valley for so many years, threatening its early development, had been lifted, thanks to changing environmental conditions and the efforts of a dedicated group of field and laboratory workers.

Chapter Five

Pioneer Families And Their Histories

ABBEY AND COOK FAMILIES
CHARLES N. ABBEY FAMILY

Prepared by Curtis C. Cook

Charles Nelson Abbey was born in Henry County, Illinois, on August 10, 1860. He moved to Iowa where he lived various places including Mount Etna and New Market. Charley was married to Rachel Melinda Peterson in Iowa, and three children were born to this union. They were Ina, Irl, and Ivan. Their mother, Rachel, died of consumption. The family moved to Grant City, Missouri, about 1895, and later Charley married Gertrude. A child named Nelson was born of this marriage.

Charles Abbey was a photographer and he worked at this calling in Iowa and Missouri. While in Grant City, Missouri, he was acquainted with Fay O. Burrell, who was a small boy at that time. Mr. Abbey made a portrait of Fay and his dog. Burrells later came to the Bitter Root where they renewed their acquaintance.

In 1902, the Abbey family left Missouri by train and came to Montana in an excursion car, a box car which carried the family and all their belongings, and settled in Hamilton in the Bitter Root Valley. For a time, they lived on North First Street, and then rented from Carrie Iddings on the westside. The children came across the mill dam to Hamilton to attend school.

When Gertrude Abbey died in 1906, Ina dropped out of school to keep house and take care of the boys. That same year, Charley was appointed Rural Mail Carrier on Rte. One out of Hamilton. He had circulated petitions in the area to get the Rural Free Delivery routes approved for the Hamilton area. He carried mail on both Rte. One and Rte. Two, but generally Rte. One, until his retirement after twenty-one years of service. Joseph Hersman was the usual carrier on Rte. Two. Charles Abbey covered his route with horses and buggy until about 1915, except for a few times when the snow conditions prevented it, and then he carried the mail on a saddle horse. Part of that time, he had a buggy with a glassed-in cab, and windows in the doors which raised and lowered by means of a cloth strap. After 1915, Mr. Abbey operated his mail route by means of a Ford automobile. In 1927, when Charley retired, Joe Hersman took over Rte. One, and Harry Robinson, former mayor of Hamilton, was appointed to Rte. Two, and Andy Bullock took his position as City Mail Carrier and Clerk (a combination position). An article in the Western News at the time of his retirement stated "It is estimated that during his service as rural mail deliveryman, Mr. Abbey has traveled about 166,666 miles, more than six times around the earth. It is also estimated that during the period of his service he has delivered more than 5,200 packages of mail. He was always accommodating, prompt and congenial, and he has won many warm friends who wish him well." Mrs.

Abbey assisted him as substitute carrier. At this time, Hamilton rural free delivery extended over 28.6 miles of road, and deliveries were made 306 days per year.

On November 1, 1916, Charles N. Abbey married Mary Ellen Withers Warren Kolpsland. Frances Abbey was born of this marriage on January 12, 1921. Mary Ellen had been born at Blue Mountain, Kansas, on March 13, 1878, and had, at age 18, come to the Bitter Root to join her brother, John Withers of Victor. She was a dressmaker and seamstress, and had a millinery shop. She first married Walter Warren and they had three children; Tom, Bertha, and Ralph. After Mr. Warren died, Mary Ellen married Mr. Kopsland and a daughter, Winifred, was born to them.

Mary Ellen died January 14, 1945, at the age of 66. Charles Abbey was active in the Christian Church serving as Elder, Superintendent of Sunday School, and president of the Upper Room Bible class.

Irl Abbey learned the painting trade and lived out his life in Missoula.

Ivan Abbey worked in Butte mines for a time, and married Pearl and returned to the Bitter Root Valley. They purchased a home in Hamilton Heights from Tom Gabrielson and Ivan worked on farms and dairies in the area. Their children, Ira, Arthur, and Millis went to school at Hamilton Heights and in Corvallis schools. Pearl worked at the Daly mansion for Mrs. Daly, during her many visits to the valley, when Fred and Rose Simmons were the caretakers for Mrs. Daly. Ivan was interested in sheep and wool and won many ribbons at the Ravalli County Fair.

Charles Nelson Abbey, Mary Ellen Abbey, Gertrude M. Abbey, Ivan R. Abbey, and Pearl Abbey are all buried in the Riverview Cemetery near Hamilton.

ALBERT L. COOK AND INA LOUISE ABBEY COOK

Albert L. Cook was born at Emerald, Wisconsin, on May 4, 1891, and came to the Bitter Root with his brother, Charles H. Cook, in 1907. Charles became a lather and moved to Missoula. Albert learned the carpenter trade and stayed in Hamilton.

Albert L. Cook and Ina Louise Abbey (daughter of Charles and Rachel Abbey) were married on May 14, 1910, in Hamilton. They lived in a house just south of Hamilton with neighbors named Ash and Poppie. Their children were Howard, Verlon, Curtis, Evelyn, and Isabel. All except Howard were born in the house still standing (1997), just north of Quality Supply, which Albert built in 1913 and 1914, to replace the small original house in which Howard was born. Howard was in first grade at Lincoln School when the Ravalli Hotel burned in 1919. He came home from school that day, after watching the fire, with his face chapped from the heat. In 1919, there was a shortage of carpenter work in Hamilton so the family moved to Missoula for employment. The home and acreage were sold to Ina Cook's father, Charles N. Abbey who lived there for many years. During World War II, the Cooks returned to the Bitter Root for a time, living on Old Corvallis Road where they did a little farming, but returned to Missoula where Albert was in the home construction business. They enjoyed visits to the valley for fairs, family gatherings and church activities. Albert Cook died in 1968, but Ina celebrated her 100th birthday on September 21, 1989, at a big party at the nursing home in Hamilton. She was one of Montana's Centennial Citizens.

Curtis C. Cook, born in Hamilton on June 28, 1916, served in the Air Force and then later completed law school at the University of Montana. He worked for the Attorney General for one year and then established a law office in Hamilton in 1948. He married Mary Lou Rasmussen, and they had daughters — Irene and Lualyce.

Howard Cook lived most of his life in Missoula. He died in an automobile accident in 1946.

Verlon Cook returned to the Bitter Root Valley and lived with Ivan and Pearl Abbey on Hamilton Heights for awhile. He died in Boise, Idaho, leaving three children.

Evelyn Cook married William Drader and had two children, Douglas and Dale. Douglas works at KUFM television; and Dale in Stevensville.

Isabel Cook married Don Graham and lived in the Bitter Root. After his death, she married Warren Heth. She is currently a widow, living in Missoula at the Clark Fork Manor.

JOHN QUINCY ADAMS, JR. AND ETHEL LEONA BARR ADAMS

by Doris Adams Lee

My dad, John Adams, born in Delta, Colorado, on Aug. 12, 1884, died on April 26, 1964 in the hospital at Hamilton, Montana. Dad was one of seven children, the youngest of which was his sister Delta, who was the first white child born in that territory, and when her parents named her Delta, the township named the town after her. This was on Oct. 21, 1882. Dad's parents had come from Russell, Kansas, but why they moved to Colorado, I never knew. Then they left Delta, CO, in the year of 1901 or 1902, and went to Corvallis, Montana, where they had a small farm just north of Corvallis.

My mother, Ethel Barr, was born in Corvallis, MT, and lived there all of her life. She was born on April 1, 1887, and died on October 5, 1971. Her father, James Barr, was a carpenter and I have been told that he helped to build the Brooks Hotel in Corvallis. While my mother was still living at home with her parents, she recalls that one afternoon her mother looked out their window and saw an Indian squaw looking in the window. Grandma Barr told her to come in. The squaw kept looking at one of mother's sisters, named Addie, who was chewing gum. With hand motions the Indian squaw made plain that she wanted Addie's gum, so Addie gave it to her. When the squaw got up to leave, she handed the gum back to Addie! My mother said a few Indians lived up around the east side and all were friendly, and got along fine.

My parents were married in Hamilton, MT, on April 19, 1908. They celebrated their 50th wedding anniversary in 1958 and all their children were able to attend to wish them much happiness. A few grandchildren attended also.

About the year 1922, my parents bought a farm just east of Corvallis which was on a small hill, and this became known as "Adams' Hill". Dad raised chickens and also farmed the land. About 1927 or 1928, suddenly Dad got up one morning and he was deaf. He had worked for the local cheese factory where the din of noise had been strong and we always figured this had a lot to do with his loss of hearing. He went to several specialists, but got no help. His sister, who lived in Spokane, Washington, had heard of a new possibility where a piloted airplane would take a free-fall and Dad went to see what would happen. The pilot took 25 minutes to gain altitude of 8,700 feet and then drop at 165 miles per hour! Remember, this is back in the 20's, and at that time, pilots wore helmets, but my Dad refused, hoping that the rush of air going by his ears would help. It did nothing for him, and Dad never went back for the second time. This was a terrible tragedy for our family. It was Mother who had the worst hardship. More responsibility fell on her, but she seldom complained.

In the mid 30's, Dad began raising guinea pigs which were used by the Rocky Mountain Laboratory in Hamilton, for developing serum for spotted fever which was caused by small ticks usually found on the Westside or in the mountains. By the 1950's, the lab quit using guinea pigs and went to eggs, as this was cheaper.

In May of 1950, my Dad was hit by a railroad train. The train tracks are east of Corvallis and bordered one edge of our farm. Dad had gone across these tracks a million times, but this one time he failed to see the train coming. Dad was badly bruised and was taken to Hamilton to see his physician, but was able to return home. His pickup truck was demolished.

There were four of us children. Frances married William Severns, Sr., and lived in Corvallis for many years. She passed away in 1965. Harry Adams died in 1990, and Dorothy Adams Hoyer passed away in 1992. I am Doris Adams Lee, and I live in Seattle, Washington, in 1997.

THE AICHELE FAMILY

written in 1974

Our father, Andrew Aichele, was born in Wiirdtenburg, Germany, in the year of 1856. The Aichele family owned a winery and sold wine and beer. Andrew, at an early age, had the job of delivering the wine in the evenings with a horse and wagon. Delivering it at night helped to keep the beer and wine cool.

At the age of 28 years, Andrew decided to leave his native country and travel to the "land of opportunity", the United States of America. He arrived in Chicago in 1884. Andrew's brother, George, and George's wife met him there. The first day, Andrew and his sister-in-law started early in the morning looking for a job. They walked all day and came home after dark. Andrew knew by this time that jobs were hard to find. They had walked all day and had found nothing.

Lena Graf was born in the town of Stuttgart, Germany, in 1864. She arrived in the states about the same time as Andrew. She was then 20 years old. Andrew and Lena met for the first time in Chicago. Then, they were married in 1887. They lived in Chicago for three years. They decided to go west as so many people were doing at that time. They arrived some days later by train in Frenchtown, Montana, just west of Missoula. Their first child, Anna Bell, arrived in 1890, and was born in Missoula.

Andrew was working hard to support his family. He was working in a brickyard, and also doing carrying for the brick layers. Andrew decided the brickyard wasn't the right place for him, so he moved his family to Victor, MT, and became a farmer as well as working at the Curlew mine. They lived in the Victor area for several years. While there a son, George, was born in 1893.

The family made another move, this time to the west of Woodside. They had a homestead near the mountains, in the mouth of Sheafman Creek. This homestead proved to be a good deal for the Aichele family. They all worked hard, raising all kinds of garden produce, setting out apple, cherry, and plum trees — and trying fruits of all kinds. The produce was harvested and hauled to Woodside with a team and wagon, and loaded on the train and shipped to Butte. The train left Woodside early in the morning and produce was in Butte by eleven o'clock. The stores had fresh produce shortly after it left the Aichele ranch.

In 1901, the home was one of sorrow. George, at the age of eight, was going to school at the Dutch Hill School and while playing baseball, was hit in the stomach. George said nothing at first, and by the time the family found out, it was too late.

A daughter, Lena Margaret, was born in 1903. Then, five years later (1908), Marie Henrietta was born at the home ranch. The family prospered, the orchards were good, and the produce had a welcome market. They added apple cider and sauerkraut to their list of products. Anna's job was cutting the kraut (cabbage), and Lena's job was tamping the kraut with a tamper in wooden barrels. They shipped up to eight, forty gallon barrels of sauerkraut at a time. The cider was made with an old cider mill and press. The mill and press are still in use at Lena's place.

The family worked hard, and Lena always had to have her lunch no matter how long or where, she was prepared for a long stay and carried a sandwich at all times! Anna says that Lena always said, "I have to have my lunch".

Anna and George started school at Dutch Hill. Lena also attended school there for four years. Then, in 1914, the Dutch Hill School consolidated with Corvallis and Lena finished school there.

Mother Lena Aichele passed away on June 14, 1914. Pa, Andrew Aichele, passed away on July 12, 1947.

Anna and Tim Garrard were married on August 10, 1919. Anna has her home north of Woodside.

Lena and Hugh Simpson were married on June 16, 1927. Lena lives on the ranch northwest of Corvallis.

Marie has the Aichele home in Woodside.

VERA BELLE ROCKAFELLOW ALBERSON

by Garry and Sandra Hildebrant

Vera Belle Rockafellow came to the Bitter Root Valley from Wahoo, Nebraska, in 1903, at the age of 12 years. Her family settled near Corvallis. She was the oldest of nine children born to Joseph William Rockafellow (1867-1952) and Mary Clarinda Linder (1866-1939). The children are: Vera Belle (1891-1975) Ethel Clare (1892 -?), Richard Samuel (1894-1935), Freddie H. (1896-1896), Elsie Marie (1897-1905), Lloyd Milford (1899-?), Arthur William (1903-?), Delbert Ray (1905-?), Estella May (Nordheim) (1908-1997).

Vera Belle married Eddy Alberson at Woodside in 1914. Eddy had come from Kermistown, Indiana, to the Bitter Root in 1912. This couple lived in the valley for most of the 55 years they were married, until his death in 1969. They adopted one daughter, Maxine Lavern Evans, whom they named Ruth Yvonne (1920-1991).

Ruth Yvonne Alberson married Earle Hildebrant and they had two children: Judith Lynne and Garry Earle Hildebrant.

Judith Lynne Hildebrant (1940), married Gary Geer. Their children and grandchildren are: Vicky Lynne Geer (1960) (1.) Mekisha Renee (1984), and Sandi Renee Geer (1962), (1.) Anthony Dain Froelich (1984), and Ricky

Ray Geer.

Garry Earle Hildebrant (1944), married Sandra Case Hildebrant. Children and grandchildren are: Brenda Jean Hildebrant (1968), (1.) Nicole LeAnn Hildebrant (1988), (2.) Carrice LuAnn Wheeler (1993), (3.) Ryan Marshall Wheeler (1994), and Shelley Lynn Hildebrandt 1971 (1.) Amanda Lynn Lamp(1992), (2.) Sarah Ann Lamp(1996).

THE ALLNUT FAMILY

by Claude Allnut

My mother's name was "Nan", at least that is what my father called her. She was born and raised in Sckyler County, Missouri. After she married my father, in Missouri, they came to the Bitter Root in 1879. They came by way of Elliston, where Dallas, Duly (Dude), and Pearl were born. My father homesteaded 160 acres, seemed like he got more later. The following children were born on this homestead: Zellie, Lily, Sally, Edward, Laura, Claude (telling this story), Leonard, and Roy.

Mr. Allnut died of Rocky Mountain Spotted Fever on June 9, 1914. Before his death, the Allnuts had sold 80 acres to the Perkins, and had built a new home just south of the log house, on the hill. Later, in 1915 or 1916, MacRae had the mortgage. Bernard Palmer paid off the mortgage, and gave Mrs. Allnut $500.00, and became the owner of the 160 acres. The next owner was Sam Samuelson.

I chewed tobacco from the time I was little and still dressed in a dress. I helped Sid Parks to plant his apple trees. He would dig a hole and I carried water in a little pail, and put it on each tree. Sid most always gave us kids the chewing tobacco and the money for the 4th of July. We all liked him and worked for him. I went after hay to Corvallis one time, and I wasn't very old.

Whenever we wanted tobacco, we went to old Sid. One day we stopped by and asked for tobacco. Sid said he was running low, and he told us to get out. We took a gas pipe, put plugs in both ends, put the pipe on an old stump, and set the stump on fire. We thought the plug would just hit the house, but the whole pipe went through the shack and landed on the floor by his bed! He wasn't even mad at us!

Sid brought some cheese...the kind that the mold is all throughout it..limburger.., some crackers, and a bottle. I took a few shots of the whiskey too. I got sick! I wanted to go home but Sid thought I should stay. I know I wasn't sick from the whiskey... but, from that cheese! Sid walked most of the way home while I drove, but I finally got him to get on the wagon. He had a hard time making it. We kids used to call him "drunkees Sid", but he was the only one that sold his ranch for a good price and got out of the country. He said, "I'm going to see my sister in Maine. She is as dirty as I am, and I like it". Asked if he was going to get married, he said, "old as I am, I'm not going to have a woman to drag around!"

Sid trapped all winter. He made $500 or $600 each winter. Sid and the kids went out for Easter, up Mill Creek. Some of us went to get water. We saw a Mountain Lion with a trap on his foot. Sid went for Jess Smith and told him to bring an axe, so if he just wounded him, Jess could kill the lion with the ax. Sid shot that lion right between the eyes! He got a pile of money for the hide.

There was always a big gang of kids around. We played baseball, coasted, or cooked wieners over the fire.

Jackson's bought the Jones place in 1912.

I remember one time, Earl Malone ran a piece of tree limb in his hand real bad, when he was trying to get a bear out of a cherry tree. We were walking along the road, when Earl tried to show me how well he could throw with his left hand...the right one being hurt. I was standing on the bank, at the side of the road, right at the turn in front of the Wolf place. Earl threw the rock...it hit me in the chest...and knocked me 10 feet down the bank !!

In 1920, I married Esther Crooks. She died on June 10, 1963. We lost two sons, but I live with my daughter, Pauline Rieker. I worked many years, and we lived on the Thousand Acre Ranch for 30 1/2 years.

ANFINSON AND BATES FAMILIES

by Gayle Anfinson Tintzman

Florence Bates came to the Bitterroot in 1899 from Wisconsin. She was three years old at the time, and the third oldest in a family of eight. Her father, Orman Bates, was a teacher who wrote at least two arithmetic books and had a law degree from Colorado, and yet he worked as a house mover and a stonemason.

Florence attended schools in Hamilton. She married Cliff Chaffin in 1915. His parents, Newton and Jossie Chaffin, lived north of Corvallis, and in 1917, both couples moved to a farm on Willow Creek Road. Newton passed away in 1921, and in 1923, Jossie passed on. There was an influenza epidemic in the twenties and after Cliff and Florence had nursed numerous people back to health, Cliff came down with the disease and died of pneumonia in December of 1924. Florence continued to run the ranch by herself with a lot of help from numerous friends.

In years past, Florence had met a train engineer from Iowa, by the name of Anfin Anfinson. He owned dryland east of Hamilton Heights. Anfin, his wife Henrietta, Cliff, and Florence had become good friends. After Cliff died, Anfin divorced his wife and in November of 1927 married

Florence Chaffin. He sold his dryland and came to live on the Willow Creek ranch. In February 1934, there was a daughter, Gayle, born to this couple.

In 1938, Anfin ran for Ravalli County Commissioner, but continued to farm the acreage. Florence was a housewife, mother, and a very good Bridge player, belonging to two Bridge clubs and playing duplicate every Wednesday night in Hamilton.

In October of 1960, Florence became sick with a cancerous brain tumor, and after two operations succumbed to the disease on March 24, 1961. Anfin died of heart failure on May 25, 1968. They are survived by daughter and son-in-law, Elmer and Gayle Tintzman; three grandsons; Terry, Steve, and Bret, as well as nine great-grandchildren.

When I was growing up on Willow Creek Road, there were about fourteen farms from the corner of Coal Pit to the end of Willow Creek. Everyone knew everyone else and the car they drove. The telephone was just impossible to get on, as everyone was on the same line together.

What fun I had tho' at haying and threshing time. I remember the long table in the front room just loaded with luscious food, and the pies were out of this world! I didn't know until I myself became a housewife and cook, why Mom hated the harvest time. All the farmers would come and help out and then move on to the next farm. To see each farmer unhitch his team, walk them to the creek for a drink, then back again to the barn, was quite a sight for a young girl like myself. All different colors and names to remember each horse by.

Starting at Coal Pit Road and coming up Willow Creek was the John Hull place. Next was Alvin and Lyle Whitesitt's farm. Down the road from them, was the Hawker place, which was Lyle's parents. The next place was the Lockwood farm. Boss and Frankie lived in the big house, and Gard and Leona lived north of them in the little house. I remember the first time I saw the Lockwood twins (Gard and Leona's girls), I was amazed to see two babies looking so much alike. I'm sure I told Mom, I wanted some just like that! Boss and Frankie were so kind and fun to visit. The farm up from the Lockwoods was the Back place. Don't remember much about them, except they had a son named Osborn. Coming east down one of the worst lanes ever, was the Reader residence. Mrs. Reader lived there with her two sons. Never knew Mr. Reader. Many a good meal was taken in her kitchen. Squib Rasmussen owned acreage just across the road from Readers. There was a house on it, but Squib lived down in Corvallis at the Brooks Hotel. My first memory of someone living in his house was the Hathaway family. They worked my Dad's sugar beets. There were nine kids, plus their Mom and Dad. I could have gone home and slept in my own big bed and ate at a table with my Mom and Dad, but when Mrs. Hathaway would ask me if I wanted to stay for supper, I jumped at the chance! We would go out after supper and play kick the can, tag, and whatever game we could think of, then maybe get to sleep four in a bed. Good memories of this family!

The farm down from us was the Emmitt Hawker place. Emmitt was a big man and from the first time I saw him to the day he died, he never aged. He looked the same to me all those years. I think I kind of made him the Grandpa I never had. Right across the road from Emmitt, was Mrs. Hainline, one of Emmitt's wives. I think he had three. This was my first introduction to divorce.

Bill Neaves lived on the corner, another great man, so kind and robust. Kind of like Santa Claus. Would run into his house every chance I got. The next farm was ours. Before I was born, Mom and Dad would take in boarders to help work the farm. Some went to school, others just stayed and worked. We had a Mexican by the name of John, who babysat me when he wasn't working the sugar beets. They tell the story of John putting me on his shoulders and trotting around the barnyard. He was a wonderful friend to me. Fond memories will stay with me forever.

Marion Gregg lived across the pasture from us. He had a daughter, Mary, who was my age, and we played with each other every chance we had. In fact, we graduated from high school together and still correspond with each other.

Our infamous neighbors, the Hightowers (Milt, Dan, and Mrs. Hightower) are covered in another article. Enough to say that my Mom was their saint. They came to see her and talk over anything that was bothering them.

Our last neighbors on the creek were Frank and Linnie Blankenship. She and Mom were very good friends. We spent many a Sunday at her house, usually eating! All I can remember about Linnie was her homemade butter. She liked it rancid, and it was just awful to eat! She had a lot of antiques that were very nice, and I would love to have them now. Her first husband, Mr. Peyton, was killed by the Indians in 1908. She was a very kind, and loving lady.

Things have really changed on Willow Creek, and they say you can't stop progress, but I do wish sometimes we could go back to the times when there were just a few of us on this road, and the old saying of "neighbor helping neighbor," was back. At least we have good memories we conjure up when that new neighbor gives you the cold shoulder!

THE APPLEBURY FAMILY

The Applebury families of the Bitterroot trace their ancestors to a Thomas Applebury who came to Williamsburg, Virginia, in 1673, as an indentured slave. He came, no doubt, from the British Isles. Henry Benson, who had been an indentured slave himself, brought Thomas to America. An indentured slave was a person who served several years as a laborer to the person who paid his passage over to this country. When his time of serving was up, he was given 500 acres of land. Thomas served for seven years in the service of Henry Benson.

The next record of the Applebury's comes from the obituary of Elizabeth M. Applebury. Elizabeth M. Rutter was born on October 21, 1843, in Palmyra, Marion County, Missouri. Her father was born on October 10, 1804, in West Kentucky, and came to Missouri in 1826. Elizabeth married James M. Applebury on May 28, 1857, in Palmyra, Missouri, and the couple came to the Bitter Root in 1884. They first settled in Victor, near the present Victor cemetery. They later established a homestead east of Corvallis. Beth Flint, a great-granddaughter, still lives on part of this homestead.

Elizabeth and James had six children — all born in Missouri. Four of these children, came to settle in the Bitter Root. John Phillip married Sallie Vance of the Grantsdale Vance family. They had two girls, Ada and Beulah. Ada married Lee Rhodian and Beulah died of Rocky Mountain Spotted Fever when she was one year old. Effie married George Million. Thomas Edward, known in the valley as T. E., or as "Ed", married Missouri Upton in Shelbyville, Missouri.

Ed and Missouri later came to Montana and settled on the Applebury homestead. They were to have five children, all born in Missouri. Eli married Maud Chaffin; James Terrill "Jimmie" married Alma Holloron; Grace married Leslie Snell; Clarence married Tillie Stangland; and Effie married Reginald Morris. Of these five families, only two of "Jimmie's" children still live in the valley. They are James Edward "Ned", and Beth Flint.

The youngest of the family, J. M. (or Marshall), was just 14 years old when he came with his folks to Montana. Marshall was later to marry Annie Glassley, and they established a homestead on the hills just east of Corvallis. Three children were born to them there. Lawrence, who married Irene Haigh; Lois, who married George Nelson; and Lloyd, who married Ruth Tabor.

Marshall and Annie later sold their homestead property in the hills to Jimmie and Alma Applebury, and homesteaded on property known as the Coal Pit. Lawrence and Irene, and Lloyd and Ruth, farmed this area for many years along with their dad. Loyd's youngest son, Denis, is still in the valley. Denis married Jeannette Wandler, and they have the Applebury Survey at Woodside. Their two girls, Darlene and Kimberly are married and live in the valley. Darlene married Theron Nelson and they have two boys, Kimberly married Kyle Winter and they have two girls.

Lloyd and Ruth also had two older boys, Rex and Jay. Rex married Janice Wildey and Jay married Jeanette Wildey, Janice's twin. Rex's daughter, Julie, married Scott Ralston and they live in the Bitter Root. Alma and Jimmie ranched on the homestead land in the hills where their children, Ned and Beth were both born. When the springs dried up, they moved down to the original homestead on Quast Lane where Beth Flint now resides. Ned married Ruth Parker, and they had five children. They are Meredithe, Terry, Brian, Alan, and Julie. Alan resides in Hamilton and has the Valley Veterinary Clinic.

BAILEY FAMILY

by Astrid Morris

In the early 1900's, the "Apple Boom" and the publicity and promotional hype of that time enticed people to move to the Bitter Root. Among those who came to the Bitter Root in response to this hyperbole were Winfield Scott Bailey and his wife, Elsie. Both were natives of Wisconsin and were graduates of Plattville Teachers' College. Their dream was to leave teaching behind and to make a living from the land. Their children, Ruth Bailey (Quast) was six and Homer Bailey was age two when the family settled on the Three Mile land in 1912. Ruth remembers seeing the Bitter Root Inn, noted in history as a Frank Lloyd Wright structure in the Stevensville area, where potential buyers were entertained. She couldn't go into the Inn, but her mother let her peek in through the door at the lavish arrangements. Ruth was impressed by a Stutz car driven by one of the developers.

It only took a few months to see that the land didn't live up to the "hype", and soon W. S. (as he was called) went back to teaching. He was hired as the Corvallis School superintendent during the time all the surrounding schools were consolidated into the one unit of "Corvallis School District # 1. The family lived in the house now known as the Brooks Hotel, and the third child, Kathryn, was born there in 1913. During this time, Bailey was instrumental in importing good teachers from his former Alma Mater in Wisconsin. Among these teachers were Mildred Chaffin and Clara Belle Lear.

After leaving the school, Bailey was part of the Corvallis Bank, which dissolved in 1924. He purchased land north of Corvallis from the Parkhurst Estate, in 1916 and he built a large two-story house which continues to be home for members of the family. In 1920, Bailey added to his holdings by buying half the Humble place from Great Western Sugar, and later bought out the other half owned by his brother-in-law, E. E. Scott.

W. S. Bailey was able to successfully pursue his dream of being an agriculturist and had moved to Bozeman to administer the Agriculture Adjustment Administration for the Roosevelt administration, when ill health forced his resignation. Son Homer recalls that, in 1916, Bailey Lane had not been built, but that Tucker Lane and Crossing were in existence. Sugar beets were taken across the river to the railroad. Great Western Sugar had plans to experiment in the raising of sugar beets and had two farms, one bought by Bailey — and one further north on Bell Crossing. GWS built a refinery in Missoula (aceing out the proposed refinery for Riverside), but World War I interrupted the plans and the project was abandoned.

In 1928, Amalgamated Sugar built a refinery in Missoula and was instrumental in getting the railroad moved to the East side of the Bitter Root River. The raising of sugar beets became a vital part of the region's economy. The Bailey farm was well suited to this crop.

Homer Bailey graduated from Montana State University in Bozeman, where he had met and married Elizabeth Harrison, daughter of the Dean of Women. The couple raised their three children on the home farm and it is now occupied by their youngest son, Robert and family. Their oldest son, John Clay, passed away from an illness and daughter Mary Lynn, lives in Hawaii.

Homer and Ruth Bailey both recall when large sheep herds were part of their lives. Ruth remembers the excitement of sheep camp and the handling of large numbers of animals. Both the Quast and Bailey families were among the many sheep ranchers in the Bitter Root Valley. The sheep were trailed or hauled to Darby where they were held until being dispersed to grazing lands on the Bitter Root Forest. The Bailey sheep went to the East Fork, and the Quast sheep to the West Fork. Homer said their camps were often serviced by way of Skalkaho road, going "in the back way" so to speak. Homer recalls that his "bride" disliked traveling the Skalkaho and was probably relieved when the Baileys stopped raising sheep in 1940. The conditions on the forest land, fallen timber and the like, deteriorated to such an extent that it was no longer feasible to graze the sheep on this land. Thus, most large sheep growers went out of business leaving a few smaller flocks which the Valley continues to support.

In talking about her growing up years, Ruth presents a nostalgic picture of playing basketball, staying overnight in the rivals towns (such as Victor or Darby), having a boyfriend give her his letter sweater, which her mother would not let her keep! Lorna Randolph was a basketball team mate of Ruth as they played for Corvallis High School. Memories were of riding the school bus which broke down and of her brother eating his noon lunch on the bus before they ever arrived at school. Ruth became an accomplished musician, attended McPhail School of Music, and taught in Philipsburg for one year. She said " It wasn't worth the sacrifice" to attempt a career in music. She returned home and had "fun" for awhile, and later married Otto Quast, who had been one of her boyfriends during those high school years.

THE BAY FAMILIES

from articles in the Republican, April 1942

Mrs. Johanna Hanson Bay was born on May 16, 1886, in Falster, Denmark, and came to America with her parents, Mr. and Mrs. Rasmus Hanson, as a child. They located in Michigan where her family started a lumber mill and built two towns, 15 miles apart, which were named after members of the family. One was named Lewistown for her brother, Lewis, and the other was called Johannasburg, for Johanna. Mrs. Johanna Bay's mother, Mrs. Rasmus Hanson, observed her 99th birthday in Michigan (Greyling, MI, Avalanche newspaper, 10-14-1944). "In accordance with an old Danish custom of having friends and family call to wish her a happy birthday. Mrs. Hanson seemed keen to visit with them all. It is the wish of the community that as Mrs. Hanson enter the centenary year of her life, she may continue to enjoy her usual good health and happiness. May she be privileged to see lasting peace restored to her native land of Denmark, and to America the country of her adoption."

Johanna married Robert Bay in 1886, and came to the Corvallis area in 1909, a year after their eldest son, Hanson, who had started a general merchandise store with William Christoffersen. The store, known as Bay Brothers, is in 1942, operated by another son, Edwin.

Mr. and Mrs. Robert Bay, their two younger sons, Russell and Edwin

"Pops" Bay relaxes and reads the daily paper.

L., came to Corvallis in 1909, after being influenced by letters from Sid Wheeler. Sid worked for them in Michigan, and his letters told them of opportunities in the Bitter Root. Mr. Wheeler owned a meat market in Hamilton in 1942. When the Bays arrived from Michigan, they moved into a house occupied by Louis Wolfe, until their own place was completed. In 1942, this house is owned by Ray Burke. During her many years in Corvallis, Johanna Bay was active in community life, and in addition found time to make 37 trips to Europe. She was a Lutheran and member of the United church, and a member of Eastern Star, Women's Club, and Scandinavian Club. At her death, on April 9, 1942, she was survived by her son, Edwin L. Bay, Corvallis, four grandsons, Fritz and Russell Bay in Vancouver, WA (sons of Hans Bay), Robert Bay, a sergeant in the Army stationed in Alaska, and Vance Bay, who is in the Air Corps at Sheppard Field, TX (sons of Edwin L. Bay).

EDWIN L. BAY AND LILLIAN MAUDE HEDGES

according to article by Mark Scharfenaker, written May 17, 1978

Edwin L. Bay came to Corvallis, MT, in 1909, with his parents, Robert and Johanna Bay. They all came from Michigan. Edwin's eldest brother, Hanson, had come a year earlier (in 1908) and along with William Christofferson, started a general merchandise store in Corvallis. This store was known as "Bay and Christoffersen." The goods for this store came from Michigan in a boxcar. Ed Bay joined the business in 1910, and the store became known as "Bay's Store," and has remained so for the last 70 years. Edwin, known affectionately as "Pops", celebrated his 86th birthday on March 24, 1978. The article mentioned above follows:

"Things have not changed too much for Edwin "Pops" Bay as far as getting goods for the Bay's Grocery Store in Corvallis. He still gets his bread from Eddy's Bakery in Missoula, his produce from Pacific Fruit in Missoula, and his meat from John R. Daily's in Missoula — just like he did when he began his career at the store in 1910. He does not, however, head out into the valley to get and deliver orders in his two horse wagon! Nor does he operate on credit terms that were payable once a year, following harvest! He does not receive all his goods in bulk and have to sack individual orders. He does not keep all his perishable goods in ice houses, nor does he find jars full of gold coins buried in his garage anymore. He also hasn't missed a day of work at the store in his 68 years there. He is now 86 years young.

The store has not always been located in the same building. According to Pops, his brother "had to chop down trees at the end of town" to put up the first store. "It was nothing but wilderness then," he said. That store burned down in its early years and was rebuilt — with the carpenters earning $1.50 per hour for a 10 hour workday. Then in 1942, there was another fire in which led to the store taking up occupancy in the present day location of Bay's Hardware store, owned and operated by Pop's son, Vance Bay. In 1964, the store was moved to it present location on the East side of the street, in the old Missoula Mercantile building.

Pop's had another brother named Russell. He died at an early age, but not before graduating from Corvallis High School as the only member of the class.

Edwin and Lillian Maude Hedges of Livingston, Montana, married in 1915. She later became a school teacher in Corvallis High School. Lillian was indicative of the wives of all the Bay brothers as "we all married school teachers" he said. Pops recalls their honeymoon in Butte, taking surrey rides around the Bitter Root Valley, and working in the store together. He also recalls naming his two wagon horses after his wife!! Pops and Lillian managed to take a few trips in their car. His mother told him, in her later years, about money being buried under the garage, and that should anything happen to her, he was to get it. Well, he dug it up, and he and his wife went into Missoula and bought themselves a touring car! That car took them over miles of back-country dirt roads to such places as Florida and New York City. Pops said the car he bought became known as "EMF", EVERY MORNING FIX'EM!! The Florida trip with his wife lasted for two months, and he nearly decided to stay. The New York trip was made with his brother and his mother. His mother was headed home to Denmark and her sons were headed to the ballpark. They spent two days watching the Yankees play.

Pops recalls apple boom days when he and his brother would take carloads of apples to the Dakotas to sell right off the car to waiting farmers. "They were the best apples, those Macintosh apples, the boxcars smelled real good. I don't know why, but they just started disappearing from the valley."

Writing his name in the ashes on the road from the 1910 fire, Indians all over, that "Big shot from Anaconda" Marcus Daly, the Depression, and seeing Babe Ruth play baseball, were just a few of the memories Pops related in the back room of Bay's Store on the occasion of the 70th anniversary of the store.

After all those years, Pops said, "I still like working and watching everything change! Most for the better, as it was a lot of work in those days, and it's easy now. Being a sickly, puny kid — I don't know how I made it"!

NELLIE HAWTHORNE BLACK

by Denise Black Severns, granddaughter (1997)

Nellie Hawthorne was born on January 30, 1877, in Vinton, Iowa, and moved to Kearney, NB, in 1879 (according to her mother's obituary). She attended grammar and high school, the University of Nebraska, and Kearney's Teachers College. Following her training years, she taught school at Kearney, then she followed the "Call of the West" and taught at a school in Nampa, Idaho. Romance interrupted her teaching career, and she and Verne Black were married in Kearney, NB, on January 27, 1909. While in Montana on their honeymoon, they stayed at the Ravalli Hotel in Hamilton, and decided to purchase land about three miles north of there. (See Grampa's story).

Nellie was one of the longtime Presbyterians residing within the area over which the First Presbyterian Church of Hamilton has jurisdiction. One article said that in the spring of 1973, she had lived in the Bitter Root Valley for 64 years, and for a goodly number of those years, was a very active person in the church, in attendance with her husband at church services and as an energetic working member of the women's organizations. Lottie Patch recalled that Mrs. Black was one of the ladies of the church who along with Miss Bessie Carpenter, Mrs. Adrian Adams, and Mrs. Patch were instrumental in the organization and continued success of the Presbyterian Women's Missionary Society, which functioned from 1922 to 1948.

Besides her church activities, Mrs. Nellie Black, throughout the years, had interested herself with civic affairs and was a charter member of the Hamilton Women's Club. She also gave freely of her time and talent to the Red Cross work before and during World War II. She served on the Corvallis School Board, probably in the early 1920's. Mr. and Mrs. Verne Black opened their account with the Ravalli County Bank in 1909. They had one son, James Henderson Black, who was born at their home on Black Lane, where they lived all their lives. She worked hard, helping with the apple work and the chickens.

MY MEMORIES OF GRANDMA:

I remember the big old trees that Gram would hide the Easter eggs around, the homemade doughnuts (she was a good cook), and her wooden cutting bowl for cabbage. Her sister, Lillian, who was from the East, decided to help her modernize her furniture that had been her mother-in-law's. They cut off the beautiful headboards and turned the bed around so the footboards were the headboards. She and her sister made many, many pieced quilts. Gram would also cut out a string of paper dolls from folded newspaper. She passed away in 1974, and my brother, Jim, my sister, Sandra, and I were able to share the old furniture left in the house. I traded property in Missoula and Corvallis for the Black home, and was able to do some renovation work on it in 1994 and 1995.

JAMES LAVERNE BLACK

"Verne", as he was often called, was born in Ridgefield, IL, on July 2, 1869. When he was 9 years old, his parents moved to Fairfield, Iowa, and then to Kearney, NB, where he grew up and was associated with his father and two brothers, Harry and Cyrus (a bird artist), in dairy farming, and in the celery growing industry.

Upon marriage to Nellie Hawthorne on January 27, 1909, they went to Salt Lake City, Utah, and on to Missoula, Montana, by train for their honeymoon. In Hamilton, they stayed at the Ravalli Hotel, and discovered the Bitter Root Valley, purchasing a home on a ten acre tract of land during the apple orchard boom, which they developed into one of the foremost McIntosh apple orchard properties. The land and home were purchased from the Daly interests. The house was a labor house of the Daly's where they fed their men, and used the front bedroom for an office. Verne and Nellie had to move into a corner of the barn on the north part of the acreage until the people moved out of the house the following spring. When they had their son, James Henderson Black in this home in June of 1910, the front office became his bedroom. The Daly barn on the north end of the property was used for working the apple crop, hay storage, and to accommodate milking of a couple cows.

Verne invented a celery seeder, a six-foot long board which poked holes in the ground to a depth of 8 to 10 inches. He grew a lot of onions and lettuce, and had a greenhouse in back of the garage near the chicken coop. The grandkids had fun collecting the eggs! I remember the cream separator in the pantry, the apple boat pulled behind an old tractor through the rows of trees, to pick up the apples. Ben and Irma Wilkerson worked for many years on this farm, as did several of the Hellman family members. Verne loved those apple trees so much, but they were gradually pulled out in the 1940's and later, due to a poor market. Apple trees near the house were left intact for Verne to enjoy, which he did until 1957, when he passed away.

BLODGETT

The family has been able to trace their lineage back to 1558 to Suffolk, England. The family name occurs in two spellings, either Blodgett or Blowgate. Members came to America in 1635 settling in Vermont and Massachusetts. The first generation that involved the Bitterroot was that of Neuman Greenleaf Blodgett. He was born in 1800 in Vermont, and represented the eighth generation born in America. He was a member of the Mormon Church and came west through Illinois and Ohio to North Ogden, Utah in 1850. His first wife died and his second wife was Elizabeth Garrett

Reed Blodgett. He had 15 children by these two wives, many of whom died in infancy, but his second wife, Elizabeth, came to the Bitterroot with her children after he died in 1882, so as to be near her son and stepson.

Joseph Smith Blodgett, one of the sons, came to the Bitterroot in 1859, bought a pack string from Major Owen, hunted and trapped for a while went back to Utah and then returned settling in Grantsdale area and farmed. He married an Indian woman who had three children of her own and later they had children together and settled finally in Arlee. He died in 1903. One of his sons, Brigham, born in 1870, married one of the Indian woman's daughters and settled in the Sleeping Child area.

Another son of Neuman Greenleaf Blodgett's first wife was Lyman Johnson Blodgett, representing along with his brother above, the second generation of the Blodgetts in the Bitterroot, came in 1868 and farmed in the Corvallis area around Quast Lane. He was also involved in building Fort Corvallis. He left in 1871 went to Ogden bought some cattle and drove them all the way back here arriving in 1872 and settled on the west side. He was responsible for establishing Blodgett Cemetery after a teenage daughter died very suddenly. His farm extended roughly from the site of the cemetery to Dutch Hill. It was for this family that Lime Creek was changed to Blodgett Creek. His wife, Mary, used to keep her cream cold in another small creek and one day the container tipped over sending the cream down the creek, so she called that one Churn Creek, which still persists. Lyman died in 1908.

Horace William Blodgett, (born 1864 died 1907), a son of Lyman and Mary Ann Parker, was one of eleven children representing the third generation. A brother Joseph Benjamin had a sawmill west of Woodside and this is how Mill Creek got its name.

Horace's son, Tom, was the fourth generation. At age 18 he had Spotted Fever. He married Oretta Dye and they had five children Violet, Clara, Ethel Bob and Don. Don and his sister Violet Rennaker still live in the valley. The others have passed on.

Don married Winifred White. Her parents built White's store at Conner in 1911. Her dad was postmaster and taught school at Baker Creek. Her mother ran the store and was assistant postmaster. Don and Winifred had seven children two of whom died. Steve, Lynda, Jan, Susan and David survive, but do not reside in the valley. These children are the sixth generation.

Tom had two brothers, William and John, and seven sisters. His brother, John, had two sons Robert who lived in Missoula and Don who lived in Anaconda, but was killed a few years ago in a snowmobile accident. He also had three daughters, but they do not live here.

Lyman also had a son Neuman Greenleaf who had a son Neuman A. and his son is Max, who lives in the valley and is the current manager of the cemetery.

Three of Lyman and Mary's daughters married into the McRae, McKillop and Shultz families.

THE BLOOD FAMILY OF HAMILTON, MONTANA

by Bobbie Blood Schrader

Varnum "Oliver" Blood and B. Nettie Peterson Blood first came to the Bitter Root in 1894. They purchased property two miles North of Hamilton on the Old Grantsdale Road. Oliver was well known as a fine horticulturist, his specialty being apples which grace the Historical Society postcards, today.

Oliver's story begins in 1860, when he was born in Galena, Illinois. He traveled the Oregon Trail by oxcart, with his family, and landed in Clatskanie, Oregon. Oliver's father and mother, Benjamin W. and Almira Caroline (Goss) Blood were one of the founding families, and had a logging company there. Father Ben hired a tiny Norwegian woman, who was a marvelous cook, to feed the loggers. When the cooking was done, she could be found greasing the skids with bacon grease to slide the logs into the Columbia River! Her name was Gertrude Johnson Peterson, and she along with her husband, Elias, and their 13 year old daughter, Nettie, had come to America from Mo, Norway in 1881.

Nettie caught the eye of young Oliver Blood, and they were married on December 24, 1889, in Clatskanie. Their children followed in the usual 1800's fashion. Herman in 1890; Ormond in 1893; Elmer in 1895; Walter in 1897; Agnes in 1899; Perley in 1902; and Clara in 1905. It was during this time they moved to the Bitter Root.

Sometime in the early 1900's, as family rumor has it, Oliver went to Alaska to look for gold. Nettie stayed home to tend the six or seven little ones and to mind the ranch. Oliver returned home without the fortune, and it was spoken of no more!

All the children attended school in Hamilton and the boys played in the High School band. Later, the boys played for local dances and it was there my grandfather, Perley, met my grandmother, Nina May Hatfield. Granddad said "The first thing I noticed about Nina was the light reflecting off her beautiful auburn hair, and those big, brown eyes! Grandmother's first recollection was, "He was so clean — his hair was always combed, and his shoes were always shined!" They married on March 28th, 1925 in Hamilton. Nina 's parents were Sidney and Ora Mae (Stallings) Hatfield of Hamilton.

Nina May was the first woman butcher in Montana, and worked in Perley's butcher shop. She was also a fantastic seamstress and sewed many of the fine dresses for the ladies of Hamilton.

The Hatfield's had three children. Marion, born in 1903; Nina, born in 1905; and Jack, born in 1907. For a time the family resided in Wibaux, MT. While there, Jack died from scarlet fever at the age of twelve. Grief stricken, the family moved back to Hamilton.

Marion was ahead of her time in finding the right man. Therefore, she was married to: #1. Bernard Taylor of Hamilton, #2. Paul White of Hamilton, and #3. Anthony DeSouza of Beverly Hills, California. The family moved to California in the 1940's to escape the winters. Sidney died in Burbank, CA, in 1943; Ora Mae died in Culver City, CA in 1963; and Marion died in Beverly Hills, a very wealthy woman, in 1973.

Nina, my grandmother, is still living near family in Tacoma, WA, as of 1993. She is a wonderfully articulate woman who has had a very full and interesting life. Nina worked for Max Factor in the wig department during the 1950's, in Hollywood. She later worked as a typist on the "Moon Shot Program" at White Sands, New Mexico.

The Blood children all married locally. Their mates are as follows: Herman married Florence Palmer and they later moved to Hillsboro, OR, Ormand was in W.W.I and he was deeply affected by it and never married. He was found dead of a self-inflicted gunshot wound, at his father's ranch in 1942, Elmer married Katherine Dowling, and later moved to Kennewick, WA; he died in 1983, Walter married Gladys Centers, Agnes married #1. Fred Modrell and #2. Frank Humble. She died in Palm Springs, CA, in 1980. Perley married Nina Hatfield, and worked for North American Aviation as a machinist, and was a talented inventor and photographer. Perley died in El Paso, TX, in 1989. Clara married #1. Ben Oertli and #2. Dr. J. W. Kilpatrick, a popular Hamilton veterinarian. Clara died in 1960 in Hamilton.

In the 1920's, Oliver and Nettie, moved to town and resided at 524 S. First Street in Hamilton. Nettie's mother, Gertrude, lived with them until her death at the age of 102 years, in 1941. Gertrude was the oldest living woman in Montana, at that time.

My father, Robert Browning Blood, was born in Hamilton on December 26, 1925. He was raised in military schools and always hoped to be a pilot. He was a step out of time, and before he could be fully trained, W.W.II was over. So, he joined the Air Force and traveled the world, but sadly was never able to fulfill his dream of flying. He died in 1989, in Tacoma, WA, leaving a wife and four daughters.

I must share a wonderful story with you that Dad loved telling. When he was a little boy, there was an Indian man in town who was known for his leather work. One day, Dad was in town with his father, Perley. They were going to buy some new shoes at a local store during a shoe sale. The Indian fellow was also looking for a bargain. He asked the clerk for the biggest pair of boots they had. They were several sizes too big for him and the sales clerk did his best to talk him out of them. His reply was "The cost is the same, no matter what size I buy, and there is twice as much leather in this pair as in my size!" Thereafter, when my father saw him in town, he would be clumping down the street in those huge boots.

There are so many family stories; Grandma Nina going up Skalkaho Pass to get the rocks for the fireplace they built; Nettie's cooking ability and perseverance; the hard winters; the crisp fall air, the beauty of the valley and the pioneer spirit that was able to bring this all about.

The older members now reside in the Riverside Cemetery, but their love of the Bitter Root Valley lives on.

BOWDEN FAMILY

From the largest wholesale dry goods house in the greatest commercial mart in the world to a similar store on a much smaller scale in one of the interior towns of western Montana seems like a long descent, when it is in fact a promotion from the position of employed to employer, from that of salesman — to owner. This long stride was made by Joseph Bowden, of Corvallis, Montana.

JOSEPH BOWDEN was born in Penzance, County Cornwall, England, on November 24, 1863, the only child of Joseph and Elizabeth Bowden, also natives of England. He attended public and private schools until he was sixteen, then served an apprenticeship of four years in a drygoods store for which he received no pay. He then went to London, and was for the next seven years, clerk and salesman in the largest wholesale dry goods establishment in the metropolis. In 1890, he resigned this position and came to the United States, locating in Missoula, where he worked six months for the Missoula Mercantile Company, and at his own request was transferred to the branch at Corvallis, where he remained until 1896. He then returned to Missoula, and in February bought the stock of the branch house in Corvallis, and with it opened a store of his own.

His years as county merchant, covering a half century, marked him as an adaptable character, linked consistently with the times. He knew the mercantile life of the Bitter Root when the 30-day credit system was practically non-existent. His early customers were in the main, farming people and when crop-time came in the fall, the annual "pay-the-store-bill" season kept it company.

Joseph was married on June 12, 1892, to Miss Anna A. Summers, daughter of William and Eliza Summers, of London, England, the marriage being solemnized in Missoula. Joseph obtained his naturalization at Stevensville in the early 1890's, when that town was the Ravalli county seat. He was a member of all branches of the Masonic lodge, affiliated with the Corvallis Blue Lodge, the Royal Arch at Missoula and the Algeria Shrine at Helena. Joseph and Anna had two sons, Jack Donald, who died at the age of

7 months, and Dudley Francis, who was born June 21, 1893, at Corvallis Montana, and attended schools in Corvallis and Carroll College in Deer Lodge, Montana, before it was moved to Helena.

After returning from World War I, Dud joined his father in the store. He later began a side line of hardware and machinery, and in the early 1930's, had the first John Deere tractor dealership in the valley.

Joseph died in 1942, and in 1946, Dud sold the store to Mr. Cushman, keeping the hardware line of the business. With the help of the American Legion members, logs were cut and peeled and a two story building was built at the northeast end of main street, which still stands today. This building became Dud's hardware store, with the upstairs to be used by the American Legion and Auxiliary for as long as they had an active organization. Also, from approximately 1946 through 1954, Dud had a set of scales which was used for weighing beet and whey trucks.

Dud was also instrumental in expanding the Corvallis Cemetery to the west. After the 1943 accidental hunting death of his only son, a cemetery

This published article included an ad for Joseph Bowden, Headquaters for General Merchandise. It was Christmas season, 1911, and at that time, he had been in business for 15 years and sold toys, groceries, and sundry items for all members of the family. He offered some items for men at ten percent off — Men's French Flannel Shirts with detachable collar sold for $2.75; fur-lined Gauntlet Gloves were $2.00; suspenders in fancy boxes were 65 cents to $1.50; and all Silk Four-in-hand Knitted Ties in fancy box were only 35 cents. Ladies offerings were handpainted China, cut glass, opera scarfs, handbags, backcombs, sidecombs, barettes, toilet sets, box stationery, hand embroidered handkerchiefs, and all kinds of fancy neckware.

plot was purchased which was covered with weeds and thistles. Many Corvallis residents volunteered their time with horses and rakes to clean and clear up a new section to the cemetery. A pump system was later installed for the irrigation of the cemetery.

In 1954, Mr. Cushman went out of business, so Dudley moved his hardware store back into the original building and expanded his hardware line to include household appliances and house and irrigation pumps. He continued with the store until ill health forced him to sell in 1964. Dud died on August 17, 1968.

Dudley was married on August 5, 1928, to Clara Dell Shriver, daughter of James and Frances Shriver of Missoula, Montana. They had two children, James Dudley and Diana Frances. Clara Dell taught school at Corvallis High from 1925 through 1928, and returned to teaching in 1962, teaching two years in the High School English Department and the following years in the Junior High, retiring in 1971. She died on February 4, 1987. Dud was a member of the Corvallis American Legion and the Corvallis Cemetery Association and enjoyed flying his own Fairchild PT 19 trainer plane. Clara Dell was associated with the Legion Auxiliary, being department President, the Corvallis Eastern Stars, the American Association of University Women and various bridge clubs.

THE BROOKS FAMILY

James J. Brooks was born in Emmet, WI, on April 12, 1849, of Irish immigrants and spent his childhood days on his father's farm. Upon reaching manhood, he followed the mining profession for most of his adult life. After his marriage to Jane Byrne, also born to Irish immigrants, James and Jane Brooks lived in the mining communities of Iron Cliff, Michigan; Silver City, New Mexico; Gold Hill, Nevada; Bodie, California; and Basin and Butte, Montana. James retired from the mining profession in 1900. Then, James and Jane purchased a cherry and apple farm west of Hamilton, in the Canyon Creek District. There they lived until James's sudden death on December 4, 1905. After James's death, Jane sold the farm and purchased a residence at 705 North 4th Street in Hamilton. This home has been owned by three subsequent generations of Brook's descendants up to the present date.

James and Jane Brooks were the parents of four children, three of which lived to maturity.

George became a prominent produce buyer and seller of MacIntosh apples during the time the Bitter Root valley was known as the "Land of the MacIntosh Red". George followed the profession of farmer for the remainder of his life which ended on March 22, 1954. He was best described by a fellow farmer as "a person who knew his business, made a lot of money, and lost a lot of it! Two of his apple box labels are on display at the Ravalli County Museum.

Anna Fay graduated in 1904 from the Deaconess Home Hospital in Spokane, WA, as a registered nurse. She married Ralph W. Barlow on November 21, 1905. Shortly after their marriage, Ralph and Anna moved to the Bitter Root Valley where Ralph worked on the "Big Ditch Operation" at Three Mile and at Eight Mile. In 1912, Ralph became the manager of the Bitter Root Irrigation Farm at Forest Hill, where large quantities of cherries and apples were grown. Anna was the cook for the laborers at this farm. It was at Forest Hill on November 6, 1916, that Anna's mother, Jane Brooks, died of pneumonia. In 1921, Ralph and Anna and their three young daughters, moved to a farm west of Hamilton. Ralph died at the early age of 41, from Rocky Mountain Spotted Fever. Anna, with three young daughters to support, sold the farm and returned to nursing at the Marcus Daly Hospital which was located on south second street. She retired from nursing when the new Marcus Daly Hospital opened. Anna died on March 13, 1952.

Ida Jane Brooks was the youngest daughter of James and Jane Brooks, and married William J. Heaney on December 20, 1899, in St. Patrick's Church in Butte, Montana. They resided in the mining community of Basin, MT, and later on a farm west of Hamilton. Ida spent the majority of her adult life in New York City.

Two of Jane and James Brooks' granddaughters, Mrs. Betty Fullerton and Mrs. Virginia Roscoe, still make their homes in Hamilton. The third granddaughter, Mrs. Margaret Corbin, lives in Tucson, Arizona.

THE BROOKS FAMILY & THE BROOKS HOTEL

by James Brooks Swanson, son of Lois Brooks Swanson

John W. Brooks (1848-1930) and Eliza A. Savage Brooks (1856-1921) were the parents of Louis Newton Brooks.

John F. Wood (1842-1923) and Mary L. Alford Wood were the parents of Lula Bell Wood.

This Brooks family came to the Bitter Root Valley by covered wagon, pulled by an oxen team, sometime between 1870 and 1880. The family journeyed here from Missouri along with several other families.

The Woods family also came to the Bitter Root Valley about this same time, but from Tennessee and North Carolina.

Louis Newton Brooks and Lula Bell Wood were married on October 16, 1898. Their story begins around 1896, when it seems that Louis went in search of work and walked about the Bitter Root Valley looking for employment. By chance, he wandered into the farm of John and Mary Wood, near the town of Stevensville, and Mr. Wood hired him on the spot.

A year or two passed, and nature took its course, and Louis Brooks courted and married their daughter, Lula Bell.

They moved to Oregon to build a life of their own, but shortly returned to the Bitter Root. They rented the Hefling house in Corvallis, and in 1916, purchased it for $4,000.00. This became known as the Brooks house and later as the Brooks Hotel. The original property consisted of five acres of bearing orchard, residence, barns, washroom, and ice house. Built originally by Mr. George W. Dougherty, (a Canadian businessman who had been hired by the Montana Mercantile Company in Missoula), in 1894, the large prefabricated Victorian structure was ordered from a Midwestern company that mass produced large homes of high quality. The Dougherty home was shipped here by rail and each piece was assembled by local carpenters who worked for $50.00 per month.

In 1916, Louis Brooks was employed as a local mail carrier. He traveled to Woodside twice each day to meet the train and carry the mail back to Corvallis. Often, passengers would ask Mr. Brooks to give them a ride to Corvallis, and from these requests, Louis started his own business of providing food and lodging for these guests. It was inevitable that the Brooks residence would become the Brooks Hotel. Thus began the 60 year reign of the Brooks Hotel where hundreds of folks slept, ate, and visited.

Louis and Mary had five children: Edna L. (1900-1993), John L. (1901-1915), Inez E.(1903-1950), Gladys M. (1907-living in 1998), and Lois M. (1921-1983).

These children continued to operate the Brooks Hotel after the deaths of their parents, and won many friends and awards for the superb old-fashioned food and genuine hospitality.

The following is a brief account of each of the Brooks children and their families.

We begin with Edna L. Brooks, the eldest Brooks child, who bore the brunt of the hard work involved in the running of the hotel. Edna quit high school to come home and help her mother full time with the endless hours of toil and back breaking work. Edna was married to Ruspor Giesy, known as R. D. Giesy, on April 20, 1921. She and her husband owned a small home on the west side of Corvallis, but spent most of their time at the hotel. They had one child, Russell, who was an excellent athlete and student. He served in World War II as a fighter pilot and was shot down behind enemy lines, fortunately returning to tell the story. Ruspor died in 1961, and Edna in 1993, and son, Russell, is still living in Whitefish, Montana.

John Lloyd Brooks, called Lloyd by the family, fell off the family porch when a small boy, and severely injured his head. Seizures and all sorts of maladies due to this injury caused his early demise at the age of 14, in 1915.

Inez Brooks like her older sister, worked very hard and her life consisted mainly of working at the hotel. She was a beautiful young woman and was said to have many suitors. Her favorite suitor is said to have left without notice, never to return. She worked tirelessly with the family, and never married. She may have died from a broken heart, who can say. She died at age 47, in 1950.

Gladys M. Brooks also worked her entire life at the hotel. As a young woman, she was a valley beauty queen, and also had many suitors. She married Hector "Squib" Rasmussen on September 1, 1942. Squib and Gladys were enamored with horse racing and traveled several states for many years, racing their beloved horses. Having no children, their horses became their love, and many ribbons and awards were garnered over the years. Squib was a real sports fan, and he and Gladys spent many hours following the Corvallis School "Blue Devils" around Montana. Gladys and Edna operated the Brooks Hotel for over 50 years, and were simply called "The Brooks Girls" or just "The Girls" by those who knew them.

Lois Marie Brooks was the baby of the family and came along late in Lula's life. In fact, Edna's son, Russell, and Lois were the same age and grew up together. Lois was the only child that escaped the powerful draw of the hotel. On March 21, 1947, Lois married Carl Swanson and moved from the hotel world into the world of farming and ranching. Lois and Carl became parents of two sons, James (that's me), and Charles. The Swanson family farm is located east of Corvallis and still operated by Charles, with his father still helping. Lois passed away in 1983.

The saga of the Brooks Hotel is one of hard work, providing a different and interesting challenge for the entire Brooks family. When age finally forced Edna and Gladys to close this establishment it was hard for the family and the community. This operation had been their whole life, and an integral part of the Corvallis community. Many famous people had eaten and stayed at the Brooks Hotel. A few that come to mind are: Mike and Maureen Mansfield, a Montana Senator and his wife. Mike later became the U. S. Ambassador to Japan. Also, Kirby Grant of "Sky King" fame in the early 60's. Mr. Duncan Hines of the famous cake mixes was a guest. Governors, important doctors and businessmen, cattle buyers, and weary travelers all enjoyed the warmth and graciousness of the Brooks family. In the early years, the Brooks Hotel served many young Corvallis School teachers, and Gladys and Edna often served as mothers who heard the troubles and problems of the local young guests. Everyone ate family style, and the days events, politics, and most any subject was open to discussion.

A unique visitor story tells of a certain Irish gentleman by the name of Shannon, who was a salesman for R. J. Reynolds tobacco. After a previous visit, Mr. Shannon returned with his family in an old Ford car with running boards. On the running board was a box with a goat in it! Mr. Shannon said he always wanted his children to have fresh milk, so he carried his goat along in the box on the side of his car!

CHICKEN EVERY SUNDAY was the menu in this wonderful atmosphere. The family would feature a full course dinner of fresh chicken, green beans, creamed corn, cole slaw, mountains of mashed potatoes and gravy, several relish plates, Parker house rolls and finally two or three kinds of homemade pie. All this food was homegrown, canned or made from scratch. Interested parties called to make reservations and often the waiting list was for several months. Guests were served family style at three large tables with another added on the porch during the summer months for friends, family and visitors. During the week,local patrons would eat an evening meal with the family. Hundreds of customers paid $1.00 to $1.50 for all you could eat of some of the best homemade food on the face of the earth. Special parties were also catered. Edna and Gladys loved to play bridge, so many bridge parties were held also.

It would take volumes to record all the people, parties, and events that happened at the Brooks Hotel, and to the Brooks family. It was my privilege to know and love these wonderful people. I miss them, and I miss the Brooks Hotel.

THE BROOKS - White Table Cloths Never Went Out of Style

an article by B. K. Monroe

The town of Corvallis is the second oldest in the Bitter Root and it has a spirit that got it's start in the late 1870's, a spirit that gives with distinction because it keeps to the neighbor context in storied reflection. One of the old homes in Corvallis has perhaps done more in the last half-century to perpetuate this little "Heart of the Valley" community's record of hospitality is the Brooks Hotel, a tall nine-room structure that was built way back in 1894 by businessman, George Dougherty.

Reminiscent conversations with Edna Brooks Giesy brought out the story of the Brooks Hotel, which had its beginnings as to public service in 1916.

Mrs. Giesy's parents, Louis and Lula Wood Brooks, acquired the old-time Dougherty residence in 1914, from Thomas J. Hefling, one-time Ravalli County Treasurer. It was the home for their family of four daughters and a son, Lloyd. The daughters were Edna, Gladys, Inez, and Lois.

Edna and Gladys (now Mrs. Hector Rasmussen) have kept the Brooks Hotel operating along the fine old-fashioned standards set by their parents. The father died in 1946, and for the next 12 years, Mrs. Brooks and her daughters went on with the business. After Mrs. Brook's death in 1958, when only the three daughters were left, they reached a decision to keep the Brooks Hotel going on, just as their mother would have wished.

Lois, by this time Mrs. Carl Swanson, had left the old home to live on an eastside ranch, but Edna and Gladys set their heads and hearts toward

The Brooks Hotel, with its olden architecture, has a dignity of service, and an air of welcome that truly marks it as a "house by the side of the road."

keeping "Brooks" in its rightful place as the number one family style place in the valley. The Brooks is the farthest thing from a short order house in all the county. It has always been a "garden to table" place to have a good dinner and fried chicken is one of the specialties that beckons many to make reservations for Sunday.

The big dining room with its one long table and a couple of smaller ones, can seat 40 diners and the old country style of heaping platters and big bowls of vegetables keeps up the tradition that Louis and Lula started more than 50 years ago. White tablecloths never went out of style at the Brooks. They have the charm that goes with pretty china and bright silver that makes the Brooks Hotel picture one never to be forgotten once a stranger has stopped by for "a good country cooked meal".

Edna Giesy has been waiting tables in the Brooks Hotel for fifty years now and Gladys, as the chief in the kitchen, has been at the big range ever since their mother died.

The Brooks Hotel, with its olden architecture, has a dignity of service, and air of welcome that truly marks it as a "house by the side of the road".

THE BULGARIANS

Thus far you have read about families, and although not really a family, the history of the Bitter Root Valley would be incomplete without mentioning the Bulgarians. The first information I could find was in the Western News of October 16, 1907, to the effect that "Thirty eight Bulgarians arrived last Thursday and are now doing pick and shovel work on the pipe lines along the Big Ditch." A good number eventually became truck gardeners, being from agricultural backgrounds and the area being much like their homeland they were drawn to the valley with dream of "a place of their own".

Partnerships were formed with three to six countrymen. Through their cooperative efforts they supplied local stores and homes with strawberries, raspberries and vegetables including their famous yellow peppers. Upon the completion of the Skalkaho Road their market was expanded to the Butte Anaconda area.

Jean Wrobel tells of her dad, Boni Fileff, who was born near Sophia in 1884 and at age 15 enlisted in the Turkish Army in order to get enough money for passage to the USA. He traveled steerage class to Philadelphia somewhere between 1905 and 1910. He worked there and in the Chicago area before coming here to be with a brother. At first he was a cook for the Big Ditch crews, then later worked for the O.W. Kerr Co. at Charlos Heights when orchards were being developed. In 1919 he married a widow, Maude McCook Holbrook, and in 1921 started farming in the Gilchrist area which is west of the present Jim Duus place and the Hamilton Golf Course. This remained the family home until he died in 1958. His wife died in 1951. Jean lives on part of the old place.

One of the earlier partnerships, Spasoff & Angeloff Company, included Evan Spasoff, manager, Spiro Angeloff, Boni Fileff, George Regis and Mike Angeloff (Big Mike also known as Muncho). They banded together to grow and market their own produce Boni was salesman during the week and stayed in Anaconda, Butte or Helena. After the Skalkaho opened in 1924, the produce would be trucked by night because it was cool and they were warned of oncoming traffic by headlights on the narrow and winding road. There was also a code of the Skalkaho; namely that when meeting a truck, the truck was to keep to the inside no matter in which direction it was going. Steve Rousoff was one of the truck drivers.

Mike Angeloff was born in 1879, came to the USA in 1907 and the Bitter Root in 1909. He was not related to Spiro, but worked with him. He was a well-known Bulgarian irrigator. He farmed in the Corvallis area. He married Viola Jessie Ohl from Sula. She died in 1951, he in 1954.

Evan Spasoff, also known as John, was buying his place, which was the old Hamilton Nursery, now occupied by other people, namely Bettye

Smith, Dick Singleton and Dr. Jim Olson. He was born in 1885, came to the states in 1910, first to Minneapolis and then here. He married Fannie Wesseling in 1930. After a while the partnership was dissolved because the others objected to the way the money was being split, thinking they were helping him buy his land while they were renting theirs. He died in 1962 and she in 1964.

Spiro Angeloff was born in 1894, came to the U.S. from Canada at age 13 with several other young Bulgarians and a man from Bulgaria who was hired to bring boys to the U.S. illegally to avoid their being conscripted into the Bulgarian Army. They worked in the mines in Minnesota, eventually migrated to Butte to work in the mines and then to the Bitter Root Valley. Early on he with others, raised strawberries in the Charlos Heights area before becoming a partner in Spasoff & Angeloff Company. About 1930 he managed another venture with four other Bulgarians on the Brooks place. This was located on Bowman Road just across from where Orchard Road joins. He and Louie Popoff also gardened on a place of their own in the Skeels Addition. He never married and died in 1966.

Louie Popoff was born in 1884, came to Montana in 1906, worked on the Como Dam then went into produce. He never married and died in 1965. Most of the time he was associated with Spiro Angeloff except the time he was associated with George Christoff, Alex Evanoff and Peter Coloff on what is now the Bill Bates place on West Bridge Road. His nickname was “Popey”. Another who worked with them was Sam Boneff. He came in 1929, and was known as Crazy Sam because he talked to himself.

Steve Rousoff was a farmer in the Daly Acres area and a salesman and truck driver for the cooperatives. He was born in 1886. He married Theresa Boice Widenbach in Butte in 1930 and moved to the valley. He died in 1947. The youngest of his three children, a son Joe, lives in the Hamilton Heights area.

Steve Encoff was born in 1888, came to USA in 1912. In the 1930s he was a salesman for the Bulgarians in Butte. He married Bertha Mabra Lambert in 1933 and decided he would rather be on the growing end so moved to the Daly place west of Freeze lane in 1939. He farmed with Frank Denchoff, Roscoe Penchoff and Steve Marinoff. Rousoff and Art Braun acted as their salesmen and drivers. He became the sole owner and the last of the "Bulgarian Truck Gardeners", retiring shortly after World War II. His step-daughter Mrs. Adam Senn, Bertie still lives in Hamilton.

Steve Marinoff came to Hamilton from Butte, where he had been a miner, in 1939. He operated a truck garden on his place on Belmont Avenue. He died in 1962

The three Steve’s posed a problem so they agreed Steve Rousoff would be “Big Steve”, Steve Encoff would be “Little Steve” and Steve Marinoff would be “Black Steve” because he was of a darker complexion.

William Daneff was born in 1897, came to the USA in 1914 and gradually came westward to the Bitter Root. He married Frances Little in 1934. They farmed their own place on the west side. He was also a salesman and truck driver for the cooperatives. He died in 1958.

Peter Coloff born 1884 and came to USA in 1910, first to Baltimore, then St. Louis then Butte and finally the valley, working on the Big Ditch. In 1911 returned to Butte worked on the BA &P RR until 1913. He returned to the valley then and worked in the orchards until he returned to Butte as a miner. In 1921 he went to Gregson Hot Springs, the current Fairmont Springs, as plunge manager. In 1930, he married Myrtle Smith, moved to Hamilton in 1933 to become a truck gardener with Christoff, Evanoff and Popoff on the Bates place. In 1934, he moved to the Sherwin place on the corner of West Bridge Road and Ricketts Road which he and his wife farmed. He also worked with his neighbor John Spasoff and partners Steve Rousoff, William Daneff and Sam Boneff for one year, but continued to farm on the Sherwin place until he moved into Hamilton in 1970. Two daughters, Mrs. James Simmons, Virginia, and Mrs. Norman Foster, Alice, still live in the valley. He died in 1979. Virginia has contributed much to this story.

There were others not involved in the joint venture. Nick Totsoff was born in 1892, farmed south of Stevensville. He later joined Mike Todoroff and Marin Mincoff to operate a truck garden on the Grantsdale Road. After he retired, he moved to the corner of Blood Lane and Highway 93. He died in 1984. Mike Todoroff also farmed out on the Grantsdale Road with George Georgeoff and Bill Dimitoff, the latter returned to Bulgaria. Mike was never married and returned to Bulgaria sometime around the 1970s for a couple of years and then returned here and died shortly thereafter.

Alex Evanoff was born in 1883 came to the USA in 1904 first as a railroader and miner in Butte then in 1930 to the valley as a truck farmer. His first wife was Eva Rennaker and after a divorce he married Irma Foster Evanoff, widow of Nick Evanoff (no relation) of Butte. He died in 1968. A stepson, Nick, still lives here.

George Georgeoff was born in 1890. He and his wife, Katherine, came here in 1941 and farmed on the Bonesteele place on Marcus. He died in 1956.

Angel Sideroff was born in 1882 came to the Bitter Root in 1910. He worked with the other Bulgarians then later farmed for himself on Big Corral Road. He died in 1956.

As you are no doubt aware by now, these fellows were not always associated with the same group each year, but moved about. Some were not even involved in the actual farming process. Jim Todoroff, no relation to Mike, was a card dealer at the Rainbow bar. Ted Todoroff, again no relation, was called Tooshka and worked for Spasoff.

Many became naturalized citizens. The following list may be incomplete: Alex Evanoff, Peter Coloff, Steve Encoff, Boni Fileff, George Georgeoff and Jim Todoroff. Although they did not want to be part of the Bulgarian Army, some served with the United States Army in World War I. John Spasoff and Jim Todoroff were two who did serve.

BURCH, CAPLE, AND LUALLEN FAMILIES

by Grace Squires Simmons and Violet Squires Rennaker Nelson

Our great grandfather, on mother's side, was Vincent B. Burch, Sr. He was born February 1837, in St. Joseph, Missouri. His son, Vincent Burch, Jr., was born in St. Joseph, Missouri on June 18, 1869. When he was just one year old, the family left Missouri on the first wagon train into the Bitter Root Valley. On the trip, his sister got sick and died. Her parents had to bury her, then run over the grave with the wagon train, because they were afraid the Indians would dig up her grave and scalp her for her beautiful blonde hair.

Vincent Burch, Sr., distinguished himself by being one of 33 men in the Citizens Volunteer Army in the Battle of the Big Hole in 1877, led by John Caitlin.

Vincent Burch, Jr., had one brother named John and three sisters, named Jenny, Bessie, and Maggie.

Great grandparents on our mother's side were Judson Fillmore Caple, who was born August 15, 1850, and he married Sara Isabell Luallen, born October 30, 1860. They married about 1876, and of this union there were 10 children. Nine were girls: Ida Ellen (2-17-1878 to 7-30-1943), Leith (Slocum), Bertha (Neaves), Rose (Humble), Annie (Randolph), Cora (Benson), Opal (O'Connell), Ruby (Sears), Ethel (O'Dell), and one son, William.

Judson Caple had a wide handlebar mustache and his grandchildren remember him smoking his pipe, and going fishing. Sara and Judson lived together for 55 years before separating. He died in his sleep on July 21, 1938. Sara died on June 12, 1960, in Hamilton, just 4 months short of her 100th birthday. Both are buried in the Corvallis Cemetery.

Grandparents:

Ida married Vincent Burch, Jr. on February 10, 1895, in Corvallis, Montana. Together they had three children: Grace Isabel (1895-1973), Roy

F. (1897-1930), and Iris (1913-1915).

Periodically, Ida had very poor health, and many of her grandchildren remember seeing their grandfather, who was a very large man over six foot tall and weighing over 200 pounds, carry her when she was too sick to walk. After "Vint" died in 1934, Ida supported herself by taking in boarders and being an unofficial doctor's aide. They were not licensed midwives at that time, but if the doctor was called at home and told that Mrs. Burch was there, he would often say "Well, I'll be along later", and tend to his other patients. Ida died in 1945.

Grace Isabel Burch was born November 14, 1895, in Stevensville, MT. She went to Hynes, California, where she completed primary school. On June 16, 1913, she married Martin Carl Moe, and together they had four children. Their twins, Carl Edward and Carlee Edna, were born on July 23, 1914, in Huntington, CA, but Carlee died as an infant.

In 1915, Grace returned to her mother's home in Corvallis, to nurse her mother as her mother was ill and stricken with grief over the loss of Grace's 23 month old sister, Iris, who died on August 25, 1915. While in Corvallis, Grace gave birth to a son, Glenn Allenon, born February 23, 1916, and a daughter, Mildred Ellen, was born on February 10, 1918, in Pasadena, CA. After the birth of their daughter, Grace worked for a dairy. When Mildred was eight months old, Grace and Martin divorced, and she returned to Montana where she worked at the Daly Mansion whenever Mrs. Daly was in residence. Grace died in 1973.

FRANKLIN LANE BURNS FAMILY

Franklin L. Burns was born at Georgetown, Ontario, Canada, on November 19, 1864. At an early age he came to the United States. While in Dassel, Minnesota, he managed a woolen mill and learned the trade of jeweler and silversmith from an accomplished German craftsman. Mr. Burns left Dassell and came to Grantsdale, MT, on October 12, 1890, broke. He was in business in Grantsdale for three months, then moved to Hamilton to open a barber shop in that same year. After two years in the barber business, he started a confectionery store, which he conducted until 1896, when he established a jewelry business. Since the first of this year, 1910, he has been an exclusive jewelry dealer. In 1906, his present building was erected at a cost of $6,800.00.

Franklin had a brother, E. R. Burns, a nephew, Ralph, of Seattle, and another brother, William Burns of Seattle.

Ada May McIntyre was born at Chatfield, MN, on Sept. 26, 1869. She lived with her sister, Mrs. Alta Paddock of Seattle after Franklin's death.

Franklin Lane Burns and Ada May McIntyre were married on December 31, 1891, in Livingston, Montana.

Frank Burns came to Hamilton in 1890. He liked the district which was only then being laid out as a town, preparatory to the development of the district by Marcus Daly. After his marriage to Ada, they made Hamilton their hometown. Frank began construction of a home, one of the first houses built in Hamilton. The couple came to Hamilton to settle on January 3, 1892. It was this home, at 311 South Fourth Street, in which they celebrated their 50th anniversary in 1941.

In 1904, the Burns block, a brick building was started and finished on Hamilton's Main Street. J. V. Burnett, well-known Bitter Rooter, was one of the masons who laid the brick. This building became the home of Burns Jewelry store which flourished for many years. On the second floor of the building was Burns Hall, the scene of innumerable dances and other entertainment's which enlivened the community over the years that followed. Also, housed in the building was the Montana Cafe. Several years ago, Mr. Burns sold the building to A. P. Nickel and Roy Milburn, who are current owners. The jewelry store had moved upstairs before that date and for a number of years the building housed the J. C. Penney store here.

Note:

This building was to be of brick, have a frontage of fifty feet and a depth of seventy feet. It would take the place of the frame buildings once occupied by Mr. Burn's store and the adjoining building used as a restaurant. There would be two stories to the structure, the ground floor to contain two store rooms, and over both a hall for entertainment's and dances. When completed, it will be one of the best in the city and will add greatly to the appearance of the north side of Main Street.

Mrs. Ada Burns joined her husband in the conduct of their jewelry store. She was active in various community undertakings, being an accomplished singer and taking part in home talent productions of the early days of Hamilton. She also participated in Rebekah and Phythian Sister lodges. She rose high among the members to become Grand Chief of the Phythian Sister organization in Montana. In her later years, she became an invalid, rarely leaving her home, but met this condition with little complaint and a rare exhibition of bravery. Mr. Burns cared for his wife, until his death in 1947. Franklin L. Burns served as a member of the Hamilton school board and on the City Council. He was a fire department member for 20 years. He served as Mayor of Hamilton in 1937 and 1938. He was a charter member of Ravalli Aerie 1693, in which lodge he long held offices. He served the FOE as its state member of IOOF Lodge No. 48, Hamilton. Mr. Burns was Hamilton's first constable, acting in that capacity when a boxcar served as a jail for offenders of the virgin peace.

Mr. Burns saw the transformation of Hamilton from a period of prairie vacancy to the automobile-choked streets. This couple prospered as they watch their city grow from a shack town with no sidewalks, to the fine community it is today. At his death in 1947, Hamilton residents paused to salute Mr. Burns, one of the men who had the vision and faith to build a new dwelling place.

HOW "FRED BURR CREEK" GOT ITS NAME

from material printed by Men and Trade on the Northwest Frontier in the Fort Owen ledger

FREDERICK H. BURR

Along with Lieutenant Mullan, Frederick H. Burr was ordered to visit the Flathead camp on the Musselshell River to obtain guides for the expedition to St. Mary's Village in the Bitterroot Valley. This they did, and they arrived at Fort Owen on September 30, 1853. Burr was second in command to Mullan, and acted as assistant meteorologist at Cantonment Stevens during the winter of 1853-54. Stevens reported that he performed his duties efficiently and with high spirits. When the surveys were terminated, Burr decided to remain in the Bitterroot in the employment of Thomas Adams, a member of the survey unit who had been appointed special agent to the Flatheads.

Fred Burr fitted well into the frontier life. In 1854, he took a Snake wife, the sister of the woman Granville Stuart later married. Owen placed him in charge of a trading expedition to the Snakes in the fall of 1854, but he soon branched out for himself. The next year he went to the "Road" and Salt Lake City, UT, where he gathered some cattle for rehabilitation in the Bitterroot. That winter, he built a log house on the west side of the Bitterroot River at the mouth of a stream, which is known today as Fred Burr Creek, about midway between the present towns of Stevensville and Hamilton. In 1856, he again went south for trade, and with the aid of James Minesinger and John Powell, brought up 400 head of cattle. By 1857, he had built up a sizeable band which he decided to herd to the California market, a goodly distance to trail a bunch of cattle — and it was twenty years before longhorns were trailed up from Texas. He left for California in March, but had gone only as far as the Snake country when all his horses were run off by a roving party of Blackfeet. This must have discouraged him, as he sold his animals to a Salt Lake concern and returned to the Bitterroot. Although Major Owen engaged Burr as interpreter and trader in 1858, he does not seem to have spent much time around Fort Owen. He was in the Beaverhead that year, and in 1860, was trading around Fort Hall.

Then Burr gave up trading for the newest pastime in Western Montana — GOLD. He went to Gold Creek in May of 1861, with Dr. Atkinson, that remarkable man who prospected with a spy glass from the back of his horse.

A month later, Burr brought his elk skin lodge, squaw, and infant from the Bitterroot and started prospecting. In the fall, he had a house built at Gold Creek for the sum of two horses and fifty pounds of flour. With a little time out working for Frank Worden and Lieutenant Mullan, he continued prospecting Gold Creek and the Big Hole from 1862 to 1863. But he never struck it rich.

Apparently, Burr moved to the town of Deer Lodge where he was appointed Sheriff by Governor Edgerton in 1864, and served as a member from Deer Lodge County to the Constitutional Convention of Montana in 1886, which was convened in Helena without authority of law by Acting Governor Meagher.

The son of Fred Burr, Dixie Burr, met his end before his father. He was hanged as a cattle rustler in July of 1884. Fred Burr was not listed as "deceased" in the register of Montana Pioneers, which was published in 1899.

THE BURRELL FAMILY

by Fay Burrell

My grandfather's name was Benjamin Franklin Burrell. They came from Ohio and Illinois to Iowa, date unknown. They ran a feed lot just south of Blockton, Iowa. They finished beef and hogs for the Chicago market. Their seven year old daughter, Rose, died and the cemetery in Blockton is named Rose Hill Cemetery after her, for she was the first one to be buried there.

My grandmother's first name is unknown, but her maiden name was Gibbons. Her family came from Ireland.

My Father's name was Albert E. Burrell (parents above).

My Mother's name was Addie Fulwider Burrell. Her father was Andrew Fulwider, from Virginia in 1912. My great grandparents were Henry and Harriett Fulwider. Henry's parents were John and Sally Fulwider and when they settled in Iowa, it was a big, prairie country. Many people would ask them how to get to Dubuque. The Fulwiders decided it would save them time to plow a furrow from Tipton to Dubuque! After that they could tell people to follow the furrow !

I was born on a ranch near Long Pine, NB, on June 13, 1894. My parents, Albert and Addie Burrell, previously resided in Wyoming, where my father was a freighter. I recall my mother telling about her dancing at parties given by the people of the Lusk community for the cowboys camped there, after driving the Texas cattle north to the summer range.

The family came to the Bitter Root in 1902, purchasing a ranch west of Woodside. Later, a ranch was purchased where I lived, and called home for 61 years. It was primarily a cattle ranch, though I ran sheep and harvested grain in the later years.

I went to grammar school on Dutch Hill. My uncle, "Win" Burrell, told me he gave the name of "Dutch Hill" to that community. I attended Hamilton High School as a freshman and graduated from Corvallis High School. I attended the University of Montana at Missoula. I played baseball, second base, first at Hamilton, then with the Ford Garage team in the Hamilton City league, and was with the Woodside team one summer when that team won the Valley Championship. I worked in a mine south of Butte, drove a school wagon (not motorized!) while attending Corvallis High School; trapped in the hills in the winter; drove cattle to the Flathead Reservation and generally participated in all the Dutch Hill events.

I served in the U. S. Navy during W.W.I., trained on the Battleship Wisconsin, shipped out on a cargo ship, and served on a mine sweeper in the North Sea. After three years service, I returned home to take over the operation of our ranch.

From 1924 to 1928, I worked at the First National Bank in Hamilton, located in the Downing Pharmacy building, and had a keepsake of a five dollar bill, with my signature on it as Cashier.

I married Helen K. Quast, daughter of Mr. and Mrs. Otto Quast, Sr., who had attended Missoula and Corvallis Schools, graduating from Corvallis where she played on the basketball team Helen worked for the Northern Pacific Railroad before going to Chicago where she received nurses training and graduated as a Registered Nurse. We married on February 22, 1926, in Spokane, Washington.

In 1933, I joined the staff of the Ravalli County Treasurer's office and was elected County Treasurer in 1936, for a two year term and in 1938, for a four year term. In November 1942, I was elected Sheriff of Ravalli County, then re-elected for two consecutive terms. I resigned in 1953, to accept appointment by Gov. Hugo Aronson to be the Warden of the Montana State Prison. During my administration, the lowest per-day per-inmate cost was $1.56 and the highest was $2.70, nearly the best record in the nation. In 1958, I resigned as Warden and was state liquor inspector for three years. When we returned to our home near Woodside, we thought our public service days were over. Not So! Being an avid and active Republican, I was prevailed upon to file for a seat in the 1961 legislature. Upon election, I served just one term and then went back to managing the farm until 1971, when we sold our ranch and retired to a new home in Hamilton.

I was a member of the Corvallis Masonic Lodge,

THE BUSENBARK FAMILY AND WOODSIDE STORE

The Busenbark family had moved west to Utah, and Henry Issac Busenbark was born in the Salt Lake Valley in 1852. He married Isabelle Burke (born 1874) in 1893, and when the railroad was being built they moved to Dillon, Montana, to farm. They had three sons and one daughter. 1. William (Roy) Busenbark, born in Stuart, MT, on February 20, 1895, and died November 2, 1957; 2. Lee Busenbark; 3. Florence Busenbark; 4. Henry Issac (Ike) Busenbark born in 1901 and died in 1970.

The family moved to Victor and Hamilton area in the early 1900's. Henry Issac and his wife Isabelle are both buried in the Victor Cemetery. Henry died in 1920, and Isabelle in 1948. Their son, Roy, returned from the Merchant Marines in 1920, and he went to work for Elizabeth Rose. Elizabeth was a widow, who had lost her husband, Ira, to Rocky Mountain Spotted Fever and was trying to keep her farm together. Her parents had left this farm to her and had moved off to Oregon. Elizabeth had six children from her marriage to Ira, four girls and two boys. In 1927, Elizabeth and Roy were married. The farm was lost, however, as many were in that era, so Elizabeth and Roy loaded their possessions and her children into a large flatbed truck and went to California to work as migrant farm workers. They were accompanied by Roy's brother, Ike, and his wife.

Sometime later, Roy and Elizabeth and the children moved back to Woodside. About this time, the railroad was being moved from its location at Woodside and Roy and Elizabeth purchased the property where the Woodside Store is now from the railroad. It had a couple of warehouses on it. Lee, Roy, and Ike worked together from one of these warehouses for a few years. Lee and Ike decided to go back to California. (Their sister, Florence, moved to Portland, Oregon.) The warehouses were torn down and the material used to build the first Woodside Store. They built a residence attached to the back of the store, and raised their children in this home. Roy also built a small home just back and beside the store, which he later moved onto a foundation a little to the south.

A son, Robert Monroe Busenbark, was born to Roy and Elizabeth in October of 1933. He was raised at the Woodside Store as his parents owned it for over 25 years. Elizabeth Rose Busenbark died in October of 1951 of cancer, and Roy missed her funeral as he had a heart attack and was unable to attend). In 1952, Roy sold the store to the Proctor family (Sally and Claude). Roy died in 1957, and both he and Elizabeth are buried in Victor Cemetery next to his parents.

Robert was a talented athlete at Corvallis High School. Robert married Phylis Smaus of Hamilton in the middle 1950's, and they moved to

Washington state, where he worked and they raised their son Bob, and daughters, Beth and Brenda. Upon his passing in 1992, Robert, who was fondly known as "Busey", was laid to rest in Victor Cemetery also.

THE CHILDREN OF IRA ROSE AND ELIZABETH ROSE BUSENBARK

1. Viola Rose Samuelson stayed in the Hamilton area and raised her children in the Valley. Children: George Roberts and Corky Roberts Pigman still live in the Valley.
2. Wilbert (Newt) Rose lives in Oregon.
3. Lena Rose Roberts moved to Oregon, and later retired in Hamilton.
4. Alvie Rose is deceased, but his wife, Irene, lives in the Valley. Their son, Larry, is a law officer in Darby.
5. Eula Rose Wetzsteon is deceased. She married John Wetzsteon from Sula, and they had one daughter, Betty, who is married to Lynn Huskinson and lives in Hamilton.
6. Vera Leone died in 1936 as a young lady.

CARLS FAMILY

John Henry Carls was born in Illinois in 1837 and came to Montana in 1862 by ox train with A. M. Holter, first to Alder Gulch at Virginia City later he went to Helena. There he married Elizabeth Euke in 1867. He was sheriff of Lewis and Clark County at one time. In 1899, he came to Corvallis where he purchased some property to which he brought his family a year later. They remained there until 1905, when they went to Missoula and later Spokane before going to Butte. Elizabeth died in Butte in 1908 and 2 years later he moved to Hamilton. He died at his son Carlos' home in 1928. The couple had three other sons and two daughters. Only one other son, Harry of Butte, stayed in Montana.

Carlos Edward Carls was born in 1882 at Willow Creek near Three Forks and came with the family to Corvallis in 1899. As an adult, he first was in agriculture and ran sheep with Jamie Lear for a couple of years. In 1909 **he married Charity Printz**, a relative of our present sheriff Jay Printz, when they lived in Missoula. Later they moved to Stevensville and eventually to Hamilton where for many years he was a barber until he retired in 1951. His first shop was next to the old Brunswick pool hall and bar, he later moved across Main Street to about where 1998 Lund Real Estate is located. He was also very much a horseman, and served many years as a racing judge at the county fair. **The couple Betty (Mrs. Max Hughes of Lolo) and Leona (Mrs. Gard Lockwood of Corvallis and Oklahoma had three children, two daughters. Son John (Bud) was born in 1914**.

Leona Carls was born April 24, 1911, in Hamilton on 9th street and she is now living in Tulsa, Oklahoma with her daughter. Leona married Gard

Lockwood (born 1912, died Nov. 21, 1987) and they had three daughters; twins — Carla and Sandra, and a younger daughter, Linda. Gard and Leona raised their family east of Corvallis on Willow Creek where they farmed. This was the former home and land of Gard's parents, Frances "Frankie" and Boss Lockwood.

Bud married Alba Feronato in 1942. Their son, John, was born in 1944 now lives in San Francisco. Bud first worked at the Rocky Mountain Lab for 5 years. He could not get into the armed forces during WWII because of ulcers, so he studied airplane mechanics, thinking to go to Seattle to work at Boeing, but instead wound up at the Johnson Flying Service in Missoula for 10 years. That job became too stressful so came to Hamilton to work with Ned Applebury at Mills Motors. Six months later he associated with Pete Staton where Mildenberger Motors was until just recently on North Second. Bud remained there for many years working for different owners such as Anderson and Ayers. He later spent some time with Charlie Stevens at his dealership until going to Bell McCall Ford until retirement.

Elizabeth (Betty) Carls married Lloyd Maxwell "Max" Hughes of Lolo. They had the Lolo grocery store and post office, a small restaurant, a service station, and also farmed two different farms. They became parents of a daughter, Ann, who married Leslie Davis and lives in McLean, Virginia.

CARMICHAEL FAMILY

by Wilma Carmichael Allen, granddaughter of Robert J. Carmichael

Robert Joshua Carmichael (b. **1819)** immigrated to America from Ireland, November 1849, with his wife and three children. Our relative, **James,** was just 3 months old as he made this trip with his parents arriving in Philadelphia, PA, in February of 1850. His father, Robert, took ill on the boat coming over, and died in 1851, leaving the mother, Jane, to provide. She took in washing, did cleaning, and used their funds carefully, but when young James was 10 years old, she put him and his brother on an orphan train to go west to find work. When the train stopped in Rochelle, IL, a local farmer chose James. **James married Alma Louise Knight** in Rochelle, IL, on Christmas of 1873, and they became parents of six children. Their eldest child, **Robert Joshua, born November 10, 1874,** was my grandfather.

Robert Joshua Carmichael met and married Jessie Edna Downs in 1905, in Lamberton, MN. He had come to Lamberton with a threshing crew and was housed at Jessie's home. They worked for a number of years in the Illinois and Minnesota areas, and then he took a position with the Sears family, traveling around the country showing their cattle. During one of these trips, "Rob" was in a train wreck and seriously injured, these injuries remained with him the rest of his life.

Jessie Edna (Mrs. Robert Carmichael) Downs at age 3 years, in 1887.

Mr. Sears sent Rob to Canada to manage one of his farms, but after a trip back to Illinois, Rob decided to move his family to Montana. **He first came alone and settled in Missoula, but then his wife and children followed by train, in 1918.** Their daughter, Dorris, relates the following story: *"Mrs. Carmichael had offended the train porter when he, unasked, took her shoes and polished them, so she elected not to tip him. Arriving in Missoula at 5 AM, this same porter avoided giving her a wake up call, so she was not prepared to disembark. With three small children, one just a baby, there was lots of baggage. Her husband, Rob, took all the baggage and the two older children, but the train began to pull out before the baby could be placed in his father's arms. The porter yelled, "Throw him the baby, and jump!". Mrs. Carmichael refused. Rob had the baby's bottle and diapers, and Jessie had the baby! Rob had to drive his old car clear to Alberton, where the train stopped next, to catch up to his wife and screaming infant.*

After a year in Missoula, the Carmichael's moved onto a farm near the "S" curve just north of Corvallis. Rob and boys did truck gardening, and Jessie worked for Pete Haas, who raised chickens. The youngest child, Dorris Clare, was born here. Later, they lived just east of Corvallis in a log home — across from what is the original Lamar Chaffin home, now the Christensen place. Lastly, Rob and Jessie owned a house that had been brought up from Quast Lane, and set on land at the corner of Main Street and Woodside Crossover. Grandma said that this was the second oldest house in Corvallis, only the Smithey home being older. Many years later this house was burned in a fire department drill to make room for the Corvallis Mini Mart. Grandma kept a beautiful garden and yard, which was enjoyed by all who passed by.

While living on the "S" curve, son Robert, known as Bob, decided to "bum" his way to the World's Fair in Chicago. Bob practiced "hooking" the train, so that he could climb on when it passed his house. Although frowned upon by the railroad owners, this was a pretty common thing. The day came, and Bob made the connection easily, finding other bums inside the boxcar. "You got on, kept your mouth shut, and protected whatever belongings you brought along," Bob said. He arrived in Illinois in just one week, wasn't a bit homesick, and loved the whole experience!

Grandpa Carmichael was disabled from a train wreck, and then from a gun accident where he accidentally shot off one hand. He lost his hearing from a mastoid infection, so had lots of physical problems. He drove a specially equipped car, remaining mobile. Today we would call him a "disabled person" and provide many forms of support, but then he just had to cope. Rob died in 1950 at the age of 75.

Grandma Carmichael was a loyal member of the Corvallis Community Church and served as Sunday school Treasurer for many years. She also cleaned the Community House and sewed rags for the Ladies Aid members to weave into rugs. She spent many hours at her sewing machine getting those rags sewed together and then rolling into balls. Often we grandchildren helped with the rolling. She loved to give tours of her beautiful yard and garden, supplying vegetables to many others. She died in 1977 at the age of 93.

Their children are: Alma Josephine married Harold Martin with sons Dale and James, **George James "Jim"** did not marry, **Edna Jane** married first to Charles Loesch with daughter Corrine, next to Gene Kraft with daughter Lorelei, and lastly to Dean Hollibaugh (no children), **Robert Downs** married Alice "Chub" White, and had two daughters, Wilma and Janice, and **Dorris Clare** married Clair Everson and had no children.

Robert Carmichael and Alice Ann White Carmichael ("Bob" and "Chub") both attended the Corvallis Schools and graduated from there. They married in 1937 and settled in a home on the eastside of town. Early years found them traveling to jobs in Anaconda and Pocatello, Idaho. During

World War II, they moved to the state of Washington where Bob worked in the atomic facility at Hanford. Relatives in Montana wished to go into the sawmill business, and got Bob involved. They returned to Corvallis in 1945, and with Loren Kraft, Gene Kraft, and Francis Frost began the CKF Sawmill Company. This was first an on-site sawmill in the Bear Creek area, but was later located at Tucker Crossing. A sawdust burner, designed and built by Bob, still stands at this site. In the 1960's, the mill disbanded. Bob then hired out doing custom heavy equipment work. He was an early member of the Corvallis Fire Department, along with his brother Jim. Alice, known to friends and relatives as "Chub", began work at the Corvallis Post Office in 1950. She served as a clerk, ran the rural route, was the CEO, and was Postmaster from 1977–1980, retiring in 1980. Bob passed on in 1992, and Chub lives in the same home in Corvallis. They had two daughters, Wilma and Janice (Judy).

Wilma married Jerry Allen (currently a Ravalli County Commissioner) and they have three children. **Bret** lives with his 4 children in the Willow Creek (Corvallis) area, **Michelle** and family are in Texas, and **Paige** and family live in South Dakota.

Janice (Judy) married Terry Park. He is retired from the Ravalli Electric Cooperative. Their son, **Bradley**, and his daughter reside near Corvallis. A daughter, **Teralee,** died very young in a car accident.

This makes five generations stemming from the Carmichael's living in the Bitter Root Valley.

CAVE FAMILY

Caroline Augusta Nicol was born in Detroit, Michigan, on June 27, 1841. She crossed the plains with her parents in 1862, settling in Fort Bridger. In February of 1863, she married George Hackleman and in that fall they moved to Montana. Her first home was within eight miles of Virginia City, and it was there that her son, Will, was born. Her home was afterwards in the Bitter Root Valley, where on December 4, 1871, she married Alfred Cave. Mr. and Mrs. Cave went to Cedar Creek at the time of the stampede and lived there until the camp was abandoned. In 1873, they moved to Missoula and she resided here until her death. She was a typical pioneer woman who endured hardships without complaint. Her tender sympathies won the affection of all. Upon her death, she left a husband, a son, Lt. William Cave who is a deputy county clerk, and two brothers, Robert Nicol of Hamilton and Alex Nicol of Iowa. She also had two stepsisters, Mrs. George B. Hartman and Mrs. H. C. Myers, as well as two stepbrothers, Lynde Elliott and D. C. Elliott, who were former residents of the Valley. Lynde Elliott was killed in the battle of the Big Hole in 1877.

THE WILLIAM TAYLOR CENTERS FAMILY

by Chuck Centers

William Taylor Centers age 27, came from Irvine, Kentucky, to the Bitter Root in 1907, with his wife Eliza, and their four children; Hugh, Jack, Dillard, and Burton. The parents had heard about a boom in apple growing and were interested in the prospects of farming a different crop than the corn they and their parents had grown in Kentucky. The boys were overjoyed when they arrived and found stones (rocks!) practically everywhere and they complained of how at their farm in Kentucky the only thing they had ever had to throw was a wet corncob!

The family settled in the Como area, where the boys went to grade school, and near Charlos Heights where Taylor was employed by the O. W. Kerr Company as an orchardist, and later as the foreman of the University Heights project with work relating to land development for orchards.

When expansion in apple production subsided, Taylor and Eliza bought a rooming house in Hamilton which they operated and also used as the family residence. This was at 315 North 2nd Street. In later years they remodeled the building into an apartment house where they continued to live their remaining years.

Taylor and Eliza consistently displayed the warm and courteous manner of Kentuckians, and were known in the community for their generosity and hospitality. Eliza cooked southern style meals that were truly memorable works of culinary art, however sad to say, nowadays, not highly recommended by dietitians! Taylor loved dogs, horses, and shooting. He was an expert rifle shot and when he showed up at a turkey shoot with his special target rifle, he brought no joy to the competitors. He raised and trained bird dogs that were outstanding performers. He brought with him from Kentucky the knowledge and experience in the training of harness race horses and the intricate equipment involved. Although there were many people here at that time who were schooled in training running horses, there were few who had experience with racing carts, and Taylor greatly enjoyed assisting during that period of time when even harness racing was given a try here in the Bitter Root.

HENRY E. "JACK' CENTERS

November 1966, newspaper clipping upon his death

Henry E. "Jack" Centers was born at Irvine, KY, on October 30, 1893, the son of the late Mr. and Mrs. W. T. Centers. He and his three brothers, Hugh, Burton, and Dillard, came to the Bitter Root with their parents in 1907. Jack was the last of the family to survive.

The family first resided in the Charlos district where the father and

Pierce Arrow, Hamilton to Missoula stage, owned and operated by Jack Centers.

sons became employed by the O. W. Kerr Co. Those were the days of the "Big Ditch" and the origin of the vast orchards of MacIntosh Red apples. As those orchards came into bearing fruit, there was much work growing the crop in the spring and summer and harvesting it in the fall. Thousands of railroad cars of fruit were shipped from the valley in the early years of the industry, most to New York City. Jack became one of the most proficient apple box makers and his services were in great demand.

He became interested in motor vehicles as the B.R.V.I. brought its big red cars to the valley to transport prospective land buyers about its domain. One of the first motor stage operators was the late Charles McMurphy, who operated motorized stages from Missoula to Hamilton, and thence to Darby. Young Centers, after returning from service with the Army in France, acquired the stage business from McMurphy in 1919.

Centers operated his stage line using a big 7 passenger Cadillac, a 9-passenger Oakland 8 in 1921, a Packard, and other cars of the biggest size then available, until acquiring his bus. The stage route then followed the main road through the Bitter Root to Corvallis, Stevensville, and via the old Bitter Root Inn — through the Three Mile country to Florence, and then into Missoula. The trip took about 3 hours including stops, providing the weather and roads permitted. Often, Dillard and Burton drove for him and Hugh also operated the bus. Hugh was engaged in the lumber hauling business in which effort Jack was his associate.

Jack sold the stage line to George Meissinger in 1926. Thereafter, he and Ben Oertli acquired a lot on the north side of Main Street and 2nd Street in Hamilton. They built a brick service station which they operated together for a number of years. Later, Centers operated the business personally before selling it to the Standard Oil Company, which later sold the lot to the late John Ford, and the building to Wilber Deffenbaugh. The latter moved the brick structure to property upon which he built Deffy's Motel on South Front Street. Mr. and Mrs. Ford had the Ford building erected upon the lot the station had formerly occupied, plus two lots to the east.

When Deffenbaugh moved the brick station down South Second and to its new location, almost everyone in the community turned out to offer advice, view with alarm and make prognostications. Despite an overwhelming fear that the move would fail, it was concluded as a satisfactory triumph by Wilber and everyone had to hear him acclaim, "I told you so!" Scarcely a brick was out of place on its new location.

Jack Centers thereafter acquired The Mint in Stevensville, which he operated for a time without signal success. Selling it, he went to California during World War II, where he was employed by the Firestone Company. He returned to Hamilton when he retired, and passed away there on November 22, 1966.

MOSES CHAFFIN

CORVALLIS, MONTANA
AUGUST 21, 1949

The Elijah Chaffin family, that is to say, my father and mother, came to the Bitter Root in October, 1864. They left Uniontown, (near Fort Scott) Kansas, around the first of May, arriving in Bannack, MT, the first of September. There were around thirty wagons in the party, many of which were drawn by oxen. My father, however, drove a team of horses. Of course, there were many loose horses in the party which were led or driven by young men of the party on horseback.

At Bannack, my father met a young miner by the name of John A. Slack, who had been in the Bitter Root valley during the winter of '63 and summer of '64. Slack had raised a small crop of potatoes, which he had hauled to Bannack. At the time of father's meeting with John Slack, it was his intention to continue with the family to Oregon. Slack talked father into coming into the Bitter Root instead of continuing on with the main wagon train, and several other families joined in this Bitter Root brigade. Among those of the original wagon party who came here with my father were two of his brothers, Milton and Anthony and their families; his brother in law, John Wood and his wife; and Alf Atkinson — who had a family, but I know very little about them.

There were several young, unmarried men in the party, among them Uncle Jim Mitchell, my mother's brother, Andy Cowan, William East, and

Isam Robinson. Joining my family's party at Bannack, and coming on to the Bitter Root with them, were my Uncle Amos Chaffin (a younger brother of father's), Aunt Polly (his sister), and Uncle Will Mitchell (my mother's brother) who had come across the plains to Bannack from Kansas in 1863.

My grandfather, Balaam Chaffin, who had been in the 1863 party died in Bannack of pneumonia, in May 1864. I remember hearing my father say, that he learned later that Grandfather Chaffin died on the very day that my family left Uniontown, KS, although he knew nothing about Grandfather's death until his arrival in Bannack.

John Slack, to be more familiarly known as Jack Slack, guided my father's party to the Bitter Root valley. My Aunt Polly, then a girl in her late teens, and "Uncle Jack", as I have always known him, fell in love and were married at a place called "Chaffinville", located on the bank of the river almost directly west of the "twin bridges", south of the Albert Wood ranch, later known as the Alex Mitchell ranch, in the early spring of 1865.

My sister, Judy Summers, then a child of three, is the only living member of that original Chaffin family wagon train, so far as I know. She is here today. There were two other Chaffin family children in the wagon party, my oldest sister, Nancy, was five, and my oldest brother, Sig, who was a little more than a year and a half old.

My family wintered at Chaffinville, where my brother Alex was born on December 21, 1864. In the spring of 1865, Father and Mother and their four children hitched up and drove on West to Oregon, settling near Salem, in the Williamette valley. They were accompanied by my Uncle Jim Mitchell

Original home of Lamar Chaffin, 521 Willow Creek Road, Corvallis, Montana, built of sandstone from the quarry in Soft Rock area.

and later that winter, in 1865, they were joined by Uncle Amos Chaffin and Uncle Will Mitchell.

I have never been able to trace any Navajo Indian blood in my family, but they certainly were of a nomadic race, for they must have loved to travel. They stayed in Oregon just about a year, returning to the Bitter Root in August, 1866.

In Oregon, my family was joined by Cortez Goff and family, Ben Sanders and family, Riles Sanders and family, William Strange (father of Elsie Magni and Gilbert "Gib" Strange), and some other people whose names I've forgotten.

I believe there was a family of Richardsons and a family of Willowbys.

Another young'n, my sister Rose, joined the family just before the folks got back home. Rose was born in a covered wagon at "Pine Hollow", just south of Stevensville, August 14, 1866.

When they came back to the Bitter Root, my family decided they'd had enough traveling and settled down on a "squatter's claim", there being no survey lines in here at that time. This squatter's claim is now the old Chaffin homestead, a mile north of Corvallis, where I now live. Where, in fact, I have lived all my life. I was born there on July 13, 1868.

Aside from those mentioned there were two other Chaffin boys: Elijah, Jr., always known as Frank (or Tam), C. C. Chaffin (more familiarly known as Eph, and now lives in Missoula), and two daughters, Margaret and Lydia. Judy and Eph and I, are the only members of the family who are living today. (1949)

REMINISCENCES OF M. P. CHAFFIN

From the Western News, December 19, 1911

CHRISTMAS OF '64, was not very merry for the new settlers. No word had been received from home for months, and the only white neighbors were five squawmen, the only other white woman being Mrs. Red Dobbins of Stevensville. Indians were encamped everywhere.

CHRISTMAS TREES were plentiful but were not very popular, there being a deplorable lack of articles to hang upon them. All big game had been driven out or killed by the Indians, and even birds except prairie chickens, were scarce. On Christmas day, the Chaffin family dined on beef, Bitter Root potatoes grown by the squawmen, coffee made from browned, dried peas, and milk from one lone milk cow.

The following summer, Mr. Chaffin raised a small crop of potatoes and wheat by irrigation and a little later a grist mill was established on Burnt Fork so that flour was obtainable at a reasonable price. In the mining district however, flour sold at a dollar a pound.

On the thirteenth day of January, '66, Mr. Chaffin purchased a sack of sugar for $66.50; tobacco brought $5.00 per pound and salt $.50. In the same year, he bought a second-hand buggy for $125.00, the first light vehicle to be used in this section of the country, and paid $40.00 for an Indian Cayuse to drive to it. The horse was purchased from an Indian named "Dominic" for whom the Dominic Mountain was named.

In the year, '65, '66, '67, great gatherings of the Nez Perce, Flathead and Pend O'Reille Indians were held in the valley and many nights did the white settlers listen to the beat of the tom-toms and fear that their last day had come.

In the summer of '66, Mr. Chaffin cleaned up $1,300.00 in gold at Henderson Gulch mine on the Deer Lodge river. He then purchased oxen and wagons and began freighting from Helena to the Bitter Root. That winter snow fell to a depth of four feet on the level and the winter was long and severe.

Early in the '70's a store, saloon and a few log cabins comprised a settlement which was named CORVALLIS by the Frenchman called Heron. In 1879, the town was surveyed.

In Mr. Chaffin's memory the first real Fourth of July celebration of Bitter Rooters was held in 1879 at Lake Como, then reached only by Indian trails. Mr. Chaffin, with several friends, made the trip on that day in a new $320.00 hack, the first vehicle ever to go to the lake. The party left the main road where Sleeping Child Creek enters the Bitter Root, forded the river and drove over the hills to Como Lake.

JOE CHESNUTT

Skalkaho Survivor

As told to Peggy Munoz, volunteer

Joe weighed nine pounds at birth on January 29, 1906, in Oklahoma. He was the eighth **of nine children of Walter and Susan Chesnutt**. Today, at 4 foot, 9 inches and 129 pounds, Joe is a survivor, a story- teller, and a pioneer in the early days of the Skalkaho area of the Bitter Root Valley.

His father, Walter learned of the "apple boom" in western Montana. It was widely promoted as a way to make money in a valley "Sun-kissed on an average of three hundred days in each year", according to a supplement of The Western News magazine, dated May, 1910. "Get rich off a couple of trees" Joe says ruefully. Walter had been trying dry land farming in Texas and Oklahoma, but had never been able to get enough together to buy his own land. He sold what they had and took the family on the train to Montana.

Joe, then four years old, remembers getting off the train by the big metal building that housed the Bitterroot Irrigation District Office and walking to a three-story hotel, probably the Ravalli Hotel that stood where City Hall now is situated. They stayed there a week and went downstairs for dinner every night. This was in 1910.

Walter got work making apple boxes and eventually heard about an abandoned claim up the Skalkaho. In 1912, he filed for the 160-acre homestead, moved the family and built a small home with the help of a son-in-law. A ninth child was born, completing the family: **Grace, Booth, Eunice, Ella, Walter, Nellie, Joe, and Helen.** The last three are still living in 1997.

Life was hard on the homestead with a few good years followed by drought and crop failures in 1914-1915. The older girls married or moved to Missoula. The father left to find work elsewhere. Booth became a sheepherder and young Walter tried farming and later was a government trapper. Susan left the homestead with the small children briefly to live in Missoula. This was about 1917, the time of the flu epidemic in the country, and Susan decided to move back to the homestead despite the near starvation that they had endured before. Grace and her family accompanied Susan, Joe, and Helen, and lived through another difficult period when Hazel, Grace's daughter, died of pneumonia and malnutrition. She is buried on the homestead on Starvation Ridge — so named on local maps for obvious reasons.

Finally, Susan was left alone with Joe and Helen and she made the decision to move once again after nine years of hardship. They moved to the McCartney place on Skalkaho Creek about 1921. The Skalkaho road was under construction and Susan cooked for the workers for a price. Joe lived there for 23 years with some time away when Booth took Joe and Helen to Grantsdale to live with him and attend the little Grantsdale School. Subsequently, they heard from Walter who had a homestead in the Haugen area west of Missoula. Joe and Helen attended school in Haugen and Joe began earning wages as the school janitor. He gave his wages to his mother.

The Haugen homestead was not successful with the men of the household away looking for work, and finally was lost for non-payment of taxes. The winters were harder and Joe and his mother moved back to the McCartney place until she died in 1949, at the age of 83. The family drifted further apart with father, Walter, living with young Walter in Gold Creek until he died in 1933, at age 78. They are buried in the Corvallis Cemetery.

Joe worked for the Bitter Root Stock Farm and for rancher, James Parr, as a ranch hand and all-around handyman. He is proud of his 63 years in the Skalkaho area. He knows the area like a book and can locate Starvation Ridge for anyone who is interested. In 1998, at the ripe old age of 91, he lives in the Bitterroot Manor. He has had several close calls, but is a true survivor. Maybe the dandelion greens, gooseberries, chokecherries, trout, and game from the Skalkaho had something to do with his longevity, or maybe it is just Joe, a big man in a small body, who never gave up.

COBB FAMILY

John Milton Cobb was born on June 4, 1858, in Callaway County, Missouri. His father was killed in the Civil War, so at the age of fourteen, he left home to shift for himself. He came to Montana in 1880. For a number of years, he worked as a freighter from Missoula to Stevensville.

On October 8, 1884, **he married Luella M. Powers,** who was born in Monroe County, Missouri. She attended an academy at Paris, Missouri, then came to Montana and taught school at Drummond. Later she joined her brother and sister at Stevensville, and taught school here also. She and her sister each homesteaded a ranch in the Burnt Fork District. In 1898, John and Luella moved their family to Corvallis.

John and Luella became parents of four children: **John J.** died in infancy, **Lillis**, who died at the age of sixteen, **Milford** who was born October 25, 1886, in the Burnt Fork area and married Lenora Emma Myers at Corvallis on January 21, 1911. They became parents of a daughter, LuRea. (LuRea married Frank Tanner and they raised their three children on a farm on Cobb Lane, now known as Popham Lane). Milford passed away in July of 1951. **Dean** married Margaret Sophonia Frogge at Corvallis on November 23, 1908, with Reverend W. D. Lear officiating, and they parented Lavern, Oreon and Leroy. Dean died on December 24, 1942. Milford and Dean and their families spent most of their lives in the Corvallis area.

JOHN HOWARD CORNISH

by Stella Cornish Kratofil

Howard Cornish was born in Missoula, Montana on November 18, 1890, his father having come to the United States in 1884, and his mother in 1890 from Cornwall, England. He moved to Hamilton in about 1915, where he was employed with Missoula Power and Light. Missoula Power and Light later became The Montana Power Co., and Howard became the Superintendent of that company.

In 1915, he married Mabel Ruth Overturf, daughter of Louis and Ella Tabor Overturf of Darby and the Como area. Howard and Mabel purchased the home at 808 S. 2nd Street in Hamilton, where their eight children were born. It was during the Depression years that John, the 4th child in the family, became very ill, and the doctor diagnosed it at first as rheumatism and treated him for seven weeks with John only getting worse. He would scream with pain every time someday would even touch his bed. His hip became inflamed and a large abscess formed. It was then finally determined that he had osteomyelitis. It was only the beginning of many years of surgeries and pain for John, until finally in the early 1940's they tried the new wonder drug, penicillin. However, it left John with one leg shorter, and a stiff hip.

Howard was known to the boys and girls for his efforts in behalf of scout work. Left fatherless at the age of six years, he had a sympathy for unfortunate children that made itself felt in countless instances. He was a member of the Boy Scout Council and devoted much of his time to securing funds and help for the summer camp. A plan to heat the swimming pool of the Skalkaho camp was one of the projects claiming his interest. when he was taken ill, and died a few days later of pneumonia at the young age of 42, in the year of 1933. The Scout Camp was named "Camp Howard Cornish" by the Hamilton Scout Council and the County Commissioners, as a memorial to John Howard Cornish.

The summer camp, at the junction of the south and north forks of Skalkaho creek, was four or five years under construction, labor being donated by civic minded citizens, scout leaders and members, and money being raised by popular subscription. The lodge building of log construction was about 20 x 40 feet, and the camp consisted of a lodge, kitchen and mess hall, housed in two buildings with neat grounds and a swimming pool, which was largely Mr. Cornish's creation. Boy Scouts of limited means were Howard's special consideration, and many were helped to spend a week in camp because of his efforts.

A fire of undetermined origin completely destroyed Camp Cornish lodge. At the time of the fire, the lodge was being used as a headquarters camp for a road crew employed by the Forest Service. The crew was out on a building project and no information was available as the origin of the fire. The loss was estimated at $4,500.00.

During the holiday season of 1919-1920, Howard made colored lights and soldered them to wires, providing his family with Hamilton's first decorated outside Christmas tree. The next year, he strung colored lights across Main Street. Every year thereafter, until his death, he and David Hope Sr., (who were both Montana Power Company employees) strung the colored lights across Main Street for all to enjoy.

Howard also served for eight years on the Hamilton School Board and was instrumental in the decision as to placement of the school in its present location. He was a charter member and an official of the Federated Church.

After Howard's death, Mabel raised her eight children by herself and with the help of the community of Hamilton. The family had a small farm in the 800 block of South Second Street, which included a barn and a chicken house, and a large garden. The family had a large trailer which they loaded with apples in the fall from the local orchards and stored in the basement for a winter food supply. They hauled sawdust every summer filling several large storage bins for fuel for heating the home, and several loads of hay and corn stalks for the cows for feed through the winter.

One Halloween in about 1944, a group of local boys took the family cow out of the barn and herded her all the way to the Hamilton High School where they managed to get her up to the second floor. This was where she was found when the school opened the next morning. It has become a favorite reflection for story telling, especially for the class of 1945.

Mabel Cornish, for a number of years, occupied herself at earning a living for her family selling household goods, as one of the operators of the school lunch program, preparing meals for service organizations, and catering for weddings and social dinners. In 1949, after the family was raised, Mabel married Archie McKillop of Hamilton.

Vivian, the oldest daughter, married Walter Shook of Conner, and lives in Darby with her daughter, Juanita Maki. She attended the University at Missoula, and in later years became a teacher in the Darby School District. She and Walter had seven children.

Luella married Menno Braaksma of Holland. She graduated from the School of Nursing at Great Falls, and became a school nurse in the California School District. She and Menno had two children.

Charles married Marianna Stilson of Colfax, WA. He worked for the Rocky Mountain Laboratory before joining the Navy during World War II, and was in on the invasion of Okinawa. He and Marianna have two children and reside in Sequim, WA

John married Phyllis Logan. He graduated from Montana State College at Bozeman, and became a teacher and athletic coach. Before retiring, he was the school superintendent at Clyde Park, MT. He and Phyllis had two children. He resides in Livingston, MT.

Bob married Jeanette Stevens of Loma, MT. He worked as a photographer until his retirement at Glendale, CA. He and Jeanette have two children and reside in Spokane, WA.

Jim married Kathryn LeClair of Hamilton, MT. He worked for A. P. Nichel Plumbing and Heating. They had three children, one of whom is John, a teacher and coach in Florence, MT. Jim resides in Stockton, CA, near his daughter, Kathy.

Stella married Ed Kratofil of Grantsdale. They both attended Montana State College at Bozeman. They have four children and reside at Spokane, WA, where Ed retired from the General Electric Co., and Stella retired from St. Annes children's Home. They have a summer home on the West Fork of the Bitterroot where the Cornish family has many gatherings.

Howard was born five months after the death of John Howard, and was named for his father. He married LaVern Hollinger of Missoula. He graduated from Montana State University at Missoula, and resides in Billings, where he is in the Real Estate business. He and LaVern have two children.

THOMAS (TOMMY) McCOTTRY COOPER

Tommy was the third child of Louella and John Fulton Cooper. He was born April 9, 1888. He arrived in Corvallis in about 1912. He married Frieda Knaak on June 11, 1915.

The Knaak family came to the Bitter Root from Wisconsin. One son, Harvey, stayed in Wisconsin; the other son, Paul, lived in the valley until moving on to Oregon. Besides Frieda there were two other daughters, Ella who married Guy Hall and Gustie who married Charles Wolff.

Tommy and Frieda were childless. She died May 3, 1946, after a long illness and he September 13, 1965.

Tommy drove the mail stagecoach between Corvallis and Woodside as the mail came to Woodside on the train from Missoula. He also worked many years at the Corvallis Cheese Factory. However, most people remember Tommy as part of their "school days", as he was the custodian at the Corvallis school for more than thirty- five years. His office was under the stairs in the furnace room. Students used to run to see Tommy when they had a toothache for he kept a tiny bottle of "stuff" he applied to the sore tooth and it helped them survive the day. He also applied many a Band-Aid to battered knees, elbows and fingers. He was not a nurse but more than once the next best thing.

He was a nephew of R. Russell Smithey, Corvallis.

COUGHENOUR

Among early doctors in this area was Dr. Joseph T. Coughenour, a veteran of the Civil War. He was born in Pennsylvania in 1844, and died at his home in the Corvallis area in 1915, at the age of 71. Dr. Coughenour had practiced medicine for forty years. He was a member of Odd Fellows and was made a member of that group in Washington, D.C., on the same night that Abraham Lincoln was assassinated.

Dr. Coughenour first came to Deer Lodge, Montana, in the early 1870's and then located in Corvallis in 1881. He was married to Eliza Shaw, who was born in Bolliver, Missouri. Eliza died in her Corvallis home on June 11, 1925. Two children were born to this couple; Joseph Tulley Coughenour and Edith Coughenour, who became Mrs. A. F. Cave.

Joseph Tulley Coughenour was born in Corvallis on October 29, 1892. He attended Corvallis and Hamilton schools and was married in 1916 to Minnie Dowling, daughter of John and Mary McHaffey Dowling of Stevensville. They lived in Hamilton for a few years before moving to his mothers ranch north of Corvallis. Coughenour had served as Clerk of Court in Hamilton and worked as a druggist for Dr. McGrath's drug store, also in

Hamilton. After retiring from farming in 1950, the Coughenours bought the Wayside Store at the corner of Eastside Highway and Bailey Lane. They sold the store and moved to Stevensville, but later returned to the store where he died in 1956. Minnie died in 1975. They had no children.

Edith Coughenour Cave and her husband, A. F. Cave lived in a home just two houses south of the railroad tracks (which are south of Corvallis) on the Eastside Highway, during the 1950's. She was active at the Corvallis Community Church as a Sunday School teacher.

THE COWAN FAMILY

by Frank T. Cowan

The Cowan family, which arrived in the Bitterroot Valley in 1879 or 1880, had its roots in Scotland on the paternal side, and in Germany on the maternal side.

Henry Moeller (Anglicized to MILLER in the United States) was born in a small village in Prussia on August 11, 1826. He emigrated to America in the early 1840's, and settled in Illinois. He applied for Naturalization papers and in 1856, became an American citizen. On December 24, 1853, Henry Miller married Nancy Jane Harper. My mother, Harriet Elizabeth, was born to them in Champaign, Illinois, on June 26, 1861.

My father, Thomas Cowen, was born in Andrie, Scotland, on January 13, 1851. The family which consisted of: (husband) Robert Cowan, (wife) Elizabeth Brown Cowan, (both born in Ireland); a son, Robert — also born in Ireland; a son, Thomas — born in Scotland; and daughter, Eliza, immigrated to the United states in 1857. They settled in Missouri, along the Merrimac River in Franklin County. Both Roberts, father and son, are buried in Merrimac Church yard which apparently does not now exist. Grandfather Robert Cowan and son Robert, had been iron miners in Scotland. It is assumed that they, along with Thomas, worked in the silver-lead mines in western Missouri during their sojourn in that state. They settled at Eureka, where the silver-lead mines were.

The family consisting of Thomas Cowan, his mother, and sister, Eliza, left Missouri shortly after the death of Robert Cowan, Sr., enroute to Utah by wagon train. Enroute they and the Miller family became closely attached and Thomas married Harriet Elizabeth Miller on June 1, 1879. Grandmother Elizabeth Cowan died in Utah and is buried in Silver City, Utah.

In 1879, or 1880, the Cowan-Miller families, along with Thomas Collins (who later married Eliza Cowan), started north via wagon train enroute to Montana and the Bitterroot Valley. The Cowan family located near Victor, along with Grandfather, Henry Miller. Later, my father bought 40 acres adjacent to the Curlew Orchard ranch and the Curlew Mines, which at that time were both owned and operated by A. M. Holter.

My father worked in the mine while my mother planted apple trees of innumerable varieties, and other fruit trees including apricot, cherries, and pears. She also planted and tended a large vegetable garden which provided food the year around for the burgeoning family. A few non-descript cows provided milk, butter and cheese, while several hogs along with an occasional deer, (my father was an expert rifleman) and chickens, both tame and wild — supplied us with meat. The house which my father built was not large, but was adequate. There was plenty of wood for the cutting, to stoke the fires for cooking and to keep warm in winter. Water was plentiful also, from the irrigation ditch in front of the house during the summer, and in the winter it was hauled in barrels from a spring about one half mile from the house.

Money was never plentiful, but while my father had work at the mine, we had enough to buy the necessities of life. With the demonetization of silver coin in 1897, the Curlew Mine closed down, and my father, and all the other workers, were without jobs. For many years thereafter, my father and a friend named George Johnson, leased the mines, along with the concentrator. They never, to my knowledge, "hit it big", but managed to eke out a living. Between leases, Father found work in other mines in the Bitterroot or at Wallace, Idaho.

The soil on our little farm was quite fertile, but it had to take a backseat to my mother. Between 1881 and 1901, she gave birth to ten children — four females and six males. Her firstborn, a girl, lived only four months, but the remaining nine all lived to adulthood. I was the "tail-ender", approximately six years younger than my brother next to me. My mother died on April 11, 1902, about eight months after I was born. Mary, who was the fifth child, and barely 14 years old, assumed the burden of running the household and rearing the remaining five children younger than she. She carried this burden until she married some fourteen years later, and raised another family of three boys and a girl of her own.

We were a close knit family, who, like most large families of that era, fought and bickered among ourselves, but were always united against any common foe! When World War I came along, four of the Cowan men joined up. Robert Arthur, the oldest, enlisted in Montana National Guard at age 34, and was wounded in the trenches in France. Elmer, next to the youngest, family member, enlisted in the "Engineer's Corps", late in 1917, and was drowned when the Troop ship Tuscania was sunk off the West shores of Scotland on February 5, 1918.

Elmer was probably one of the finest high school athletes ever produced in the Bitterroot Valley. He demonstrated his abilities in 1916, his last year of eligibility, by winning the individual championship in track at the County Meet. He was second in the 50 yard dash, first in 100 yard through

880, and the javelin throw, with record performance in the 440 and 880. He also played baseball and basketball.

Albert, the third son, because of his prior military service with the Wisconsin National Guard while attending school at Beloit College, was called up shortly after war was declared in 1917. He was assigned to the 91st Division at Fort Lewis, Washington, for much of the duration. He later was sent to France and was commissioned second Lieutenant just before the Armistice was signed in 1918. Albert was also a fine athlete in track and later in football at Beloit College. *(See story on Albert A. Cowan Family.)*

Henry, the 2nd oldest son, was well known in the Hamilton area for his work at the Spotted Fever Laboratory. He contracted the fever through his work and died in the old Hamilton Hospital on October 29, 1924. Henry was known for his 6 ft, 4 inch, 250 pound size, his even disposition and his profound devotion to his work, his family, and his friends. He stood out in a crowd.

Walter enlisted in the Marines, and spent his period of service in southern California. He saw no active service. He died June 8, 1966.

Blanche married William S. Jones on November 24, 1903, and had a large family. She died December 26, 1967.

Mary married John Smith on July 1, 1915. They continued to live in Victor all their married life, raising a family of three sons and one daughter. Mary passed away on September 28, 1963.

Ellen married Arthur Fifield on March 3, 1908. They also continued to live in the Bitterroot Valley, raising a large family. She died on March 19, 1964.

There are many nieces, nephews, and grandnieces and nephews still living in the Bitterroot.

For myself, Franklin T. Cowan, I have outlived all immediate family members and many of the second generation. I was married in 1924, to Elva Ayler, my college sweetheart, and raised one son and one daughter. We celebrated our 61st anniversary on April 7, 1985. I had a most satisfactory career with the U. S. Department of Agriculture as a research entomologist on grasshoppers and mormon crickets. I retired after 40 years of service, in 1967. I live in Bozeman, Montana.

THE CRUTCHFIELDS OF MONTANA

by Virginia Crutchfield Walton and Jack M. Crutchfield

"I cannot tell how the truth may be; I say the tale as 'twas said to me"

For a number of years, we have been asked by both family and friends to record some of the events in the lives of Mother and Father when they came to Montana to live. Realizing that is it is not written now the story would be lost for future generations, we have collaborated in re-telling this story for you.

In no way is this considered a "literary gem" by us, but it does record some of the stories as told us by Mother. Much, of course, is lost in the retelling for she was a witty and interesting conversationalist. Father died when we were too young to remember him, so events in his life are lost. Mothers story is a follows:

It was 56 degrees below zero that winter night in January, 1893, when Father, Charles M. Crutchfield, stepped off the Northern Pacific train with his bride to introduce his friends to her. Many of the young people of the town of Missoula had braved the cold to come to greet the young Virginia woman who, at last, had consented to come to the West to share fortunes with the handsome bachelor attorney.

Charles Manson Crutchfield born on June 19, 1863, the eldest son of George Knox Crutchfield and Virginia Alice Denoon Crutchfield of Richmond, Virginia. After completing his education in Richmond, where his father was connected with a newspaper, he matriculated at Washington & Lee University in Lexington, Virginia, to study law. It was then that he met and fell in love with Lena Robb Payne of Warrenton, Virginia, who was spending the winter at the home of her sister, Mrs. M. B. Hardin. Col. Hardin was Professor of Chemistry at the Virginia Military Institute, and Mrs. Hardin was Lena's only sister; and twenty years older.

Mother was young and gay and pretty, so did not lack admirers from the V.M.I. and W.&L, both mens' schools. However, she was inclined to favor a student at the Episcopal Seminary in Alexandria, Virginia, where she often went to visit her maternal grandparents.

Lena Payne was born May 4, 1867, in Warrenton, Virginia, the daughter of Inman Horner Payne and his wife, Mary Ann Massie Payne. Her father was a merchant and owned a number of farms in Fauquier County. The home place, known as "The Pines", was located on Academy Hill, just out of Warrenton. She attended a private girls' school, for "young ladies" just didn't attend public schools! Her education lacked many of today's frills, but she received much better basic education in academic subjects than today's children. The Bible, the classics, and the dictionary, were thoroughly studied as were mathematics, science, etc. She also was an accomplished horsewoman.

Mother was the youngest of ten children, five born before the Civil War (or as she always said "the War between the States!), and five after. Father was the oldest of thirteen children.

When father finished law school at Washington & Lee, he returned to Richmond to practice briefly. In the meantime, a college classmate of his was urging him to come to the Montana Territory to practice law with him. So, in 1887, he arrived in the town of Philipsburg — a wide open town where no holds were barred, and where silver mining was at its height. It was quite a revelation to the non-athletic, refined young Southerner. On the trip to Philipsburg, the train was stalled by a rockslide that closed a tunnel on the Mullan Pass, so the passengers had to hike over the mountain to catch the stagecoach on the other side. According to a letter written to Mother, which we found not long ago, he was sure it would be the last mountain he would ever climb! And it was!

He stayed in Philipsburg only two years and then moved his law practice to Missoula, a much larger and more refined town. Fort Missoula was then an active Army Post, and there was more cultural and social life. Several old-timers described him as handsome, cultured, and intelligent — beside being a Southerner, which was quite a distinction.

In the hope of eventually getting Mother to marry him, he built a large home where he and three or four other young lawyers kept "bachelors hall" with the help of a Chinese cook named "Sing". For those of you who know Missoula, the house was the first house on the southside of the river, on the eastside of Higgins Avenue — on the corner of what is now Ronald and Fifth Streets. The house has since been torn down and replaced by an apartment house.

IN 1892, one of the classmates from law school, Asa Duncan, who was practicing law in Missoula, returned from a visit to Virginia. He told Father, that Mother, had decided that she wasn't cut out to be the wife of a missionary; so Father made a hurried trip back to Virginia to plead his case. As he often quoted later, "the race is not to the swift, nor the battle to the strong, but to him who endureth forever!"

They were married January 11, 1893, in St. James Episcopal Church in Warrenton. When they returned to Missoula, the bachelors had moved out of the house, but the loyal Chinese cook remained to help Mother start the housekeeping career for which by temperament and training, she was unprepared.

Living in the West was quite an adventure for her. The house was isolated from the rest of the town, which was divided by the Clark Fork River. It was located on a flat by itself, and she often said, "there was nothing to break the cold winter winds out of Hellgate Canyon, but a baseball fence, and that blew down!"

The Flathead Indians camped near the house each spring, and in exchange for sugar, tea, etc., they gave her many artifacts which we still have.

In order to cross the river to go to the main part of town, or for calling at the Fort, she took the local "street car" — a mule drawn vehicle! The driver always parked beside the building where Father had his office, so Father would call him to say that Mother wanted to go calling, and he would leisurely drive his mules across the bridge. He would deliver her at her destination, and then wait until she was ready to return home. Business wasn't so rushing that he had to hurry, for to keep his franchise he had to make only a trip or two daily!

One winter day she decided to walk across the bridge. After she started the wind began to blow the snow, and since she had heard stories of Montana blizzards, she became worried and "hitched" a ride. Father looked out his office window to see his bride perched upon a load of logs on a bobsled, riding down the main thoroughfare of Missoula!

The southside residential section had begun to grow, and three or four new houses were built adjacent to their home. The grocery boys called it "Bridal Row", but the occupants called it "Mortgage Row", for each house — including Father's — was heavily mortgaged at 12% interest.

While living in Philipsburg, Father met Marcus Daly, one of the outstanding mining men of the state, and later considered one of the "Copper Kings." When Father moved his law practice to Missoula, Mr. Daly retained him as his attorney.

Mr. Daly wanted to buy a large acreage in the Bitter Root Valley, a beautiful spot south of Missoula, to establish a ranch on which to breed his race horses. He also planned to build a lumber mill so it was important to have the town adjacent. He instructed Father to negotiate the purchase of the land, admonishing him, "Crutch, offer them a fair price, but don't let them hold you up." He then started his own town, and called it Hamilton, the name of his ranch foreman. It was a "company town" in every sense of the word. Besides owning much of the adjacent acreage and the lumber mill, he started a store and a bank, of which Father was one of the directors. In later years, the mill and store were sold to the Anaconda Company.

It was at the beginning of this venture that Daly asked Father to move his office to Hamilton for he wanted a resident attorney. He said he would have a home built according to the plan Father and Mother wanted, and they in turn could buy the home from the Company. He also built houses for the managers of the store, the mill, and the ranch, with the same provision that each buy them back as he was able. These houses are adjacent to ours. Our home was to be finished in six weeks, but it took six months. In those days the carpenters worked seven days a week. The same carpenter was building the Christian Church at that time, and since they would not allow him to work on the church on Sunday, he built on our house then. Mother said that she guessed our house was either the best or the worst house in town, but she didn't know which!!

Father, Mother, and their two babies — Virginia and Inman moved to Hamilton in 1895. Once again, the house was in a section by itself, but as in Missoula, was quickly followed by others. Since the house was built to accommodate a large family, Father and Mother set the goal at thirteen, it was built accordingly! It is typically Victorian with large rooms and high ceilings. It is still the family home.

Before they moved to Hamilton, Father had come up the valley on business so he brought Mother along — a days trip by train. That evening he went to the Company office (where Dowling's Mortuary is now located), leaving Mother at the Page Hotel, a false-front building in the middle of the embryonic town. It was Saturday night, payday for the ranch hands, mill workers and "river pigs" (the men who rode the logs down the river as there were no logging trains). That night the twenty-ninth saloon opened, and men were riding up and down "main street" in "Dead-X " wagons, shooting off guns and generally celebrating payday in Western fashion. When Father returned to the hotel, Mother had pushed the dresser in front of the door and was sitting in the middle of the bed, frightened and crying. She wanted to go back to Virginia!

Although she had household help, Mother was so busy taking care of their fast-growing brood she had little opportunity to take part in the few activities of the new town of Hamilton. She also was saddened by the death of her baby, Virginia, who died of spinal meningitis on April 23, 1896, the year they moved to Hamilton. She was buried in the little cemetery on the west side of the river.

To join Inman Payne were: Charles Manson, Jr., born June 27, 1897; Mary Hardin, born March 20, 1899; Lena Robb, born December 27, 1890 (who died February 21, 1901); (Miss) Jack Massie, born on February 28, 1902; and Virginia Dannon, on June 17, 1904. Of course, there were no hospitals, so doctors delivered babies in the home and a woman was hired to "live in", until the mother was able to take over the household duties. Mother said she was required to remain in bed for at least two weeks after the birth of each child and was not allowed to go down stairs for four weeks!

When they were married, Father promised Grandfather that he would see that Mother returned to Virginia each year to see her mother. This she did until her mother's death on October 7, 1890. It was a hard trip by railroad, which took seven days each way, so she told her father that he would have to come to see her as it was too difficult for her to make the trip with several children. Grandfather then came every year until his death. He died while visiting in Hamilton, on October 10, 1905.

After Grandfather's death, Mother's bachelor brother, whom she adored and who idolized her, came every year. This was the time of celebration for the Crutchfield tribe — for in our young minds, no other person held such a place! When the local train pulled into the station, all five of us, plus all the neighborhood children, were waiting on the platform to greet "Uncle Jack" with squeals and bear-hugs. He always brought two trunks. One held clothing for each of us and this was, of course, a big help to Mother. But when the second trunk was opened we hardly could contain ourselves. There, before our very eyes, were many large boxes of candy which he had purchased wholesale from Hutzler Bros. in Baltimore! This candy was not given out indiscriminately — for each piece had to be earned. We were given such jobs to do depending on our size — perhaps raking the lawn, piling wood, painting the fence at the back of the house, etc. Even the neighborhood children worked. As we look back on it, we doubt if we accomplished very much, but we tried hard — with an eye toward our reward! The thought of Jack's story-telling hours are still a delightful memory for us. We climbed on his lap, the arm of his chair, and sat at his feet to be near while hour after hour he spun tales of how he and his imaginary pal, "Billy", became involved in many escapades. Why, they even took and "a-e-reo-plane" trip to "Roosia" (Russia) — unheard of at that time!

When we were small, Mother's one interest outside her home was her Church, for which she worked faithfully all her life. When they moved to Hamilton, there was a Christian Church or a south Methodist Church at Corvallis, a small early-day settlement six miles to the North, and a Presbyterian Church at Grantsdale, five miles to the south. The closest Episcopal Church was in Missoula, fifty miles away. She had been a devout Episcopalian all her life, as were all of her family in Virginia, so she could not bring herself to rear her family in another church. Finally, she wrote the Bishop of the Diocese asking permission to gather a group together to form a small mission. This she did with great zeal! Whether the men and women were originally Episcopalians we do not know, but she enlisted their help. They met in the living room of our home to form the nucleus which was to become St. Paul's church, a mission of the diocese of Montana. Father was a member of the first Vestry.

Mr. Daly gave two lots to each denomination that would build a church in his new town. However, he gave a full block to the Roman Catholics at the request of his manager, who was a member of that denomination, as was Daly. In order to finance the Episcopal Church building, many, many, ice cream socials and pancake suppers were held at our home, since it was the only home large enough to accommodate the people. At this time, all of the denominations helped each other. Mother often said, "The Episcopal Church in Hamilton was built using pancakes as bricks and ice cream as mortar." She maintained her loyal interest in her Church during her lifetime and was grateful to know that her children and most of the grandchildren remained in the Church, with of course, a dissenter or two.

Father's main interest, aside from his family, was in his law practice and politics. He was an ardent Democrat and worked hard for his party. He served in the legislature for the State of Montana during the first, second, and sixth sessions representing Granite, Missoula, and later Ravalli County. He was also a member of the Masons and the Elks. He was popular with all who knew him and was always know as "Colonel" Crutchfield. This was due to the fact that he was a Colonel on the Staff of Governor Robert B. Smith, third Governor of the State of Montana, and also his reputation of being a courtly Southern gentleman. His untimely death on August 25, 1910, at the age of 47, was a shock to all who knew him. He was buried in Riverview Cemetery next to his two little daughters, Virginia and Lena.

Mother had been an invalid for about five years before Father's death.

Charles M. Crutchfield, April 28, 1905.

Miraculously, she soon was back on her feet and became a forceful mother, as well as a father, to her brood of growing children ranging in age from six to fourteen. Many and varied were the problems confronting her, but with an iron will she surmounted each situation. Both her family and father's offered to help educate us if she would return to Virginia, but she chose to rear her family in Montana, as she and Father had planned. By that time, she had become a loyal Montanan.

Since she always had had household help, she had never cooked a meal! She learned the hard way and became an excellent and economical cook. She began taking an active interest in civic affairs as well as her Church. She served on the local school board for eight years, was Home Service Chairman for the Red Cross, Past Matron of the Order of the Eastern Star, a member of Daly Hospital Guild, the Women's Club, and P.E.O. In most instances, she was a charter member and was always an active enthusiastic member.

In later years, she continued her interest in affairs around her, her many friends and her family. As she often said, "I love my children, adore my grandchildren, and idolize my great-grandchildren." She spent many hours crocheting and making pieces of needlepoint, as well as collecting antique oil lamps and finishing old furniture. On May 4, 1956, her birthday, the women of St. Paul's Church gave a tea for her and her many, many friends gathered in the undercroft of the Church to greet her. It was a fitting tribute to her long and active life. On November 5th of that year, at the age of eighty nine, and with mind still clear, she died and was buried from her beloved St. Paul's Church. Her grave is in Riverview Cemetery next to Father, and their daughters.

THE CRUTCHFIELD CHILDREN

INMAN attended Washington & Lee University in Virginia, Father's alma mater, for a year, leaving to serve as a Lieutenant in the U.S. Army during World War I. He was wounded in France, and spent two years in Army hospitals. Upon discharge, he studied at Georgetown University and received his MB from the National Law School in Washington, D.C. He began practice of law in Jacksonville, Florida, in 1925, and continued there for the remainder of his life. He married Christine Inman Payne, Jr. and their children are Christine Dearing (now Mrs. Charles L. Keyser whose husband is a Chaplain, U.S. Navy) and Garold McLane (Mrs. John H. Fewell of Jacksonville). Inman died in Jacksonville on December 23, 1963, and is buried in Jacksonville.

CHARLES married Selma Satter of Canby, Oregon, October 14, 1930, and they became parents of Jacqueline Lena (now Mrs. Richard Hendershot of Orange, CA); and Charles M. III. Charles was always interested in aviation and served as a Sergeant in the Air Service of the U.S.

Army during World War I. Following the war, he worked in various capacities at airports in California. His last years before retirement were spent with the Helicopter Service of Los Angeles. He died in Long Beach, CA, on October 20, 1974.

MARY did office work until June 7, 1924, when she married Howard Nelson Bates, formerly of Missoula, Montana. They became parents of a son and a daughter. Howard Nelson Bates, Jr. (better known as "Jerry"), and Virginia Lee (now Mrs. Robert W. Minto of Seattle, WA). Mary worked in the office of the family owned business, Bates Fuel Service, as well as keeping her home and garden. She died on September 5, 1958, and is buried in Hamilton. Mary had a unique history of having been baptized, confirmed, married, and buried in and from St. Paul's Episcopal Church.

JACK (baptized "Miss Jack") received her B. A. from the University of Montana and M. A. from Teacher's College at Columbia University in New York. She taught commercial subjects and was the Girl's Counselor in Montana schools until her retirement in 1945. She served as an officer in the Women's Army Corps during World War II, for three and one half years. She died on August 6, 1996, in Hamilton, and was survived by nieces and nephews.

VIRGINIA, better known as "Dutch", remained at home in Hamilton, living with and caring for her Mother. She began work in a jewelry store, then became Assistant Cashier of the Ravalli County Bank, where she was in charge of the insurance department. She resigned from the bank and established her own insurance business, continuing until October 18, 1966,

The Daly Mansion, about 1905.

when she married Frank J. Welton, a native of New York City. They had a ranch on the Sleeping Child Road.

MARCUS DALY

Marcus Daly was an early pioneer of the Bitter Root Valley. In 1872, he met and married **Margaret Evans** in Utah. At this time, she was eighteen and he was thirty. While working for the Walker Brothers in 1876, as a roving prospector, Marcus was sent to an area now known as Walkerville (north edge of Butte, Montana), and by the 1880's came to the Bitter Root Valley scouting a supply of timber for the mines in Butte. His personal and business life stories are covered in many articles and books, and it would be redundant to go into those details. His influence in the Valley, whether praised or pandered, cannot be denied. The following books are available at the library: "War of the Copper Kings", "Green and Silver", "Daly's of the Bitter Root", "Anaconda, Life of Marcus Daly the Copper King", as well as coverage of the Daly story in "Land of the Giants", and "Montana, a State of Extremes", and "Battle for Butte".

GROWING UP WITH THE BITTER ROOT VALLEY

August 1970, by Pearl Dinehart

My father and mother, Mr. and Mrs. Allen E. Shapee, had lived in Wisconsin, but since my father's health was not good, the doctors advised him to go west, where they considered the climate to be more beneficial.

At that time, a telegraph operator — depot agent — was needed at the Stevensville station, so my father took the job. In the back of the depot there were living quarters for the family and that is where I was born. I recall my father telling about taking me "piggy back" to town as we had not even a horse or buggy in those days.

When Ravalli County was established, Stevensville became the County seat and my father became the Clerk of the Court. Later, when the county seat was moved from Stevensville to Hamilton, my father was still the Clerk of the Court and my mother was his deputy.

I started school in the old Washington school building. We lived in a house half-way between Grantsdale and Hamilton, right by the road next to the Big Ditch.

It was about this time that Hamilton had an epidemic of small pox. We children rode to town with our parents every day when they went to the courthouse to work as by then we had a horse and buggy. On one of these trips we met Dr. McGrath who was on his way to the "pest house" with a patient. He stopped us and asked my parents if we children had been vaccinated. I had, but my brother had not, so the doctor said we had better get it done. He took out a sheet and placed it over the buggy, and vaccinated my brother right there on the road!

Another thing I remember from this period of my childhood was a trip to the Daly Mansion, in which the playhouse was the important thing to me. It was built just like a big house, only on a smaller scale — a most delightful place for a child to play.

I was ten and my brother eight when our mother died and father took us to our grandparents in Wisconsin. After three years there, my father sent for us and we came back to Hamilton where I entered the sixth grade. We lived at the Vincent Boarding and Rooming House, which is now the Dowling Funeral Home. I remember playing in the big yard with Geneva Lundgren, where we had a hammock under the pine trees.

Then came Hamilton High school trips to Stevensville in the Galloping Goose, a train consisting of an engine and one coach, which ran from Missoula to Hamilton. We rode on this to ball games and other school activities. Our debating team, of which I was a member, was defeated by Stevi, who won the debate on Women's suffrage. Graduation exercises in 1911, were held in what was then the Lucas Opera House (Downing's drug store) and which is now the skating rink.

I took the teachers' examination in the spring and got a school at Charlos Heights. One room and seven grades, at $70.00 per month, with $5.00 extra for doing the janitor work. At first, I roomed with a woman who was very nice to me, but she always had a headache and used camphor. When I opened my lunch pail all I could ever smell and taste was camphor! My father drove to Charlos Heights each Friday night and took me home to Hamilton, returning me to Charlos Heights every Sunday.

After teaching at Charlos Heights, I enrolled in the Minnesota State Teachers College in Winona, ten miles across the Mississippi River from Wisconsin, where my grandfather still lived on the farm. He drove his two spirited horses to Marshland Junction to meet us in his "surrey with the fringe on the top".

After graduation from college, I taught for four years at the old Washington School in Hamilton. Then I was married, in 1917, to William H. Dinehart, and we lived in Wallace, Idaho; Spokane, Washington; and South Dakota where our eldest daughter, Carol, was born. Back in Hamilton four years later, our twins, Alma and Wilma, were born. When they reached first grade, I went back to teaching. I spent twenty-five years in the Hamilton schools and ten years substitute teaching — ending my career last year in 1969. I AM GLAD TO BE LIVING IN THE BEAUTIFUL BITTER ROOT VALLEY AND AM ENJOYING THE ACTIVITIES AT THE SENIOR CENTER.

By Willie Dinehart Hammer:

My mother, Pearl Dinehart, was born in October of 1894. She taught school off and on in the valley, then steady over 25 years here in Hamilton and Grantsdale, mostly 2nd grade. When she retired, she couldn't quite accept retirement, and continued to teach as a substitute. When asked to "baby-sit" a class for a day, she would remark emphatically, "I don't baby-sit. I have a program", and she would stay up late getting ready. Later, I remember her sitting in the yard at my sister's, and students coming by to say "hello" after graduating High School. They all loved Mrs. D., and she would think a minute and come up with their name every time.

Pearl was born in Stevensville, and died in Stevensville in April of 1984, at the age of 90. She was certainly a part of the Bitterroot and active in the community, a true lady with high principles. So many of her friends have come into the Daly Hospital Gift Shop, where I volunteer, and tell me what a great lady she was! It brings her right back, and I am filled with pride.

Her oldest daughter, Carol, died in April 1989. Her twins, Alma and Wilma, still live in Hamilton and love it. Alma, the talented twin, retired artist from Rocky Mountain Laboratory, is involved in miniatures. She has a complete doll house all handmade, a bakery, banquet room, Spanish apartment, hunters retreat, child's nursery, and her latest is a farm produce stand with every fruit and vegetable there is, all handmade and "tiny". Willy, the "talkative" twin, I remember mother saying I was born talking, is active in the same Presbyterian Church she attended so many years. I have always been into music and make cassettes for everyone. My 460 cassette collection is all cataloged, being a retired librarian from Rocky Mountain Laboratory. I enjoy playing bridge and spending summers at our cabin on the East Fork, where my family gets together every year. You can see why I am a lover of this Bitterroot Valley, and have watched it grow into something very special.

DOWLING

The Dowling family has had three John W. Dowlings in the Bitterroot so I will identify them by; first, second and third.

John W. Dowling, the first, was born in 1859 in Gays River, Nova Scotia. He came to the United States in 1880, to California where he was involved in the lumber business for two years. He then went to Butte where he was involved in contracting. In 1884, he arrived in the Bitterroot and purchased a ranch which he planted with 4000 fruit trees. In 1887, he was elected County Treasurer of the new Ravalli County. This was the same election of the famous "Capitol Fight" between Marcus Daly championing Anaconda and W.A. Clark with Helena in the contest for state capitol. At the conclusion of his term, he purchased an interest in the Amos Buck Mercantile Co. of Stevensville. Three years later, he sold and then started his own mercantile store. After a year, he sold his interest to the Stevensville Mercantile Co. which he and the May brothers had started. This company then bought the Missoula Mercantile, Stevensville branch and John became manager, later disposing of this also. He built a business block and owned and managed a funeral home, which in those days was almost a natural outgrowth of the furniture business.

He married Mary A. McHaffey, a native also of Nova Scotia, in Butte in 1883. They had eight children, including son John W. II, a daughter married to W.T. Whitesitt, and another daughter married to J.T. Coughenour, brother of Dr. Coughenour. John I died in 1945.

John W. Dowling, the second, was born in Stevensville in 1895. He was active in athletics during school years, and was always a lover of the outdoors. In 1917, he married Mabel "Murph" Burnett and that same year moved to Hamilton where he purchased the Wagner Funeral Home and continued in this profession until his death in 1957, which occurred when he, along with the sheriff, went into the mountains to bring out the body of a hunting fatality. He attended the University of Montana in Missoula and also the Chicago School of Embalming. Besides his profession, he was very

The invitation to visit the new Dowling Funeral Home in Hamilton during its opening, November 20-21, 1937.

active in community affairs, serving on the school board, Chamber of Commerce, Lions Club and seven terms as County Coroner before it was merged with that of the Sheriff's office.

He and "Murph" had four children, John W., the third, Alpha Iline who was married to Missoula dentist Dr. David Tawney, but she in now deceased; James Howard, Captain U.S.N., who died in 1975; and Donald Burnett, still living in Hamilton.

John W. Dowling, the third, or Jack as he was usually known was born in 1918 in Hamilton. He graduated from Hamilton High School, attended St. Johns Military Academy in Wisconsin, the University of Montana and San Francisco College.

He married Peggy Carrigan in Butte in 1940. Her father was manager of one of the mines in Butte. That same year, he became associated with his father in the Dowling Funeral Home. Jack and Peggy had four children, three sons John, Michael, Tim, and a daughter Kathleen. None of the children reside in Montana.

Following his service in the Navy during World War II, Jack returned to Hamilton and was associated with his father until his father died, at which time he and his brother, Donald, purchased the business from their

A horse and carriage funeral by the Dowling Funeral Home.

mother. This partnership continued until 1971 when Donald purchased Sanderson's Hardware. Shortly thereafter, Jack had Ed Leach help him, but after a few years Ed started his own mortuary.

Shortly thereafter, Donald rejoined him and they continued until Jack's death in 1989.

As a young man while in school, Jack was active in athletics and in later years very active in community affairs.

Donald was born in 1934 and continues in the business today. He and his wife Shirley, whose maiden name was Evans, have four children, two of whom live in Hamilton. A daughter, Charlene, and a son, Gregg, who is a pharmacist at the Bitterroot Drug.

The history of the present Dowling Funeral Home in interesting. It was built in 1892 for Marcus Daly's family, but they never lived there. It became the office of the Bitterroot Stock Farm and was eventually used by the Bitterroot Irrigation Company land developers during the apple boom from 1905 to 1914. It was purchased in 1926 by John W. II and served as the family home as well as the Mortuary.

DOWNING

Do Downing Mountain and Downing Street in London have anything in common? Well yes, according to some members of the Downing family they are both named after the family. Albert H. Downing was born at West Andover, MA, March 26, 1857, the son of Samuel and Rebecah Downing, whose ancestors came from England in the 17th century, landing at Plymouth Rock. Downing Street in London is named for them. Rebecah's family, the Baileys, have their lineage documented back to James Bailey (b. 1612), England who came to Rowley in the Massachusetts Bay Colony around 1640. Rebecah, a sixth generation New England Bailey, married Samuel Downing, a shoemaker, on Oct. 23, 1845. Seven other children were born to this couple, Eliza, Eben, George, Horace Laura and Gertrude. Albert was the seventh.

The family moved to North Andover when Albert was quite young. He finished eight grades of school there. At age fourteen, two years under the legal age, he became a machinist's apprentice in the iron works of an uncle. Upon completion of his four year apprenticeship, became restless and having had three other uncles who had gone "out west", two of whom had returned, so he bought a ticket to San Francisco.

On his way to California, at age 20, he got as far as Salt Lake City by train, changed his mind and went to Corrine, Utah, then by wagon to Butte. He arrived there when it was a one street town in 1876. He became a range rider during the Nez Perce emergency, patrolling from Deer Lodge to Flint Creek hills. He then worked in Butte at just about everything until he was able to buy a team and head for the Bitterroot in 1882. He went through the valley all the way to the Big Hole and saw only one person, Billy Edwards. He returned and stopped at the Eastland Place (Now View Acres on South 8th) and was told about claims available across the river, and he homesteaded 160 acres there.

He built a log cabin, as well as furniture and cabinets with an axe and chisel. The cabin featured a cook stove which was unique on the west side at that time. He spent eighty-five dollars, ordering a No. 7 stove from Salt Lake City. It was delivered to the Skalkaho Post Office.

In 1886, he married Mary Baldwin, niece of George Orr, who was the discoverer of gold in Alder Gulch. They had five children, all born on the homestead. Their four daughters were Margaret (William) Huebner, Estes Park, CO; Gertrude (Alexander) Bett, Chehalis, WA; Susie (Herbert) Carroll, Kelso, WA; Alma (Robert) Bailey, Hollywood, CA. Their son, the youngest, Samuel Albert, ran the ranch after his dad retired. Albert and Mary built a new house in Hamilton around 1910. Mary passed away in 1919 and Albert later married Caroline Nicel. He lived to age 92.

Samuel Albert (Sam) married Margarete and they had two children. Samuel Deane, (Dean or Sam), a watchmaker and jeweler in Hamilton for years. He and his wife, Nora, had two children Mark and Nordeane (Hedditch). Sam's other child is Alma Rose Vining. Her husband, Charles Eugene (Gene), died in 1990. Alma Rose and her son and his children, Tifani and Ryan, still live on parts of the old ranch.

Albert's brother George S., his wife and daughter, Ada, left North Andover in May 1883, arrived via train at Bearmouth, and stage via Missoula to Big Corral on the R.W. Nicol ranch, who was also the postmaster at the Skalkaho post office. He took them by boat over the river to Albert's place. He took up a timber claim and homestead next to his brother's and built a log cabin for his family. It stood until the 1970s or 80s on what is now Trudy Shatzer's place, also known as the C.W. Ellingwood place. They had two more children, William, (born 1885, died 1904) and Lewis E. (born 1887). He took up another claim across the road, built another home which burned in 1891, rebuilt that same year and lived there until he died in 1939. That also burned in 1947. Downing mountain is named for the two brothers, Albert and George.

George's daughter Ada was married to Murray Grant son of H.H. Grant, for whom Grantsdale is named. Henry Grant was born of this marriage ranched on the land that George had across from his first place.

Lewis became a pharmacist and established his pharmacy, Downing Drug in 1917 in the old Lucas Opera House, which he owned. Lewis died in 1981, his wife Florence in 1960. They had two children, son William and daughter Elizabeth. His son, William (Bill), was also a pharmacist and practiced along with his dad. The building burned down in 1986, the upstairs had been a roller rink for years, but his son built a new one story brick building to replace it. It has since been named Hamilton Pharmacy. Bill married Marguerite and they had a son, Gregg. Marguerite still lives in Hamilton and son Gregg in Boise. Bill died in 1996. Lewis's daughter, Elizabeth, married a physician, Dr. Lockridge, who practiced in Whitefish before he died in the late 1950s. She now lives in Lubbock, Texas.

Lewis had many interesting stories to tell about early Hamilton. He and his brother and sister went to school at the Sawtooth School, a log cabin structure built in 1886 near the Brennan and Kress sawmill on Roaring Lion creek. The structure was 18 'x 30 'x 10 'tall, was moved four times and finally wound up on the east side of the Westside Road on what is now the Storm King Ranch. It was in poor shape and was torn down a few years ago. His first grade teacher in 1893 was a Mr. Simpson. Marcus Daly brought 60 jockeys to the area and 40 of them had to go to this school. The law at that time was go to school until eighth grade or age 18. They came to Lewis's third grade one day, next day went to the fourth grade, next day to the fifth and so on until at the end of six days they finished the eighth grade.

The Brennan and Kress sawmill was built in 1886. A bridge was built across the river so they could take lumber over to the railroad. This came out at about where Blood Lane in now located. It was then the Henry Chambers ranch and also Skalkaho post office. Marcus Daly wanted a lumber mill in the Bitterroot so he started by building a dam where Main Street bridge is now located. The Brennan and Kress mill, which Daly later bought, supplied the timber for this dam and after completion the mill was dismantled, although Brennan and Kress and many of the crews worked for Daly at the new mill. Logs were floated from Sawtooth, Lost Horse and the East and West Forks until 1905, when the railroad reached Darby and then came to the mill by rail. The spur to the mill came down Pine Street. This mill closed in 1924, and the work shifted to Bonner.

FRANK H. DRINKENBERG

Frank H. Drinkenberg suffered a traumatic experience in 1904, which seems now a humorous story. While Drinkenberg was attending a function at the Lucas Opera House, some personal foe went to extensive measure to inflict property damage to this man. The Western News headlines read, "Frank Drinkenberg's machine blown into fragments — an unprecedented outrage — believed to have been perpetrated by some personal enemy — giant powder did his business". Mr. Drinkenberg had the first automobile in Hamilton and someone either didn't like the machine, or the man, or possibly both, and successfully dynamited the car while it sat in a shed behind the Drinkenberg house.

F.H. Drinkenberg built his first commercial block on a lot directly behind the Lucas Opera House at 162-164 S. 2nd Street, in 1909. Mr. Drinkenberg built this building as an investment with the Drinkenberg Rooms and a photo gallery on the second floor, and a movie house occupying the first floor. One year later, with the First National Bank solidly established, he built a new bank directly across the street from his Drinkenberg Block, a building which currently is occupied by Haigh's Pool Hall. This building at 163-167 S. 2nd St. was not a solo venture. Owners were T.L. Humble, J.A. Summers, C.C. Chaffin, and F.H. Drinkenberg. The new masonry building replaced a frame building whose second floor formerly served as Hamilton's first city hospital, c. 1895. By 1896, the hospital had moved to the Ravalli House on South Fourth Street (no longer in existence). At the time of removal of the earlier building, it was occupied by a bicycle shop and Hub Clothing.

The First National Bank offices, which replaced the bicycle shop and Hub Clothing, would return to its same location in the new building. This new building had a distinct style, with defined masonry piers, squarish windows accented by brick voussiers. The masons delineated the first and second floor with a strong corbeled banding and the cornice was distinguished by a playful pendant-like arcade. The power of the new architecture closely resembled other buildings of the period designed by A.J. Gibson. This new style sharply broke away from the simple vernacular style of its adjacent neighbor to the south, the Doran Block at 169 S. 2nd St., built as the first masonry building on South Second Street, c. 1895.

Later in that same year of 1895, Drinkenberg joined with R.B. Bell and C.C. Coulter to build additional buildings on the block in the same pattern as his First National Bank building, thus completing the block with the same pattern except the Doran Building. In looking at the block, one wonders whether Mr. Drinkenberg anticipated acquiring the Doran Building to continue the facade and create the largest building block in Hamilton.

The new commercial blocks, unlike their predecessors (which usually were erected on a single lot), would have multiple lot frontage. Two beautiful and nearly identical examples were the George McGrath Block at 215-217 Main Street, and the Bitterroot Stock Farm Office at 166-170 South Second Street, erected 1910 and 1909 respectively. Both building were designed by A.J. Gibson. Other prominent commercial blocks erected in 1909 were the First National Bank Block, Drinkenberg/Bell Block, Drinkenberg/Coulter Block, 165-179 South Second Street, and the Daly Block at 123-127 West Main Street, done for Margaret Daly by A.J. Gibson, c.32.

A number of the new buildings on South Second Street were backed by F.H. Drinkenberg. Drinkenberg's investments in the north side of Hamilton prior to 1900 had provided an excellent return, allowing him to start the First National Bank in 1909. The bank opened July 30th, and had R.L. Perkins as Cashier, F.H. Drinkenberg as President, and W.B. Harlan as Vice President.

Although a very affluent man by 1909, F.H. Drinkenberg did not reside in the prestigious south side, but remained true to his north side affiliations by residing at 505 North Second Street, in a brick home he had built in 1898.

Mr. Drinkenberg's first home may have originally been built by Martha Allison. Records indicate that Martha Allison and F.H. Drinkenberg collectively owned the north side subdivisions. The chain of title shows Martha Allison or Martha Allison-Reinkeh to hold first title and F.H. Drinkenberg listed as second owner. Records indicate that Mr. Drinkenberg purchased an entire city block from Ms. Allison and paid the sum of $25,000.00. Considering land values of the period, even in the city, this was a sizable sum, which strongly suggests that the residence may well have been in the purchase. After Drinkenberg sold the property a man named Trelor occupied the residence. Mr. Trelor was the band leader for Mr. Daly's horse races each Sunday.

Note:

For additional information on Hamilton area buildings, see "Hello Hamilton Walking and Driving Tours" by Ada Powell and Carolyn Jones

THOMAS HARPER and BESSIE ELLIOTT DUNBAR

Thomas Harper Dunbar was born on August 31, 1871, at Downing Missouri. At the age of 14, he came to Deer Lodge, Montana, and worked on the Tom Elliot Ranch at Racetrack, MT. He came to the Bitter Root in 1885 with a brother, James Dunbar.

Thomas worked for the Dunbar and Johnson Sawmill in the Blodgett Creek area until 1904, when he married Bessie Elliot. They went to the St. Louis World's Fair for their honeymoon. They came back and took up a homestead in the Christaisen Creek area of the West Fork. He operated the homestead and a sawmill, cutting lumber for other homesteaders in the area. Bessie worked lots of days in the mill along with household chores.

Bessie told many interesting stories of the early days of the West Fork, about the Indians that used to camp on the upper end of their place. She told of the long dusty trips to Darby for the supplies. They would drive the wagon to town and stay all night at the Hart Hotel and get their supplies and go home the next day.

I remember one story about the Indians. She was busy in the kitchen, she heard the door open and when she turned around there stood two large Indian men. One had a knife in his hand and was rubbing the blade with his thumb and pointing to the door. She was too scared to scream. They realized they had frightened her, so they backed out the door while motioning her to follow. They pointed to a grindstone that stood near the house. They were asking permission to sharpen their knives. She said it was quite a sight to see them when they came up in the spring for Bitter Roots, and in the fall hunting. Horses, kids, and dogs, all having a good time, quite a sight.

Tom moved his mill up to Hughes Creek and cut lumber for the dredge, but never got paid for that summer's work.

In 1911, he bought a timber claim in the mouth of Blodgett Creek and moved his mill down and built a house on what is now called Alvista Drive. In those days it was called Kenney's Hill. In 1912, Tom and Homer Elliot sawed lumber and built a house for his and Bessie's mother, Laura Elliot. The first son, Thomas Jr., was born in 1916.

In 1918, Tom, Bessie, and Tom Jr., bought 20 acres of land in Woodside. This was the year their second son, Charles, was born. On the northern part of the land they built a lumber yard. They hauled lumber to this site, where it was piled and dried before shipping. They also leased part of it to some of the other mills for the same purpose. There were several mills in this area that loaded lumber on the railroad in Woodside. In those days, mills were fairly portable; they would move to a timber claim, cut it, then move to another location. Tom moved his mill from Churn Creek Ranch to Woodside, where he cut lumber for the Iman Ranch and also for the Woodside Clubhouse.

In 1920, their third son, Doyle, was born.

In 1925-27, he built the potato cellar that is all of the local store and the apple packing house that is now Dunbar Building Supplies store. The railroad notified him that they were to relocate the road to the east side of Corvallis, so the building stopped. The cellar was used for cabbage storage for many years, and the packing house was a dance hall during the depression years.

In 1926, Tom moved his mill to Mill Creek and sawed for a couple years, then sold the mill to Kim Hickey, who moved it to the Bear Creek area, and later to Victor.

In the fall of 1934, Tom and Tom Jr. started a small mill at Woodside, powered by a steam tractor. It was operated until 1942, when World War II came along and all three sons went to the service. Tom then took care of the ranch and the cattle, the mill stood empty. In 1946, the boys came home and the mill was started again. Tom Sr., worked the mill until 1955 when failing health caused him to retire. Tom and Bessie lived in the brick house that they built in 1918, for the rest of their lives.

Thomas Harper Dunbar passed away in 1957, and Bessie Elliot Dunbar passed away in 1961.

DUUS FAMILY

by Eva Duus

The Peter Duus family arrived in the Bitter Root Valley in March of 1916 during a huge snow storm. They were dryland ranchers in Bickleton, WA, before moving to the Bitter Root. That spring in below zero weather, they lambed out the sheep they had brought with them from Washington. My name is Eva Stoll Duus. My parents, the Stolls, moved from Fort Collins, Colorado, and arrived in the Bitter Root the same year. We lived in Stevensville first and then in the Three Mile area for a year or two; I went to school there, and ultimately, we moved to Hamilton. The ranch was purchased from Daly around 1917 and the deed was transferred to Peter Duus in 1921.

I was born in Russia in 1902. My folks came to America when I was three. I grew up on a ranch. My folks didn't land at Ellis Island. They sailed clear around to Galveston, Texas. My mother said it was not a very clean ship. There was a man who met the boat and he was trying to get some of the people to settle in Texas. He said he would furnish everything if they would stay. But, my mother said there were too many fireflies at night and they spooked her too much to stay there. They had plans to settle in Windsor, Colorado. My dad had a brother there who had a job for him right away in the sugar factory. So, they were prepared to farm sugar beets when they came to the Bitter Root Valley. At the smokestack on the Jack Fitzgerald place, there used to be a log cabin. The field boss in Colorado had told Dad he could bring his family over here free if we would work for him in his sugar beet fields. The beets were pretty rough; they were all quackgrass. Some good ones were raised in Corvallis, though. They never did finish the factory. One was built in Missoula instead.

I came from a big family of seven children. I was the oldest. Then there was Kathryn, Pauline, Phil, Minnie, Harry, and Albert. When we first came, the three girls shared a bedroom. We didn't get our own bedrooms until I worked at the seed house, sorting peas. The seed house I worked in burned down. It was about where the Coffee Cup restaurant is now. That's where I worked in the winter time. I worked on the Duus ranch in the summer to help cook for the crew. I also worked at the Bitter Root Laundry, pressing shirts. Zelma Hartley's dad had the laundry at the time. It was located where the Citizen's Bank is now. I was 18 when I first started working at the laundry.

Pauline married Bernie Yerian. She is gone now. They lived down the road here. My brother, Harry, was a retired Navy man. He enlisted when he wasn't even of age and served in the Philippines. Phil almost died of malaria while there. When he came back to the Bitter Root Valley, he worked in the Forest Service. Albert Stoll, my brother, still lives down in Hamilton.

My husband's name was Clarence Duus. Clarence and I were married May 26, 1924, in Deer Lodge. We had two boys, Jim and Charles. The house I'm living in now and the barn were purchased from the Dalys.

Even before I knew my husband, I was working on the ranch for the Duus family. One fall, I came out here every day and picked potatoes working most of the time until dark. The men harnessed their horses and were out in the field by 7:00. That meant the women must prepare breakfast for the men at 6:00 a.m., a big lunch at noon and supper was at 6:00 p.m. sharp. The meals were served like clockwork, we couldn't be late. At haying time, we served around 15, threshing time, 25. We raised grain and butchered all the meat for the ranch including sheep, beef, and pigs. I made our own butter, you couldn't buy it. It was a lot of very hard work to keep everyone fed.

There was a Stud Barn Ditch, Mountain House, and shearing camp east of our ranch that was part of the Daly Ranch. We heated our house with wood and coal, then a big oil heater, and now baseboard electricity. Clarence and I had a Model T pickup. We finally got a Model A Sedan. I was so proud of that. Dr. Hayward, our doctor, had a black coupe with white wheels. It was the first coupe I saw and I really admired it.

Clarence went hunting for enjoyment. There was a lot of game. We could go right up here on our land and the pheasants were thick in the field. Clarence was very good at training dogs for hunting or herding.

Mountain herding is a lot different than flat land herding. It was hard to find help. One year we had 3,000 head of sheep to shear. It rained every day for two weeks solid. We had employed 8 shearers, two wool tiers, a wool tramper, the boss of the shearing crew, two herders, two camp tenders, our sons and a lot of ranch help making around 20 people to feed and there was no work getting done. I had to feed all those workers while we all waited for the rain to stop. We took some chickens with us for the first day but, after that, Clarence had to go into Darby every day to get meat. The oven was not good at our cabin across from the Darby Cemetery.

We finally got a truck load of lumber and built tent frames where we put 300 sheep in there a day to dry out and shear. In comparison, the Stock Farm used to shear 10,000 head at a time. There were rats up there around those old buildings. One night, one ran across my bed!

We raised black "marker" sheep, too. We used one marker for every 50 sheep and we would count the markers to determine if all the sheep were in the herd. The black ones would wear different bells, with their own individual sound. In this way, the herder could walk through them at night and listen for the various bells.

Ned Hobbs was the camp tender's name. One day, he was found all bent over and staggering. He had gotten ptomaine poisoning and almost died. The herder stayed with him for two or three days and just let the sheep go.

When the sheep were counted at East Fork Ranger Station, there were 350 sheep missing. Clarence eventually offered $1.00 a head reward to find the lost sheep. Some men even flew over the area to look for them. Loggers at Harper's Camp found about one-half of them. Darby Ranger, Clyde Shockley, found the rest. We only lost 50.

Clarence died May of 1973.

THE DYE AND ODELL FAMILIES

by Hazel Blodgett and Violet Rennaker

George Tolson Dye, Sr., was the 6th child of David Stitchacomb and Christina Ann Barr Dye. He married Aquilla Odell on June 13, 1875, in California. Aquilla was born on December 29, 1856. They had eight children: Maudie, Tabitha, George Ward, Elmina, Isabella Ann, Bert Andrew, Ona Eva, and Oretta Dye.

The Dye family came to Montana in 1882 or 1883, living first in Anaconda, Montana. They came with Aquilla Odell's parents, brothers, and sisters. Her father was Harris Walter Ward Odell (born in Orange County, NY; died 9-17-1898). He married Isabelle White Fergerson on November 25, 1852. (She was born in Glasgow, Scotland on May 11, 1832).

Harris and Isabelle had nine children: Harris Walter, Sarepta, Aquilla, Lillie, Sarah, Elizabeth, Alfreda Sarah, Alfred, John Ferguson, and Wallace Byron. The Dye and Odell families had contracted to cut railroad ties for the Railroad Company. They had been having so much bad luck, they decided a change of scene might help. The Dyes lost two little girls in infancy. The Odells lost three children. One was a year old. The boy, Alfred, a twin, came to his folk's bed one night feeling bad. They told him to return to bed and in the morning he would be alright. Next morning he said, "You don't know how sick I was, I thought I was going to die!" He died a few minutes later.

One day, the women were washing clothes along the banks of the Sacramento River. Little Lillie was making mud pies. They saw her slip into the river and rushed to her rescue, but she was gone. When Harris Odell, her father, came home, he tried frantically to find her body. He dove to the bottom of the river many times before he gave up.

They owned a lot of land along the river. The county had many problems with flooding. The county built a levee to contain the water, and along the top of the levee they planted willow trees to make the levee stronger. Harris Odell's sheep ate all the willows and the county sued and took their land away from them. It was taken to court and Harris pleaded his own case. They lost, and decided to move to Montana. They made the move in 1882 or 1883, by covered wagon. In 1886, because they were farmers at heart, they moved to the Bitter Root Valley.

As they entered the valley, it was filled with sagebrush and pine trees. They drove their wagons until the ground appeared to be good to farm, and settled at Camas Prairie — now known as Charlos Heights. They lived in their wagons until they built log cabins. They bought adjoining farms, and had several experiences while living here.

The Indians were still crossing the valley going to the reservations. One day, the children saw an Indian coming toward the log cabins. The oldest Dye boy, George, Jr., told the children to hide under the bed and he held his finger in the latch so the Indian couldn't open the door. Aquilla Odell Dye always said to feed the Indians, and be kind to them and they would not get hurt.

One time, George Dye, Sr., went to town and by the time he came home, the creek had risen. There were no bridges. His team would not cross the high water. As George sat there deciding what to do, he listened to the water rushing over the rocks. He said it sounded like a roaring lion. And, that is what it became know as, The Roaring Lion Creek.

The river bordered their places and they experienced a lot of high water. It was a common sight to see a chicken coop go floating down the river with a rooster crowing for dear life on top. Bunches of hay would come floating down also, and they would take large poles and pull the hay to shore and it would help supply them with food for their stock for the winter. Because of the high water situation, they moved down east of Corvallis, where the soil was richer. Each family rented their farms in this area for a short while, and then bought farms down on Hawker's Lane.

George Tolson Dye was a small, neat appearing, mustached man. He was very particular about his clothes and the way he looked. He was a jolly, friendly man, always jigging or acting up in some way. He loved to make up and tell stories. He was hard working, honest, a good man, and a helpful neighbor. He loved horses and took pride in them.

After Aquilla's death at age 48 on October 7, 1904, George made a trip to Salt Lake City and met and married Johanna Pauline Browsky. She was a nurse who had come over to America from Germany. She and George raised a second family of four girls. George soon acquired a nice herd of dairy cattle. The children milked these cows each morning before school and at night. George built a large box to hold a five gallon cream can. He would put the can full of cream in the box and pack ice around it. He took this to Woodside and put it on the train and shipped it to Butte. A man in Butte would pay him for this cream and in this way he helped support his family until the time came that he failed to get his pay for his cream. He decided to quit shipping it and began making his own dairy products and sold them in the Bitter Root. In those days, people went to the river when it had frozen, and cut big chunks of ice and hauled them to their ice houses on the farms and put sawdust around it so it wouldn't melt. This is how George Dye got the ice to put around his dairy products.

The Dyes raised alfalfa, hay, oats, and wheat. When it was harvest time, it was quite a sight to see the threshing machine come to take its turn at each farm. The binder machine would cut the grain and it would fall in bundles ready to be shocked. After it was shocked, it was gathered and brought in to the threshing machine to have the grain separated from the straw. The women worked hard preparing food to feed all the working men. They had no electric stoves, no refrigerators, and no electric lights.

In spite of all the work the was done in those days, they also found time for fun. George Dye had a bunkhouse built and that is where they would gather to have their parties. All the girls in the family could play the organ, and the boys played the fiddle. It was a time of dancing, singing, and fun for all.

The Dye family lived and died on their farm on Hawker's Lane and were buried at the Corvallis Cemetery. The Odell family moved back up to Camas Prairie. Harris Walter Odell died there and is buried at the Corvallis Cemetery. Isabelle Fergerson Odell died in Hamilton and is buried in the Corvallis Cemetery, also.

WILLIAM EDDY FAMILY

by Grandson, William N. Eddy on May 18, l997

WILLIAM EDDY was born in Vermont, in the late 1860's. In the early 1890's, he and his brother, Herbert, came into the Bitter Root Valley by wagon. In 1895, Herbert Eddy married in Stevensville, and later moved to Canada.

WILLIAM EDDY married RETTIE M. RALL in June of 1899, at the Victor residence of her father, Thomas Rall.

William and Rettie acquired a ranch at the mouth of Fred Burr Creek, where they lived until moving to Victor in the late 1940's.

They had nine children: Alice, Clarence, Flora (Mrs. Bill Ferth), Helen (Mrs. Kenneth Hinman), Arthur, Bob, and Jean (Mrs. Joe Dugal). Two children died — one of Spotted Fever and one with the Flu.

Mr. William Eddy farmed and ran a sawmill utilizing the timber on his ranch.

In 1927, William Eddy shot a grizzly bear that was attacking his cattle, inside his barn. This is believed to be the last known grizzly killed in the Bitter Root Valley.

William died in 1951, and Rettie died in 1967. Both are buried in the Victor Cemetery.

The last grizzly bear killed in the Bitter Root. This bear was shot by William J. Eddy in 1927. The bear was in Eddy's barn molesting his cattle. The Eddy's ranch was at the mouth of Fred Burr Creek.

THE PETER ELLIOTT FAMILY

by Harvey C.Elliott in 1971

Here are just a few memories of the school day.

When we packed water from the ditch over the hill south of school and one dipper hung on the side of the pail to serve everyone. When the well was dug, and everyone wanted to pump water for awhile. When the high board fence was built to separate the boys and girls playground. HA, HA!! The old outhouses, the horse shed, and the pile of slab wood along the west fence to feed the central heating plant between the three rooms. When Earl Malone brought the cub bear to school. The coyote and hounds race. Bill Garrard was the coyote and we were very late getting back, long after the bell rang and had to contact the trustees before we could return to school. When every boy brought powder, blasting caps, shotgun shells or anything explosive and put it in a pipe, plugged both ends, built a fire and threw it in just as recess was over. It sailed into the air, broke a board on the fence and caused a runaway with a horse and buggy.

I could go on and on for many pages! But, we all have many memories of school days on Dutch Hill. After all had grown up, they were a bunch of good citizens.

I was born on Nov. 21, 1898, at the west end of Sears Lane on what was known later as the Keeling place. Later dad bought a small farm and built a house about two and a half miles north of the school house. One time before this we lived on the old Jim Dunbar ranch, now owned by Henry Oppegaard. This was a long hike and I started early and got home late.

At our home place the Garrard, Lockwood, Bill Johnson and Little Johnnie Johnson kids usually got together near our place and trailed along together. When the snow was deep and the roads were not plowed the big kids would break trail.

In 1974, it has been a long time since the days of Fairplay School on Dutch Hill. Therefore, any of the girls I mention will be called by the names we knew them by at that time. This will not be in sequence but only as I remember things.

Miss Sherwin was my first grade teacher. It would be interesting to know how many she taught during her long career. A wonderful woman! Miss Cramer had a room and boarded at our place. My father was operating the farm known as the Bill Turnage place, adjoining the school grounds which were then owned by W. T. Tyler, and later sold to a Chicago lawyer named Boyce. I'll wager you all remember Jimmy Boyce! Ed Mills came here as kind of a caretaker for Jimmy. Bethel Irwin also put in sometime teaching. I will not name the boys who "bugged" her swivel chair and caused her to fall over backwards when she sat down! Mr. Cope was the teacher when I graduated from the eighth grade. He got a bad start and was given a bad time for awhile, but was a very good teacher. Earl Malone would sneeze and wake up all three rooms! Of course, he didn't intend to!! Edna Lyle could out run any body at school, Ruth Pierce could whip most of the boys. Bob and Dink Hall came here fresh out of some boys school and what the other kids couldn't think of, they certainly could!

I walked two and a half miles to school which was only a short distance as many walked five or more, including the Talbots, the Garrards, the Bill Johnsons, and the Johnnie Johnsons, Dave and Nora Buckridge and many more. Kids are badly abused if they have to walk one half mile now.

What about sanitary conditions? Two outhouses separated by a high board fence, a water pail with a tin dipper which everybody used, later a well with a long handled pump. One would work the pump while another would cup their unwashed hands and drink while getting spattered from the overflow.

Mr. Keeling had a peach orchard at the end of "Sears Lane" as we called it then. Many of his peaches were harvested after dark! Many pranks were played around the neighborhood. Stealing was practically nil, there was no vandalism or destruction of peoples property. Cabins in the area were left with bedding and food, doors were never locked and the latch string was always out if you were hungry or in trouble. Things are much different now. In many, many ways the good old days were much better.

JOHN ELLIOTT FAMILY

by Tom Dunbar in 1993

John Elliott was born in Lynchburg, Virginia in 1856. Laura Keays was born in Elinorah, Missouri in 1865. John and Laura were married in 1880.

To this marriage were born 7 children: Homer in 1883, Bessie in 1885, Vista in 1888, Hazel in 1895, Jess in 1899, Willie (died as an infant), and Freddy (died as an infant).

They moved to a homestead near the mouth of Mill Creek from Rathdrum, Idaho, in 1887

John Elliott died on December 11, 1900, at age 44.

Laura Elliott married Carl Bertelson on May 20, 1918. They operated an orchard and dairy until retiring in 1940. Laura died in 1943 and Carl in 1948.

Laura was my grandmother and I stayed with her when my brothers were born. It was always a pleasure to go stay at Grandmother's. Their home was always a gathering place for all her children and grandchildren. Many Christmases and Thanksgivings were spent there. Their home was always open for their friends and neighbors and the hospitality was unexcelled.

ENGLERS CAME WEST

By Bill Engler, in 1997

My parents, Mr. and Mrs. Frank Engler, with their 3 year old son, Walter, came to Montana in 1908, from Orchard Park, New York.

My father worked for Harper & Beard Logging Company. He hewed railroad ties for them. In 1908, they homesteaded in the Dominic district, east of Corvallis. It cost $8.00 to register for a homestead and $2.50 per acre for the land. It was dry land and their principal crop was wheat. My father also worked for the newly formed Forest Service at the Butterfly Ranger Station, up Willow Creek.

There were quite a few settlers up east of the Buttes, so they formed a school district (Dominic). My brother, Walter, went to school there for one year and my mother was clerk of the school board.

The farming was all done with horses and the transportation was by horse and buggy. My mother and Walter would take the horse and buggy down to Corvallis to buy our groceries. They most always stopped at the Jim Rawlins ranch to rest as that was about half way mark.

My brother Bob was born up on the homestead in 1912. The people up there had to cope with many hardships and I'm sure a new baby just added to this.

In 1913, my father sold out and moved down to Corvallis. He continued farming and rented land to raise potatoes, cabbage, and squash. He hauled these by team and wagon to the railroad at Woodside. Harry Thrailkill bought most of the produce and shipped it to Butte, or back east. Also, Dad would work at most anything he could get and was foreman of the Corvallis Road district for a number of years.

Corvallis was quite a large town, two general stores (Bay's and Bowden's), three churches, one hotel, a barber shop, grade and high schools, bank, cheese factory, garage, drug store, dentist, Odd Fellows Lodge, and three barns. It was a friendly town and community. Everyone knew each other and they were always ready to help each other when a disaster occurred. There was no fire department, but when a fire occurred everybody came to help. They would remove the contents out of the house, then the bucket brigade would start. Someone would pump water from their well, and people would stand in line passing the bucket from one to another and get the water to the fire.

I was born in 1915, in Corvallis. My sister, Dorothy, was born in 1918, so our lives and the Great Events of the world, our country and Corvallis all meshed together. We all attended Corvallis schools, starting at the old schools where the first three grades were. We drank from a tin dipper and the toilets were outdoors.

The Corvallis Bank went broke in April 1924, and most of the people lost their money. It was quite a shock to the community and several old people committed suicide as they were despondent from losing their life savings. One of them was a good friend of mine.

Another event that made an impact on our lives was the loss of our high school to the fire in 1930. We went to school in the old Equity Building, and the grades went to other places in town.

The stock market crash came in 1929, caused the Great Depression. People were losing their farms, there was no work in the factories, there were soup lines in the cities, and no jobs. The election of President Roosevelt was the best thing to happen in 1932. He had many good programs to help the people to get work and recover from the Depression. He was a good leader and had good men to implement his programs. One program was the CCC, in which I enrolled. It took the young people off the streets and gave them all a job. They paid $30.00 a month, $5.00 of which went to the kids — and $25.00 was sent home to their parents. We also got clothes and board. President Roosevelt created Social Security, a work program called the Work Projects Administration (WPA), the Tennessee Valley Authority (TVA) which is a series of dams and hydroelectric power, the Rural Electrification Administration (REA), and many other programs that are still in effect today. Perhaps the most outstanding still with us today are the REA and TVA.

The World War II, also made a very large impact on our lives. Everyone was patriotic and all came to the aid of our country by serving in the Army, Navy, or Marines. Also, people went into construction jobs, built ships and war supplies and bases in the Pacific, Alaska, the Aleutian Islands and the South Pacific.

President Roosevelt didn't have any Political Action Committee (PAC) money to get elected. He used the radio to present his fireside chats with the people. He had several slogans such as "Every dog a bone, every kid an ice cream cone," and "Happy days are here again".

Corvallis was a sports minded town. The people supported their teams, and football, basketball, and track were the main school events. We always had a town team in baseball and we played Hamilton, Victor, Stevensville, Ronan, and went to Salmon, Idaho, occasionally. We have seen Corvallis School in Class C, then Class B, and now is going to Class A.

The hunting and fishing were always good. There wasn't much crime committed. There was only one Sheriff's Deputy for Ravalli County. He didn't get to Corvallis very often, so the parents took care of their kids problems.

The roads in Corvallis were all dirt, and in the spring of the year when they thawed out they were muddy and hard to get around on with the teams and wagons. In those days, the road department was divided into districts, and my father was hired to take care of the Corvallis District. The bridges and culverts were all made out of timber. They also had road graders for grading the roads and plowing the snow in the winter. They were powered by a 4-horse team. Nick Blindaur was the county road boss, and later, it was Homer Benson.

The railroad was on the west side of the river, and the depot was in Woodside. It was later moved to the east side. The railroads were constructed with horses and fresnoes. The building of the Big Ditch was a boom to the valley. It provided water for many farms. Also, there were orchards and fruit. The Summerdale orchards were just east of Corvallis.

Looking back over my life, Corvallis has been a nice place to live and raise a family. The people are friendly, and we have a lot of recreation in the beautiful Bitter Root Valley.

THE LEVI ESS FAMILY

by Levi Ess, Victor, Montana

I was born in Plains Valley, then called Horse Plains, in Missoula County — which is now Sanders County. I started to school when I was 7 years old. The school was across the Clark Fork River from where we lived. There were no bridges then, so I had to go to school in a rowboat. My first teacher was Miss Jessie Davis. I still have the report card she gave to me with her picture on it!

My mother came to the Bitter Root Valley in 1868, from Kansas, in a covered wagon and she didn't beat me much as I came in 1900, but only part of the way in a covered wagon. My folks left Plains on November 7, and when we got to Ravalli it was snowing a little. Mr. Gibbons, who had a sawmill there let us sleep in his barn. That was good, otherwise we would have been a bunch of popsicles. Next morning it was two degrees below zero, and there was a thirty mile an hour wind. Mother and four kids got onto the train and came on to Victor. John Skaggs, Arthur, and my father brought teams through.

We moved into my Granddad's house and I went to school at the Pleasant View School, which was only three-fourths of a mile to walk to. That was wonderful! The teacher was Miss Butler, a wonderful little gal. Then my Father got a place about four miles North and West of Fairplay School on Dutch Hill. There I went to school for 7 terms and had four teachers. They were: F. Clifton; J. Jones; G. Wold; and Miss Baily and C. Jackson. I sure enjoyed going to school at Fairplay. I never had a teacher I didn't like, and all the people were my friends and still are. I never had an enemy. A stranger to me is a friend I haven't met. I have gone by where the old school house used to stand, but it is gone now and so are the Dutch. I met many nice people where I used to live.

THE FIERCE FAMILY

Harrie Edwin Fierce was born November 14, 1885, in Castana, Iowa. He graduated from Castana High School, and soon after moved with his father to Wyndmere, North Dakota, where the family worked together on a large wheat farm. He did some house painting as a sideline and played on the local baseball team. It was here that he met and married **Mary Ethel Duffy** (1885-01967). In 1910, they moved to Helmville, Montana, where his father was Manager of the Day and Hanson Ranch (the "Company" ranch). Harrie was foreman, and for the next nine years, supervised the crews who worked the cattle, sheep, hay and grain. During this time, he planned for the future by buying in 1915, the Sig Chaffin place at Corvallis, Montana. It was leased to Jim Lupton until March 1, 1920, when the family moved to this new home. **Besides Harrie and Ethel, there were four children; Francis Myron** (1908-1986), **Mary Elmore (Black)** (1910-?), **Knowlton Edward** (1912-1981), **and Frederick Sterling** (1916-1944).

Harrie bought the adjoining acreage to the north and land across the road from George Schwab, so had about 200 acres of usable and pasture land in the "Heart of the Bitter Root Valley".

The homestead cabin of Mr. and Mrs. James Everly, who lived in the Corvallis community for over half a century, in 1889. This cabin is still standing at the Bob Smyth ranch on the Eastside Highway.

His first big crops were potatoes, hay and sugar beets. He also had a small dairy. Later, he had a band of sheep, and enlarged the dairy enough to put in a milking barn with milking machines. His trips to the Corvallis Creamery to deliver the milk, and to pick up some groceries, were a daily routine after Barney Smyth retired from his creamery route.

Ethel had chickens, geese, and a large garden. Ethel taught school for five years before her marriage. She liked club work and was active for years in the Corvallis Woman's Club, serving several terms as President. She also belonged to the Corvallis Grange. She and Miss Hoyendahl started a well-child clinic, where mothers could bring their children for a free check-up, and for medical care. It became an important part of the county health service. Support for the project was the Food Cupboard, raffled off at the Ravalli County Fair each year. Ethel liked acting, and gave "readings" at club and Grange programs, and also took part in some home talent productions.

The children attended the Corvallis Schools and the Federated Church. Harrie was elected to the school board and served for twenty-five years, part of that time as Chairman. When his youngest son, Fred, played basketball he became an ardent "Bluedevil" fan.

A ten-acre plot on the Northeast corner of Cobb Lane (now Popham Lane) was sold to Ethel's mother and stepfather, **Mary Jane and Myron Knowlton Sargent.** They built a small home and lived there until Mary Jane's death in 1927. Some more land was trimmed from the farm by a boundary adjustment between the Schwab and Felix places.

After Harrie's death, Ethel and Francis kept up the farm for several years, but Ethel finally sold it to Russell (Bum) Lairy, keeping a small lot and the "little house" for herself and Francis.

THE FOLEY FAMILY

JOHN M. FOLEY was born in 1882, and came from New York State. His bride, ELLEN, was born in 1890, and came from Montana. They were married in Butte, Montana, on December 31, 1908. They came to the Bitter Root Valley in 1910, when Mr. Foley was named foreman of the Bitterroot Stock Farm.

Later, they purchased their own farm southeast of Hamilton in the Grantsdale area. In winter months, Mr. Foley went to Butte to work for Mr. Thee Hennessy. His job there was driving an 8-horse team on an ore wagon. In the spring he would return to the Bitterroot and his farm where he raised potatoes. Then he got started raising cattle and even later raised entirely cattle and saddle horses. He broke these saddle horses for riding. Cattle and horses were what he loved to raise and be around.

This union produced nine children: Elizabeth (Keith); Ella (Culbertson); Harriet (Tell); Mildred (Curtis); John; William; Marion (Anderson); and 2 infant daughters who died in infancy. Elizabeth was born in Butte, and the remainder of their family were all raised on the ranch.

Ella and Harriet became school teachers and both taught at the Jefferson School on 5th street in Hamilton. Elizabeth was a clerk for J. C. Penny Co., and Mildred was a beautician in Hamilton from 1937 until retirement in 1990. Marion, the youngest daughter, served in the U. S. Army, later becoming a teacher and also deeply involved in church work in California.

The two sons followed their father. They stayed in the valley, with their own families, and continued in the cattle business. Bill stayed on the home ranch and John has a ranch on Hamilton Heights.

Mr. and Mrs. Foley have a lane named after them. It is a lane connecting Skalkaho Road and Fish Hatchery Road, named Foley Lane.

WILLIAM JOHN FULLERTON

"William John Fullerton was an industrious and capable citizen who owned the respect of all who knew him", according to the obituary which also named him "as a remarkable man". He was born on February 12, 1857, in Milwaukee, Wisconsin, and at the age of 14, accompanied his parents to Toronto, Canada, where he made his home until he came to Hamilton, Montana. While in Canada, he met and married Annie James Stewart who was a native of Cincinnati, Ohio. They were wed on August 3, 1882. Mr. Fullerton came to Hamilton in 1905, to accept a position as head of the plumbing department of Marcus Daly's Valley Mercantile Company. His family joined him after he established a home for them at the end of South Second street in Hamilton.

In 1908, the youngest of the couples thirteen children, Theodore Hamilton Fullerton, was born. Theodore was their only child to be born in Hamilton, Montana. In 1910, William purchased the plumbing and sheet metal business from the Valley Mercantile interests of the Daly family. He continued the business which was later operated by his two sons, William, Jr., and Theodore. In 1953, Theodore bought out the interest of William, Jr., and became the sole owner. At that time, the name was changed to Fullerton's Plumbing and Heating. The business was expanded to include many major construction projects throughout Montana. In 1967, Theodore was killed in an auto accident, leaving his widow and four sons. The ownership of the business was transferred to his widow, Elizabeth (see Brooks, Barlow) and later bought by their oldest son, Dennis. Eventually, the business and the building were sold and the business re-located at 401 West

Main. Mabel, the widow of William, Jr., died in 1995, at the age of 98. Elizabeth continues to live in Hamilton.

William John Fullerton was a resident of Hamilton for 41 years after his arrival in 1905. He died at the age of 89, in 1946, having been in ill health for a number of years. For many years, he maintained a hobby of raising fine chickens which he took delight in exhibiting at the Ravalli County Fair. Before coming to Montana, he was noted in Toronto for his prowess as a foot racer. He was a member of the Episcopal Church, as was his wife. In 1932, Mr. and Mrs. Fullerton returned to Toronto to visit children, relatives and friends, and there they celebrated their Golden Wedding Anniversary. After returning to Hamilton, Mrs. Fullerton died the following year (1933). They are both at rest in Riverview Cemetery just West of Hamilton.

Two granddaughters, one grandson, one great-grandson and a daughter-in-law still live in the Bitter Root Valley. They are as follows: Lillian Peterson (daughter of Harvey), Zoe Wetzsteon (daughter of Margaret), James Hartson (son of Evelyn), Steve Fullerton (grandson of William, Sr.), and Betty Fullerton (widow of Theodore).

THE JOHN T. GARRARD FAMILY

(as of 1974)

John T. Garrard was born in north Ogden, Utah, on December 2, 1865. Not much is known of his boyhood. After coming to the Bitterroot Valley, his folks owned the place now owned by the Ravalli County Fair. They sold the farm for thirty ($30.00) dollars.

Jane A. Miller was born April 10, 1875, in the Cherokee Strip in Kansas. Before her family left Kansas, they saw Jesse James and Frank James, they were operating in an area near their home. On their way west, the family met Buffalo Bill Cody and Wild Bill Hickock. The pair was sent out west to kill some of the thousands of buffalo that had wrecked a Union Pacific train. Their wagon was held up for several months in Utah because they had run out of funds to finish their trip. It was here that they heard about Montana, so they decided to come here. There were Indians all the way, they were all friendly. The family came down the Bitterroot Valley and found their new home near Victor, which consisted of 160 acres. They traded a Spencer rifle and thirty dollars and took over their new home.

John (Jack) Garrard and Jane A. Miller were married August 13, 1890. They lived in the Victor area and Jack worked for the farmers around Victor

Tim Garrard, their first son, was born on October 3, 1891. At this time the family lived west of Victor, near Sweathouse Creek. The family moved south of Victor in the river bottom now. Here, on August 9, 1893, their second son, George, arrived. On November 14, 1895, a third son was born, John William. At this time the Curlew Mine was in its boom, and Jack moved his family to the mine housing area and worked in the mines. It was here that Tim attended his first year of school. The mining company had built a grade school for those working for them. From here the Garrard family moved to a farm west of Woodside. On June 28, 1898, Nancy L., a daughter was born. The Garrards lived here and raised their family. Tim, George, William and Nancy got their schooling by walking, riding horse back or driving a horse and buggy to the Dutch Hill School.

Tim married Anna Aichele on August 10, 1819. Tim passed away January 15, 1963 and John T. Garrard passed on May 4, 1920. William married Cora Miller on November 26, 1926. William died on October 13, 1973. George married Mildred Boyer on February 14, 1928. George passed away on November 25, 1972. Nancy married Myron Davies on September 5, 1929, and in 1974 made her home in Castle Rock, Washington. Jane A. Garrard passed away in January of 1944.

AUGUST HENRY GEYER

by Helen Jean Kress Wilson

The year was 1875; Ulysses S. Grant was President of the United States and Utah was a territory where families were passing through on their way to settle the Wild West.

Such was the case of **August Henry Geyer,** an immigrant from Germany. He met **Martha Lunicia Busenbark** in Happy Hollow, Box Elder County, Utah Territory, and **they married there on February 10, 1875.** August was 27, and Martha 19.

In 1885, the family came to the Bitter Root Valley via stagecoach and ended up on a farm south of Darby. But, August was a businessman, and in 1886, leased a boarding house from the Henry Grant family in Grantsdale. Then in 1890, August Geyer was picked to help plat the new town of Hamilton, and he chose one of the best lots for his new boardinghouse he named "Geyer House". He also served as Justice of the Peace in Hamilton. In 1892, he traded the boarding house for a piece of land at Victor where he farmed. If you go into the Farmers State Bank, behind the teller windows is a very large photo of the Victor Schoolhouse. Two of the girls in that photo are **daughters of August and Martha. Their names are Marie Pearl Geyer-Kress and Jessie Claire Geyer-Carey**.

On a very hot day in July 1900, two farmers got into a fight over irrigation water. August Geyer ended up getting hit on the head with a shovel. The following account appeared in the Ravalli Republican newspaper,

The Geyer House, Hamilton, Montana, Territory. Built in 1890 by August Henry Geyer. Traded in 1892 to the Messer Family for a farm in Victor, Montana.

dated July 20, 1900:

"A case from Victor was tried in Justice Morris' court last Monday, by a jury, the case growing out of a scrap between parties named Jergenson and Geyer, in which the latter is said to have gotten the worst of it. Jergenson afterwards had Geyer arrested for disturbing the peace. The jury found the latter, "NOT GUILTY", and assessed the costs to the complaining witness."

Two days later, Geyer disappeared, and family members speculated he had amnesia from the hit on the head with the shovel. There was no trace of August Geyer until a letter written to his daughter, Jessie Claire, dated April 25, 1901, states that he had bought a farm adjoining Jake Sorensen's ranch in the East Fork Valley. Family members have never been able to determine where August Geyer died, or when. Martha remained on the farm in Victor until her death on December 10, 1917, and is buried in what is called Kresston Cemetery on the Kress ranch West of Hamilton, along with seven other members of the Geyer-Kress family.

JOHN EDWARD (ED) GIBBONS

Ed Gibbons was born July 14, 1876, in Monroe County, Missouri into the family of Thomas Gibbons. In 1879 the family of five children left by railroad for the end of the line in the Dakotas. From there they continued by ox train to Butte where Thomas had a brother in the wood business. From this brother they acquired a team and wagon and continued on to the Bitter Root. The rivers at Missoula and in the Bitter Root had to be forded, as there were no bridges. They wintered in Stevensville in 1879 and in the spring moved to Corvallis. There, his father Thomas filed on a homestead and built two cabins on eighty acres, just south of the Glenn Chaffin or now the Connolly residence on Willow Creek Road. Thomas then fenced ten acres "coyote proof" so they could raise some calves, chickens and pigs. In 1880, Ed's father returned to Butte to work in the mines as a carpenter until 1882 when he returned to Corvallis.

Ed recalls the first school as a log cabin with a sod roof located west of the present school. However when he started school it was a frame building and in a different location. He took many lickings from the teachers. His first teacher was Sue Jones. She then taught several years in a two- room school building in the 1880s located where the present grade school stands. Some of the families living in Corvallis when his family arrived were: Jacob Goff and family including Bently Goff; Elijah Chaffin and family including Mose and Frank; John Slack and family (they lived where the Slack house is located on the Teller Wildlife Refuge); W.E. Lear, father of Paul and Jamie; John Wood, father of George and Doc Woods and Lulu Brooks; Josh Woods, father of Addie Wood and Daisy Goff; Lyman Blodgett, father of Mrs. Vic (Clara) Shults; Robert Meyers a blacksmith, father of Mrs. Lee Simmons; Gilbert Simmons father of Lee, Ole and Mason; James Barr, father of Josie Cochran and Mrs. J. Q. Adams; R. Parkhurst.

Ed says in 1886, when he was ten years old, that one night at midnight his father awakened him and told him his mother was very sick and he would have ride to Stevensville to get Dr. Gwinn. His father had a tough bronco saddled so Ed started out. It was a moonlight night and as he was going through the trees north of Corvallis he thought the moon cast shadows were Indians chasing him. Hence he really laid it on the bronco and got to the doctor. Coming back he rode with the doctor, trailing his mount. They arrived back early in the morning.

Ed was married to Louise Johnson July 18 1897. She passed away in April 1949. They were parents of one son, Gerald, who was killed in a construction accident in 1965. In 1952 he married Hazel Boyer.

Ed was a resident of Corvallis for eighty-eight years and saw many changes in the community, some of which he had a hand in. For example he helped haul rock from the Soft Rock area to Corvallis for the construction of the buildings, one of which now houses the Corvallis Drug store. The structures were built for Dr. Charles Thornton and Guy Cochran. During the building the contractors built an incline plane in order to barrow the rocks up to where needed. This ramp stretched across the street almost to the Bowden or later Bay's store, so that there was barely enough room for a team and wagon to pass.

In the 1930s he worked for the Ravalli County Road Department and was eventually the Road Boss for the Corvallis District. In those days, the roads were mainly gravel and most of the work was done with a shovel. A farmer could hire out himself wagon and team for two dollars an hour and have the sum deducted from his taxes.

There were many stories associated with Ed, as one might expect as he spent 87 years in Corvallis, and I'll let you in on three of them. Ed's father had built the Methodist Church in Corvallis and remained quite active in the church activities. On this particular occasion they were having a big picnic for some visiting church dignitaries. Ed and a buddy were in a devilish mood and stole all the watermelons that had been accumulated for this picnic. Of course this upset the congregation and a reward was offered for the recovery of said watermelons, but this did not produce any results. Sometime a day or so later Ed's dad was showing some of these visiting notables about his farm. Upon showing them his root cellar the missing watermelons were discovered. I did not hear what happened to Ed and his buddy.

On another occasion Ed was working in one of the local logging camps and the hands were in the habit of teasing the Chinese cook by the name of Wong by doing such things as nailing his shoes to the floor. They decided to call a truce and told Wong they would not tease him any more. Wong replied, "Velly nice no tease Wong. Wong no pee in soup anymore."

Ed also had a filling station just across the street from the Methodist Church to the south and following his marriage to Hazel Boyer he started going to church. However, after a spell he told the congregation he was not coming to church anymore, because none of the congregation bought any gasoline from him.

He retired in 1950 and passed away in October 1967 at age ninety-one.

DAVID CLARK GRAY FAMILY

David Clark Gray came to Deer Lodge, Montana, from Missouri. Emma Louella Mallory came from Illinois.

David and Emma met in Deer Lodge and were married there. Their first son, Clark, was also born there in 1891. Mr. Gray was a butcher and delivered meat. He sold his butcher shop and bought a dairy farm, later selling the farm and moving to the Bitter Root in 1899, with their five children.

They purchased 160 acres on the Westside from Mr. Rennick. Henry Grove had been the original homesteader of this property. The family lived in a small log house until 1910, when a larger house was built. This house is still standing, and lived in.

The children walked to Canyon Creek School which had grades on through seventh grade, then went to Hamilton schools for eighth grade and high school. The Canyon Creek School only had one room to begin with, and later a second room was added. This building later became the first Public Health Laboratory in the Bitter Root Valley.

The children were: Ethelyn, Clark, Edith, Fern, Ernest, and Ruth.

Clark married Irene and they stayed on the farm and had an orchard. After many years they sold the farm and moved to Hamilton. He worked for Montana Liquor Store.

Ethelyn married and remained in the Bitter Root.

Edith went to California and became a milliner.

Ernest went to California and worked for California Electric.

Ruth married Miles Romney, Jr. They lived in Washington, D.C., where he worked for the IRS. They returned to Hamilton where he published the Western News, was a State Senator, and a Constitutional Convention Delegate. Ruth still lives in the family home. She is 96 years old.

GRIMES FAMILY

As told to Bob Talbot by Edward F. Grimes, In February 1998

William H. Grimes was born in St. Cloud, Minnesota, on March 29, 1872. He died in Hamilton, Montana on March 13, 1944.

William first came to the Bitter Root Valley in 1909, to work for the O. W. Kerr Company at Charlos Heights. He came from Glenwood, Minnesota, with **his wife,** the former **Anna Briese**.

William and Anna lived at Charlos Heights for two years where their first child, a son, died at birth. They then moved to 519 N. 3rd Street in Hamilton, where **a son, Edward F. Grimes, was born on May 21, 1913.** While still living in Hamilton, Mr. Grimes bought and sold real estate. He at one time owned over 200 lots in Hamilton. He worked in the Ravalli County Assessor's office and was under-sheriff for four years.

Having purchased the "old Gibb's place" on the southwest corner of Hamilton Heights Road and Wilcox Lane, William operated it for 17 years, until 1943, when he sold out to Frank Mihara. In 1931, while on this ranch, **the son, Edward F. Grimes,** bought 17 guinea pigs from Jim Pickerill for $11.00, and started raising them for sale to the Rocky Mountain Lab (U. S. Public Health Service) in Hamilton. Ed continued to sell these animals to the Lab until 1937, when the Lab began raising their own. They hired Ed to take care of them. With the exception of four years spent in the Navy during World War II, and time spent going to college, Ed continued his employment with the RM Lab, as their Animal Husbandman, until he retired in 1971.

Edward F. Grimes married Kay Weimer, who came to Hamilton from eastern Montana to work at the Rocky Mountain Laboratory. They were married in 1941, and at present they are living at home in Hamilton.

HAGEMAN FAMILY

The Hageman name was usually associated with a colorful character by the name of Sid and many scattered Hageman owned lots and structures.

Ernest O. Hageman was the father. He was born in Wisconsin in 1873 and came to the Bitter Root in 1896. He first settled in Stevensville and opened a photography studio. Two years later, he moved his studio to Hamilton where he remained until he died in 1944. He was well known for his scenic photos of the Bitter Root Valley. In 1900, he married Louise Juliana. They had a son, Sidney, and two daughters, Irene Louise Sterner of Missoula and Harriet Cline of Long Beach, California.

Louise was born in 1870 in Wisconsin. She became a shrewd businesswoman and acquired much real estate and was one of Hamilton's wealthiest women. She died in 1954.

Sid was born in 1902. He was a hard worker and accumulated a large amount of real estate until he owned 30 lots in the city and other holdings outside of the city. He also liked a good time. In 1958, he married Georgia Gerleman Biggs at the Rainbow Bar. Miles Romney wrote an article in the Western News on April 3, 1958, about the wedding, stating in part: "after the wedding the judge was packaged home via taxi and the ante-bellum festivities started around a large bouquet of Four Roses." The bride in years past had been engaged in growing strawberries and selling strawberry plants, hence she was known as the Strawberry Queen. Unfortunately, she died three months later and he died about a year later.

Three years later, to settle his estate, 13 parcels of property were sold at auction. They netted $26,440. This gives you some idea of property values at that time.

JOSEPH AND EMMA HAIGH AND FAMILY

JOSEPH HAIGH was born at Alma, Wisconsin, on February 22, 1877, and was one of 18 children, nine boys and nine girls, born to John and Mary Haigh. Joseph grew to manhood in Wisconsin and came to the Bitter Root on March 17, 1899, at the age of 22 years. He worked for the famous Daly racing stable until it was disbanded upon the death of Marcus Daly. He

Joseph and Emma (Koepp) Haigh. Married January 5, 1904.

then went to Florence, MT, where he was employed by Swan Johnson. When Swan came to the Hamilton area to take charge of a portion of the Daly Stock Farm, Joseph Haigh came with him. One of the Daly ranches was named after Swan Johnson and it was not long before Haigh was named foreman of the Johnson ranch. At the end of 1903, Joseph returned to Wisconsin where he married Emma Ida Koepp, the sweetheart left behind when he first came west. She returned to the Bitter Root with him. (Emma Koepp was born in Nelson, Wisconsin, on November 30, 1882.)

Three children were born to this union: Irene Verna born on October 29, 1904, on the Bitter Root Stock farm and married Lawrence Applebury on February 6, 1927; Ruth; and Herbert.

In 1907, Mr. and Mrs. Haigh left the Bitter Root to return to their native Wisconsin, thinking of relocating there. But, the Bitter Root had grown to be their favorite spot on earth, so they returned here and Joseph became a foreman of a crew engaged in building part of the "Big Ditch". When that job was completed, he bought a ranch on the Skalkaho, situated between the Hauswirth and Shuland places. Later this property was sold and the family moved to the Doran addition with Joseph going to work for a number of years at the ACM mill, then operating west of Hamilton on the Bitter Root River.

In 1915, he bought a cigar store from M. L. Kelly. This store was located on North Second Street, where the Rainbow Bar is now situated. He ran it until 1922, when he sold the business and bought a farm west of Grantsdale, which he operated for three years. About this time "Bud" Frogge died, and Joseph purchased his cigar store which was located in the building now occupied by the Signal Bar. After operating in this location for several years, Joseph moved to the former First National Bank building, which has since been known to everyone in the community as "Haigh's". Mr. Haigh bought the north half of the building in 1935, and the rest of it in 1950. He sold it to his son, Herb, and son-in-law, Lawrence Applebury, on March 25, 1952. He had retired from active management of the business in 1946, devoting himself to his family, his extensive flower garden and his lodge work.

Mrs. Joseph Haigh, after a number of years of illness, died on September 3, 1939. She was buried in the Riverview cemetery at Hamilton.

In the 1950's, the "Liberty" theatre stood just to the south of Haigh's bar, and patrons of the theatre would stand on the sidewalk outside, near an open window into Haigh's, and buy their popcorn to take into the theatre. The smell of this warm, succulent popcorn tempted anyone and everyone near this old landmark.

CHARLES EDWIN HARTLEY FAMILY

by June Hartley Howe

Charles Edwin Hartley was born February 25, 1878, in Marshfield, Missouri. After graduating from Southwest Baptist College in Bolivar, Missouri, he taught school for two years. Since boyhood, he had dreamed of going to Montana and his dream was realized in 1901 when he boarded a train for Missoula, Montana.

After spending a year in Missoula and two years in Dillon, he moved to Hamilton in 1905, and bought the Chris Sandven Laundry on South Second street. In 1908, he built a two story brick building on the north corner of Main and First Street (now the Citizens State Bank location) and established a modernly equipped laundry which he operated for 44 years. In 1946, he sold his Bitter Root Laundry to Glen Mitchell.

Mr. Hartley was intensely interested and very active in the civic, fraternal, and religious life of the community. He served as President of both the Chamber of Commerce and the Lions Club. He held many offices of the Masonic Fraternity — Master of Ionic Lodge No. 38 A.F.&A.M., high priest of the Hamilton Chapter of Royal Arch Masons, and was a member of the Algeria Shrine, Helena, Montana.

He was an active member of the American Baptist Church, being instrumental in the merging of his church and the United Methodist in 1931. Both he and Mrs. Hartley were longtime members of their church choir. Mr. Hartley was chairman of the local Chautauqua Association, which was successful in getting Hamilton placed on the Chautauqua circuit during the 1910-1920 era.

For many years, Charles Hartley was active in Republican politics and was a valued director of the Ravalli County Bank.

In 1905, Charles Hartley married Anna Svoboda in Missoula. Anna was born on July 8, 1883, in Prague, Bohemia, and the following year her mother brought her and her two sisters to America to join their father.

Anna Hartley spent much time assisting her husband in the operation of their laundry. She held the office of Worthy Matron of Leona Chapter of Eastern Star. She was an exceptionally fine seamstress and her needlework was exquisite. Also, she loved to care for her flower garden.

A daughter, Zelma Jeanne, was born to the couple on February 25, 1905, which was her father's birthday. Another daughter, June Evelyn, was born on June 10, 1911.

The first family home in Hamilton was an apartment at the Ladd Flats, now the Vintage Villa. In 1910, they purchased a home then located where the high school now stands on South Fifth street. In 1920, they purchased the house across the street at 206 South Fifth, which the Hartley family has

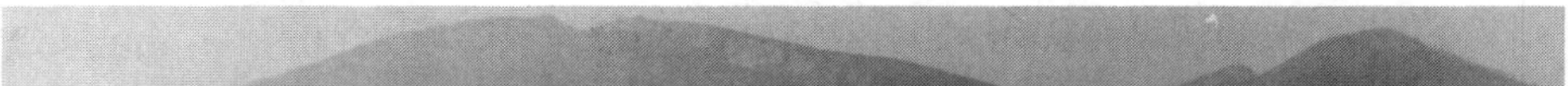

Bitter Root Steam Laundry, 1908. Located on the northwest corner of Highway 93 and Main Street, Hamilton, Montana.

continuously occupied to the present time.

Charles Hartley died November 3, 1958, at the age of 80. Anna Hartley passed away on March 11, 1979, at the age of 95. Both were interned at Hamilton's Riverview Cemetery.

Family members surviving are daughters Zelma and June; June's husband, John Howe, Jr. and their children, Jeanne Howe Hargett of Hamilton and Robert Hartley Howe of Washington D. C.; also, two great-grandsons, Christopher and William Hargett.

THE JOHN HAUF FAMILY

by Jane Hauf

My grandfather Hauf was born and raised at Eichetadl, Germany. His name was John Hauf. He owned and operated a store and armory, where all kinds of guns were sold. He had the required education necessary in those times. He was married to my grandmother in the 1850's. Her name was Theresia Schloss Mitler. She was born and raised in a castle, Schloss, Von Schloss, still standing, used as a fort in the wars. She died when my father was two years old. Later, John Hauf married her sister, who raised Dad and a family of her own.

My father was born December 21, 1860, served in the military academy, and came to the United States by boat when he was eighteen. Landed in New York City, later went to Johnstown, PA, where he mastered the English language, took French and Latin later. He became an engineer on the railroad, followed the occupation until coming to Anaconda, where he was employed on the concentrator of the A.C.M. Company.

While he made many trips to the Bitter Root, in time he bought four ranches, one at the entrance of Darby, the old Buhl place, the George Bender place (for which he paid $500.00 and the ranch he later lived on until his death. He took over the homestead rights from the Scholl family, proved up on it and made it his home and never went back to the business world.

He improved his ranch, diversified farming with a 41 acre orchard, raised hay and stock and truck gardened. As improvements were made, orchards planted, more and more hired help was needed. He took in five boys who weren't his own and raised them until they went out on their own. Work increased, it became the bread basket of his neighborhood, as he gave work to all men, boys, and women.

He was married on December 29, 1890, in Alamosa, Colorado, to Margaret Whitelon Smith, came back to Montana on January 7, 1891, to spend the rest of his life on the place he loved. To them were born five children: Theresia, Jane, Arthur, Rupurt, and John Jr.

Both my Grandfather and my Grandmother Smith were born in Mount

Vernon, Virginia, in 1816. Grandma's name was Lucy Lebecca Winter. Grandfather Smith's name was Daniel Deleancel Smith. He had three brothers, a doctor, a judge, and a preacher. Grandpa Smith started to school when he was 10 years old, never missed a day until he was nearly 13, an ardent reader and retained what he read, taught others in his neighborhood, later became a Clerk of Court in Lancaster, Missouri, a position he held for 35 years. They married in 1840, and became the parents of nine children — girls and 4 boys, of which my mother was the youngest.

My mother graduated from the local schools (Missouri), went to Normal for 2 years, became clerk in her father's office until she moved to Colorado to teach school. At that time she was paid $45.00 a month, good wages then. She lived and boarded with Jennie Cole, a friend from whose house she was later married. Ranch life was a new experience for her. She conquered it, raised her family.

Dad died of gangrene on April 26, 1939. Mother continued to live on the ranch until her death on March 23, 1949. Both are buried in the Corvallis Cemetery.

Our Grandfather and Grandmother later came to the Bitter Root and dad gave them what is now known as the Bender place. We walked across Mill Creek to visit them often.

My father donated the land to have the Fair Play School built. I think my mother was on the school board at one time. All of us went to this school. Theresia and I later went to Sacred Heart Academy in Missoula for some time. I took piano lessons and learned to do "fancy work". After Arthur finished school, he went to Mechanical school in Spokane. Rupert went one year to the University after graduating from Corvallis High School, and then to Montana State College for awhile. Johnie went to a Portland Mechanical school after he graduated from Corvallis.

One of the greatest aids to farming was the irrigation systems that were used. Dad had "Hauf Lake" on Mill Creek, which supplied us with water when "high water" was over.

There were amusing things that happened. There were always black bears in the orchard in the fall. Earl Malone caught a small one and John Garrod raised it.

Theresia married John Young, a friend of Roy Pierson's from Chicago. John helped plan and build the "club house" at Woodside. After their marriage, the Young's went to Chicago where John was born and had lived for many years. They had one daughter. Theresia died of cancer on July 31, 1954, and was buried in Chicago. John Jr. was killed outright in an auto accident, May 21, 1972, and buried in Yakima, WA. Survivors are Jane and Rupert in Hamilton, and Arthur in Missoula.

HAWKER FAMILY

by Wilma Whitesitt Rasmussen

John Henry Hawker was born November 17, 1852, in Marion County, Wisconsin. He grew up in Missouri and married Virginia (Jenny) Caroline Burch. They had four children: Emmett A. Hawker, Alice Hawker Ward, Myrtle Hawker Ward, and Minnie Hawker Southmayd.

Jenny died of pneumonia in 1890. Her sister, Mary Elizabeth (Lizzie) Burch Pond, later became John H. Hawker's second wife. Lizzie had lost two husbands in Missouri. The first one, Mr. Swigert died of an illness. He had fathered one son, Burch Swigert. Her second husband was a Mr. Pond, who fathered two daughters, Lula and Grace Pond. He was accidentally shot in a hunting accident. Lizzie, then a widow with three children, decided to move to Montana in 1888, as her brother had moved here earlier. She homesteaded on Gird Creek, east of Hamilton.

John Hawker and his four children moved to Montana in 1890. Shortly thereafter, he married Lizzie in May 1891. He went to work on the Gilchrist Ranch and Lizzie became the ranch cook. Their son, John E. Hawker, was born August 8, 1892. When young John was 9 months old, they sold the Gird Creek homestead to Marcus Daly and it became part of the Bitter Root Stock Farm. They then rented a place from Will Kraut. In 1894, they bought the place including the large house which is still a

Barn on the John Hawker Ranch.

landmark place south of Corvallis on Hawker Lane just west of the Eastside Highway.

Three more children were born of this union. They are Lyle Leona Hawker (Whitesitt), Clarence Hawker of Missoula, and Milburn Hawker of Tarreton, Idaho. The children attended school at Willow Creek until its consolidation with Corvallis. Lula Pond and Minnie Hawker went on to the training school in Stevensville and both became teachers. Lyle Hawker Whitesitt graduated from Corvallis in 1912. All together, there were eleven children with two sets of cousins in one family.

One son, Clarence, had tuberculosis of the bone in his leg. The family moved to Sleeping Child Hot Springs so the lady who owned the springs could put poultices of hot mineral water on his leg. After many months the leg got better, but was always smaller than the other one.

John Hawker loved music. He had a Victrola and bought all the records that came out—Golden Slippers, Three Black Crows, etc. He also had a piano with a player attachment, which the grandchildren nearly wore out. He made music on a comb and gave the kids pennies to try and jig. He could beat his sons at horseshoes and foot races. He was of small, trim stature with pretty blue eyes, white hair, goatee and mustache.

He raised bees and there was always plenty of honey in the cellar for Grandma's hotcakes. She was a very good cook and had a special touch with her oatmeal that simmered on the back of the stove. Her hands and arms were always bruised from the hens pecking her when she yanked them off the nest. She always had warm bricks or irons for the kids to take to bed to keep their feet warm.

The Hawkers were all excellent farmers and pictures of their ranch are on display at the Ravalli County Museum.

There are only two descendants remaining in the valley. Wilma Whitesitt Rasmussen lives on Hamilton Heights Road. Gary Hawker is employed as jailer at the County Jail, and is the son of John Hawker the third, better known as Jack.

THE HEAVILIN FAMILY

by Eva Heavilin Roberts

Mr. and Mrs. A. J. Heavilin came to the Bitter Root Valley in 1888, establishing a homestead at Charlos Heights, then known as Camas Prairie. They lived on the ranch of 160 acres for six years, moving to Hamilton where they lived ten years. While here, Grandma and Grandpa ran a restaurant where the Mildred Foley beauty shop is now, and Grandpa had a hamburger stand up town. They left here and lived in California, Lewistown, Butte and Philipsburg, then returning here to retire. They lived on Adirondac Avenue for a number of years before going to Missoula, where they both passed away. Grandpa was a veteran of the Civil War. There were 12 children in the family. His brother, Frank J. Heavilin, was owner of the Sleeping Child Springs.

Grandpa and Grandma Solberg came to the Valley from Butte in 1888, and took up a homestead of 160 acres on the west side of the Bitter Root River, where they lived until they passed away. There were four children in the family: Ida, Ada, and Ivy, and a brother named Johnie, who passed away before they came here.

My mother, Ada, was just ten years old when they came here. She married Oliver Heavilin at Corvallis, MT, the ceremony was performed by Rev. B. F. Morris in July 1895. There were 5 children in our family; Sam, passed away in 1967, Alice Gardner of San Leandro, CA, who had 2 children, and her husband Ray, passed away May 1972; Helen Pauline Fundenberger has one daughter, husband Lyle, passed away June 1972, now lives in Las Vegas, NV; Edith Smith moved back here in Oct. 1973, lives at 311 N 4th St, with her husband Clifford, has one son, Les Busenbark, who lives in Oakland, CA; and Eva married Roy Roberts (writing this account).

The Andrew Heavlin family, early 1900s.

Roy Roberts and I were married in 1922, at Missoula. We have two children, Roy Junior, who lives in Kelso, WA, and has two children; and Audrey Babb who lives in Hamilton and has a daughter named Cindy. Roy passed away in 1964.

Oliver Heavilin, my father, passed away in 1938; Mother, Ada, died in 1968 at the age of 90 years.

Dad built a log house on the west side where we lived for many years. We also lived in the brick house. Our sister was born there. McCleod owned the place at the time. Dad hauled the brick for the house. It was a beautiful house then. Dad was just 17 years old when he came to the Bitter Root and lived here the rest of his life. We lived near Woodside for many years. Nat and Mary Levstick were our neighbors. They came from Austria to Butte, then here. They had two children who died at birth, so they took three boys to raise, Johnie, Luie, Rudie Porch-Avenica.

Dad was born in Butler, Missouri. He came out west in a covered wagon with his folks. Mother was born in Butte, MT, and came to the valley when she was ten years old.

We all went to Fair Play School, but Helen Pauline. We walked part of the time and part of the time, we drove. Our horse's name was "Punk", and when we got in the school yard the kids would holler and our horse would stop. We were about six miles from school. That was the good old days! So many are gone now.

HESS FAMILY HISTORY

by Jennie Huls Lilyquist, & Frances Hess Reilly

Albert George Hess was born in 1877 in Illinois. He moved with his family to a farm in Missouri, where he grew up. Upon reaching 21 years of age, he left home with a new suit and $50.00 and a strong desire to have his own farm someplace in the west.

His first stop was in the St. Ignatius, Montana area. By the time he reached Missoula, he had accumulated his own team of horses and a freight wagon. It was while he was in the Missoula area that he met and married Hattie Stockman Atherton in 1906. (Hattie had a daughter named Beatrice Atherton by a previous marriage. Beatrice was born in 1896 in Missoula, and died in Butte in 1932.)

About 8 years was spent in leasing farms near Lolo and on the Indian Reservation near Ronan until he had enough money to make an offer on the 1000 acre ranch, which was part of the Albert Wood place. The land was located just north of Tucker crossing, bordering the East Side Highway, and extending to the west across the Bitterroot River (163 acres was hill ground to the east of the highway).

Along with several neighbors, Albert worked with a committee to influence Montana Power to extend the power lines to that section of the valley so they were all able to enjoy the wonders of electricity. This also enabled Albert to start a dairy of 50-75 cows and build a huge red barn. This barn was the pride of his life, but a single bolt of lightning struck it one fine spring day in May, and it burned to the ground. Friends and neighbors were so wonderful and came to help milk the cows until a new, much smaller structure was erected. The Hess's milked cows and raised hogs. The boys hauled cans of milk to the cheese factory in Corvallis and brought back whey, which was fed to the hogs. In 1936 they remodeled the farmhouse.

The east end of Tucker crossing separated the ranches owned by Albert G. Hess and John S. Treece. Albert's stepdaughter, Beatrice, married John A. Treece. Their daughter was named Harriet and she married Val Loesch. The buildings on the Treece place are no longer standing, but the Treece's lived there from 1905 until the place was sold by C. M. "Dick" Treece, about 1950.

Albert and Hattie Hess had six children: Charles, William, Ted, Dorothy, and twins Herbert and Frances. All the Hess children graduated from Victor High School, and their father, Albert, served on the Victor Board of Trustees for many years. Will's wife, Ida, (the former Ida M. Johnson), was a teacher at the Etna school on the East Side Highway, between Corvallis and Stevensville.

Charles married Ernestine "Ernie" Richards, whom he met when he was in Butte, and there were four daughters born to them: Judy, Clara, Deanna and Ernestine "Tina". Dorothy Hess married Claris Glidewell and they had two children, David and Jeanette. Will and Ida gave birth to a daughter named Karen, and a son named Jay. Ted had also married and had two sons, Ted and Chuck. Frances married Tom Reilly, and they had three girls and one boy. They are Carol, Kathleen, Sarah, and Tom. Will passed away in 1955, and Herbert died in 1995. (Albert and Hattie moved to Missoula in 1942, and resided on Edith Street. In 1953, Hattie died at the age of 74, and Albert died in 1972, at age 95).

Charlie and Ernie had been renting the O'Brien place located on the Eastside Highway. Their first three daughters were born there. Charlie and Ernie moved in 1942 to the farm north of Tucker Crossing and there they raised sheep and beef cattle. Ernie always raised a big garden and canned lots of food for winter. Tina was born in 1942. Ernie was very active in the Corvallis Community Church, and every Sunday she would gather up all the children in the neighborhood and take them to Sunday School. She drove a pick up most of the time and the back-end was often filled with children. This worried her husband a lot, because one day Judy reported one of the older boys sitting on top of the cab while they were traveling down the road! She was very musical and played the piano for Sunday services.

Charlie became ill, so they sold the farm in the late forties and bought a home in Missoula right across the street from their church. Charlie passed away in 1948. Ernie became the organist at the Bethel Baptist Church at that time, and she still plays the organ for their services!

THE HIGHTOWER FAMILY

by James Robinson, once a neighbor

It is difficult to know where to begin with DAN AND MILT HIGHTOWER, because even those who knew them best can only guess at the beginning.

By most accounts they came to Montana from Missouri, where Milt was born on July 15, 1890. They came with their mother, Mary Josephine Hightower, and probably their father, though little is known of him. They came to the Bitterroot Valley partly by train, partly by wagon train. Dan was born in Jamestown, N. D., on March 8, 1898, probably where the family spent some time before moving to Willow Creek in 1902. Why they came to the valley is equally sketchy. Their closest neighbor, Marion Gregg, said they followed another group of Hightowers who didn't want anything to do with them, but the only connection acknowledged between the two groups is that they all came from within a 30-mile area in a rural section of Missouri.

What is clear about Dan and Milt Hightower, however, is that somehow they never made it into the 20th century. It was this ignorance, and innocence, that both attracted and repelled people, and made the Hightowers a legend in the Bitterroot Valley. "They're two people that if you ever met them, you'd remember them," says Ned Applebury. "The two greatest hillbillies in the State of Montana."

They did not work with any regularity or pleasure, and subsisted on a monthly welfare check from the county. "They got $15.00 of County money the first of every month, and lived for two weeks and starved for two weeks," is a quote from Dan, according to Squib Rasmussen, a neighbor who got to know them when as a boy in the 1910's. Neither Dan or Milt was educated past the 3rd grade. It's guessed they wore out a pair of overalls before they washed them. They were regarded as odd, even dumb. This led to charitable offerings from local residents, which Dan and Milt sometimes used to prove that despite appearances, they were not dumb! "I remember one time when Dan was sitting in the barbershop in Corvallis getting a haircut", says Applebury, "Of course, he'd get a haircut probably once every two years." The barber gave him a haircut, and Dan got up and asked "how much do I owe you?" The barber said, "Oh, that's free," so, Dan got back in the chair and said, "I'll take a shave!"

"They just weren't bright," says Edna Geisy, who attended eighth grade with the Hightower's sister, Elizabeth. Elizabeth was befriended by a local family and lived for only a short while in the shack. She eventually became a nurse.

Their mother died in March of 1944, but they lived in the two-room, tar paper-roofed shack until Milt died in 1969. They heated the shack with two wood stoves, one of which they cooked on. In spite of a power line running over the roof to houses up the creek, the shack did not have electricity or running water. "It was two little rooms with three beds across the back of the room" said Applebury, who met Dan and Milt as a boy and remained friends with them until they died.

"It was just made out of rough boards, that's all the walls were. One slight partition between the kitchen and the living room. The kitchen was probably 10 x 10, with an old wood stove in it. The living room and the bedroom was a combination of maybe a room 20 x 20, with the beds in one corner and a couple old chairs in the other corner. They bought canned goods, and the cans for many, many years, were thrown out in the same pile — a mountain of tin cans!"

Another neighbor, Gayle Tintzman, remembers them from her early childhood. "My first recollection is that we would go up there and eat. I presume we were invited. I'm sure we just didn't go up there. And I can remember Mrs. Hightower, she was small — say five foot tall. She always wore a black dress with a white apron over it, starched. She just rustled when she would walk! She had her hair back in a bun, and she smoked a corn cob pipe, and she chewed tobacco. There was a spittoon across the hall, now I don't know how far — you know when you are little, it seems like a long ways — but, she could hit it! And you could have eaten off her floors, and they were wooden floors. Very nice lady. In fact, sometimes too nice, because she'd want to give you a kiss and here would be this tobacco. I'm sure I always let her kiss me, probably"!

"Ma chewed, and Milton smoked a pipe, and Dan had cigarettes", said Marion Gregg. "Ma did some crochet work and as she sat there in her rocker, she kept her foot over a knothole — then when she wanted to spit — she moved her foot, and hit the hole every time!"

"Milt was the worker of the two, Dan wouldn't do much. At that time, we stacked hay and used a staking pole, and he would drive the derrick. Wasn't much work to that. Milt would work, but we had to really brag on him," Rasmussen recalls. They would hire out to do odd jobs for neighbors on Willow Creek, mostly during haying season. "I remember one time," says Applebury, "probably after I got out of high school, I went up to Anfinson's to do the thrashing. Dan was out pitching bundles onto the wagon. They called them spike pitchers in those days. And you'd brag on him and he'd work like a madman. He'd throw the bundles clear over the wagon, so you had to be careful that you didn't talk too much." "Dan wasn't the worker, like I said, but Milt was," says Tintzman. "Milt would come down to my Dad's and a lot of times Dad wouldn't even ask him. He'd just know Dad was going to start haying or thrashing, and he would be down."

While Milt could or couldn't work, Dan COULD WALK! "I can remember all my younger years seeing that guy going down the road, he took steps that must've been six feet apart. I'm sure he could go five miles per hour — he was a fabulous walker," said Applebury, who manages the Ravalli County Fair. "He would walk to Hamilton every Saturday morning and buy their groceries, and this was after he was a pretty old guy. They didn't think anything of walking 10 or 12 miles to town!

WALKING surrounds one of the most famous stories about Dan. He'd taken sick and wasn't satisfied with the treatment he had received from the County Doctor. He decided to go to Missoula (50 miles away), to see the doctor there. According to Mr. Gregg, Dan walked all 50 miles except for the 15 miles from Corvallis to Stevensville, where he got a ride. However, in his unkempt condition, he attracted some attention as he entered Missoula. Approached by the Missoula police, he became upset and refused to say anything other than that he was from Willow Creek. They called Willow Creek, Montana, to see if a character of his description lived there. In the meantime, they took Dan's clothes, stripped him, sent his clothes to the laundry and put him in jail. Eventually the police called Anfin Anfinson, Gayle's father, who was a County Commissioner at the time. Three days later, the Ravalli County Sheriff picked Dan up and brought him home!

The Hightowers, at home on Willow Creek. Left to right are Milt Hightower, Julie Applebury, Countess Margrit Sigray Bessenyey, and Dan Hightower.

"Milton laughed about that," said Gregg, and told Dan, "That will teach you to stay home!"

After sometime, Gregg was going to Missoula, and there was Dan going down the road. "I picked him up, but when I reached Corvallis, I said, "I'm going down to Missoula, you can ride along and see the town." "Nope", said Dan. "Why not," I asked. Then Dan replied, "You know when that fellow opened the door and let me out of there, he said he would keep me for 30 days if I ever came back, and I don't want to stay that long!"

The two strange men attracted the attention of the late Margit Bessenyey, granddaughter of copper baron Marcus Daly. A friend of Applebury, she asked to be taken along on one of his visits to them. "Margit was the kind of person who was very sympathetic to that type of people...." said Applebury. "She didn't go up there at all with the idea of joking with them or making fun of them, or nothing like that. She was very serious, and just sat and talked to them about the old days, where they were born, and we must have spent three hours just visiting. They just loved it!"

Milt's health began to fail in the late 60's. Their living conditions didn't help them to stay healthy. The neighbors and friends watched closely. The shack insulated with newspapers, was tough to keep warm. On January 9, 1969, Dan came to Marion Gregg's log cabin and told him Milt was in trouble. "Milton's on the floor and I can't get him up," said Dan. Gregg called the Welfare people and went to help Milton. "The squalor, it can't be described," said Gregg. Milt was on the floor, and he looked up and said, "There's a chair over there, find it and sit down." He was passing and made that attempt to be civil. I got him up in a chair and set him next to the little stove (somebody had traded them out of their good big one!) and that night the welfare people took him to the hospital and he died." Shortly thereafter, Dan was placed in a home in Hamilton and eventually moved to the North Valley Nursing home. Applebury would visit Dan and sometimes drove him back out to Willow Creek, but sometime later the place burned down and he never wanted to go back after seeing the results of the fire. Nobody knows who burned the shack down. One day in town, Dan approached Gayle and asked "Gayle, is the shack gone?" "Yes, it is Dan," said Gayle. "Oh why did they do that?" Dan asked.

"I think their friendliness," said Applebury, when asked what attracted him to the Hightowers. "When you'd see them, they'd just bubble over like you were just a great pal of theirs. Your natural reaction to a person like that is to like them...that's a great quality in people. I know that's what attracted me to them...they just made me feel like I was one of their very, very great pals."

"I looked at 'em different than probably a lot of people," says Vance Bay, whose father and he sold and delivered groceries from Bay's Store in Corvallis, to the Hightowers. "To me they were kinda neat people. I liked them, I really did."

"A lot of people said they wouldn't trust them," said Tintzman. "I don't think they would really hurt you. But, it was just in our day and age, mine especially, maybe not my mom's, people were being educated and yet here were two who were so illiterate and backward, backwoodsy."

Dan died on May 15, 1975. He and Milt are buried in the Corvallis Cemetery.

Today, if you drive up Willow Creek Road about five and a half miles, you will come to the last mail boxes and the road turns right up a hill and then down and left and up again past Gregg's log cabin on the right. But most of all, you will notice the cans; rusted tin cans with two triangular holes punched in the tops. A small mountain of them at the base of the lilac bush and the rose bush. If you have a good eye, you will see a red Prince Albert pipe tobacco can. Its contents were smoked by one of the two greatest hillbillies in Montana.

A. A. HOBBS

from the Western News, February 25, 1926

Angelo Albert "Powder River" Hobbs, as he was known to a wide circle of friends, was a true trail-blazer in every sense of the word. Born at Chavie, on Lake Champlain, 59 years ago, he began a life that was productive of good to all who associated themselves with him. When still a lad, he turned his face toward the west, coming to eastern Montana in good turn and following the life of the range.

The west of forty years ago (1886) was a land that called for a hardy spirit. "Powder River" lived the rugged life of the days. There we see him with others of those empire builders taking great herds of beef cattle all the way from Texas to Miles City. Here we see him called by death.

Mr. Hobbs looked upon life with a smile. His good humor did much to rub the rough corners from the lives of his friends. Not with a trumpet, but with kindly good deeds modestly directed, did he guide his life. He was a fine man. He was constructive. Words cannot express the superlative.

The deceased is survived by his widow, Mae Wilson Hobbs; two sons, Will and Ned, all of Hamilton; and a daughter, Mrs. M. Knowles, who arrived here today from her home in Wisconsin.

NED HOBBS

Son of A. A. Hobbs, obituary August 12, 1972

NED HOBBS, age 70, died on August 12, 1972 in Hamilton, Montana. He was born on February 27, 1892, at Manson, Iowa, to Angelo

Albert and May Wilson Hobbs, and came to Glendive with his parents when he was 16 years old, then moved with them to the Bitter Root on July 4, 1919, locating in what is now the Doran addition. They then moved to the west side of Hamilton and lived there for years. He married Chloe Mathews at Hamilton and after her death he married Gussie Hobbs, who preceded him in death August 1957.

Ned Hobbs had many friends. They were not only Bitter Root residents but people in many states, for Ned traveled about the west a great deal. He was an outstanding horseman, knowing horses with the eye of an expert. He broke numerous horses in his many years of work with them. And he helped train and care for race horses from Calgary to the Mexican boundary, working with race strings at most of the principal race tracks in the west. It was not only that he knew horses, he loved them and was able to bring the most out of them in performance.

Ned was a man who asked no one for an advantage but was willing to lend a helping hand. His last years were not easy as he was attacked with his fatal illness of cancer long before it claimed him.

Surviving Mr. Hobbs are his sister Mrs. Claire (Merna) Knowles, from Reno, NV; and nephews, Raymond and Ralph Hobbs of Hamilton; nieces, Mrs. Lee (Irma) Miller and Mrs. Ralph (Ruth) Springer of Hamilton, Mrs. Joe (Maxine) Fetterhoff and Mrs. Gordon (Maybelent), both of Reno, and Mrs. James (Jerry) Coats of Tonapah, NV.

THE HOBLITT FAMILY

by Donna Sutherland Copeland, 1997
Great-granddaughter of Daniel Seward Hoblitt

Corvallis History of now 268 Hawker Lane.

Daniel Seward and Amelia Bailey Hoblitt bought what is now 268 Hawker Lane farm in 1907. Their youngest son, Allen (known as Billy), age 17, was with them. Daniel and Amelia were 58 years old.

Daniel Seward Hoblitt was born the 8th of 9 children to Mahlon Seward and Mary Ann Thomas Hoblitt on September 20, 1848, in Atlanta, Illinois. His father was a friend of Abraham Lincoln and he was a cousin of William Seward, who was Lincoln's Secretary of State. His father established the first meat market at St. Anthony Falls, which is now Minneapolis, Minnesota. When grown, Daniel moved to Otsego, Minnesota. Daniel always smoked a pipe.

Amelia Bailey was born to a Methodist minister and wife on July 30, 1848, in Elgin, Illinois. Amelia was a school teacher at Otsego and married Daniel S. Hoblitt on March 19, 1870, at Bailey Station, Minnesota. Daniel and Amelia were 22 years old.

Daniel and Amelia had 6 children: Alvin Bailey (known as A. B.) and Louise Elmina were born at Otsego, MN; Carrie Mahitabel (known as Cad) was born at Lily Pond, MN; and Carl Daniel was born at Petosky, MI. Daniel and Amelia then moved to Monticello, MN, and cleared a farm of timber. Haner Deighton and Allen Talmadge were born at Monticello. They adopted Bertha. They lived in Monticello for 25 years.

When Daniel and Amelia came to Corvallis, Montana, four of their children and Amelia's brother, Thomas Clement Bailey, were in the Bitter Root. Carl had come in 1899 to help his Uncle Tom hay west of Stevensville, and had married Grace Conner in 1903. A. B. and wife, Florence, had come to Darby about 1901 or 1902, to teach school at Darby. A. B. also taught 7th and 8th grades at Corvallis for three years. Cad came to visit A. B., and married Robert E. Tompkins on March 25, 1904, and lived at the Bass ranch at Stevensville. Louise, her husband, E. C. Sutherland, with children Bill and Margaret, had come in 1903, to farm two miles south of Stevensville.

Daniel, Amelia, and Billy farmed the land with horses. Then, Amelia died suddenly on September 29, 1910, at the farm, and is buried at the Corvallis Cemetery.

A. B. went to the University at Missoula to get a law degree. Billy married Naomi Tevis at Lolo on March 22, 1912, and Haner married a school teacher, Ina Buckmaster, on July 10, 1912, in Monticello, MN. Haner and Ina came to farm at Corvallis.

Haner and Ina returned to Monticello, MN, in 1917, to farm Amon and Beatrice Buckmaster's farm when Amon and Beatrice family went to work at Ruth, Nevada.

Carl and Grace farmed the land with Daniel. Carl and Grace had three children: Daniel Aaron (known as D. A.); Grace Eva; and Julia. D. A. graduated in 1922, Grace Eva in 1924, and Julia in 1926, all from Corvallis High School. From 1920 to 1925, four sons were born to Carl and Grace: Carl, Douglas, Gene, and Lewis.

For 16 years, Daniel helped Cad, whose husband had become an invalid after a runaway horse accident. Robert Tompkins died on March 26, 1925.

On April 24, 1927, Daniel at age 80, had to see a doctor for the first time as he had a paralytic stroke while helping Cad to prepare to entertain 27 relatives to meet his 85 year old brother, Mahlon Seward Hoblitt and wife, Mina, who had visited a son in Oregon and were returning to Monticello. After just 5 days in bed, Daniel recovered.

The men raised feed for the cows, horses and chickens plus a big garden. The men brought home lots of fish, hunted deer, elk, and pheasants. The women cooked and baked plus canned the garden produce by boiling the jars for three hours on a wood stove. The cellar was always full of good food. Every September 20th, on Daniel's birthday, a family potluck dinner was held. The family grew to 24 grandchildren and 20 great grandchildren by the time Daniel was 93 years old.

In the 1930's the railroad went through the middle of the property. And in 1934, Carl and Grace moved to Darby to farm the Conner farm. Haner and Ina came back to Corvallis from Monticello.

Haner and Ina raised sugar beets until the sugar factory closed. They also raised the best tasting strawberries, and a big garden. Ina's nephew, George Haner Buckmaster (known as Bud), came to live with them after his mother died. Bud graduated from Corvallis High School in 1940. A kitchen sink replaced the pump, an electric stove was added to the kitchen, then a bathroom. Haner and Ina always had a Buick car. Ina drove and Haner was the passenger. Haner died on October 28, 1967, at the age of 62, and is buried in the Corvallis Cemetery.

In 1939, when Daniel was 90 years old, he moved to 706 W. Main St., in Hamilton, MT, to live with Cad, her daughter, Virginia Tallent, and Virginia's daughters — Connie, Carrie Lou, Kathryn, and Geraldine. Daniel died on January 1, 1944, at the age of 95, and is buried beside his wife Amelia, in the Corvallis Cemetery.

Ina leased the farm to George Brown. Joe and Ruby Sutherland helped her take care of her yard and house for 20 years. Ina was able to always get a driver's license, so went to church and quilted at the Community House every week. In 1983, Ina fell, breaking her hip for the second time, so had to go to the rest home. Ina enjoyed playing bingo and embroidering pillow cases and dish towels. Ina's mind was sharp, and her eyesight and hearing were good. In 1986, the farm and possessions had to be auctioned off to pay for Ina's rest home costs. Roy Wolff bought the farm. Ina died on September 29, 1987, at age 99 years, and is buried beside Haner in the Corvallis Cemetery.

HOLLORON FAMILY

James B. Slagle was born in Delta, Fulton County, Ohio, on December 11, 1845. He was a farmer and enlisted in the U. S. Army, December 16, 1863. He was wounded in the ankle severely on October 13, 1864, near Richmond, Virginia.

James Slagle's father died in the Mexican war and young James was adopted when he was a year old (1846) by Walter and Elizabeth Coleman. They lived in Euclid, Cuyhoga County, Ohio, and Pike Township, Fulton County, near Delta, Ohio. In 1862, he rejoined his own family in LaSalle County, Illinois, and resumed the Slagle name. **He was later to wed Mary Jane Foley** on May 24, 1866, in Allen Township, LaSalle County, Illinois.

Five children were born to Mary Jane and James Slagle: Elizabeth (Libby) born in 1867, **Ambrose** (Henry) born in 1869, **James** in 1871, **Juanita** in 1877 and **Frank** born in 1879.

Mary Jane and James Slagle lived in Sioux City, Iowa, for 20 years with their young family. James returned to St. James Soldiers Home in Ava, Missouri, in 1904, because of his injury. His last years were spent in Corvallis, Montana, near his daughter Elizabeth. He died July 20, 1917, and was taken back to Quincy, IL, for burial.

Elizabeth Slagle married James Holloron and they had 11 children: Alma Juanita born in 1887 in NB, Hazel **Deanne** born 1891 in Iowa, Blanche **Irene,** born in 1889 in NB, Maurice **James,** born 1893 in Iowa, Hobart **Howard** in 1898 in Iowa, Edward **Lloyd** in 1900 in Idaho, **Veta Yvonne** born in Granite, MT, in 1902, **Maxine Isabel** born in Corvallis in 1904, **Kathleen Clover** in Corvallis in 1905, **Donald Slagle** born in Corvallis in 1908, and **Robert Wayne** born in 1910, in Corvallis, MT.

James Holloron was a mason by trade. He worked at many mining communities and when the job was completed he moved to another mining camp. In 1904, he came to Corvallis to work for Jim Rawlins. Mr. Rawlins owned a livery stable and a dray business in Hamilton, where the present post office is located. He also owned a ranch east of Corvallis.

The story is told that as Mr. Rawlins left the train depot at Woodside, headed for his ranch east of Corvallis, he stopped to give a ride to a woman walking. It happened to be Mrs. Holloron on her way to join her husband. She had five children with her and carried a baby and a birdcage. Thus began a lasting friendship of the Rawlins family and the Holloron family. Mrs. Rawlins and Mrs. Holloron became very close friends and the two families have spent all holidays together, even today. Maxine Holloron used to say that she was born in a stable. She was born on the Rawlins place, in quarters fixed up for the family until they had a place of their own. Later, the Holloron family moved to what is known as the Fierce Place, north of Corvallis, where Kathy was born. Jim Holloron and Libby later homesteaded a ranch east of Corvallis, where Donald and Robert were born. Mr. Holloron soon left again for Canada, and Libby, with the help of her boys, made a living on this homestead. She even drove a horse drawn school bus along with raising cattle, until the boys were old enough to take over. The horse drawn school bus had a small stove and runners that were used in the winter. Clothes were home made and Mrs. Holloron said she would cut out six patterns at one time when making shirts for the boys. Later, Blanche took over the sewing for the family and as a seamstress for other people as well.

Alma, the oldest of the children, married James (Jimmy) Applebury in February of 1912. Jimmy bought a ranch on the hills east of Corvallis from his uncle, Marshall. It had been a log house and Jimmy rebuilt it and added a porch on the front and side. It was here that Beth and Ned were born, with no doctor attending. Beth weighed mere two and one-half pounds, and was kept on the warming oven of the kitchen stove.

Hazel was the second child of the Holloron's, and died when she was nine years old, in Burke, Idaho, of diphtheria.

Maxine and Kathy went to Dillon to get an education, but Maxine became homesick and left for home. She opted to go to Missoula Beauty College and became a beauty operator. She rented a shop in back of Emmett Smyth's barbershop, which she operated until she was able to buy the shop, purchasing Emmett's small house at the rear also. Maxine ran the shop for 52 years, after which she rented it to Nancy Hall. She was still living in the house with the beautiful yard full of flowers that she lovingly cared for until she died in 1991.

Kathy graduated from Dillon, which was then a Normal College, and taught third and fourth grades in Florence, the West Fork country school, Grantsdale, and Corvallis. She retired in 1967. She married Gerald Gibbons on June 5, 1938. Gerald (Gib) was killed in a construction accident in Corona, CA, in 1959, and Kathy came back to Corvallis and moved in with Maxine until her death in 1990.

Maurice, the oldest of the Holloron boys, farmed on ranches near Corvallis. He married Dora Smyth Wallace in 1925. Dora had two children, Alice and Wesley. In later years, Maurice and Dora bought a home in Hamilton, where Maurice died at the age of 90.

Hobart left Corvallis when a young man and worked in the mines in Butte. During World War II, he worked for Boeing in Seattle, and died there in 1944.

Ted (Edward Lloyd) worked in the smelter in Anaconda, and married Annetta May Wallace. They had three children: **Betty Ann, Eddie Lloyd, Jr.,** and **Sharon.** Ted died while attending a 4th of July picnic at his niece's home, Beth Flint, in Corvallis in 1983.

Donald (Dee) and Robert (Bob) stayed on and worked the homestead ranch until 1996, when they rented it to Lee Erickson. **Veta** kept house for Bob until she was confined to a rest home, where she died on April 6, 1997. Dee built his own home next to the original Holloron home and married Ruth Whitlock, a Corvallis teacher, in May of 1939. **Dee and Ruth had two children, Phyllis Kay and Jerry.** Ruth died in March of 1997, but Dee and Bob are still on the Holloron Ranch.

JOHN G. HOWE, SR. FAMILY

John George Howe was born on February 9, 1879, in Kellogg, Minnesota, and graduated from Minnesota State in 1899, where he was captain of the basketball team his senior year. He started his career with the Winona Creamery at Winona, Minnesota.

In 1904, he married Ruby Parson in Kern, MN. On October 13, 1905, their son, Warren, was born. In 1906, the family moved to Spokane, WA, where Mr. Howe was head of the butter department of Hazelwood Creamery. On April 1, 1908, they moved to Stevensville, Montana, where John managed the Bitter Root Cooperative Creamery. This creamery building was destroyed by fire in 1911, and rebuilt of cement blocks in less than a month. To celebrate the completion, Mr. Howe staged a "creamery picnic, with free ice cream and buttermilk to everyone in the community". It was such a success that it became an annual event (and is still carried on in 1997).

John G. Howe, Jr., was born in Stevensville on September 21, 1910, and another son, George Quenten, was born on May 14, 1919.

The family moved to Hamilton when Mr. Howe took over the Ravalli Creamery on September 1, 1926. After the sale of the Creamery to the Kraft Company, Howe was in charge of the company's Western Montana interests. In 1933, he built his own Ravalli County Creamery on the north corner of Main and Fourth Streets.

In its greatest productive years, this plant would produce 2,500 lbs. of butter per day; 500 lbs. of cheese; and 500 gallons of ice cream. Many international, national, state, and county awards were received. His butter exhibit received first place at the 1904 World's Fair in St. Louis, MS. The Ravalli County Creamery team won the triple crown of excellence at the 1967 Montana State Fair for the finest butter, cheese, and ice-cream in Montana. John Jr. and George were members of that team and later became co-owners with their father.

The creamery was sold in 1967 to John Greer.

Mr. Howe always found time during his busy life to devote service to the communities in which he lived. In Stevensville, he was a city councilman and school board trustee. In Hamilton, he was a member of the Board of Directors of Marcus Daly Memorial Hospital for 27 years, much of the time as Chairman. For twelve years, he was a member of the Board of Trustees of School District No. 3. He was also a member of the Ravalli County Bank Board of Directors.

Ruby Howe kept busy raising three sons, sewing, working in her flower garden, and keeping an immaculate home. Ruby Howe died the day after her 100th birthday in 1983.

John G. Howe, Sr., lived to be over one hundred years old, passing away in April of 1979.

One son, George, passed away in 1991. Warren and his wife, Phyllis, live in Walnut Creek, California. John Jr., and his wife, June, live in Hamilton.

There are four grandchildren: Jeanne Howe Hargett and Robert Hartley Howe, children of John Jr. and June Howe; and Patricia and George Howe, children of George and Rosemary Howe.

There are also three great-grandchildren: Christopher and Bill Hargett; and Allyson Howe.

HOW A PIONEER CAME TO MONTANA

"Aunt Rose" Hull

from The Sunday Missoulian, Sept. 23, 1928
told through her sister-in-law, Mrs. J. B. Mitchell

"Aunt Rose" was born in Alabama in 1839, and was taken to Missouri a year later by her parents. In 1855, they moved to Kansas and preempted a farm near Fort Scott. There, Aunt Rose grew to womanhood and married. Her husband enlisted when the Civil War broke out and she remained on their farm and kept the home fires burning. Her first child was born before the war, and another came after its close. These are the children she mentions in her account of a trip up the Missouri river in 1869, a journey that ended in the Bitter Root Valley. After ranching for a number of years, her husband moved to Gibbonsville. Later, the family lived at Corvallis, and her husband died there in 1906.

"In May of 1861, my only sister and younger brother started to the then Far West. The feeling of utter loneliness that came over me as I bade them good-bye, caused me to resolve that some day, I too, would follow them into that unknown land. It was a dangerous undertaking to brave the perils of the plains as hostile Indians, sickness, death, might end the journey before the goal was reached.

My oldest brother had gone to California in '49, and never came back, finding instead of the gold he sought, only a lonely grave. To my loneliness was added the fear of what might happen to those I love.

My sister and her family reached the Bitter Root Valley, and six years later the opportunity came to me to join them there. A brother had come all the way back from Montana to see us in Kansas and to marry the girl of his choice who lived there, and the tales he told of that country — land for the taking, gold for the digging, and plenty of work and good wages for all who cared to work! This so excited my husband that he consented to go and we began discussing ways of getting there. My father was a helpless invalid who was never to walk another step, so over the plains could not be thought of by us, and we decided to go to Fort Benton by boat. Fort Benton was 1,300 miles distant on the Missouri River and we were to make the journey by team, about 300 miles farther into the Bitter Root. My married brother, his wife, and two younger brothers with a party of friends preceded us in that way. Also, we had 30 head of cattle they drove over the plains for us. We had 120 miles to Kansas City before we could take the boat to Fort Benton. The boats had to wait until the Missouri was navigable and they generally made only one trip a year.

We hired a neighbor by the name of Copes to take us to Kansas City and, as we could only take necessary things, preparations were simple and soon made. Hoop skirts were out by that time, so we were not bothered by them, but wore our calico homespun and straw hats.

A bed was made in the wagon for my father, my husband and I, with our two children, Johnny, age 9, and Daisy, a babe of nine months, bade farewell to sunny Kansas and started our long journey. My husband had been a soldier in the Civil War so he was used to fighting and was well armed if the Indians became hostile. We arrived in Kansas City one May morning, and found we had to wait until June 16th, to take the boat to Fort Benton. In the meantime, we boarded at a small hotel run by a woman by the name of Hicks. Mary Hicks had a young sister, Etta Bacus, who upon learning we were going west, wanted to go too. My sister had written me asking me if I could find a girl to help her, to bring her along if I could, as a single woman coming to Montana at that time was soon sought in marriage by some eligible bachelor. We told Etta if she would promise to remain single and work for my sister until her fare was paid, we would buy her a ticket and take her along. She consented and she was a help to me, a comfort in that long journey.

After leaving Kansas City, it took the boat a month to reach Fort Peck, a government station kept by a man by the name of Farwell, who had an Indian wife. As the water became low in 1869, the boat was obliged to stop there, not being able to navigate farther. In traveling on the boat, we would be obliged to stay a whole day at a time on a sandbar. One day the captain had a small cannon put on the top of the boat, more to frighten the Indians, than for actual use. My husband had fired cannons in the Civil War and he told the captain: "You had better chain that cannon to the boat, for if it ever is fired — it will fall off." An egotistical gentleman from New York City said, "I bet that man never saw a cannon, it's all right." The captain took his word and left it as it was. On the Fourth of July, wishing to celebrate, they fired the cannon and it went down in a deep hole in the river and was never recovered! The Captain had an imitation cannon made and placed on the boat, thinking to fool the Indians, but they were not fooled, and made sport of it by saying "Uh, Uh." One day, they let a party of Indians come on the boat to look for a man they wanted to scalp, but he was not there and so trouble was averted. One place we stopped for wood, several Indians were buried in the trees and we were afraid the fool New Yorker would make trouble, as he tried to reach a rope hanging from a body, but he could not reach it and so we were saved.

We arrived at Fort Peck and unloaded our goods and waited there for the team, owned by the Diamond R. outfit that was to convey us on to Fort Benton. As our fare was paid to that place, they promised to furnish us a wagon and team. My husband was to drive to that destination. At the time we were detained at Fort Peck, our supplies became very low. Mr. Farwell told us we could get flour, sugar, and coffee in the fort, but would have to furnish everything else for ourselves. Wild meat was easy to get but one had to go outside the stockade and the Indians were troublesome, so we had to be very careful.

WILL DICKINSON

In Kansas City we had been joined by a young man by the name of Will Dickinson, who had the western fever and he had come with us. Will said to my husband, Joe, "You can't hunt for you have your wife and children and your helpless father-in-law to leave if anything should happen. Now, I have only myself to consider. I'll do the hunting and you provide the rest of the food". Joe agreed to this and the adults of the party were well provided for, but my poor baby nearly starved, as condensed milk was then unknown, and fresh milk could not be obtained. I could nurse her no longer and all she had to eat for two months was coffee with a little sugar, and with dry bread crumbled in it. No vegetables being obtainable, she had none of the things considered so necessary to the babies of today.

Of course she grew very thin, but came through all right and in time grew to womanhood and had a family of her own. The Indians who lived at the fort were much taken with her, as she had red hair and they are particularly partial to that color. They offered to buy her, offering six of their best ponies for her, and I watched her very carefully while they were around, fearing they might steal her.

One day Will said to my husband, "Joe, you hunt today." Joe said "No, I can't go out today, Will." "I'll go then," said Will, and he could not be persuaded to stay in camp. He borrowed a rifle and several rounds of ammunition and started out. Walking farther than he thought, he started back to camp. He had used all of his ammunition but one bullet. Hearing a noise, he looked around just in time to see painted Indians coming toward him. One of the braves fired at him, hitting him and making a long gash on his face from which the blood flowed freely. He shot the Indian, killing him, and before the other Indians could molest him, he pulled up his gun as if he would shoot them too, and they, thinking he had more ammunition, rode off. The dead Indian had had his horse tied to him with a short rope, as in those days the Indians on the plains often looped a short rope around the jaw of their horse and looped it into the belt that they wore, so if they were shot, their horse would drag their body away. Will cut the rope and, taking the brave's pistol, knife, and other belongings, he rode the pony into camp where his wound was dressed by a doctor who had come up the river with us and he was all right in a short time.

My brother from Fort Benton came to meet us and take us to the Bitter Root. In those days, there were no telegraph wires, railroads, telephones, or any way of communication but by messenger. A man by the name of Healey (who was the first man to discover gold in Idaho) carried his message to us. On the first of September, the Diamond R outfit of 100 wagons had come to take us to Fort Benton and on the way we met him. This outfit was comprised of 100 wagons hauled by oxen and they hauled freight and passengers between Fort Benton and Fort Peck. They had furnished us with one yoke of oxen and one wagon and Will had his Indian pony to ride. We were cautioned three times by the manager of the outfit to start at 1 A.M., and not to make a noise of any kind in passing the Indian camp, "For if the Indians discover you, you are gone sure!'

TO THE BITTER ROOT

We made the trip to Helena without anything of special interest occurring. We traveled in sight of the mountains all the way and when we passed through the Hellgate Canyon and through Missoula into the Bitter Root Valley, we were surrounded by the Bitter Root range, whose canyons with their purple shadows, tipped with snow-capped mountains, were a beautiful sight. We followed the Bitter Root River, catching the gleam of its restless waters as it wound its way down to join the Clark Fork at Missoula, and at last we arrived, weary, dirty, and happy, at the home of my sister in Corvallis, on October 22, 1869.

As Will Dickinson was a generous man, he and my two brothers rode the Indian pony into the Bitter Root valley from Fort Benton by riding and tieing. In that day, one horse could do the work of three by riding and tieing. It was accomplished by one man riding a mile or two, then tieing him and walking on, leaving the horse for the next one who came, and so on, until the process was repeated.

Will married Miss Emily Slack, Missoula's first teacher, and they lived in Missoula all their married life.

The girl, Etta, kept her word, but in the year following was married to a young man who was a member of my sister's family and founded a home of her own in the Bitter Root, where her descendants still live.

HULS FAMILY HISTORY

by Jennie Huls Lilyquist in 1998

The earliest record of the Huls family is found in an obituary article in the St. Charles Chronicle, dated June 30, 1905, relating information about the life and death of Spencer Booth Huls. The article states that he came to

St. Charles, Illinois, from Seneca County, New York, with his parents Mr. and Mrs. Deacon James Huls in 1843. They resided on a farm about two miles west of town. Spencer B. Huls married Mary Jane Mallory in 1854. They had one son named Spencer "Smith" Huls, who was born and raised in St. Charles. After Spencer Booth Huls died. Smith was the sole member of the family living, as Mary Jane Huls had passed away in 1894. They had sold their dry goods and notions business, "Huls and Kelley", and moved to Marshalltown, Iowa, in 1903. The following are direct quotes from that article:

"Spencer B. Huls, father of Spencer Smith Huls, of the firm of Huls and Son Grocers, of Marshalltown, Iowa, was thrown from his delivery wagon June 22, about 11 o'clock in the morning. Meeting Hagenbeck's circus parade, the horse became unmanageable. Harvy Henderson, who is employed at the store was with Mr. Huls at the time of the accident, and when the horse began to plunge in fear, jumped out and caught hold of its head. His efforts proved fruitless, however, and when the animal ran him into a telephone pole he was compelled to let go, and the loose horse, dashing through the parade between the elephants and the zebras, wheeled in front of the Friend's Church, across the street toward the Burkhart residence, up on the walk and across main through the parade again! Mr. Huls was thrown out when the wagon struck the curb, and his leg was fractured by the horses kick, while his head was injured by striking either the curbing or a dray wagon, which was standing near. The horse which caused the accident was a new purchase, and while seemingly gentle was very spirited".

"After suffering almost a week, with short intervals of consciousness, Spencer B. Huls, one of St. Charles' old substantial citizens, died early Wednesday morning from injuries received. Smith Huls brought the body of his father back here to his old home for burial. His residence here spanned fifty-two years. There was perhaps no man in St. Charles better known or more esteemed by his friends than "Spence" Huls."

"Mr. Huls has been closely identified with the growth of the town, was the first treasurer after the city of St. Charles was incorporated, and was an alderman and member of the committee that installed the first electric light plant. There is no man in town more familiar with the history of the place and its people than was he."

The following entries are taken from the Spencer Booth. Huls family Bible: Spencer Smith Huls married Sarah Gallogher, July 3,1887. A son, Mallory Smith Huls, was born to them, January 10, 1889. Sarah Huls died in 1895. Smith married Inez Shibley, April 14, 1897. A son, Alfred "Spencer", was born to them on March 8, 1901. A daughter, Constance Inez "Connie", was born August 2, 1903.

In 1908, Smith and Inez Huls, along with their 7-year-old son Spencer, and 5-year-old daughter, Connie moved to the Bitter Root Valley. They came here from Marshalltown, Iowa, where they had been owners of a grocery and dry goods store. They first moved into a stone house on the west side on what is now called River Road. (Inez had a twin sister named Irene, who, of course, stayed behind in St. Charles. The separation from her family proved to be very hard for Inez.) Smith Huls owned the first school bus for the Corvallis district. It featured a wooden coach for the children!

In 1910, they settled into a home they built on land they purchased for taxes on the east bench 5 miles northeast of Corvallis, on what is now Sutherland Road. Their friends Robert and Lynette Snow, who had also moved here from St. Charles, helped them because he was a carpenter by trade. They planted fruit trees, and raised hay and pasture for a few head of cattle. Spencer graduated from Corvallis High School in 1919. He enjoyed baseball and played on the Corvallis team. His teammates nicknamed him "Pickles" because he was a base runner who took daring leads, causing the opposing crowd to yell "Pick Huls". He was also on the track team.

On September 16, 1924, Spencer **secretly** married Corvallis second grade school teacher Marie Louise Sutherland. They continued to live in their respective homes for the first year of their marriage because a schoolteacher could not be married!!! Marie was a Bitter Root native, having been born in Stevensville on April 22, 1904. Marie graduated from Corvallis High School in 1921 as valedictorian of her class.She and her best friends, Kathryn Weber and Connie Huls, attended Normal School in Dillon, now called Western Montana College, where they earned their teaching certificates. Upon graduation, they returned to Corvallis and taught school.

In 1925, Smith and Inez moved to Divide to run a grocery store, which allowed Spencer and Marie to move into their home. Marie's little sister, Pauline, came to live with them as their mother, Louise Hoblitt Sutherland had passed away. A son, David Spencer, was born at home, delivered by Dr. Browning, February 16, 1928. The doctor bill for his services was $45.00. That summer Pauline became ill with polio and died August 13, 1928.

In 1936, Spencer and Marie harvested logs to build a home of their own. Spencer helped to remove some of the old flumes owned by the Bitterroot Valley Irrigation District and he built his first cow barn from reclaimed flume-lumber. The planks were eighteen inches wide, twelve feet long and three inches thick. They milked Shorthorn cows, separated the milk, and sold the cream in Corvallis. They raised hay, grain, pigs and chickens. Marie traded eggs for groceries at Bays Store in Corvallis. Spencer and Marie's second child, Margaret Elaine "Peggy", was born on June 30, 1937.

Smith Huls died in 1945, in Havre, Montana, and Inez passed away in 1963. Spencer Huls died January 18, 1986. Marie died July 20, 1988.

JOHN LAFAYETTE HUMBLE FAMILY

as condensed by Doris Humble Babcock

The Humble family came to the Bitter Root Valley in the 1870's from Missouri. John Lafayette Humble (better known as "Fate") was quite a colorful character. He was a native of Tennessee, born November 19, 1846. He went with his parents to Springfield, MO, and it was there he enlisted when the Civil War broke out. He served with the Sixteenth Missouri Cavalry and was on Price's raid through Missouri. At the close of the war, he married Caroline Wilkerson, and in 1870, brought his young wife to Montana Territory. They settled north of Corvallis on what later became part of the W. S. Bailey farm and the Zito ranch.

During the troubles with Chief Joseph's Nez Perce Indians, Fate was one of the leaders in organizing for the protection of the settlers, serving as Captain of the Corvallis Company and helping to establish the fort in Corvallis. Later, he, with others, founded the Christian Church and was involved in buildings and businesses in Hamilton.

Fate was the first President of the Citizens State Bank, and remained a stockholder for several years. As a rancher and farmer, Fate was the owner of large flocks of sheep and other livestock. He sold his ranch to the Great Western Sugar Company in 1918, and thereafter resided in Missoula.

Fate passed away on February 16, 1939. He was the last surviving member of the Bitter Root Post of the Grand Army of the Republic. At his death, he was survived by his third wife, Jessie Brown Humble, and her two daughters, and a nephew, John Lafayette Humble, Jr., whose story follows.

JOHN LAFAYETTE HUMBLE, JR.

John Lafayette Humble, Jr., was the son of Michael and Ruth Humble, and was born on October 12, 1872, in Marshfield, Missouri. In 1878, his family came to Montana by railroad as far as Deer Lodge, and by sled from there to the Bitter Root Valley. The parents bought 160 acres of pre-empted land at $1.25 per acre, in the Florence area, and commenced living there. The actual purchase being completed May 21, 1887.

As a youth, John observed the early development of the Valley, and soon was engaged in helping his family produce a living. As a youth, he drove a team from Florence to the old grist mill on the Burnt Fork, the trip requiring two days. Later, he drove teams hauling wagon loads of materials and food to the Hughes Creek mining camp, which was then being operated by Pete Flugstad. He recalled that a Yellowstone Kelley was hired by the miners to kill deer as meat for the camp of about 300 workers. Kelley killed as many as 10 deer per day at the price of $1.00 per head. Humble recalled that during the migration period, when the deer returned to Idaho's Selway country after summering in the West Fork of the Bitter Root, he had seen as many as 2,500 to 3,000 deer in a single day!

John Humble married Rosa Caple at Corvallis on December 9, 1900. Rosa was the daughter of Judson Fillmore Caple and Sara Luallen Caple, and had come to the Bitter Root from Missouri when she was just two years old. Before and after his marriage, John ranched on the Willow Creek. He helped to build the "Big Ditch", and in 1910, when that job was completed, the Humble's bought a place south of Corvallis, where they resided for many years while John worked as a road supervisor.

In 1919, John leased a ranch northeast of Hamilton, and farmed it until 1923, when he became foreman of the Steele Ranch which was just East of the Daly Mansion. He worked for the Bitter Root Irrigation, and later for the Associated Seed Growers.

John and Rose had eleven children. One son died at birth, and the others were: Lawrence, Clarence (Shorty), Lewis, Joseph, Caroline, Lucille (Spud), Marjorie, William, John, and Marian.

IMAN

by J. R. Iman

John and Wilhelmina Iman, with their 5-year-old son, **Russell,** moved to Montana, from Council Bluffs, Iowa, in 1902. They operated a livery stable in Missoula, that was located across the street from Hellgate High School on Higgins Avenue. **They moved to the Bitterroot Valley in 1910.** They purchased ranchland and a general store, post office, blacksmith shop and slaughterhouse at Woodside. The store was located at the northwest corner of the Highway 93 and Corvallis Road intersection. The slaughterhouse had a walk-in freezer. In the winter, ice was cut from a pond on the Iman's property and packed in sawdust for cooling. They shipped fresh fish and meat to Butte (for the miner's use) on the Northern Pacific Railroad, located where Hwy 93 now runs. Ranch work in these early years consisted of breaking horses, raising livestock and hay and clearing land for farming. Livestock included 150 head of goats that were used to clean up the brush on their property. John and Russell continued to purchase land for the Woodside Stock Farm.

Russell Iman courted Grace Leavitt, daughter of F. J. Leavitt who owned a ranch at the mouth of Sleeping Child Creek. They were married in 1918. Mr. Leavitt wondered aloud why his daughter would want to live in "stump town", as Woodside was referred to at that time. The young couple lived with John and Wilhelmina on the ranch. **Jack Iman was born at the ranch, in the Iman home, June 1920.** In the early 1920's, the NP Railroad was moved to its present location on the East Side, and Highway 93 was built on the rail bed to Hamilton. Without a railhead, the post office and many Woodside stores and businesses closed. The Iman family continued to improve and expand their ranching operation.

Jack attended Corvallis Schools, and graduated in 1938. He played sports and participated in school play productions. After graduation, he attended some additional classes at Hamilton High School. He then entered the Armed Services in 1941, joining the Air Force and serving as aircraft mechanic in several locations in the South Pacific, including the Marshall Islands. He later watched the television program "Baa Baa Blacksheep," which was based loosely on Pappy Boyington's Air Force exploits, and remarked that much of what was portrayed in that program was very similar to the kinds of experiences he had in World War II. **John and Wilhelmina passed the ranch on when she died in 1946.**

Jack married Patricia Joselyn, daughter of Jerry and Edna Joslyn of Hamilton, **in 1948.** He and Pat lived with Grace and Russell for a short time while they built their own home next door. Expanded swine production at the ranch improved the operation, and many champion hogs were displayed at the Ravalli County Fair. In addition to the ranch, the families were very involved in water resource planning and community development. They were members of many task forces and groups involved in local and state issues, including the Montana State University President's Advisory Board; the Governor's Commerce Committee and the Montana State Grange. **Jack and Pat had two children, J. R. and Jessie.**

Russell died in 1965, and Grace continued to live in her home until she died in 1987. Pat died in August of 1995, and Jack passed away in August of 1997. Jack died in the same house where he was born.

JOSEPH ITEN

from his obituary in The Western News

Joseph Iten, a Swiss immigrant, walked down the gangplank of a steamship into New York City in 1899. He didn't speak English, was 19 years old, having been born on December 13, 1880, at Underageri, Switzerland. He was not armed with a college education but he possessed native ability in abundance, a determination without limit, which led him to accomplishments that could be the envy of any man.

He traveled to Gallatin County where he worked on a farm belonging to an uncle, and left to come to the Bitter Root in 1900. He has related recollections of his arrival on the evening passenger train with little money, unable to speak the language, and dismayed at the celebrating lumberjacks in the public houses and upon the streets.

It so happened that he became observed by Rory McLeod, who ran a farm and dairy near what is now the Hamilton airport. McLeod sized Iten up as a man who would work, and learned he could depend on him. McLeod's sons taught Iten to speak English and made him aware of the ways of the world in the rough and ready Bitter Root of those days.

Joe went to work for the Bitter Root Stock Farm in 1902, where his foreman was the late Joe Haigh.

In 1905, Joe returned to Switzerland to visit his parents, and while there met Katharine Iten (no relation) and they became engaged, making plans for her to come to America later. In the meantime, Iten acquired cement and a machine for making cement blocks which he had done in Missouri, and went into the contracting business. His ability to accomplish work quickly and well brought him lots of business.

In 1907, it was time for him to make another trip, this time to New York, where he met Katharine upon her arrival by steamship. They were married February 7, 1907, and came to the Bitter Root Valley, which has ever since been the Iten home. Joe built their home of cement blocks on North First Street, in which they resided for many years, and raised their children. These children are: Walter, Josephine (Mrs. C. C. Tefft), Helen (Thompson), Tillie (Mrs. S. T. Carlson) and Doris (Mrs. R. W. Richardson). Joseph and Katharine Iten celebrated their 50th anniversary in 1957. Katharine passed away on April 21, 1962.

Iten's works as a contractor defy comparison in this area. He would engage in most any building effort and their are numerous testimonials in these works standing as monuments to his craftsmanship.

He furnished the blocks for the Smith & Brown building (now the basic part of the Eagles hall) when the original contractors failed to complete the structure. He constructed the first cement sidewalks in Hamilton. He contracted cement paving on Hamilton's Main Street, Second and Third Streets in 1927, and was chiefly responsible for construction of the west addition to the Hamilton City Hall on South Third. He built Daly Lake, the tennis courts and swimming pool at the Daly mansion and helped to build the present mansion itself.

Raising a fine family, belonging to the Catholic church, the Elks Lodge, and doing his construction were not enough for Joe. He also found time to serve the city of Hamilton for five terms (1939, 1941, 1943, 1945, and 1947) as Mayor, longer than any other mayor. His administrations were soundly conservative with the taxpayer's dollar, it being stretched to get a dollars worth of value "until the eagle screamed!" He was also twice elected on the Republican ticket as a Ravalli County Representative in the state Legislature in 1950 and 1952.

During World War II, he served as one of the men who undertook the difficult task of administration on the Ravalli County Ration Board. In this work he had to step on many toes, but he seemed to be able to do it with a smile which satisfied all but the most obstreperous.

Determined to make another trip to Switzerland, he did and enjoyed visiting with his remaining relatives.

The past few years had not been so kind as he gradually deteriorated in health until finally dissolution claimed him. Burial was in the Riverview Cemetery.

THE JENKINS FAMILY

by Thomas M. Jenkins and Marjorie Jenkins Hilliard

The Jenkins belong to pioneer families, their ancestors were prominent in American frontier life in Pennsylvania, Kentucky, Illinois, Iowa, and Kansas for more than two hundred years. Oscar Warren Jenkins' father, Warren Y. Jenkins, served the Union Army in the Civil War from April 1861 to January 1864. His mother, Susan Virginia Boone Jenkins, was the grand niece of Daniel Boone of Kentucky. His parents were married in Illinois and later moved to Altoona, Kansas. Oscar, born January 20, 1885, and the sixth of ten children, married Mina May Smith on April 9, 1874, at her parents home in Neodesha, Kansas. Mina May Smith had been born in Knoxville, Iowa, on August 17, 1875. They made their home in Altoona, where the first two of their seven children were born. Vernon Ellsworth was born December 18, 1895, and William Oscar (Bill) on October 27, 1897.

Mina's brother, Charles E. Smith, married Oscar's sister, Amelia, on March 7, 1895, and in 1899, came to the Bitter Root Valley. Their being in the Bitter Root, no doubt aroused Oscar and Mina's interest in moving here also, and they arrived in Victor by train on March 30, 1900. Vernon was four and Bill was two at the time. After a short time in Victor, they moved to the Pete Wall place on Owing Creek, just West of Hamilton. While residing there, Oscar (who was an accomplished stone mason) secured work at his craft in the construction of the Ravalli County Courthouse in Hamilton. He worked as an assistant to Sherman Gill, handling the heavy stone foundation, and did other work on the building, including construction work on the roof. He walked to work in Hamilton and elsewhere. While in the Hamilton area, their next two children arrived. Rollin Avery was born December 26, 1901, and Cora May — the only daughter — was born on September 23, 1903. Both youngsters were born in Hamilton at the home of Mina's brother, Elmer Smith.

Later Oscar engaged in work in the woods of the area, which were then being harvested of the virgin crop of yellow pine that covered most of the Valley and its mountains. From time to time, he also worked as a stone mason on other buildings then rising in the new town of Hamilton.

In 1903, the family moved up Elijah Gulch, now called Soft Rock

Creek, east of Corvallis, onto a 172.9 acre homestead. Here, the last three children were born, Joseph Ardin, on November 19, 1906; Delwin Young on February 10, 1912; and Clayton Boone on September 19, 1914. On the homestead, Oscar grew wheat and Mina raised chickens for eggs. There were also milk cows and a large garden to provide food for the growing family. Mina was an excellent cook, and her cottage cheese was considered the best! She was also a good seamstress, and her dish towels were gleaming white.

Spring water was available for the homestead house, and Vernon told of how his mother called him one day to go get some water as his grandmother was "choking to death". He ran frantically to the spring, got the water and ran back to the house, to find that grandmother was very thirsty, but not dying!

One old-timer said there were rattlesnakes "as big as your arm", until the sheep were run in the area. The sheep trampled the rattlesnakes and ridded the countryside of them. There were also Columbia Sharp Tail Grouse in the area, but were over-harvested and became extinct.

Oscar and Mina Jenkins, on dryland homestead in the Soft Rock area.

The older children attended Willow Creek and Dominic elementary schools. After graduating from Dominic School, Vernon started high school in Corvallis. He saddled up old Betsy, took a lunch, and headed out early in the morning. Upon arriving, he found no barn facilities or feed for his horse. He decided this would never work, and left for home by noon.

Among the neighbors up Soft Rock were the Appleburys, Englers Luedeckes, Reinkes, Tews, and Charley Smiths.

The drought in the mid 1920's brought crop failure and the bank foreclosed, thus taking the homestead that had been mortgaged to purchase more land. In 1928, they acquired farm property under the "Big Ditch", in the Summerdale area. Living at first in a two-story house on the hill above their property, then on the Robbins place which was about 1/8 mile south on the west side of the road, while they built their home. This was about 1934, and Oscar obtained the lumber for $16.00 per thousand feet for clear lumber. Here Oscar operated a dairy, ran a small band of sheep, and was a school bus driver for Corvallis School. In 1951, they moved to Hamilton and retired.

THE JENKINS CHILDREN

The oldest son, Vernon, worked on a ranch in Ross' Hole, and for the Forest Service. He also worked for Albert Groff in the Stevensville area, and one year, hey herded cattle to the Big Hole for the summer range, then he began his life-time vocation as a professional sheep shearer. On March 18, 1927, he married Nina May Parker, who was from the Stevensville area. They first made their home in that area, and a short time later moved to Corvallis. In 1933, the family moved up Cobb Lane (now Popham Lane) on the Bigelow place and raised sheep and operated a small dairy. "Doc" Bigelow was an old-maid doctor, she adopted two girls and after returning to New York, never returned to the Valley to practice. In 1944, Vern and Nina moved into the Hamilton Heights area, where they purchased a small farm, to go along with their dry-land on the northeast side of Palmer Butte (now known as Chaffin Butte). Vern was very interested in civic affairs and always enjoyed his year as "wrangler" at Lost Trail Camp. Nina and Vern were both 4-H leaders for years, she with sewing and he with the sheep. At age 76, he sheared sheep the day before he passed away. They had three children: Marjorie Mae Jenkins Hilliard, Thomas Marvin, and Vernon Lee.

William (Bill) lived in the Bitter Root his entire adult life. When the automobiles first came out, it was told that when Bill came upon a team ahead of his car, he didn't think about the brakes, and just kept hollering "Whoa". It is not clear what the outcome was! Bill owned land in the Mountain View Orchard area, where he farmed and raised cattle. He was very good with animals, and the veterinarian responded quickly if Bill could not handle the situation. His marriage to Lillie May Holt Kelley took place November 10, 1940. He had two step-daughters, Adra Foard and Norma

Morris. In 1957, he retired and they moved to South Ninth Street in Hamilton.

Rollin was the third child, and Vernon said that he was in inquisitive child. If they wanted him to do something the brothers told him not to do it, like putting his fingers in a mouse trap. "Ma" however understood the technique well, and the result was more than they anticipated. Rollin attended Corvallis grade school and graduated from Mount Ellis Academy in Bozeman, where he worked his way through school. He worked in the Forest Service some and continued his education at Union College in Lincoln, Nebraska. Here he met and married Ethel Percy Dunks, a native Texan. Afterward, he attended Walla Walla College in Washington. He and Ethel both taught church school for the Seventh-day Adventist Church in Montana and Texas. In the 1950s, Rollin was ordained as a minister and served his church in Texas, New Mexico and in California. Ethel was a great help to her husband, organizing whatever needed to be done. They had two children, a son, George Everett and a daughter, Joanne Mae Jenkins Cleveland.

Cora May, the only girl, with six brothers, was very talented and the family enjoyed her music when she played the piano. "Falling Waters" and "The Robins Return" were two pieces that enchanted her nieces and nephews. Graduating from Corvallis High School in 1923, among her classmates were Otto Quast, Ralph Erickson, and Maxine Holloron. While teaching school at Lone Rock, she met Paul Newton Barker, from Stevensville, and they married in 1926, and moved to Washington state. During WW II, Paul was away from home as a master machinist at Boeing in Seattle. They had three children, Corrine Mina Copeland; Pauline Augusta Barker Tolle; and a son named Robert Leroy Barker.

Joe Jenkins worked for the Forest Service and manned the Sula Peak Lookout Station one summer, carrying his twin babies on the trail. You can drive up to the lookout now, but not in those days. His eyesight required him to wear glasses constantly, and when he took them off he couldn't see to find them. He attended Mt. Ellis Academy in Bozeman for a short time. One time, he rode the freight train going east to Livingston and nearly fell under the wheels when he tried to jump off at the top of the pass to catch the westbound train. In 1927, he married Helena Candace Douglas, who was born in Crawfordsville, Indiana in 1909. They had four sons, Joseph Warren, the twins, Ralph Arden and Robert Oscar, and Leslie Thomas. He purchased some acreage near his parents home and later traded property with his brother Del, in the Mountain View area. He married Maybell Eggers from Hamilton in the mid 1930's, and when WW II started, they moved to Seattle area where Joe worked in the defense plants. After this marriage failed, he joined the Merchant Marines, and in Seattle, he met Cora Esther Halverson Carlson. Cora was born in Watertown, South Dakota, and the family called her "Cora Joe" to distinguish from their sister Cora. After they married, Joe now had two stepdaughters, Eilene Harriet Carlson Davis and Vivian Olivia Carlson Barron. He was a kind person and when given the task of reprimanding the girls, he would start by saying, "Now little honey-bunch!" He came back home one time and, with his brothers Del and Clay, drove up to the old homestead. It was interesting to hear the three brothers talking about where the house, barn, and fields were when they lived there, and some of the antics they did.

Delwin lived all his life in the Bitter Root. He went to the Corvallis schools, and also attended Mount Ellis Academy. In 1932, he married Gertrude Mae Hulshizer from Missoula. They lived in the Corvallis area and Del farmed. They had two children, a daughter Margaret Lorraine Doty, and a son, Russell Del. After this marriage broke up, Delwin continued to work on the farm and later married Ruth Montana Wagoner. Ruth loved the outdoors, she was raised in northeastern Montana, and preferred the plains country. Del also was a guide and outfitter for hunting and pack trips for a number of years. He furnished horses for Lost Trail camp in the 1970's. Their two boys were Eldon Delano and Verlon Young. When Ruth passed away, he married Wilma Ross Nicholson and her son, Robert Nicholson (a neighbor), became his stepson. Del had a sense of humor and it was interesting to hear him tell about his adventures in the mountains.

Clayton was the youngest child, and was called "Babe" until he was about four years old, when he finally became Clayton Boone. He was educated in the Corvallis school system. He drove their newly acquired motor car when he was so young he had to look through the steering wheel to see the road. In 1933, he married Helen Mabel Haley from Stevensville. After their marriage in Missoula, they ranched in Mountain View area northeast of Corvallis. In 1946, they moved to Sula, where he continued to ranch. He worked as a carpenter, and managed the Lost Trail Camp for 21 years. He was an avid hunter and prospector. For 36 years, he drove school bus for the Corvallis and Darby school districts, and in 1964 was honored with a 25 year service pin and life membership in the Montana School Bus Drivers Association at the 11th annual conference. In 1976, he retired and they moved to their new home up Willow Creek Road. Helen, who was of pioneer stock, worked hard both on the ranch and at the Lost Trail Camp. They had four children; Dorothy Marlene Jenkins Johnson and Barbara Elaine Jenkins Kline, and sons, James Clayton, and Donald Leroy.

Now, Oscar and Mina and all seven children are no longer with us, but one thing they had in common was their love for the Bitter Root Valley.

CHARLES G. JOHNSON: 1875-1953

by Edna Johnson Thomas in 1970

My father, Charles G. Johnson, was born on the island of Borholm, Denmark, in the Baltic Sea east of the Danish Peninsula of Jutland and south of Sweden. It is rugged and picturesque, its granite cliffs rising abruptly out of the sea. My father often told us stories about the ruins of castles left by the Vikings who had in early history inhabited this place. The people were intelligent, industrious, and made bold, hardy seamen.

At the age of sixteen, my father left his homeland and went to sea on a sailing vessel. While still in the Baltic Sea, a great storm came up and washed away the cargo. The crew barely escaped with their lives. They sailed then to Brussels, Belgium. Here, my father ran away and hid until the vessel sailed because the captain of the ship was a very cruel man. Later, he sailed on another ship which was going to the west coast of the United States. It took seven months to sail around the Horn (southern tip of South America). They crossed the equator twice as there was no Panama Canal at that time. The sailors had to drink lime juice to keep from getting scurvy.

After landing in Seattle, which was a small town at that time, my

Charles G. Johnson home, located just west of Corvallis High School.

father worked his way east, finally arriving in Missoula. He walked to Hamilton, sleeping in haystacks along the way. There he worked for a time at a mill. This was in 1893. He became a citizen of the United States soon after he arrived.

Later he worked for the Wan family, who lived where the Jack Morris family lives now. The Wan's were great-grandparents of Jack Morris. My father became acquainted with the Benjamin Strange family, who lived nearby. In 1897, he married Sarah Magdaline Strange. He was twenty-two and she was twenty-one. They farmed at various locations in the Valley, but finally settled near Corvallis. In 1909, I was born and my sister, Irene (Mrs. W. G. Hickey), was born in 1913. She now lives in Stevensville, retiring with her husband after thirty years of having a business in Bozeman.

Father was among the many men who were hired to plant trees along the roadways of land owned by Marcus Daly.

In 1918, our mother passed away and in 1919, our father remarried. His bride was Ellen Stade, who came from Denmark. She was our mother for many years, passing in 1963.

Father was a Ravalli County Commissioner for six years during the Depression. At that time, there wasn't much money to spend except for bare necessities. We all had to be very frugal. Before that, in the 1920's, the Corvallis Bank went broke and many families lost all their money, including our family.

In 1922, our brother, Robert E. Johnson, was born. He now lives in Stevensville and works at the Corvallis School.

My sister, brother, and I attended the Corvallis Schools and graduated from there. We were taught in our home to consider it a privilege to get an education. My sister and I became school teachers.

In 1943, our brother enlisted in the Air Force. After training at the various Air Force bases, he went to the European theatre of war in 1945, and served as a co-pilot on a B17 bomber. During the last months of World War II, he was in the squadrons which flew by way of France, Germany, and back to England — flying over the island of Bornholm where his father was born. After the war, he was stationed in Munich for a year. Pilots from here flew to Casa Blanca in Africa.

Our father was active in community projects. He served many years on the Corvallis School Board. He was an honest, friendly, hard working man who appreciated being a citizen of the United States. He was well known for his very strong sense of humor. He passed away in 1953.

THE NAAMEN JOHNSON FAMILY

as related by Ruth Rawlins Johnson
and from local newspapers of that time.

NAAMEN JOHNSON was an early day philanthropist. He was a pioneer in every sense of the word. Born in Rochester, New York, on August 9, 1835. He, while quite young, went to Illinois and shortly thereafter made the long journey around Cape Horn to the gold fields of California in 1850. He came to Montana in 1863, during the gold excitement at Alder Gulch. Naamen died in 1907 in Corvallis.

Emma Johnson was born in 1852 and died in 1904.

Naamen returned to Illinois just before the Civil War and enlisted in the Army and served until he was taken sick and sent to the hospital. He came to the Bitter Root in 1882, from Bozeman, settling in the Corvallis area. He and his wife, Emma, came together and they acquired farm land on the eastside of Corvallis which included the Hay place. They donated the land where the "old Corvallis School" (present site of the Quentin Brown School) was built, and land to a church (where the present Community Church now stands).

They also sold lots in Corvallis, creating the Emma Johnson Addition.

They were the parents of eleven children: 1. Charles M. Johnson, 2. Thomas C. Johnson, 3. Robert Johnson, 4. A. C. Johnson, 5. Sidney Johnson, 6. Edward Johnson (married Ruth Rawlins and lived out their lives in Corvallis, and had one daughter, Mary Jean, who married Robert Miller, living in Hamilton and operating the Ford dealership with their son Neil.), 7. Mrs. C. F. Daly, 8. Mrs. J. E. Gibbons, 9. Mrs. Roy Myers, (whose daughter, Ann Mary Dussault, is active in Missoula County politics), 10. Lydia Johnson, 11. Bessie Johnson.

THE KEELING FAMILY

by Anne Keeling Woodruff

My father, Charles Franklin Keeling, was born in 1873, at Grayville, Illinois, on the banks of the Wabash River. At the age of 19, he joined the U. S. Army and was sent to Fort Logan, near Denver, CO, where he served the four years of his enlistment, being discharged just before the Spanish-American War.

My mother, Della Myrtle Hill, was born in 1877, near the town of Phillipsburg in northwestern Kansas. She was the eldest child of Alfred and Annie Hill. When Mama was thirteen years old, the family moved to Denver by covered wagon. After graduating, she went by stagecoach to Vernal, UT, where she taught school for two terms. Papa and Mama met at a church social in Denver and were married there in 1897. From there they went to Bozeman, MT, where Mama taught school and Papa worked in a logging camp. I was born there in January 1898. They lived in Butte for a short time before moving to Missoula. Papa worked for a truck gardener near Missoula, before he bought a relinquishment on a 160 acre homestead, two and one half miles west of Woodside, from a man named Felch, who had bought it from the Peter Elliotts. The Elliotts had filed on the place and built a two room log cabin on it. (In later years, this property was known as the C. B. Kenck place.)

The Bitter Root Valley was enjoying Indian Summer that fall of 1899, when my parents came to Woodside from Missoula on the branch line of the Northern Pacific. It was then routed up the west side of the valley. Dad had engaged a man with a wagon and team of horses to haul their furniture and baggage which was following in a freight car, up to the new location. Mama was six months pregnant and I was only 22 months old, but they were so eager to see the homestead that they set to walking up Dutch Hill. They later told of Mama sitting down and having a good cry when she saw the cabin that was to be her home. It was a typical bachelor's den — dirty windows, greasy floors, cupboard fouled by the leavings of packrats and mice as well as of the cats that were expected to catch them!

The following February 7, their second baby girl was born. The Indian wife of Bill Turnage was the mid-wife. Tragically, the little one had three vertebrae that were filled with fluid rather than normal bone. The baby died the following week and was laid to rest on the south side of Mill Creek near a big fir tree that still stands. (This is just north of the present Forest Service road.)

My first and happiest memories began in that summer of 1900. The place was a wonderland to a very small child — big pine trees to call friends as well as support for a stout rope swing. There were buttercups and other wild flowers to be gathered and pine squirrels and chipmunks and dear little birds that nested in the trees, in the grass and under the eaves. The drawbacks were the no-see-um gnats and nightly ritual of kneeling face down on Mama's lap while she searched my curls for wood ticks. The cabin had been made snug and neat and the folks spent many long days planting orchard and berry fields as well as vegetable gardens. They raised fruit and vegetables that were shipped to Butte and Anaconda. At one time, Papa had a lovely little peach orchard that thrived for a number of years. He grew early tomatoes and cabbage plants in a big hot-bed that was heated by two stoves with pipes under the length of the beds.

In the fall of 1900, Mama began teaching at the Fairview School, a one-room white building perched on a bare hillside a few miles south of Victor. She drove a horse and buggy to her work and sometimes I would go with her. On cold days, we took hot bricks to keep our feet warm. In 1901,

Mama taught summer school at the Fair Play School which was just one mile east of our place. That November, my brother Ralph was born. Again Mrs. Turnage did the honors.

In 1902, Jim Horn set his sawmill on our land south of Mill Creek when much of the virgin timber of that area was logged.

My sister, Mildred, was born on February 23, 1904. Our nearest neighbor, Mrs. Chris Wolff attended the birth. That night, we had a big snow storm. That morning, frost glistened on the kitchen walls and ceiling and snow reached the window sills. I still recall the deep and narrow paths that Papa dug across our yard.

Although we had neither radio nor phonograph, the long winter days and evenings were seldom dull. We had sleds and skates and numerous games to play and we pulled taffy and popped corn, but best of all were the times when we were cutting and sewing rug rags or piecing quilts while Papa read aloud to the family.

By 1906, we had outgrown the log house, which was replaced by a four room frame building. In 1908, Papa came down with the dreaded Spotted Fever from which he recovered after many weeks of illness. He was attended by Dr. C. R. Thornton and visited by Dr. Howard Ricketts, who was researching the fever here in the valley.

In 1909, Joe Blodgett set a sawmill near the mountain just to the northwest of us. Much of the surrounding land was logged, including the north half of our place. How we children hated to see our friendly old pines yield to the cross-cut saws and be hauled away to the heartless mill! "The trees will grow back", they told us — and they have.

In 1910, the four-room building was made over into a six-room house that Mama designed and Papa built, mostly from lumber from our place. They built a fireplace faced with attractive native rock. In 1912, Grandpa and Grandma Hill came from Denver to buy 30 acres of our land on the south side of the creek. They built a three-room cottage there but Grandpa's health also failed and they returned to Denver where he died. Mama's health also failed and she died in July of 1916. Soon afterwards, the family moved to the West Coast.

Mildred died in Seattle in 1946. She left three sons. Ralph died in Chicago of cancer in 1952. He left a son and a daughter. He had won a four year scholarship to Yale University from West Seattle High School in his youth. Papa lived to be 83 years old, and died of a sudden heart attack in 1956. He had returned to the town of his birth in Illinois.

KEIRNS AND COWAN FAMILY HISTORY

by Kamai Van Aken Rhodes, great-granddaughter of E. H. Keirns

Edwin Hamilton Keirns was born February 7, 1852, in Hamilton, Ohio, to John Nixon Keirns and his wife Sara Shaner Keirns. Edwin married Rebecca Ellen Johnson on February 16, 1876 in Casey, Iowa. They had a son, Lester Carl, born January 20, 1878, in Casey, Iowa who died January 12, 1879. Their second son, Carl DeLoss, was born October 12, 1879, in Osborn, Kansas. Carl died July 9, 1880. Their third son, Frank E., was born April 18, 1887, in Osborn, Kansas.

According to a personal journal kept by John N. Keirns, Edwin Rebecca, and Frank left Kansas on March 26, 1888, on their way to Montana. They traveled by train and arrived in Victor on or before April 7, 1888. John received a letter from a friend that told him of the death of baby Frank on April 7, and that he was buried in Victor, Montana, on April 8, 1888.

Edwin and Rebecca acquired 120 acres near Victor and built the Keirns Ranch house in about 1898. It still stands today at 1374 Red Crow Road, in faint resemblance of the original structure shown in a photo which hangs in the Victor History museum, and in the homes of most of the grandchildren of E. H. Keirns. Edwin built the house with wood from his own sawmill and used only prime lumber without any knots in it. They also planted a large apple orchard and Edward was a member of the Bitterroot Fruit Growers association. By 1925, most of the orchard had been taken out due to winter freeze and lack of water.

Edwin and Rebecca's fourth child, a girl named Gladys Mildred, was born on August 5, 1893, and two years later came Frances Louise, born March 14, 1895. Unlike the short lives of the three boys, both girls grew strong and left a story of pictures for generations to follow. During this time, they both attended Victor school when it became the first consolidated school district in Montana. Gladys and Frances rode to school in horse drawn school wagons.

Rebecca had a great interest in flowers and shared this with both girls. They entered flower shows and state fairs, collecting many prize ribbons. Frances later became a certified flower judge and was asked to suggest a state tree for Montana. She suggested the "Ponderosa Pine", and was honored by winning with her choice.

Gladys Keirns graduated from Victor High School in May of 1916, and attended Montana State College, then taught at Woodman School west of Lolo. **She married Albert Ashley Cowan** May 5, 1919, in Victor. They had two daughters. Altha Bernice born on August 31, 1920, and Frances Luella born May 9, 1926. They attended all 12 years of school in Victor, riding however on motorized school buses.

Albert Ashley Cowan was taken abruptly from his family when he was shot in the back and killed while separating milk in the kitchen of their family home. This shooting took place on December 25, 1929, by a ranch hand employee. The fellow confessed to the crime and was sent to the Montana State Penitentiary and later to the state mental hospital.

Gladys Cowan remarried to E. Clayson Payne in 1933. Born to this marriage was Gail Yvonne on October 31, 1934. Despite losing her hearing to scarlet fever as a child, Gail went on to graduate from the University of Montana and taught at schools for the deaf before marrying Ray Mederios on August 5, 1964.

The ranch was divided between Gladys and Frances after Edwin H. Keirns died of a heart attack in 1924. Rebecca died in 1925 after falling down a set of stairs. They are both buried at Victor Cemetery. Each daughter lived in the house with their families, at different times, following the death of their parents. Although sold from the Keirns family in 1949, its history lives on today.

Gladys Keirns Cowan Payne passed away November 1964, and is interred in Victor Cemetery. Clayson Payne died in 1977, and also is buried at Victor. Gail followed in death on March 16, 1997, succumbing to cancer while living in Las Vegas, NV.

Frances Louise Keirns graduated from Victor High School in 1917, and went to teachers training in Eastern Montana, then taught school briefly. She married Edgar Lloyd Puyear on August 25, 1917. They lived on the Keirns Ranch after Edwin H. died. Edgar became a livestock dealer and was well known by ranchers and farmers of the Bitterroot Valley for his honest bartering. Born to this marriage were Gwen, Mildred, Barbara and Gerold.

Edgar Puyear died while he and Frances were living in Kennewick, WA, and is buried in the Keirns plot in Victor Cemetery. Frances passed away in June of 1989, and is buried next to Edgar.

This history of Edwin and Rebecca Keirns is a reference for their great-grandchildren. There are many generations of people and other relatives throughout the Bitterroot Valley and across the country. Thank you for reading our story.

SLAVIC PEOPLE IN THE SKALKAHO AREA

by Edward Kratofil

About the beginning of the 20th Century, several Slavic families started to settle in the Skalkaho area.

Most of these hard working people had first settled in Butte and Anaconda where the men worked in the mines and the smelter.

They were hard working people and the mines had work available and they could work for a decent wage. Most had come from Croatia or

Slovania, which at that time was under Austro-Hungarian rule so they were called Austrians. After World War I, the area was combined into Yugoslavia.

Because of the terrible economic conditions in their homelands, many of these people migrated to America for better living conditions and to find their pot of gold. Mining and farming were the main ways of making a living in the old country, so these were the jobs they sought when they came to America.

Mining in those days was less than desirable, and their dream was to save enough money to buy a small farm and move out of the unhealthy conditions of the mines and smelters.

Some people started to settle around the Skalkaho area where land was available at a reasonable cost. A few would farm their small acreages from spring to fall, and go back and work in the mines at Butte during the winter, until they could pay off their farms.

Among the first family names to arrive were Strnisha, Miller, Thompson, Fortune, Antonich, Frankovich, Cash, Shragel, Marvin, Kobe, and later came Barich, Kratofil, Perusich, Novak, Kudasic, and Bolf. Several of these names were Americanized. Many descendants are still living in the valley.

Due to their ethnic background and language they found security and communication easier by living near each other. They were all hard working, fun loving people. They worked long hard hours, but Sundays were set aside for church and socializing with each other. Around the 4th of July, quite often, the neighborhood would have a picnic. Usually a lamb or a pig was butchered and some of the men would set up a barbecue. Early in the morning, they would start cooking the meat on a spit over an open fire, while the women prepared the rest of the meal including many ethnic foods. By noon all would be ready to eat. Everyone would have a very good time playing various games and just visiting. Then all would go home to milk the cows and do various chores. Of course, the work was much harder to do in those days as there wasn't electricity and very few had tractors so most work was done by hand or with horses.

Money was very scarce so many men paid off their water bill by using their teams and manpower to clean and repair the irrigation ditches in the area. Many farm buildings were built of used flume lumber which could be bought at a very reasonable price.

When extra labor was needed, such as haying or threshing grain, neighbors would often help each other and the women would serve a feast for the noon meal. Normally, only one neighbor had a binder and would cut and bind the grain ready to thresh. Another neighbor would come with his threshing machine to each farm to do the threshing.

In the fall, a truck would make a trip to California and bring back a load of grapes and many of the families would purchase these grapes to make their Vino, which was a staple on the table both in the old country and also when they came to this country.

Pork was the main source of meat as it could be cured to last all year when made into bacon, hams, and sausage. Later, when freezer lockers came into being, beef was butchered and frozen. Of course there was also fish, pheasants, deer, and elk to be had in season.

THE BEN KRESS FAMILY

by Helen Jean Kress Wilson

Bernhardt Kress was born to German immigrants, Bernhardt and Anna Gehla Gontner-Kress on December 8, 1857, in Mesomenie, Wisconsin. His father left the family in Wisconsin to go to the aid of a brother in Florida. His father never returned, and Anna Gehla was left with several children to raise by herself.

At the age of 12, "Ben," as he was best known, started work in a nursery to provide for the family. It would be at his first job that Ben would get experience that would influence his life forever.

At about the age of 20, he came west with a brother, Theodore, working to build the railroad. They landed in the Black Hills in the winter of 1878-79, and went on to Miles City, MT, where they learned the trade of cutting railroad ties, as well as the trade of logging. From the time he came west until 1902, he worked in or owned sawmills.

In 1891,Ben Kress set up a sawmill with a man named Ed Brennan. It was located on the south side of Roaring Lion Creek (now part of the Henry Grant place). The mill was purchased in Philipsburg and brought to the area to cut logs for the railroad, and to help settlers with their houses. When Marcus Daly came in with the ACM mill at the end of Main Street in Hamilton, the Brennan-Kress Mill folded, and they went to work for ACM.

Ben Kress needed a place to stay and took room and board at the new GEYER HOUSE. It was there, he fell in love with the proprietor's oldest daughter, Marie Pearl Geyer. In a letter dated September 26, 1893, written to Pearl while visiting in Deer Lodge, Ben proposed. One week later, Ben received this reply-"YES"! But, there was a catch. Marie was still paying on an organ, she had a $15.00 balance, and her father told her that a young lady does not go into marriage with a debt, so the wedding would have to wait awhile. They were married January 1, 1894. Their marriage license was number 29, in the new Ravalli County, issued on December 27, 1893, and filed January 4, 1894.

Ben bought a piece of land from Newman Blodgett, in May of 1894, on the west side of Hamilton, about three miles northwest of town. It was 80 acres of bench land with irrigation rights, and cost $10.00 an acre. A family home was built, and Ben continued to work at the ACM Mill while establishing his farm.

In a 1910 supplement of the Western News, there was an article written about my Granddad, and I quote, "I became interested in fruit growing at the first fair held in Hamilton, in 1894. What I saw at the fair set me to thinking about raising fruit, and nothing else. In the spring of 1895, 112 trees were set out. I knew nothing about varieties or the business. Where I made my mistake was planting the wrong varieties. I had planted 24 varieties in all. By 1910, I had nearly 40 acres all told. I practiced clean cultivation from the start, and the trees thrived nicely. I began to get returns on the fourth year of planting, and the fifth year was good enough for a commercial crop. I settled on the MacIntosh Red variety and one year sold $1,700 worth of apples that were produced by 130 of these trees. My success came by "Cultivation which makes the orchard; and hard work with little common sense."

Ben Kress learned grafting when working as a young man at the nursery in Wisconsin, and from this knowledge, developed his own MacIntosh Red. Start Brothers had an exclusive on the sale of the trees and this is their description: "This is a double-red color improvement of the MacIntosh apple, which had retained its position as one of the top ten apple varieties, for more than 150 years. Popular on the markets because of its uniformly large, brilliant over-all color. Tender white flesh makes this variety a favorite for eating, pies, cobblers, jelly, cider, sauce and jelly. Extremely hardy tree. Ripens late August to early September in the Midwest.." Trees sold for $6.95 each. There are still a few of these trees in the Swanson Apple Orchard in Corvallis.

An interesting story that many farmers loved to tell was of the schemes used to lure easterners to come to the valley and buy land. It goes like this: "There was a well-managed five year old orchard, ready for sale. It was awfully rocky, so the seller took a pitchfork and made a row of rocks down every other row of trees. The buyer said, "We'd like the orchard, but what about all those rocks?" The fellow selling the land told him, "Oh, you use them, the heat from the rocks is what makes our apples so red." The apple boom ended in the 1930's, when Washington and Canada were able to ship the fruit at cheaper rates.

At the home place, Ben and Pearl raised four children: Jessie Marie (Beechwood), Herbert Theodore, Robert Bernhardt "Benny", and Elsie Marie (Brooks). I can remember that my dad, Herb, hated the farm because he had picked so many rocks off the land for the orchard, using the rock for fence lines.

The Kress's won many awards for their apples, sending carloads of hand picked and wrapped apples all over the Northwest. They were also members of the Horticultural Society. In 1902, Ben gave up the sawmill and devoted full time to his growing family and orchards. Ten grandchildren loved romping on the big front lawn of the farmhouse on special occasions.

The Kress's sold the ranch, due to failing health, in 1942, and moved into town. They celebrated 52 years of marriage before Ben passed away in February of 1946. Pearl died in April of 1957. Both were charter members of the Christian Church in Hamilton.

LAGERQUIST FAMILY

The Lagerquist family was known in the community primarily for their involvement in lumber manufacturing. J.O. Lagerquist (John) started the family on this route in 1904. He was born in Sweden in 1865. At age 16, he was a carpenter apprentice to an uncle. After becoming a carpenter, he served in the Swedish Army. He came to America at age 22, first to Minneapolis, then in 1889 to Butte and Anaconda being employed by the ACM Company in construction. In 1891 he came to Hamilton and was in charge of constructing the Daly home. In 1904, he and Eric Erickson became partners in a lumber manufacturing business. He bought Erickson out in 1908 and continued the business as Riverview Manufacturing Co. located on North Fourth Street. The company made boxes for the fruit growers.

He married Sarah K. Perkins in 1900. They had six children. One son, Elmer (Duke), eventually moved to Los Angeles and was involved in the furniture business. He died in 1970. Two other sons, Victor (Luke) and George, stayed in Hamilton and helped their dad and eventually bought him out when he became too ill to run the business anymore. A fourth son, John Albert, died in 1910 at age five. The two daughters were Ruth Nugent of Elko, Nevada, and Nancy of Missoula. Their mother, Sarah, died in 1971 at age 101. Father John died 1948.

The two boys added a sawmill to the business in 1938. Prior to that, it had been mainly a planer mill and box plant and was located across Fair Grounds Road from the fairgrounds. In 1952, they replaced the circular saw with a band saw in order to be more efficient in cutting logs. By now, Luke had bought out his brother. One year later an interesting piece appeared in the Western News. It appears that a massive Ponderosa tree was cut up Laird Creek. It was about 150 feet tall and 400 years old. It was cut into sixteen-foot sections, but the butt log and the one adjacent to it were thought to be too big to cut at the mill, so they had been left in the pond. Finally, it was decided to cut the one next to the butt log, so by much struggling, precutting with chain saws and maneuvering, it was placed on the carriage and run through the saw. It almost wrecked the mill, but it was cut. I don't know when if ever the butt log was cut. They said that the tree yielded between six and seven thousand feet of lumber. Luke entered into partnerships with Milo Wilson and Dee Shook as the Bitter Root Timber Industry in Darby, where they built a plant including a dry kiln. Luke eventually retired from this venture and closed the Riverview plant as well. He died in 1968 after being ill for a number of years.

George had sold his interest in the mill to Luke before entering the service where he taught instrument flying. In 1958, he bought the Bates Fuel Service on North Third. An interesting sidelight was also his sale of the lots on the northwest corner of North Third and Pinckney to the Mountain States Telephone Company. The company used these lots to build a structure to house the dialing equipment, which was supposed to be operational in 1964.

George was also a charter member of the Hamilton Golf Club and had started playing when the club was located where the Rocky Mountain Laboratory is now located.

In 1945, George married Emma Raudabaugh. She had been a lab tech at the Rocky Mountain Laboratory and then worked at the Marcus Daly Memorial Hospital as lab tech, x-ray tech and EKG tech until the 1960s. They had a daughter, Dr. Lenore Tsang, now residing in Palo Alto, California. Emma died in January 1985 and George in October 1985.

THE LAWS and KANE FAMILIES

Information by Jim Kane

My grandfather, James Bernard Laws (aka "J. B."), and his wife, Frances, moved to the Bitter Root in 1894, from Chetopa, Kansas. They were accompanied by their three children: Ralph born in Chetopa in 1884, Robert born in Chetopa in 1886, and my mother — Grace, born in Altamont, KS, in 1889. Grandfather's sister, Mary Laws Greenup, had moved to the Bitter Root and it was her invitation that encouraged him to move here also. Mary and her descendants have lived in the Darby area.

Grandfather's first job was shooting elk for local boarding houses, and he spent some of those first years cutting stulls for the mines in Butte. My grandfather and his family first moved to the Darby area, and then to Corvallis where he had a small farm and operated a hay baling operation.

He always loved the Bitter Root very much, and one of the reasons was that he had had seven consecutive crop failures in Kansas, so the irrigated ground of the Bitter Root Valley looked very good to him! Grandfather Laws was one of the founders of the Corvallis Presbyterian Church, which was later part of the United Church. He was a remarkable old man and I remember him riding a pretty salty horse and driving his Model T, when he was in his late seventies.

My Mother, Grace, attended elementary school in Corvallis riding in via horseback, and later went to Hamilton where she graduated from high school. Her classmates, the Myers sisters, the Lear and Cobb boys are shown in some wonderful old pictures. Grandpa Laws gave my mother a horse and buggy for a graduation present, and she went around giving piano lessons in people's homes — at fifty cents each. She was a good piano player and played in the church for many years, and at more funerals than I can count, never charging one cent. My mother's brother, Ralph Laws, lived most of his life in the Darby area where he both farmed and worked in the lumber business. He married Margaret Nicholson and they raised three children. Her brother, Bob, never married, lived in the West Fork and raised horses and cattle, and worked in the local sawmills.

My Father, Thomas Kane, was born in Kingston, Ontario, one of nine children. I am not sure when he became a U. S. citizen, but I know he went to college two years in Canada, and then taught school in Minnesota. He mustn't have liked teaching school, because he then moved to the Bitter Root, in about 1904, where his first job was herding sheep. A definite improvement over teaching! He had a brother, Simpson Kane, who also moved to the Bitter Root and lived in the Woodside area. Sim never married.

My parents, Grace and Tom, met while Tom worked for my grandfather Laws baling hay. They were married in 1909, and moved to the family farm in 1910. My brother, Tom, was born in 1910; my sister, Clare, in 1912; another sister, Doris, in 1920; and I (Jim) in 1925.

My father was very interested in politics. I'm not sure just when he first ran for office, but I think it was as early as 1912. I know he served continuously as a Senator in the State Legislature from about 1912 until 1934, when he retired from politics. He was President Pro Tem of the Senate for several terms. After his retirement from the Legislature, he held several appointive state positions. He always said his success in politics was due to the fact that when he was running for office, he went to Hamilton every Saturday (so did everyone else, apparently) with a pair of gloves and a pocket full of cigars. He would hand out cigars to the men, and crank the women's cars! A sure winning recipe! No big fund raising scandals in those days. He was also known for doing all sorts of Irish dances — jigs, reels, clogs, hornpipes, etc.

My father told many interesting stories about the "Boom", as he called it, when the Big Ditch was built and so many orchards were planted. He knew almost everyone from Sula to Lolo, and had stories about most of them, interesting observations on how the people moved to, and lived in, the Bitter Root Valley.

About myself and my siblings: Tom never married (deceased), Clare married and had one child (deceased), Doris married and had two children (deceased), Jim (That's me) married Marilyn Murphy in 1954, and we have three children. I am living in Pleasanton, California, in 1998.

LAY AND GILMORE FAMILIES

Montana Pioneers

written by Presley E. Lay, on April 22, 1958

George Lewis Lay was born in Kirksville, Missouri, on January 24, 1868. His great-great-grandfather, Thomas Lay, fought in the American Revolutionary War, having enlisted in Grainger County, Tennessee. In the early 1840's, Thomas Lay and his family migrated west from Tennessee to Missouri, locating at Kirksville.

When George Lay was a boy of ten years, his father, Lewis E. Lay, decided to go west. So, by wagon train — with their train consisting of twenty-eight — they left Kirksville, Missouri, on May 7, 1878, and arrived in Bozeman, Montana, on August 3, 1878.

In May 1888, George Lay came to the Bitter Root Valley. His sister and brother-in-law, Mr. and Mrs. B. Frank Heavlin, came to the valley soon after they were married in 1882, at Bozeman, MT. They homesteaded on what was known as Camas Prairie, presently known as Charlos Heights. In 1888, George's brother, Ike Lay, was living south west of where Hamilton is, on a ranch that in later years has been known as the Lay Ranch. George Lay's son, Presley E. Lay lives on the old Ike Lay homestead.

In 1888, George Lay worked on the first Northern Pacific railroad bridge across the Bitter Root river at Woodside, Montana. During 1888 and 1889, he carried mail from Corvallis to Riverside.

In 1893, he returned to Bozeman and went down the Yellowstone river near Big Timber where he took up a stock ranch. This ranch today is known as one of the fine ranches along the Yellowstone River.

In 1903, he sold his well improved stock ranch to his brother-in-law, Sid Fraser, and Sid Fraser, Jr., operates this old ranch today. For a time then, George went into Canada and upon returning went to Twin Falls, ID, where he homesteaded. Selling out in Idaho, he returned again to the Bitter Root Valley where he purchased an interest in Sleeping Child Springs from his brother-in-law, B. Frank Heavlin. He continued with the operation of this health resort until 1907, when he sold his interest back to Mr. Heavlin. Mr. and Mrs. Heavlin sold their homestead on Camas Prairie (now Charlos Heights), purchasing Sleeping Child Springs in 1904. They sold the springs in 1931, and moved to Missoula to live.

George L. Lay and Miss Kate Gilmore (from another pioneer family) were married November 28, 1907, at Hamilton. They became parents of two sons; Presley E. Lay and George G. Lay. In 1958, Presley Lay operates the ranch which was purchased by his father in 1907. George G. lay is an operating Engineer at the U. S. Public Health Service Laboratory in Hamilton.

George L. Lay was always interested in government, state and national affairs. He served on the school board, also as chairman of the board of Dist. #27, which now is a part of Dist. #3.

The following is from the obituary of George L. Lay, which appeared in The Western News on August 23, 1956.

" Friends of Mr. Lay gathered at his home on January 24, 1956, to congratulate him on his eighty-eighth birthday, little thought it would be his last natal day. Mr. Lay said upon the occasion, "This has been the best birthday of my life". Much reminiscing was done upon his life that day and the Western News was pleased to run a story of the birthday festivities and of various phases of his life. It was noted that he was especially fond of horseback riding and he pursued that pleasure in the hills and mountains of his loved valley until he was in his eighties."

W. P. GILMORE

Willis Presley Gilmore was born at Kirksville, Missouri, on August 19, 1847, the son of Thomas P. Gilmore who was born in 1807 in Kentucky.

Willis P. Gilmore and Zeralda Carter were married in Green Castle, Missouri, on March 13, 1872. She was born July 31, 1855, at Keokack, Iowa.

The W. P. Gilmore family left Kirksville, Missouri, May 26, 1876, for the Territory of Montana. Their wagon train consisted of four wagons and teams. The Gilmore wagon train pulled into Gallatin Valley on September 1, 1876.

Upon reaching Montana, the Gilmore's first stopped at Pony, Montana. This was a new mining camp at that time and reported to be very rich. Some of the party found work but Willis found nothing, so he and his family immediately left for the West Gallatin where work was reported to be plentiful. Mr. Gilmore had two nephews there, Lewis and Zack Lay. The Gilmore's located at Salesville, some years later the name was changed to Gallatin Gateway.

In 1882, W. P. Gilmore purchased the first twine self binder on the West Gallatin. He hired help, and with the use of lanterns, they cut grain day and night. The price charged was $2.00 per acre.

THE AVART COURIER of Bozeman, told of the appearance of the first steam threshing machine in the Gallatin metropolis, in August 1884, as follows:

"Great curiosity was manifested by citizens of Bozeman in a steam engine threshing machine which passed down Main Street Saturday, and remained in front of Cook's blacksmith shop for some repairs until Sunday afternoon, when it moved down the Valley to Bogel's ranch for the purpose of threshing his excellent crop of fall wheat. What excitement and unusual curiosity was the fact that the engine used to run the thresher furnishes also the necessary power for moving itself anywhere on an ordinary road and from farm to farm. When ready to start, the engine, tender and separator were turned around on Main Street with as great apparent ease as a span of horses attached to an ordinary wagon. The novel threshing machine is owned by W. P. Gilmore and J. C. Carter."

In 1890, the Gilmore family sold their holdings at Bozeman and moved to Boise, Idaho, where they purchased a farm. They remained there until 1900, when they again sold their property and came to the Bitter Root Valley by wagon train over what is now called Gibbons Pass.

Mr. and Mrs. W. P. Gilmore purchased the ranch of John O'Dell at Camas Prairie, later called Charlos Heights. Upon retiring from the ranch, the Gilmores purchased property in Hamilton where they spent their remaining years. This is where they celebrated their sixtieth wedding anniversary on March 13, 1932.

Willis Presley Gilmore passed away on February 8, 1934, at the age of 86 years.

Zeralda Carter Gilmore passed away on April 27, 1939, at 84 years of age.

Their children consisted of three daughters: Maud Gilmore Shawver, who died in November 1956 (Como, Montana, had been her home for 56 years), Kate Gilmore Lay, and Cora Van Duesen.

REVEREND WILLIAM D. LEAR AND ALICE MYERS LEAR

by Alice Lear Wheeler and Lois Lear Shuland

Reverend William Daniel Lear was born February 17, 1844, in Lancaster, Kentucky, and was one of a family of eight children of William and Elizabeth Adams Lear. His father operated a southern plantation and practiced general farming, specializing in the breeding of fine horses, in which his son was always interested. His father died when young William was just 12 years of age. The family went from Kentucky to Missouri, where William Daniel Lear received his higher education in a Canton, MO, university, and at the Christian University at Lexington, KY. He was ordained into the ministry in 1877, and began preaching at the age of thirty-three While teaching school in Millport, Iowa, **he married Alice Myers,** one of his pupils, in **1879.**

The following year, he came west with a group and they arrived in Beaverhead in April 1880, with the snow four feet deep and no shelter available. Soon after, he was called to a Christian church in Helena. That fall, he came to Missoula on horseback, riding on up the Bitter Root Valley to take a position as a school teacher at Corvallis. During the winter **of 1881, he organized the first Christian Church here. This was the first Protestant church completed south of Stevensville.** There were seven charter members, and in the same year the church edifice was built. The

Reverend William D. Lear.

building which housed this church was later used as a community hall in Corvallis, and still stands in 1998. In 1997, it held a business called "Mrs. McGregor's Garden".

Reverend Lear went back to Iowa in March to join his wife, and he remained for a year to preach in the church at Moulton, Iowa. He returned to the Bitter Root Valley with his wife **and his son, Jamie,** in 1883, making the journey by covered wagon to Deer Lodge and from there to Missoula on the first passenger train to run over the Northern Pacific tracks in that section. The Corvallis church welcomed the minister and his family.

In 1884, Reverend Lear organized a church in Missoula, and two years later established one in Stevensville. He secured a lot from the Hamilton Land Company for a church site in Hamilton, and a few years later he organized a church in Florence. Twice he served as Chaplain in the Montana State Legislature. He held pastorates in the Bitter Root Valley for over 50 years, pioneering in teaching the gospel.

The family made their homestead just Northeast of Corvallis, where they built a log cabin and later built a two-story home, a large barn, milking shed, and other outbuildings. Reverend Lear practiced farming while engaged in his church work. The couple had four children: **Josie,** the oldest son, died before they left Iowa (February 21, 1882), **Lea,** born February 3, 1885, and died in Corvallis in 1887**, James,** born in Iowa, and **Paul,** born in Corvallis. James and Paul were raised in Corvallis. "Jamie", as he was called, recalled many hours of riding horseback up the Willow Creek to watch the Indians, who had camped there, rope wild horses and break them to ride. As a boy, Jamie exercised race horses for Marcus Daly.

In later years, Reverend Lear was associated with the United Church, in which the Christian Church body was affiliated, and for which he served as an elder for 15 years. He was an honorary elder until his death on October 11, 1936, at the age of ninety-two.

Mrs. Alice J. Myers Lear died on July 7, 1936, and was known to the entire community as a kindly, sympathetic lady, with a love of life, and an interest in her family and friends" according to her obituary.

JAMIE AND PAUL LEAR FAMILIES

Jamie and Paul stayed in the Corvallis area and each married Corvallis schoolteachers. **Jamie married Katharin Haines** of Ennis, Montana, **and Paul married Claribel Hafflee** of Shullsburg, Wisconsin.

Jamie and Katharin, or "Kittee" as her family and friends called her, made their home on the old homestead of Jamie's parents, except for seven years spent in Ennis. They farmed their 160-acre dairy ranch until 1948, when they sold it and moved to a home on the corner of Highway 93 and Shady Lane in Hamilton. When the new highway came through, their

James D. Lear driving freight wagon from Virginia City, Montana.

home had to be moved. Today it is located off Westside Road.

Kittie's mother died shortly after her birth and Mr. and Mrs. William Ennis, for whom the town was named, raised her. When Jamie and Kittie lived in Ennis, they leased and ran Mrs. Ennis's ranch and Jamie also drove the freight line with wagons and a team of six horses, from Norris to Fort Benton, Montana.

Jamie and Kittie had five children. Joseph and Lois, born in Corvallis, Paul and Alice, born in Ennis, and Gene was born on the ranch in Corvallis, after they moved back from Ennis.

The oldest son, Joseph, died in Phoenix, AZ, in July of 1989. Paul Jr. and his wife, Marie, live in Seattle, WA. Gene and his wife, Helen Jean, and family live in Spokane. Lois Shuland and Alice Wheeler both live in Hamilton in 1997.

Katharin Mary Lear died March 22, 1966, and James D. Lear died March 28, 1977.

Paul D. Lear, Sr., and his wife Claribel also ranched in the Corvallis area. Paul worked eleven winters in the Ravalli County Treasurer's office in Hamilton. He was a clerk at farm auctions for a long time, and was a member of the Corvallis School Board and several other boards and organizations. Paul Lear Sr., died March 10, 1954, and Claribel on January 1, 1977. Paul and Claribel had one son, Lee, who was born on June 26, 1927, and died September 23, 1995.

JOHN G. AND CARRIE LEIBEL

John G. Liebel was born in Austria, Bohemia, in 1854. In 1866, at the early age of 12, his father sent him with a guardian to the United States in search of a sister with whom he was to live at Oskegan, Michigan.

He married Carrie Bolton in 1879, at Little Falls, Minnesota. She was born in Joliet, Illinois, in 1858.

John G. and Carrie Leibel came to Hamilton in 1895. They became parents of three boys and two girls. They are: George, John, William, Ethel, and Winifred. Mr. Leibel and sons worked at the A.C.M. Company at the west end of Main Street. John was the Justice of the Peace from the 1920's until 1935.

LEONARDI AND BOSCHET (BOSKET) FAMILIES

by Pierina Leonardi

My maiden name in Italy is Boschet. In America, they spell it Bosket. Italian language does not include a "K", thus it is spelled Boschet in Italy. My Dad's name is Pete Boschet. Dad and mother were married in Italy in

1902. I was born on the 23rd of November, 1906, in Zurich, Switzerland, right over the border from our Italian home of Feltre. The female name for Pete is Pierina, so being the first child, I was named Pierina, after my father. Most people called me Pauline because it was too hard to say Pierina. Rose and Fostino were born in Italy, Albert was born in Washington, Frank was born in Idaho, and Adeline was born in Corvallis.

Dad heard about the Bitter Root Valley from his brother who was working in a dairy in Corvallis at the time. He wrote to Dad to come over here. There was work in the sugar beets and there was lot of good hunting in the mountains. My dad came from Italy in 1912. He worked in Washington in the summer of 1912 and then worked at Potlatch, ID, in the mines. After about a year, he decided that mining was not for him, he wanted to work in the fresh air. He was heading to California when he heard of a free pass and train ride being offered to Montana. Mother followed in 1913 and my sister and I were to come over in a year or two with an Aunt. There were strict health regulations about who could make the journey. We were about to board a boat for the journey, when the authorities noticed my aunt had pink eye. We were told we couldn't leave. But then WWI started, and we were stuck in Italy for another 7 years.

On the July 28, 1920, we arrived at Ellis Island, New York Harbor. It had taken 16 days to reach America. I was 14 and my sister was 13, and I remember it well. We had never been away from our home in Italy. The authorities found that somebody in the boat had some head lice. My sister and I didn't, but they had to treat the entire boat load of people anyway. They took a bucket of kerosene and swabbed it all over everyone's heads. It was very hot in the sun. It seemed almost 200° and the kerosene was dripping down our faces. If somebody would have lit up a cigarette, we would have all gone up in smoke!

That night, they put us to sleep in the women's dormitory at Ellis Island. It was a great big room with iron bunk beds. The next morning, when we awoke, I didn't see anyone but my sister around. The night before at bedtime, there had been 40 or 50 women in the room but now they were all gone. We were really scared. We found a large door and pounded frantically on that door for maybe 10 minutes, to us it seemed an hour. Finally, someone opened the door and gave us something to eat. The next morning, a big matron took a huge old iron bar and hit the iron beds so loud they could have wakened the dead.

The third day, they released us to our uncle, who had been staying in the men's dormitory. They put tags on us like baggage so everyone would know our destination and we wouldn't get lost. We had to buy enough food to last for the long train ride. It took us two days to arrive in Montana. We were about an hour from Butte, conversing in Italian when this Italian man across the aisle heard us and he started talking to us. He said, "When I get to Butte, I'm going to buy you something real good that I don't think you ever had before." He brought us a pie, I remember it was some sort of berry pie because it was very red so it must have been a cherry pie.

We thought that pie was the best thing we had ever tasted. I didn't think about asking for his address because I would like to have called or written him to thank him for that. It really meant a lot to us.

The next school year, we started school in Corvallis. Because we didn't know English, we had to start in first grade for two weeks. We had gone to the fourth grade in Italy, but then WWI started. By 4th grade there, we had learned as much as 8th grade over here. When you don't speak the language though, it is very tough. The other children continually teased us because I was as big as I am now, as big as the teacher.

During 3rd grade, at age 15, I had written a letter in Italian. During recess, my sister and I stayed in because all the kids would just make fun of us, because of our size and our language. They couldn't understand the Italian language. One day, I had started to write a letter to my girl friend in Italy. This boy came around and just grabbed it out of my hand and they all started laughing, making fun, and showing the letter to everybody saying, "Oh, look at all the gibberish that she wrote." Miss Cora Quast, our teacher at the time, found out what had happened. After recess, she took this youngster up in front of the class and said to him, "Here read this!" He replied, "Oh, I can't read this, it is rubbish". And, of course, he couldn't read it, so she then said to him, "You see, she knows this language and now she is trying to learn our language, you should never make fun of somebody because they want to learn more than one language." She really gave him the third degree. They left us alone after that. She was very nice and I will never forget that. We learned to speak English, but our mother continued to speak Italian at home.

I married August Leonardi in 1924. The first year we were married, Mrs. Daly's grandson and Crawford's daughter came to our place in a cart. He was around 10 years old and he always had to have a man with him—guarding him, you know, to see where he was going. We have lived in different places in the valley. We were down in Corvallis for a while, up to the Glass place for a couple of years and then Shambeau's place. After that, we bought this ranch from Daly. Actually, we bought it from Mrs. Daly and then we farmed up here all those years.

August bought two mules from somebody in Corvallis to help with sugar beet farming. Their names were Jack and Jenny. The ground was always so muddy and wet, but the mules were so strong, they could pull the trucks out. The sugar beets were loaded by hand onto the truck. Because of the mud, some of the beet growers had to take the beets out to the road on a "stone boat" and then load them on a truck. We kept Jack and Jenny until they got so old we had to retire them. They had truly earned their retirement.

When the Amalgamated Sugar Company in Missoula was sold, that signaled the end of the sugar beet farming in the valley.

We cooked for 8 to 10 men during the summer haying season and 18 to 20 men during threshing time. The cows needed to be milked twice daily and separators and milk machines had to be cleaned after each use. We purchased a washing machine around 1935. We couldn't have it inside the house because it was run by a gas motor. Everyone had to put their washer on their front porch. Water had to be heated on the stove top and then taken out to the washing machine.

Montana Power put in electricity in 1937. I remember just a bare light bulb. Missoula Mercantile was promoting a Jacuzzi pump at this time. They talked to August about putting one in. In those days, the money was pretty short, so he offered to put in a pump for cold water in the house for $125. We had to heat all the water for bathing and dishes. In another couple years, we put in a bathroom and plumbing. Elinor and Irene got to take the first bath in the new bathtub.

We grew almost all of our vegetables and fruit for our family, especially in the thirties during the depression. After graduating from nurses training, our daughter Rose, went to California to work. When she came home for vacation Rose said, "My girlfriend in California said they really had a great depression over there and a lot of them could not get enough milk or meat and I told them we did not have a depression in Montana." I was sure to tell her, "Oh, yes we did!" "And, it was only because we were living on a farm, that we had milk and meat—pork and beef—and we raised all our own vegetables and fruit so you children didn't know there was a depression or food shortage elsewhere." We had to make clothes out of printed flour sacks but our family had plenty to eat. We had a great big garden. I remember my husband taking down sacks of wheat in exchange for flour.

August helped Bulgarian friends take produce to Butte over Skalkaho Road, which opened in 1924. They would travel all night so the produce would be nice and fresh in the morning when they arrived. I stayed home with our five children. Our oldest child is Rose who lives in Denver now, then Elinor and Irene, and sons, Pete and Robert. Our son, Pete, died in 1979 at the early age of 51. Robert is retired and lives on the family ranch which he purchased from us in 1972. Mother died in 1956 of cancer and father passed away in 1978 at the age of 98.

GRANT AND NELLIE LE SUER

The year was 1903, and Grant LeSuer at age 25, has come west to Oregon to see what the "New West" was all about. Eighteen months later, he returned home to Pennsylvania to find a beautiful young school teacher named Nellie Billings, age 20, living with his parents in Town Line, PA. They were married on July 12, 1905.

Their first child, a daughter named Helen, was born June 3, 1906. Grant had been impressed by what he saw on the earlier trip west, and in 1909 they moved to Hamilton, Montana. Grant picked up any kind of work he could get, such as digging ditches, cutting wood, pruning orchards, and picking and packing apples. Nellie forgot about being a school teacher, instead joining her husband picking apples and fruits, or being a cook for the hired hands on ranches. Then came an opportunity for the two of them to cook at Medicine Hot Springs. They had been told they would cook for about 20 people a day — it turned out to be more like 60 each day! It only took four days of preparing and cooking food, baking bread and desserts, and they quit!

Next, they cooked on the Marcus Daly ranches during the haying season for hired help. But this time they got "flunkies" to help in the kitchen. ("Flunkies " was the term used for extra kitchen help). Again, they had 60 people to cook for but the flunkies did the dishes, prepared the vegetables, and helped in the dining room. Grant and Nellie were paid $125.00 a month for the two of them, plus board and room. Flunkies were paid $25.00 per month.

A son, Andrew, was born on July 22, 1914, in Hamilton. Grant and Nellie continued to help on ranches in the area until 1917, when they went to Seattle, WA, where Grant worked in the shipyards as a riveter. In 1918, they again returned to the Hamilton area where they established a small fruit and vegetable farm on the Grantsdale Road. Grant bought a Ford truck, and freighted over the Big Hole Road into the town of Wisdom.

In 1921, they bought a home in Hamilton, where the high school now sits on the South Fifth Street. Helen graduated from high school in 1924, (which was then the Lincoln School building on South Second Street, and the new County Courthouse occupies the space). Grant continued in the trucking business until 1925, when they returned to Edinboro, PA, to take care of his father who was in failing health. Grant decided to become a bow maker and maintained a small store in Edinboro, to sell his bow and arrow products and teach classes in archery. He was also a very good rifleman, going to Ohio in 1927 to a National Rifle Shoot where he won several trophies.

Grant's father died in 1930, and once again the call of the west brought them back to Hamilton, Montana. They purchased an apartment house on South Fourth Street. In 1932, Andrew graduated from the new high school on South Fifth Street.

Grant had become interested in natural crystals and would spend hours out in the hills, looking for outcroppings. He had an extensive collection when he died on December 10, 1943. To preserve them, his son-in-law, Herb Kress, created a headstone for Grant — using many of the crystals.

Nellie LeSuer continued to operate the apartment house until she passed away on July 3, 1957. Both Grant and Nellie are buried in the Riverview Cemetery just west of Hamilton.

THE JOHN ERNEST LOCKWOOD FAMILY

by Clyde and Evelyn Lockwood in 1974

The Lockwood family came to the Bitter Root Valley in 1900, from Vermillon, SD. They bought what was then known as the Crippen home and orchard. It had a huge white house, barns, sheds, root cellar and apples. Theodore, Lloyd John, and Hazel were born in South Dakota. Clyde, George and Glen were born on Dutch Hill in the Bitter Root. The children all went to school at Fair Play School until they were of high school age. Then, they went to Corvallis. Clyde drove the school bus which had a home-made body and solid rubber tires.

The family was engaged in growing fruit. Apples were the largest crop. When pectin came on the market, all the crab apple trees were pulled up. The family also had a large garden. Clyde said they had to hoe the

Putting up hay on the old Lockwood Place on Dutch Hill. A. M. Moore, photographer.

beans, peas, etc., all summer long. Then in the winter evenings they sorted many beans. They would get a bucket of apples to eat while sorting the beans. The vegetables were shipped to Butte and Anaconda every three or four days.

Mr. T. W. Lockwood, father of John Ernest Lockwood, was from Holly, Michigan. Mrs. Lockwood's parents, Mr. and Mrs. John Hundley, lived with the John Ernest Lockwoods. Mrs. Hundley was known as "Grandma" to all on Dutch Hill. Clyde said she did all the patching, and was forever sewing on buttons. Grandpa fished a lot, and enjoyed a wonderful life.

Ernest Lockwood was a good father. He made a swimming hole for his children, and all the neighborhood kids would come to enjoy it. In the winter they skated on it. They also had a pool table, which drew a lot of young people to the Lockwood place.

In 1918, the Lockwood's bought a house in Missoula. Clyde and Hazel moved down and lived in the house a year until the folks came. Hazel was going to the University, and Clyde was in his senior year of high school.

Clyde's mother told of all the bread she would bake each week, always sixteen loaves. Then when apple-picking time came, it meant more baking and cooking. Many of the neighbors were employed during the fruit season.

Theodore was born in 1893, passed away January 23, 1961, in Yakima, WA; John was born in 1896, passed away May 18, 1931 in Portland, OR; Lloyd was born in 1896, passed away May 16, 1970 in Portland, OR; Hazel was born in 1899 and passed away in 1967 in Seattle, WA; Clyde was born in 1901 and he is the only one of the family left in March of 1974; George was born in 1905 and died on his 21st birthday; Glen was born in 1909 and died February 1967, just one month after Hazel's death.

Clyde and his wife, Evelyn, live on the East shore of Flathead Lake. He is retired now.

The Clyde Lockwoods have two children, Billie Jean Noe, who teaches in Edmonds, WA; and Clyde Lockwood, Jr., who is chief ranger of a national park in Philadelphia, PA. Billie Jean Noe is the mother of four children. Clyde Jr. has two daughters.

THE LUDERMAN FAMILY

by May Talbot Luderman in 1975

On November 12, 1892, I made my advent into this world arriving at the Christy cabin near the main highway at Woodside. Shortly after my birth, we moved to Corvallis. My first teacher was Miss Nora Smithy. Poppa completed our home at Woodside, and I lived there until I married. Life on Schiffman Creek was interesting and also hectic, for I was the only girl in the family with eight mischievous brothers. (Note: see Talbot and Moore families). Kept me busy, trying to hold my own, and many's the tale I can tell about those days. My brothers were: Otis, Elmer, Joseph, David, Charles, Curtis, Ralph and Emmett. Life always has its tragedies, and we had our share. The year 1909, there were many spotted fever cases, and my two brothers, Elmer and Ralph, were victims. Elmer survived, but Ralph lost the battle. Then, in 1919, Joseph died of the flu. But life must go on, and so it did. We had plenty to do, as three months of the year, Poppa worked a gold mine in the Eight Mile area, so us young ones were left with responsibilities at home. We gardened, built walls of rocks, hunted, fished, or whatever was required to keep our family busy. In the summer time, when the creek dried up, my brothers and I would fish in the holes with buckets and cans. I wore an apron dress, and would hold it out, and then the boys would lift the buckets up, fish water and all, and they would pour them into my apron. Did you ever get hit in the belly with fish? Well, I did, and believe me the neighbors knew where the Talbot kids were, for there was plenty of noise created!! Come winter, fishing became another story. My father and brothers would catch trout and whitefish. We ate the trout, and the whitefish they would freeze, then pack them in snow in apple boxes and send them to Missoula. We were paid fifteen cents a pound for these fishing efforts.

At times in the winter, we would be snowbound and couldn't get to school. There were steep hills and many fences to cross. We would remove the lids from our "lard bucket lunch pails", and along with the Garrett kids we'd sit on the lids and slide down the snow covered hills to school.

School memories at Fair Play were many and varied. My father made us go a certain way to avoid the dangers. We would go down by the Johnson place and cross a swamp and negotiate many hills and fences in a given length of time. Many a rousing baseball game was played with a butter paddle used for a bat. School life was made interesting at Fair Play when we and along with the Garrett kids we'd sit on the lids and slide down the snow covered hills to school.

When the snows left, the Lockwoods, Gerrard, Garretts, and Talbot clan would climb the bull pines, and just like monkeys we would swing from one tree to another, playing "follow the leader". First guy to fall was no longer the leader

For entertainment, my brother, Elmer, and John Lockwood would fight for ten minutes every night. I used to tend my brother, Curt, and I would put him and Clyde Lockwood in an apple box, load them on a cart and go to the orchard. I'd pour Whitney crab apples on top and around the two boys, until they could hardly move. Then Theodore Lockwood and I picked pie cherries, and would squirt juice in each others eyes!

School memories at Fair Play were many and varied. My father made us go a certain way to avoid the dangers. We would go down by the Johnson place and cross a swamp and negotiate many hills and fences in a given length of time. Many a rousing baseball game was played with a butter paddle used for a bat. School life was made interesting at Fair Play when we were recessed in order to go to the Relief Stations! These were separated by a high board fence. There was one for "George" and one for "Georgette"! The fellows always taking careful aim to hit the "little house" with rocks, just as the girls would be inside resting!

It was in the second grade when a good looking, black eyed, boy came to school, and we became friends. This friendship matured into courtship, and when Fred Luderman and I were nineteen years of age, we boarded the "Galloping Goose" and went to Missoula and took the "fatal step". Fifty years and five children later we celebrated our Golden Wedding in 1962. I will never forget the day we returned from our honeymoon, we were met by school friends and given a ride on a hayrack. We went to Fred's parents home and rolled up the rug and danced. That party was something else. Fred bought a keg of beer, and a box of MacIntosh apples. Along with a wedding cake that Fred's mother had baked, we had a fun evening! Brother Otis, had a wild horse and he rode it backwards going home. Too many hops had gotten to him, I think.

The Ludermans came to Woodside from Butte, Montana. Fred was born in Butte on September 20, 1892, to George Edward Luderman and Georgia Bell Wallace. The Ludermans had previously lived in Oregon, California, and New York. Fred had one brother, Dean. Fred's father was a plumber in Woodside.

Following our marriage, we lived on Grandpa Moore's farm at Sunnyside. We then moved to Hamilton. From there, we moved to Bridger, then to Billings. In 1937, Fred was transferred to Greybull, Wyoming, as field manager for Michael Leonard Seed company. We purchased a ranch out on Shell Creek, and it kept us busy at both places. Fred passed away August 17, 1965. I still live in my home in Greybull, at 325 North 3rd Avenue.

WILLIAM WALLACE McCRACKIN

by Trudy Bassett

Civil War service on a Union gunboat on the Mississippi, raising sheep in Montana in the 1880's, and association with Marcus Daly were among the interesting experiences of William Wallace McCrackin, pioneer banker of the Bitter Root Valley.

He was born in Indiana, PA, on June 28, 1842. After his father's death, the family moved to Fairfield, Iowa,in 1855. At the start of the Civil War he enlisted in the 4th Iowa Cavalry, and later became mate on the gunboat. He returned to Indiana, PA, shortly before the Battle of Gettysburg, re-enlisted in the infantry and again saw service on the battle front.

After the war, he worked as a surveyor for the Burlington Railway, which was extending its line into Iowa. When the Union Pacific was constructing its tracks through Nebraska and Wyoming he worked for the railroad as a telegrapher and storekeeper, part of the time in Utah.

His banking career began in Fairfield in 1876. In 1878, he married Gertrude Junkin, daughter of the publisher of the Fairfield Ledger. Like many others living in the Midwest, they hoped to make their fortune in sheep-raising. They came to Montana in 1880, and began their venture at Sand Coulee. Severe winter storms killed most of their flock — and their expectations of profitable ranching.

After working for a short time in an Omaha bank, William came to Butte to be employed by Clark Brothers Bank. Then he was assistant cashier in the First National Bank in Butte, was instrumental in organizing the Silver Bow National Bank there, and became its President when it opened on May 2, 1890.

Marcus Daly was impressed with McCrackin's integrity, abilities, and personality, and urged him to come to Hamilton in 1894, to help organize the Ravalli County Bank. The first bank in the county, the institution opened for business on April 1, 1895. Daly was the President, and McCrackin the Cashier. Actually, he was the one-man force conducting business! Funds deposited the first day totaled $45,846.95, a substantial sum then. Local businessmen joined McCrackin not long afterward in obtaining control of the bank, and he then became its President.

His public service included three terms as Mayor of Hamilton, elected the third time term without opposition. He was a leader in the Chamber of Commerce, a member of the Hamilton School Board, and active in other community organizations. Wider recognition came to him as President of the Montana Bankers Association, and as the Republican candidate for State Senator from Ravalli County in 1906.

In World War II, a Liberty ship was named in honor of McCrackin. It was commissioned October 6, 1943, in Portland, Oregon, and saw service in the Pacific and was sunk on the Pacific Coast in 1962.

Mrs. McCrackin also had interesting memories of the days in Iowa. As a child she had helped her father in preparing the issue of his newspaper which told of Lincoln's assassination. She shared the difficulties of Montana pioneering and the uncertainties of their early days in the state.

They celebrated their silver wedding anniversary in 1903, with more than 100 guests, many coming from a distance to attend. The flowery newspaper account tell how she "wore her wedding dress, both garments and

Children of William Wallace McCrackin and Gertrude Junkin McCrackin. From left are Virginia McCrackin (White, Mortimer A.), Helen McCrackin, first student to register at the University of Montana, and Wallace McCrackin.

the wearer being wonderfully well preserved from the ravages of time." The McCrackin's home was not only a center of hospitality for their local friends, but a place where many others were house guests through the years. She was an active member of the First Presbyterian Church, and the Montana Daughters of the American Revolution elected her State Regent.

Besides being an ardent outdoorsman, McCrackin was a baseball fan. He had intended to see the World Series in 1913, but died on May 31 of that year. A full-length portrait, painted by R. V. McBain, another early-day resident of the valley, shows him in sportsman's garb. It hangs in the foyer of The Banque Club, the restaurant in the former Ravalli County Bank building.

The McCrackin's had three children: Helen was the first student to register at the University of Montana, became a teacher after graduation from Bryn Mawr. She was principal of Hamilton High School at the time of her death in the flu epidemic of 1918. She led students in the founding of The Hamiltonian, the school paper.

Wallace and Virginia, twins, were in Hamilton High's first graduating class. Wallace studied later at the University of Chicago, and Armour Institute of Technology, and received his degree in engineering. After travels in South America and Alaska he went to France in the summer of 1916, to serve in World War I, with a volunteer ambulance unit from Canada. Later he transferred to the American forces. He was with the Army of Occupation in Germany and was discharged as a sergeant. In 1920, Wallace was named president of the bank. He married Frances Underwood, a teacher, who still resides in Hamilton. He was a charter member and the second president of the Lions Club, a director of the Chamber of Commerce, and a member of the American Legion, and Masonic Lodge and Helena Shrine.

Virginia McCrackin became the bride of Mortimer A. White, who was the bank's president after William McCrackin's death. He was the office boy when the Silver Bow Bank was organized and came to Hamilton to be the cashier of the local bank. He served as president of the Chamber of Commerce and was chairman of Liberty Bond and Red Cross drives, and of the Hamilton Library Board. Mrs. White was active in the Presbyterian Church, President of Hamilton Women's Club and of Chapter AF of P. E. O. They returned to Hamilton to live after several years in California.

Their oldest daughter, Catherine, was the wife of Milton Byrd, also a Hamilton mayor for three terms and auditor for Citizens State Bank. He lived on the ranch of his parents, Mr. and Mrs. John Byrd, near Darby in his youth. Mrs. Byrd has been president of AAUW, Ravalli County Child Health Council, Chapter AF of P. E. O., Marcus Daly Memorial Hospital Guild and Hamilton Hikers Club. She is an elder of First Presbyterian Church and a member of the Hamilton Library Board, of which she is past chairman. She organized UNICEF "trick and treat" program, the

International Relations Club and Friends of the Hamilton Library.

The White's second daughter, Gertrude, worked in the Ravalli County Bank during summer vacations while a student at the University of Montana. After her marriage to Hugh Bassett, a copyreader for the Los Angeles Times, she later was editor of three papers in Bell, CA, Madison County, MT, Welfare Supervisor, and Society Editor of The Missoulian. She returned to live in Hamilton after retirement from work as a Supervisor in San Mateo County, CA, welfare department.

Like her sister Catherine, Virginia White was a graduate of the University of Southern California, and a teacher. She resided with her husband, Bernard Bordeau, in Oregon before going to live in Arizona, at Apache Junction and Lakeside, after their retirement.

WASH McKINNEY HISTORY AS I KNOW IT OR HAVE BEEN TOLD

by Merle McKinney, March 1997

Wash McKinney, Grant McKinney, Theodore McKinney, their mother, Phoebe Williams McKinney and her brothers came west by wagon train shortly after the Civil War. Wash's dad had died from an illness he got during the Civil War along with two other brothers. They came to Beaverhead County, Montana. Wash had a butcher shop in Dillon and probably ranched also. Wash was born in 1856, and died in 1928. I don't know how old he was when they came to Montana, I think from Illinois. In Dillon or Argenta, he married Olieve Pilon. I don't know the date, but Bertha was the oldest of their children and she was born in 1885.

Bertha first married Troy Williams, who was her first cousin, and they had 4 children. I'm not sure in what order. Ruben, the first son, died as an infant. The children I knew were Abe, Tom, and Ernestine. Troy was born in 1867, and died in 1914. Bertha then married Lynn Scharmota, and they had two more children, Elsie and Leonard. Bertha died in 1975.

The first four children of Wash and Olieve were born in the Dillon area. Troy was the second child, born in 1887. He married Etta Bradley and they adopted a baby boy, Troy Dee, who had six children. Troy Dee died in 1979.

Perry (Peg), the third child of Wash and Olieve, was born in 1890, and married Eva Hannon, probably about 1910, for a few months. They had a girl, and she was raised by her mother (Eva) and her step-dad, Clarence Hart. She had several half sisters and a brother.

In 1915, on November 25, which was Thanksiving Day, Perry married my mother, Grace Alice Sorensen. They had two children, Merle and Beryl. Grace died in 1938, in Tacoma, WA, from an operation for a tumor in the

Wash McKinney
1856-1928
Early 1900s.

brain. Perry died in 1950, in Longview, WA, from a self-inflicted gun shot.

Merle met Lucille Lowery in 1935, and they married in Darby in 1937. They had three boys, Larry, Michael, and Gordon Wayne (who had the first name initials as his great-granddad, George Washington McKinney). Larry married Thea Thompson in Darby in 1962 and they have two sons, Jason and Chad. Jason has almost identical twin boys named Bret and Kyle, born in 1988. Michael married Janet Lagrimas in 1970. They live in California and have no children. G. W. married Nancy Evers in Darby in 1974, and they have three children; Gwyn, Adam, and Christie.

Beryl married Q. B. Nelson in Longview, Washington, in 1946. They have two children, Teri Jo and Randy. Teri has three children; Jason, Megan, and Jared. Randy has two children; Brian and Jennifer.

Alice was the fourth child of Wash and Olieve, and born in 1893. She died in 1986. She married Wade Shockley in Darby, and they have one daughter, Bernice. After many years, they separated, and Wade later died. Alice married Charley Smith, who was her daughter's father-in-law. Bernice had two children, Jimmy and Sandra. When Alice was two years old, in 1895, Wash and the family loaded their wagons and came to the Bitter Root Valley where they homesteaded 160 acres, at the mouth of Rock Creek, in

Ravalli County. They came through the Big Hole Valley. There must have been a wagon trail from the Big Hole down through Rye Creek, south of Darby, and on to Como. This is where the rest of the children were born.

Blanche was the fifth child born in 1895, and died in 1985. She married Dewitt McGaughlin in Darby. They had one daughter, Beatrice, and she had two boys. Dewitt died in about 1919, in the flu epidemic, and later Blanche married Charles (Chic) Neaves. They later divorced and after that she married a man whose name was Warrick, and I don't know what became of that. She joined the WAC's and served in the Army in World War II.

Sadie was the sixth, born in 1896, and died in 1991. She married Gabe Harmon in Darby, when she was quite young. They divorced about 1925. About 1938 or 1939, she married Hub Summers and he died around 1944. There were no children by either marriage. Hub owned the Darby Merc for many years.

George Wesley, Wes for short, was the seventh and born in 1898, and died in 1944. Wes married Bernice Edson in about 1928, and they had one daughter named Berna. She has two children: Kasey and Kelly. I remember for my ninth birthday, in 1925, Uncle Wes and my folks bought me a .22 pump Winchester rifle. I think it cost about $22.00, and we still have it.

Irene was the eighth born, in 1900 or 1901, and died in 1993. She first married Harry Young and they had four children. Ruben died as an infant, don't know what order. The ones I knew were: Willard, Doris, and Wesley. Willard had 6 children and Doris had 3 children and Wesley had none.

Olieve was the ninth, born in 1906, and died in 1984. She first married Dave Coons real young, in Darby. It didn't last long and she went down to Lamont, Idaho, where she married Elton Bailey. After a few years, they divorced, and she went to Ogden, Utah, and married Dick Alberts. They adopted a boy, Armond.

There were two other boys in Wash's family that died as infants when they were still living at Como. One I think was Ike, and the other Alex. All the others all started school at the Como Schoolhouse, (except Olieve), which is still there. Grandma Olieve died at Como in 1906, when daughter Olieve was born. A few years after that, Wash sold the Como place to the Henault family, and bought a place up the East Fork above White's Store, which is on the cut-off road from East Fork to West Fork of the Bitter Root River. In fact, I was born on part of the Williams homestead, just south of White's store and post office. Beryl was born in Darby on South Main Street.

When I was born, Bella Ruark came and delivered me and took care of Mom for a few days. Bella was very pregnant at the time. She gave birth to Bud Ruark just 20 days after I was born. Dr. Hayward came by horse and buggy a few days after Bella left, to check on us.

The place that Granddad bought was part of the Williams homestead, and they were Phoebes family, their places joined my Grandpa Sorensen's and his folks' homesteads. They had 320 acres just to the south.

The younger ones after Granddad sold the Como place, moved up East Fork, went to the Rye Creek School, which is now the residence of Florence Wolfinbarger, along Highway 93, close to White's Store. There was no high school at least in Darby area in those days. The first high school in Darby, I think started in 1911. I have a folder of all who have graduated from Darby High School from 1915 through 1989. Wash, in the early 1920's, sold the ranch in the East Fork. I think to Jack Coultas, who already owned the Sorensen's two homesteads.

Wash then moved to Darby. In 1928, he was irrigating farm land on the University Heights up on Camp 2, when he dropped dead in the field, on July 6, his old horse standing close by waiting to go home. I remember, Granddad didn't have any love for banks. He lost what money he had in 1922 or 1923, when the Darby Bank went broke.

McKILLOP FAMILY

by Helen McKillop

Archie McKillop was born November 3, 1872, at Cape Breton Island, Nova Scotia, Canada. He came to Boston at age 17, and worked two years as a carpenter. He then went to Billings, Montana, and later to the Bitter Root Valley. During the early development of the valley under Marcus Daly he built many barns and buildings on the Stock Farm. He also helped build the St. Francis Catholic Church and helped construct the first Daly Mansion. Archie also built many houses and other buildings in the valley. Archie married Minnie Blodgett. They made their home on the west, on the Blodgett homestead, which was given to them by Minnie's father, Lyman Blodgett. Lyman gave all his children equal value of land. **Archie and Minnie had 3 sons — LeRoy, Hughie, and Herbert.** Minnie died leaving 3 small children. Archie married Tillie Strifert and they had one daughter, Catherine.

Archie and Sons had the Churn Creek Dairy and raised purebred Jersey cattle. Hughie took the cattle to the fairs around the state, loading them into cattle cars at Woodside. Traveling by train, he would be gone for 6 weeks at a time to Missoula, Helena, Great Falls, and Lewistown. They won many ribbons and trophies.

Hughie McKillop married Mary Kobe and they had two daughters, Helen and Barbara. Archie sold the ranch to Hughie and Mary and it remained in the family for three generations, but was sold in September of 1988.

LeRoy McKillop worked at the Bitterroot Stock Farm and other ranches in Montana.

Herbert McKillop was in car sales and real estate businesses. He married Mable Stockman and they had two daughters, Judy and Nancy.

Catherine McKillop married Walter Fortman and they had two daughters, Darlene and Julie.

THE MACE AND WARD FAMILY

by Ira L. Mace

Bengerman Franklin Mace was born September 5, 1837, in Braton, Virginia. Caroline Perkins was born April 10, 1838, in Carter County, Tennessee. We have no record of their marriage date.

My dad, Willard Perry Mace, was born December 10, 1861, in Unionville, Missouri. He left home and came to Deadwood, SD, in his teens. He hired out to a cattle company by the name of Conrad and Pearly to herd cattle. He loved to ride horses and bucking broncos. He worked around there for about three years. He knew Calamity Jane and Wild Bill Hickock while in Deadwood. He quit his job there and rode his saddle horse to the Bitter Root in the fall of 1883. He stayed with his riding and breaking horses in the Bitter Root. In fact, he spent his life in the Bitter Root. He met Margaret Ann Ward, my mother, two or three years later and they shared each others company until 1938. They got married in Corvallis on November 29, Thanksgiving Day, by the Rev. W. D. Lear, an old time minister in Corvallis. The house where they were married is still standing a quarter of a mile south of town, the place known in later years as the Everly place. Their marriage license is recorded in the Missoula Court House. That was Missoula County at that time, also, the Flathead Reservation was in the Bitter Root then. He made friends with the Indians. He broke for them. They gave him a pony, he said he had gotten as many as eleven ponies from them.

In 1890, they filed on a piece of land southwest of Woodside, known in later years as the Sid Parks place. I was born on that place on July 6, 1891. We lived on that place until 1893, then we moved to Riverside to work at the Daly residence. Brother Charlie was born there on April 19, 1893. Two years later we moved west of Hamilton, the Canyon Creek area. Dad worked at the Hamilton Sawmill. Brother Roy was born May 28, 1895. Three years later, sister Nell was born on September 12, 1898. In 1900, we moved to the Woodside area. That is where George, Earl, Callie, and Orvie were born.

We all attended the Fair Play School. Dad was caretaker on the August Christian ranch until it was sold to the Al Burrell family. Later, Dad did contract work picking rock. He cleared a lot of land for several neighbors.

He made a lot of rock fences along the highway and on the Bently Orchard Road. The rock fences are still standing. Our neighbors were the Ollie Heavlin family, the Duncan McCleods, the D. D. Moores, the Archie McKillops, and the Hod Blodgett families. My folks sold their place in 1913, and moved east of Corvallis on a dry ranch, raising mostly grain and livestock. In about 1924, they moved to Hamilton. Dad passed away January 2, 1939, and Mother on May 7, 1944. They are in the Hamilton Riverview Cemetery.

MATT WARD AND RHODA COOPER WARD

This is my mother's history. Matt Ward and Rhoda Cooper were born in the state of Kansas, in Carter County in the mid 1830's. There is no record of their marriage to be found.

There were five children born to them, my mother, Margaret, Mary, Reece, Charley and Matt, Jr. My mother, Margaret Ann Ward, was born August 2, 1871, in Kansas, Carter County. The parents and the five children all came to the Bitter Root by covered wagon. They came in about 1879. They settled on Gird's Creek that is east of Hamilton. That was the Flathead reservation then. Mother said the Indians were very sociable. They lived here for about 5 years. The children went to a little one room school near there. During the five years, they had two daughters born. Soon after that, Grandpa Ward passed away leaving Grandma with 7 children. But, everything turned out well. Their two older sons were nearly grown up and they were old enough to be a lot of real help. So, they located on a large place. It was on the west side of the river, near the mouth of the Blodgett Canyon on 160 acres. They had quite a struggle for a couple of years, but they kept at it and it paid off later on. Getting living quarters was the main part of it. After a year or so, the house, a few out buildings and the fencing done, the living came much easier. As the years rolled by, the older children quit school. They decided to go on their own. They wanted to make their own money. Uncle Reece and the two younger girls were in school. They tried to keep up the place, but it was too much for them, so they decided to sell off most of it in 10 or 20 acre tracts. They sold all but a few acres near the home. They kept enough ground for garden and small fruit trees. Grandma and Uncle Reece and the two girls lived there until 1905 when they sold the home and moved to town. The home was occupied by the County Poor Farm. After they moved to town, Uncle Reece went into the building business. He built many nice houses in Hamilton. He retired about 1912. He lived with his mother until she passed away in 1932, at the age of 96 years. Reece sold the home and moved into furnished bachelor quarters. He was in his mid 80's when he passed away in 1952. All of Grandma's folks were laid to rest in the Hamilton Riverview Cemetery.

After moving from the Sid Parks place where I was born, we moved to west of Hamilton in 1893. We lived up on the hill overlooking the old river bridge. My father was employed at the old sawmill. About 1896, we moved to a place near the old county poor farm. The land was purchased from my uncle. I went from there to the Canyon Creek school for nearly two terms. In the spring of 1900, Dad sold the place and we moved to a place one mile south of Woodside. There were 6 boys and 3 girls in our family. We all grew up there. I started to Fair Play School in September of 1900 and I completed the 8th grade in 1907. I never went on to school as transportation wasn't available. So, I went to work for my father. He was foreman for a ranch that later belonged to Fay Burrell. After working there for a few years, I took off on my own. I had many occupations through the years. In 1916, I met Maude Wilcox, now my dear wife, and we were married on April 8, 1918, at Missoula. We came back to the Corvallis — Hamilton area and about 10 years later, we moved to Bonner in 1928. I was employed by the ACM CO. for 17 years. In 1936, we built our home at East Missoula. We had three lovely children born to our marriage: William L., Charles E., and Florence May. They are all married and have families. They live near us.

MACLAY — BRUTTO

from the obituary of Sallie Brutto,
Ravalli Republic, June 24, 1992

Sallie Sinclair Maclay Brutto was born at Lolo, Montana, on April 20, 1908, and was the daughter of early pioneers Samuel and Nellie Sinclair Maclay. She was educated in Florence-Carlton and Missoula, and graduated from Montana State University School of Journalism.

In 1933, she married Frank Brutto who served as a war correspondent for the Associated Press in the 1940's. Their daughter, Marta, was born in 1940, and the spread of the war kept this family apart for five years. A second daughter, Elisabeth, was born in 1947.

The family returned to Hamilton in 1958 and Sallie founded the Hamilton Little Theatre Guild. Next came a trip to Rio de Janeiro, Brazil where Sallie taught Journalism while Frank pursued his career with the press. It wasn't until 1967, when Frank retired, that the couple could return permanently to the Bitter Root Valley. They settled in Hamilton, and took up very active roles in the community. Sallie was founder of the first Senior Citizens group in Ravalli County, and was President of the organization for four years at its inception, and for another six years later. She and Frank established a Senior Center in O'Hara House and helped organize numerous events there including the first Art-in-the-Park. She was active in the formation of the Bitterroots Art Guild and a board member of the Friends of the Library.

Frank and Sallie were active members of the Bitter Root Valley Historical Society, and as such campaigned to save the "old Courthouse", which was then converted into a home for the Ravalli County Museum.

Sallie edited the "Western News" for its publisher, Miles Romney, during his term as a Montana State Senator, and again during his final illness. She was a publicity director for the American Cancer Society after surviving a bout with cancer, and found relaxation in horseback riding with the "Saddle Tramps".

In 1992, when Sallie Maclay Brutto passed away, she was survived only by her two daughters, and her sisters, Nelma Maclay and Annie Leffingwell, and her brothers, Samuel and David. In 1997, only her sister, Annie, survives. This grand old family has deep roots in the Bitter Root Valley, and will be covered more thoroughly in history from the far north end (Lolo) of the valley.

JOSEPH MAKI (Jarvimaki)

Joseph Jarvimaki was born the son of Klara Elma Piikila Jarvimaki and Anders Jarvimaki,in a small village at Karvia, Finland, on December 17, 1870. The farmland lay outside the perimeter of town and each owner of each small plot had to go outside the town to work his farm. This system had come down through the years. For safety sake, the people gathered together at night to be able to fend off wild animals and roving bands of thieves and thugs. Joseph worked for a wealthy man who drove a spirited team of horses. His job was to keep the horses, carriage and harness in tip-top condition. When the "Boss Man" was ready for a ride, he came out with his white gloves on his hands and ran his hands over the entourage. If there were the smallest amount of soil on the gloves, Joseph was reprimanded and had to wash the whole outfit again with soap and water. He did not like this job at all. His older brother, Vilhelm (Willie), came to America first. In 1892, with the help of his brother, Joseph followed the trail to a seeming "Rainbows end". To further make him anxious to leave home was the fact that every young man had to serve a period of time in the army. His time was getting near so he decided to take off for a better life. He arrived at Ellis Island in 1892. He often told of how he and three other men came to the United States on just one $20.00 bill! The first man would be answering the official's questions, when asked if he had any money to live on, he would show the twenty dollar bill, then he would fold the bill and quickly slip it to his friend. The second man repeated the act, and on and on, until the four men had presented his wealth. The trip across the ocean took thirteen days.

From Ellis Island, Joseph went to Michigan, then to Belt, Montana, and on again to Philipsburg, Montana. Here he joined a large encampment of men cutting wood for the Daly smelter in Anaconda. Most of these men were not married so lived in very primitive style, some in tents, some in small cabins and shacks. Sometimes many men shacked together to save on expenses. Wages were as low as .50 cents per cord of wood. The hours of work were long and hard. Most of the timber had to be cut with axes, as saws were expensive and not many were available. The hillsides were covered with snow and ice in the winters. The cordwood logs were often set loose at the top of a hill and went sliding to the bottom sometimes at great speed. In some places and during the summer, there were flumes formed of logs and filled with water. These flumes floated the logs to a landing deck where they were loaded on wagons and later rail cars for delivery in Anaconda.

In 1899, Joseph came to Hamilton, Montana, to work in Marcus Daly's big lumber mill. He worked in the planer section, which was still hard, long hours, but better than in the woods. He lived in a large boarding house until he married Lydia Houtamaki on March 2, 1900. He then moved to 225 N. Eighth Street. That house is still standing, and in very good condition. From where he lived he could walk a half block, roll under a tall wooden fence, and be at his place of employment. While living in this home, three children were born; Jacob, Lydia, and Hilda. Hilda died of pneumonia when less than a year of age.

In 1904, Joseph received his citizenship. In 1907, Joseph and family moved to Victor, Montana, where he purchased 40 acres of land on Bear Creek. Here an additional eight children were born: John H., Walter, Elma, Lillian, Bertha, Joseph U., William and George. To make a living, Joseph, with the help of wife and family, farmed his land and milked cows, raised hogs and beef. He rented additional acreage and worked in the nearby timber for the sawmills. His was a hard life with not much play, but he was never too busy to help a neighbor or a friend, and dearly loved to sit down and visit over a cup of coffee. On his farm, Joseph built a "Finnish sweat bath". It was a small building in the corner of which was constructed a heating device built of stones. A fire was built in this, and heated with wood until the rocks were very hot. Dippers of water were tossed onto the rocks, which created dense steam. There was a seating arrangement built across the end of the room. This was similar to a grandstand. The heat on the lower level was not bad, but the higher you climbed — the hotter it got — until it could not be endured. After a good sweat came, a bath of cold water. Wood had to be cut and water hauled for this bathhouse, but any and all were welcome to use it. Neighbors and friends came from miles around to take a good old Finnish bath!

Joseph was a man to be admired, a true friend, hard-working, and as honest as the day was long. One must marvel at the courage and hardiness it took to leave home and all he knew, to cross the ocean, and make a new life for himself in a strange world. Joseph died on March 27, 1959, at Victor, Montana and is buried in the Victor Cemetery.

Joseph had siblings; Emma, Maria, Vilhelm, Hilda, Alesandra, Lempi, and Vilhelm (an adopted child).

THE WILLIAM W. MALONE FAMILY

by Nina Rummel and Earl Malone

William W. (Billy) Malone was born in Lansing, Michigan, on February 22, 1862. He came to Montana in 1882, coming up the Missouri River on a steamboat to Fort Benton. He worked his way up, working around Missoula and working some for the railroad. He worked on the line from Missoula to Spokane. He had a contract to get out ties for the railroad and had some Chinese people working for him in Noxon. He came to the Bitter Root Valley in 1885, and worked for Marcus Daly and also some in the woods.

Margaret Couch Malone was born in Albina, Missouri, on March 30, 1869. She was the daughter of Luther and Mary Couch. She came to the valley in 1887, with her sister, Jennie, and Jennie's husband. Her folks came about a year later and lived on Camas Prairie, then in Grantsdale. Her father died at the age of 46.

William Malone and Margaret Couch were married November 16, 1890, in the Grantsdale Church. The church is still in use, and is now known as the Grantsdale Community Church.

They lived in Hamilton and William worked in the woods. Later, he went to work for the big mill and "drove the river", which meant riding the logs from the pond to the mill. Earl, Edith, and Nina, were born in Hamilton. At the time of his birth, it was understood that Earl was the first white boy to be born in Hamilton. William and Margaret took up the ranch in 1894, which was all timber. They had to clear a place to build the house, which consisted of one room. More rooms were added later. They moved on the place in the winter of 1898. Earl had to stay in town with his Grandma Couch, she lived on Fifth Street, to go to his first year of school. William continued to work at the mill and drove a team of horses to work. He worked most of the time at night. He cleared his ranch and cut logs and sold them. In 1908, he got out logs and had a mill on the place. He cut out enough lumber to build a new two story house with six bedrooms, living, dining room, kitchen and bathroom. However, the bathroom was never finished, since there was no electricity in that area at that time. The house was built in 1910, and the family moved in that fall. In 1911, the phone was put in.

Ed, Cora, Muriel, and Ione were born in the first house. Marie and Harry were born in the second house. There were nine children and all are still living in 1974. Earl the oldest, was born in 1892 and Harry, the youngest, was born in 1913. All are married and there are 21 grandchildren.

Earl, Edith, Nina, Ed, and Cora want to the Fair Play School. William was a trustee for the school for several years. Margaret was a trustee when they consolidated. There were three women on the board and they were instrumental in getting a well dug for the school.

William sold 80 acres on the north side of Tagalder Creek to the ACM Company. He then bought 80 acres from Sid Parks. He used Tagalder Creek for water, then later had a ditch from Mill Creek. They planted an orchard of 12 varieties of apples, several kinds of plums, peaches, pears, cherries and strawberries. They raised some hay. Some days, they would pick up to 100 crates of strawberries, and ship them all over the state by train. They would ship on the 12:30 train and on the 6 A. M. train. They made two trips a day to Woodside. They would pick until noon on Friday to ship, then not again until Monday noon (they never picked on Sunday). The berries that were picked Friday after the noon shipment, were taken to Hamilton and peddled on Saturday. Sometimes throughout the week, they would sell berries in Hamilton, too. They always put up nice berries.

They used the 3-gallon crates, which sold for about $1.50 per crate. They paid $.25 a crate for picking. All the young girls and some women and boys picked. In those days, everybody worked. They sold several car loads of apples every fall. One year, they loaded over 900 boxes of apples, one of the largest car loads ever shipped out of Woodside. All the neighbors came to help, bringing a team and wagon. Then, the Malone family would help their neighbors in turn. For two years after her husband died, Margaret took a car load of apples to Aberdeen, South Dakota, and would sell them right from the car. She had a nephew there who helped her.

O. L. Kenney was their closest neighbor. They came there sometime around 1895 or 1896. They had a boy, Alfred, who died at the age of 17 and a girl, who died at the age of 15. They lived on the ranch until Mrs. Kenney died. Then, Mr. Kenney sold the ranch and moved to Hamilton. Other neighbors were John Elliott, John Alnut, Jim Smith, Bay Lyle, John David, Sid Parks, and John Dunbar. Neighbors were really neighbors in those days!

William Malone died on December 11, 1923, of heart trouble, leaving six children still in school. Margaret stayed on the ranch about two years, and then sold it. It has changed hands several times since then. One party sold the house and moved it off the property. There is no house there at this time. Margaret Malone moved to Missoula and died there on September 22, 1944.

Back on the subject of school, they lived about four miles from the Fair Play School and walked a good deal of the time. By going across the fields and cutting the corners, it made it a little shorter. They did drive some of the time if the horses were not needed for work. There was a long shed on the school grounds for horses, since several of the children rode horses to school.

They had a Sunday School at the school house most of the time. Sometimes they could get a preacher to come and preach.

They had neighborhood parties, school parties and box socials. It was quite an outing for families to go up to the springs for a few days after the harvest and just before apple picking time. One Fourth-of-July, Edith and Nina had gone to Hamilton to a celebration dressed in lovely summer dresses. On the way home (about 4 o'clock) it started to rain, and before they got home it was snowing! They were in a buggy with no top, so needless to say, they were drenched and cold by the time they arrived home.

GEORGE MEESER, SR. AND MARIA GRAFF MEESER

as told to Francis A. Dunwell by Mrs. Roy Barnett 8-8-1976

GEORGE MEESER, SR., (pronounced Meser), was born in or near Wittenberg, Germany on May 27, 1858. He migrated to the United States about 1883 or 1884, and probably debarked at New Orleans, as he went directly to Kansas City and was employed as a cabinet maker there. The call of the west must have reached him, as he moved to Victor, Montana, about 1886.

He must have been interested in prospecting and mining as he sold his 1/9 interest in the Pleasant View Quartz Claim, between Sweathouse and Bear Creek, to Washington J. McCormick and C. P. Higgins, old Missoula pioneers, on June 11, 1886. He received $400.00 for his share. He also filed a claim in 1892, called the Blue Jacet, about six miles east of Stevensville on Spooner Creek.

He acquired a sawmill in partnership with Al Fowler on Sweathouse Creek, west of Victor, in 1886 or 1887, and had about fifty men working for him. Logging was done with horses.

His future wife, Maria Graff, came to Victor from Chicago where she and her sister, Magdalena, had been working in a restaurant of a hotel. She arrived in the caboose of a freight train in late 1886, and worked in the sawmill boarding house where she met George. They were married at Victor in May of 1887. Marie had been born in Strassburg, Germany, April 29, 1868, and came to the United States about 1885. Their first child, a daughter, was born in Victor on October 3, 1889, and named Estella Meeser. A second daughter, Anna Meeser, was also born there on May 21, 1892.

The Meeser's bought the Cowan place west of Victor (160 acres) and had as neighbors the Blakes, Cates, Poindexters, Woodmaceys, and Koeshners. Mr. Blake married an Indian woman and had several children. Mrs. Barnett says that they always remembered her Dad. Mrs. Koeshner was the local midwife for babies delivered in that area.

There was much Rocky Mountain Spotted Fever in the early days causing many deaths. Mr. Meeser, being a cabinet maker, usually made the caskets, the women lining them in black, and the hearse was usually a buckboard wagon.

Burials were in the cemetery northwest of Victor.

George Sr., joined the Masonic Lodge while a resident of the Victor area. He had a sister, Margareta, who arrived in Kansas City about a year later than George. She did housework and menial tasks for those people needing emigrant servants, before marrying George Aichele there. The Aichele's came west about the same time and both worked in the sawmill boarding house at Victor. George Aichele contracted lung fever and had to give up his duties. George and Margareta moved to Helena where he ran a butcher shop. He later died there, and Margareta married a second time, to John Kofen, a butcher in Missoula. He was accidentally killed and she married again to Henry Hubert, an artistic painter from Missoula. His paintings are in the Elks Temple in Missoula. Henry died in Missoula in December of 1924, and Margareta died on December 16, 1944.

Maria Graff's sister, Magdalena, married George Aichele's brother, Andrew, at Victor, while working in the boarding house. They later moved to Missoula where he worked at the Missoula Brick Plant west of Missoula near the present airport.

George Meeser, Sr., dissolved his partnership with Al Fowler in the sawmill business, and acquired the Geyer House in Hamilton in 1892. It was a hotel and boarding house that housed the new Hamilton Sawmill workers and also the Northern Pacific railway people. George and Maria owned and ran this hotel for approximately five years. Their third daughter, Louise, was born there on January 21, 1895.

The next venture for George was the acquisition of forty acres of Sawtooth Creek land next to the foothills. The land had been logged off and a log house and well were in place when he traded or sold the Geyer House for the rural atmosphere. Maria preferred the town living, but never the less stuck with her man.

For a short time, they lived in a house at 303 South 7th Street, in Hamilton, while the log house was remodeled by adding a combination kitchen and dining room and a rock root cellar. Daughter four, Marv, was born on March 21, 1897, at the South Seventh location.

The family lived at the Sawtooth ranch for about twelve years while George cleared the land, planted MacIntosh apples, and raised produce to sell in Hamilton. Maria would occasionally tell the daughters to each take $.25 from their produce selling income for lunch at "the Chinaman's" (Lee Hom's) restaurant. Estella still stops in at the present restaurant for an occasional meal when in town. Many rocks were picked on the forty acres in the process of cultivating and farming the land, and became rock fences. The children all assisted in these chores.

George Meeser, Jr., was born on the Sawtooth Ranch on January 14, 1904.

Estella, Anna, and Mary went to the Sawtooth School which was located across the road on the corner southeast of the present Henry H. Grant property.

About 1909, Mr. Meeser decided to sell or trade his Sawtooth Ranch for a house at 108 Pennsylvania Street in Hamilton, and also Butte property that consisted of a residence on Nevada Street, a lodging house on East Broadway, and a house in Walkerville. George and Maria lived in Hamilton until 1913, when he went to Butte to work at his carpenter trade. He also worked in Idaho for about one year during the construction of the Arrow Rock Dam.

In 1919, they decided to give up the Butte property and return to live on Pennsylvania Street in Hamilton. George Sr., died there on October 1921, at the age of 63. Maria did some nursing, later moving to North Third Street where she passed away in the summer of 1952, at the age of 84.

WILLIAM HENRY MILLER

as told to Sally Turner, in 1950

The boy who walked all the way from the Missouri-Kansas borders to the Bitterroot Valley in Montana. I was born near Springfield, IL, in 1865, the year Lincoln was assassinated. When I was only a few months old, my family went by covered wagon to southeast Missouri.

In the spring of 1874, we joined a 29-team wagon train headed for California. Father drove our team, and my job was to walk behind our wagon and keep our stock from straying. I was nine years old and had never worn a pair of shoes. The first few days I suffered with sore feet, then the soles of my feet got as tough as shoe leather.

In Colorado, we spent the night near a Government Scout Camp. **Two fine looking scouts gave us several bags of dried buffalo meat. I was mighty pleased to learn they were Buffalo Bill Cody and Wild Bill Hickok. My family called me "Willie". After meeting two great "Bills", I never let anyone call me Willie again. I informed everyone my name was just plain Bill.**

After many months on the road, we arrived in Salt Lake City, Utah. What little money we had started out with was gone. Father got a job in a coal mine. Mother and we children worked in the potato fields. I had never seen such wonderful potatoes. When mother asked how such fine potatoes were grown, a man told us how water was brought in from nearby streams to irrigate the land. Up to that time, we had never heard of irrigation.

On April 1, 1876, we headed north, our destination Butte, Montana, and the richest hill on earth. We had plenty of food and as usual, I walked behind the wagon to look after the livestock which consisted of one blind and one balky horse, which were pulling our covered wagon, two yearling steers, and two milk cows. While we were camped along the Idaho-Montana border, a man by the name of Bassett stopped to visit with us. When father told him we were headed for Butte, he had a serious look on his face. He said, "You know nothing but farming. I believe if I were you, I would go to Magic Valley — west of the mountains, and raise vegetables, wheat, and corn." Father explained he had had all the farming he wanted. Mr. Bassett insisted that a gold town was no place to raise children, and with mother's help, Mr. Bassett persuaded father to first try his hand at raising vegetables in Magic Valley (Bitter Root Valley).

The Bitter Root was truly Magic Valley. The mountains on the west looked like giants wearing huge white caps. The wooded valley floor was covered with beautiful wild flowers and luscious grass. I could hardly keep the livestock moving, as we had never had them where grass was so plentiful. We traveled on down the Valley, to where Victor is now. There were a few settlers who had already taken up homestead land and doing pretty well at raising vegetables, grains, and fruit. A man came to our tent and wanted to know if we were looking for a location. In a short time, he had traded his land to father for our Spencer rifle and thirty dollars. We moved into the poorly built log cabin already on the 40-acre place and began a new life in a new country.

We cleared land and trapped that winter and the next spring we traded furs for garden seed, fruit trees, and a little farm machinery. We children tied gunnysacks on our feet until we raised enough vegetables and fruit to buy shoes. We hauled vegetables, fruit, pork, and beef to Deer Lodge, and sold everything we could raise in the way of food. At that time, the Bitterroot Valley was called "The Bread Basket of Montana."

We had the finest neighbors to be found anywhere. Mrs. Smith taught me reading, writing, and arithmetic. In those days there were no schoolhouses. That is, there were no schools where we lived. The Smith's little daughter was the most beautiful little girl I had ever seen! She was two, and I, at that time, was twelve. Her name was Julie, and she loved to run away from home, a very bad habit in bear and cougar country. I can never forget the look of horror on Mrs. Smith's face when she came to our place to tell us little Julie was missing. We all went out to search for Julie. I happened to pass by the sturdy log fence that corralled a vicious old sow and pigs, and there laid Julie, sound asleep with her head resting on the old sow's belly. How I was going to rescue her I did not know, but I would make a try at it. No one dared go near the animal when she had piglets because of her mean temperament. I didn't dare call for help, as I would awaken the sow. I slipped around back of the sow and grabbed Julie and dragged her over the fence with the vicious sow after me. I was so frightened, both Julie and I fell to the ground after we made it to safety. Mrs. Smith called me a hero, and I am not ashamed to admit I was the most frightened hero in the world! When Julie grew up she married a man by the name of Groff, longtime banker in Victor, MT. (Both Julie Smith Groff and her husband confirmed the story of Julie being rescued from the vicious old sow by 12 year old Bill Miller.)

Not too long after that, my Father helped to build the first schoolhouse. It was a one-room log building that later became the townsite of Victor.

Everything the man Basset told us about the Bitterroot Valley proved doubly true. We really prospered. At the age of 18, I bought a fine team of horses, a new wagon, and a plow. As long as the weather was not too severe, I made regular trips to Deer Lodge. It took me around two weeks to make the trip. I followed the river road to Missoula, then over Hellgate Pass to Deer Lodge. Remembering how the potato farmer in Utah had irrigated his ground helped us to raise the best of fruits and vegetables. I raised fine watermelon and cantaloupe. It was September of 1886, when I loaded my wagon with watermelons and headed for Missoula to sell my melons and take in the Barnum and Bailey Circus. While there I met two Garrard boys, and their 15 year old, sister Maragaret Anne (Annie) Garrard. I made up my mind right then and there to marry Margaret Annie. On October 13, of that same year, I did just that, but not without a bit of trouble.

I drove to Missoula to buy a marriage license and to my surprise, a girl under eighteen could not marry in the state of Montana. Whether the clerk told me I could marry Annie with her parent's consent, or even if there were such a law, I was too disappointed to remember. I left the courthouse feeling mighty blue. I ran into an old friend by the name of Goff, who offered to go back to the courthouse with me and talk to the clerk. All Goff said to the clerk was, "I have known Annie for over eighteen years. Bill was very excited when he was here before, and gave Annie's age wrong." On October 13, 1886, Margaret Annie Garrard and I were married at the Garrard home by Justice of the Peace, Edward Green of Hamilton. We were the third couple to secure a marriage license in Missoula, MT.

Later, Annie's parent's sold their farm for $30.00, and it is now the Ravalli County Fairgrounds at Hamilton.

Annie and I built a two-room log house, two miles south of Victor, on what is now Highway 93. The buildings are still there. We lived a normal happy life, but like most people we had our disappointments and heartaches. Often times, I went to Father Ravalli for advice and comfort. My being of the Mormon faith made no difference to Father Ravalli. He always advised me wisely. Many times I hitched up my team to the wagon and took Father

Ravalli to see an Indian who was sick, or maybe in some kind of trouble. Once while driving along, I saw tears in the good priest's eyes. "Why are you crying?" I asked. "My heart is sad because I have no more medicine for my beloved Indians," he replied. It was not only Indians he helped — it was anyone — regardless of his color or religion. When Father Ravalli died, the Bitter Root lost a true friend, and the greatest man who ever walked on the green carpets of Magic Valley. Not only was he a kind priest and a faithful friend, he was good for the soul.

I bought a bigger and better farm near Blodgett Mountain, where my children helped me raise good crops of fruit, vegetables, and grain. The Valley became noted for the fine crops grown here, especially for the MacIntosh apple, the finest tasting apple grown anywhere.

I well remember the first automobile that came through our county. My wife and I had driven up to Curlew gold mine, a few miles from Victor, and on our way back home we heard a noise. We looked back and all we could see was a cloud of dust. My team ran away, and I was unable to stop them until we arrived at our gate. It was a man by the name of Drinkenburg, who owned the first gas wagon and the first car I had ever seen. It was a Model-T. I thought it a pretty nice thing to have, so I went to Hamilton and bought a Franklin. I tried to drive a Model-T, but to save my life I could not drive one. I did pretty well with the Franklin, and I was happy and proud to load my family into the car and drive them around the country they had never seen before. Once, while on one of our pleasure trips, the car got balky and I stopped at an old man's farm and asked him for some motor oil. He was as green as I was about a car. All he had to offer me was some bear grease. It stunk to high heaven, but I put it in and the car worked just fine on the bear grease!

I have spent many years in the Bitterroot Valley. My children, grandchildren, and great grandchildren come often to see Anna and me. In this year of 1950, Annie and I have been married for sixty-four years.

MITCHELL FAMILY HISTORY

by Lorena Mitchell Erickson

WAGONS HO! That was the call, booming out that spring day of May 14, 1864, from Bourbon County, Kansas, **as seven wagons began their way west.** My great-great-aunt, **Margaret Alabama Mitchell Chaffin,** her husband, **Elijah Chaffin**, children, **Nancy age 5, Judah age 3,** and **Balaam Siegel age 17 months** (whose twin, **Joseph Lincoln** had died when about one year old), were in this wagon train, along with great-great uncle, **James Mitchell.** Thus began the journey west for the Mitchell clan.

Many hardships were endured with the crossing over the plains

and mountains to Bannack, Montana Territory, arriving in September 1864. At the prompting of John Slack, the wagons proceeded to the Bitter Root Valley to winter. Makeshift log cabins were hastily built to protect the families. Food was scarce, but the settlers bartered with the Flathead Indians for beef and potatoes. During that first winter, Margaret gave birth to Alexander, her fifth child, acclaimed as the first white boy to be born in this Bitter Root Valley.

In the spring of 1865, the Chaffins, along with several other family members, moved on to Oregon, but being disenchanted with the rainy weather, came back to the Valley in 1866. On their way back, just south of Stevensville at Pine Hollow, **Rosanna Mary,** the sixth child of Margaret and Elijah, was born. Traveling south to Corvallis, they established their permanent home. A dairy was started and butter and cottage cheese was stored in a water-cooled milk house. At monthly intervals, the dairy products were hauled to Stevensville and Missoula, or by packhorse train to Deer Lodge. The family prospered, expanding their farm ground, crops and cattle. The family also expanded with the birth of another son, **Moses,** in July of 1868. The life of this pioneer family was hard, filled with tedious manual labor. All the clothing was sewn by hand, the food grown in gardens and generally preserved by drying and salting, and great quantities were laid by. But, there was still time for visiting and helping family and friends. Margaret did miss her family and must have been very persuasive in her letters to them to come to Montana.

On May 17, 1869, my great grandfather, William L. C. Mitchell, and his wife, Mary Elizabeth (Molly), Cowan Mitchell, his brothers, Campbell L. and Alexander E. Mitchell, the William Chaffin family, and four single men, left from Kansas to begin their journey west. This journey was well documented with two journals kept along the way by Campbell Mitchell and T. B. Reeder. (I will not record the journals here, that will be another chapter, another day.) The way west was fraught with many perils and adventures, but they were heading for the Bitter Root Valley to join their sister, Margaret Chaffin. They arrived at the Chaffin homestead just after sunset on September 1, 1869. What a joyous greeting welcomed them.

In June of 1869, Rosanna Maldenettie Mitchell Hull, her husband Joseph, son, Johnny aged nine, and infant daughter, Daisy, along with "Aunt Rose's" father, Cowan Mitchell, who was an invalid, started their journey to the Bitter Root, coming by boat up the Missouri River to Fort Benton. The river was low that year, so their journey was cut short at Fort Peck, and they had to go on to Fort Benton by freight train. William Mitchell came from the Bitter Root to meet them and help them on this trip west to Margaret's home. They arrived happy to have ended their journey, now that most of the brothers and sisters were together. (Two more brothers, John and Samuel, did not come to the Bitter Root, as John died on Donner Pass, year unrecorded, and Samuel died in 1904 in Oakland, CA, and a younger sister, Sarah, died in 1862, the same year the great-great grandmother, Ellen Weir "Nellie" Cowan Mitchell died. Samuel's remains are buried next to his father, Cowan Mitchell in the Corvallis Cemetery.

All of the Mitchell's homesteaded in the Corvallis area, building homes and starting farms. By the 1870 census, the families were prospering, with a dwelling and acreage in farming and stock raising. The Mitchell's were known for their affection, hospitality and generosity. They were stalwart community members, opening their homes and sharing meals with their neighbors and anyone passing through needing a meal and /or a bed. In 1872, the Independent Ditch was built by J. S. Humble, the Mitchell brothers, Joseph Hull, Elijah Chaffin, John Slack, John Goff, and W. Humble. This made it possible for the farmers to grow wheat, fruit and other irrigated crops on their land.

The pioneers were reaching out for a true social branch to cling to, and on May 15, 1874, the Corvallis Grange No. 17 was chartered. Charter members included C. L. Mitchell, W. L.Mitchell, Rose and Joseph Hull and Margaret and Elijah Chaffin, among others. Organizational officers elected that first meeting included Elijah as Master, and Margaret as Lady Assistant Steward.

By 1877, William and Molly had four children, three girls and one boy, my grandfather, Burton Luther. Margaret and Elijah had three more children and all the families were prospering. During the summer of 1877, word came to the valley that the Nez Perce Indians were on the move, and dressed in war paint, and fully equipped to battle. They were headed toward the valley. A makeshift fort was constructed in Corvallis, and many of the women and children took refuge there when Chief Joseph and his people came through the Valley. It is said that my great grandmother, Molly, was very "strong willed", and refused to go to the fort, feeling safer in her own home. There was destruction from the Indians as they passed through, breaking into homes and stealing what they wanted, and destroying what they didn't.

In February 1878, Margaret gave birth to her eleventh child, Elijah "Frank" Chaffin. Nine days after his birth, Margaret died, leaving her loving family behind. She was remembered as strong, healthy, and brave, with the Mitchell disposition, always jolly, calm, never out of humor, and always uncomplaining.

James Mitchell returned to Kansas in 1881, **to marry Katherine Reeder**. Their first child**, Harriett**, was born there in 1882. Two more sons, **Robert** (1883) **and Archibald** (1886) were born in the Valley before the family moved on to Camas, WA, where their last two children, **Wilbur** (1892) **and Margaret** (1894) were born. The family returned to the Valley in 1897, where Jim and Kate lived out the rest of their lives.

Joe and Rose Hull continued to live in the Valley until Joe's death in 1906. They farmed and were very active in the community, taking care of Rose's father until he died in 1886, and was buried in the Corvallis Cemetery. Aunt Rose joined her daughter, Daisy, in Eugene, Oregon, to spend her last years.

After the battle of the Big Hole, **Alex Mitchell** settled on a farm south of Victor on the Bitter Root River. **He married Nancy Summers in 1884**. Four sons were born there: Henry, **Samuel, Thomas, and John.** They lived there until 1909-1910, then moved to Calgary, Canada, where Alex died in 1915.

I must thank Leda Reed for her wonderful book, "The Song of the Bitter Root," and Glenn Chaffin for his book, "The Last Horizon," for providing me with valuable information, and wonderful family stories and memories.

ALBERT MOORE

Early Photographer

Compiled from the Western News 9-10-1959

Many of the pre-1900 families of this area have pictures of relatives labeled to show they were the work of A. M. Moore. **Albert Moore** left his mark on the Bitter Root Valley from 1891 to about 1902 or 1903.

According to an article in the Western News, dated September 10, 1959, Moore was born in Walnut Grove, Missouri in 1870. He came to the Bitter Root in 1891, as Marcus Daly was platting and settling Hamilton with new buildings, and operating his race horse farm out of Riverside. *"It was a ripe time for a photographer to arrive, as the period was one of the giant boom, inspired largely by Daly's racing operations, but also because of the harvesting of the native forest of the area. This employed a small army of jockeys, trainers, managers, hangers-on for the racing plant, and a large army of "river pigs", lumberjacks, millworkers, carpenters, and all sorts of similar professional workmen. At the same time, there was a building boom in the construction of a new town of Hamilton, and a fight over the county seat's location brewing in which Stevensville, Corvallis, Grantsdale, and Hamilton, were all implicated."*

Although his residence here was fairly short, he must have taken thousands of photographs. In the later years of his time spent here, he became associated with E. O. Hageman in the photography business. Before leaving Hamilton, Moore sold his share to Hageman, who continued the business for many years.

The immediate occasion for Moore to leave the Bitter Root was the death of Marcus Daly on November 12, 1900, and the subsequent sale of Daly's racing stable by his widow. The sale of the numerous Daly horses was held in two separate parts: the sale of the running horses being made first, at Madison Square Garden in New York in 1902, and the sale of the harness horses at the same place in 1903.

Moore secured a job of accompanying the horses east when they were shipped to the sale. He never came back to the Bitter Root to reside, but his pictures were left as an enduring monument. He spent the latter part of his life in Florida, dying there at the age of 84, in 1954.

Albert Moore was an uncle of Charles and Otis Talbot, sons of Mr. and Mrs. J. R. Talbot, who resided in the Bitter Root for many years. Mrs. Talbot was a sister of Albert Moore.

THE RUTH MOORE FAMILY

by Ruth A. Rockafellow Bartlett

My father, Charlie Moore, came from New York State and mother, Libby Thompson Moore, from Vermont State. I was born on May 3, 1886 in Anaconda. The Moore family arrived in the Woodside area in 1898 and settled on a homestead on which we lived until Mother's death in 1933.

My brother, Howard, and I attended elementary school from 1st thru 8th grade at Fair Play School. We enjoyed our school building, for all our holiday entertainments were held in it. Also, church services and funerals, etc. Mother usually played the organ at most of the services. My father was a carpenter and he worked much of the time helping build the Anaconda smelter and other buildings in Butte, Montana.

I attended business college in Missoula during 1917-1918. Then, I worked as a clerk in the Montana Hotel, Anaconda, for 2 years. Richard S. Rockafellow and I were married on September 7, 1920, in Anaconda. To our union, two boys were born, Howard Douglas, May 10, 1925, and Ellis Dee, September 23, 1929. We were living on a farm at the time of Dick's death on August 23, 1935. After his death, I moved to Hamilton to work for the Security Abstract Co. for six years. Then, I worked for Selective Service in the War Department in Missoula, eventually transferring to Helena in February 1947, retiring from there in December, 1965.

Winters were spent in Arizona and on June 2, 1969, I was married to George E. Bartlett from Rapid City, South Dakota. We then took up residency in Mesa, AZ, and have lived there since.

My oldest boy, Howard D. Rockafellow, lives in Burlington, WA, and has 7 children. And my other son, Ellis D. Rockafellow, lives in Livingston, Montana, and has 6 children.

In my youth, I remember that I worried about walking through the woods and seeing wild animals, but the thing I most worried about was a porcupine. I thought I could outrun any other animal but figured the porcupine would throw its quills at me if I was a mile from it. Fortunately,

I never ran into one.

We never rode to school. If the weather was bad, someone would come to meet us so we wouldn't get lost. We came through many blizzards. The Hauf family would take us home with them. They lived just a half mile from the school. We really enjoyed school picnics, usually the last school day of the year—that was a big day for us. We played ball a lot, girls and boys both. We had a big wide board for a bat, couldn't hardly miss the ball. That was fun. We enjoyed walking to school as we went with the Rummel, Blodgett, Shults, Severns, and Mace children, and Fay Burrell.

THE FAMILY OF LUELLA BELLE AND ROBERT BRUCE MYERS

by Loyce Simmons Teller, granddaughter

I am going to start this family history with the year 1730, the year that Robert Myers' great grandfather, Jacob Myers, was born in Westphalia, Germany. He brought his family to the United States in 1763. Jacob served in the Revolutionary War. Then next was Robert Myers' grandfather, William Myers, who was born in Germany in 1762, and he served in the War of 1812. After the death of his wife, Jennie, he married Jane Monroe, and from this union Robert Myers' father, James Myers was born on January 1, 1829, in Kentucky. James married Frances Isabel Short who had been born on July 14, 1841. James and Frances lived in Edenburg and Greensburg, Missouri, where their six children were born; Alice Jane, Robert Bruce, Amy Lillian, Martha Caroline, Mary Evaline, and William Roy.

IT WAS THE YEAR 1889, OR 1890, when James and Frances moved to the Bitterroot Valley and settled in Corvallis, Montana. Four of their six children came with them; Alice, Amy, Mary, and William. Martha stayed in Greensburg, married, and never came west. Robert, known as "Rob" or "Bob" stayed in Greensburg and married Luella and they moved to Corvallis area in 1891, just a little later than his parents.

They homesteaded 160 acres just east of the Bitter Root River, with the land running to the north and the south. Bob worked to clear the land for his home, barns and such. The road in front of his place was nothing more than a wagon trail at that time, and with no river bridge Bob and his family had to ford the river to get to Woodside and the train station. The train station was also a grocery store, and for many years was owned by the Pierce family.

Not long after they returned from Missouri, another daughter was born. She was named Mary Frances, born on February 26, 1893, and the last child to join this family. They now had Rea, Lenore, and Frances.

Bob built a blacksmith shop east of his home, along the side of the graveled road, and worked at blacksmithing for many years. It had to be moved when the present highway was under construction, and was purchased by a neighbor, Bill Engler, and moved to his property just a quarter mile east. Bill used it for a garage and shop for years, and it is still visible from the highway.

Bob's old horse barn still stands northwest of the house. He also farmed some, and had a garden, but mainly loved the blacksmithing and music. The Myers Band often played for dances in the Victor area.

The old paint shop is still on our property. My mother, Rea used to paint buggies there, and Lou had her big old loom in this shop, too. Grandma wove many a rug for family there, and as a child I would sit on an apple box and watch her weave. I would fill the shuttles for her as she needed them. There are names such as Lee (Simmons), Gil (Chaffin), Glenn (Chaffin), Paul (Lear), Roy (Myers) and BK (Bessie K. Monroe) and others painted on the walls inside this old building. They were all young then, single girls and boys.

Ice cutting days. After the ice reached 8 to 10 inches thick, the men would all meet at the Red Bridge and saw blocks of ice, small enough to handle by hand or by ice tongs. They would load them into wagons and take them home to their ice houses where they would bury them in the sawdust. The ice would keep all summer.

SIBLINGS OF ROBERT BRUCE MYERS

Sisters:

ALICE JANE MYERS LEAR: Alice Meyers was born on September 6, 1860, in Edenburg, Missouri. She married William Douglas Lear (born February 17, 1844 in Lancaster, Kentucky). This was my Aunt Alice and my Uncle Will. Uncle Will was called to the valley by Elijah Chaffin to set up the first Christian organization. He helped build the first church edifice, in Montana at Corvallis in 1881. He served two terms as Chaplain of the State Legislature of Montana. William was also a descendent of John Quincy Adams. Aunt Alice and Uncle Will lived in a small house in Corvallis on what is now called Water Street. This house still stands, is being lived in, and in good condition. Their children were: James (Jamie) D. Lear, Paul Lear.

MARY EVALINE MYERS CHAFFIN: She was born March 14, 1873, in Greensburg, Missouri, and died on October 11, 1958, at Corvallis. Aunt Mame married Moses Lord Chaffin, son of Elijah and Margaret Chaffin on January 8, 1893 at Corvallis, MT. Uncle Mose was born July 13, 1868, in Corvallis, and died on June 15, 1956, at Corvallis. They lived in the Elijah Chaffin home most of their married lives. This house still stands in 1997, an is now part of the Teller Wildlife Refuge and in very good condition.

AMY LILLIAN MYERS FROGGE: She was born on October 15,

1866, in Greensburg, Missouri, and died April 20, 1950, at Corvallis. Amy married Drewry R. Frogge. He was born on February 9, 1854, and died in Missouri on August 17, 1925, buried in Corvallis Cemetery. Aunt Lil and Uncle Drew used to live east of Corvallis on Willow Creek and our family loved to visit them usually staying overnight. Aunt Lil ended up living on Church Street across from the elementary school, where her house still stands, and is in very good condition.

Brother:

WILLIAM ROY MYERS: Was born August 14, 1879, in Greensburg, Missouri, and died on November 19, 1957, at Missoula, Montana. He was a blacksmith, salesman, and deputy sheriff. Uncle Roy married Agnes Ainslee Johnson in Corvallis. She was born March 31, 1886, in Corvallis. They spent most their married life in Missoula.

The wedding gift each child received from their parents, Bob and Lou, was a COW! Each sold the cow to purchase something really special, which in Rea's case was a sewing machine.

The three Myers daughters:

1. REA MYERS SIMMONS: Rea married Lee Elijah Simmons, who was born March 29, 1884. Lee's parents were Nancy and Gilbert Simmons. His maternal grandparents were Elijah and Margaret Chaffin of Corvallis. They were married April 14, 1912, at her parent's (Bob and Lou Myers) home, which was then known as "River Ranch". They became parents of three children; Walter Robert, Marylee, and Loyce Lenore. It is Loyce Lenore telling this story.

A. Walter Robert met Ethel Elvera Swanson while she was teaching school in Corvallis. They were married in Anaconda, and had two girls; Lenore Lillian and Jo Anne.

B. Mary Lee Simmons was born June 27, 1915, in Corvallis and married Thoralf Johannes Lee at Spokane, Washington. They had three boys; Robert Bruce, Gordon Craig, and Alan James.

C. Loyce Lenore Simmons was born September 28, 1922, in Corvallis and married Leighton A. Teller. They had three children; Vicki Lee (deceased), Leighton Stephen, and Janet Lynn.

2. LENORE EMMA MYER COBB: Born in Missouri, married to Milford Ezariah Cobb on January 22, 1911. Lenore was a school teacher before she married Milford. They had one daughter Luella Rea (LuRea) Lu Rea married Willard Frank Tanner at Spokane, WA. They have three children; Marilyn Jean, John (Jack) Milford and Mart.

Milford and Lenore spent most of their married life just two miles north of Corvallis, on the old family residence on Cobb Lane, now known as Popham Lane. Milford was a rancher and a dairyman. He played the tuba in the band organized for Corvallis musicians. He also loved to hunt coyotes. He and Bob Myers each had their own hound dogs for this purpose. Lenore was a fine journalist and wrote for the Western News.

3. MARY FRANCES MYERS ELLIOTT. Born in Corvallis on February 26, 1893, she married Howard Everett Elliott at River Ranch on January 6, 1919. They met in Dillon where both were attending school. She was a teacher and he was a 2nd Lt. in the Army when they married. They settled in Deer Lodge, MT. After many years in the school system as Superintendent of Deer Lodge High School, he returned to school and became a licensed optometrist. Frances was an accomplished artist and had a lovely singing voice. They had three children: Bruce Madison, Paul Roy, and William Schuyler.

Many delightful Sunday dinners with homemade ice cream were enjoyed by the siblings and their relatives at the home of their parents, Bob and Lou. The men, after a nap, indulged in horseshoes while Grandma Lou read the funny papers to the grandchildren.

NEAFUS — WOODS FAMILY

by Amy Lee Rockefellow Felix, Great Granddaughter in 1998

William Henry Neafus was born in Kentucky on March 10, 1840. Cornelia Woods was born in Missouri on September 28, 1842.

They married on May 8, 1864, in St. Joseph, Missouri, just one week before they departed from thereby covered wagon train for Alder Gulch and Virginia City, in Montana Territory.

To this couple were born nine children: Anna Dixie on March 3, 1865 (died July 17, 1887), Marion Wallace on August 7, 1867 (d. August 16, 1869), Harry Edwin born February 13, 1870 (d. September 21, 1944, unmarried), Nellie Ernestine on April 11, 1873 (d. October 6, 1897), George Allen on August 20, 1875 (d. June 25, 1897, unmarried), Twins — on August 4, 1878 — Richard Marion (d. August 26, 1910) and Mabel Claire (d. in 1978 at the age of 99 or 100 plus. Married a Reynolds from Corvallis), Laura Elbert on October 21, 1882 (d. January 5, 1952) married Robert Russell Smithey on April 16, 1901, Edith Bradley on January 8, 1888 (d. December 30, 1987. Married Fred Simer of Salmon, Idaho. She was planning her 100th birthday party at the time of her death. The youngest in the family, she was always known as "The kid" until the end. Nieces and nephews called her "Aunt Dollie".

The Neafus name has been traced to 1594, with the first immigration to America in 1650. There have been numerous spellings. The 1880 census spells it "Nafus". Carlis Neafus, a grandson, was the last to carry the name in this branch of the family. Granddad Neafus became an orphan between the ages of four and five, and we have no further traces of his immediate family.

I found the Neafus family to be "colorful". Never knowing Granddad, I gleaned from others that he had a great sense of humor. He was a big man at six foot tall, but wore a size six shoe. It was a standing offer that he would give his shoes to any man who could wear them! He was known for his ability to broadax logs for building. He apparently built their homes in this manner wherever they lived and helped others to build their log homes, also.

They arrived in Virginia City, Montana, and moved to Last Chance Gulch and Townsend, and to the Sun River area, arriving in the Bitter Root in 1891. Most of the land on the Eastside of the valley was taken up, so they settled about a mile north of Woodside. Though they watched three granddaughters grow to adulthood, they also saw five of their nine children die. Two of their daughters lived to age ninety-nine.

They came to Montana at the insistence of Cornelia's widowed father, Patrick Woods. Patrick Woods was a man of considerable means who seeing the South losing the Civil War, sold his plantation and freed his slaves, purchased trading goods and formed a wagon train to bring his family West. He must have been a man of strong will as his family did not want to move West. He married a widow who had joined the wagon train and the last that was known of him prior to his death was, he ran a trading post in Augusta.

The Neafus family was taught to work hard, be honest, and to keep their word. I knew the four remaining children and learned this at an early age. They were good examples.

Great Grandmother Neafus was spunky and strong, but she never gave up on the fact that she would have been a "Southern Belle". She never accepted the fact that the South had changed. Instead, she simply disliked living in Montana and longed to return to the South, as she had known it — and as it could never be again. She was proud to have attended a boarding school. When her picture was taken, she nearly always held her Bible. She wanted people to know that she was educated. She read her Bible and did not waste her eyes on "fancy work", but she had to sew for her family.

Cornelia had been known to pull up her skirts and wade through a mud puddle to keep from walking under the "Yankee Flag". All the slaves had been freed except a man and a woman who had been brought along on the wagon train. The woman offered to teach Cornelia how to cook. Still the sassy one, Cornelia swore she would never cook so long as there was a black around. I've been told that she should have taken the lessons for she never did learn to cook. Granddad took it in stride by explaining she had gotten the shortening in upside down! To her death, at 94 years, she maintained that apples should be cooked in a copper kettle over the open fire. She always had peppermint candy on hand for her great grandkids, but I don't remember eating anything she had made.

WALTER AND KAY NELSEN

Walter Nelsen was born in Hamilton in 1910 to Lars P. and Lucy Jergensen Nelsen, the last of eleven children. Chances are that Walter would have been a citizen of Denmark had it not been for his uncle, Jim Jergensen, who was disillusioned with the economy in Denmark, where it took a year to earn enough money to buy a cow — so Jim came to America to "check it out".

Jim Jergensen homesteaded in the East Fork. There remains even now an apple tree which he planted. The tree is located just northwest of the Medicine Tree, and has a sign which reads, "This apple tree planted in 1890, by J. A. Jergensen, Homesteader". After Jim settled in the Bitter Root Valley, he sent money to bring the rest of his family to America, including Walter Nelsen's mother and father. Jim went on to become a State Senator. Lars and Lucy settled in the East Fork area, and established a truck farm. Walter recalls stories of hauling the produce to the Big Hole:

"Sometimes ranchers would buy the whole truckload, and other times, they would have to go to several ranches. They would chop down a lodgepole and attach it to the rear axle of the wagon so the tree would act as a brake, going down the steep grade into the Big Hole. When you got to the bottom of the hill there was a huge pile of trees left by other drivers," recalls Nelsen.

Lucy, the young Mrs. Nelsen, didn't know quite what to think about the Indians who traveled through the East Fork country in those days. Walter recalls his mother's story about one Indian who frightened her by peaking through the window at her. She was home with the babies that day, and cautiously went to the door. The Indian indicated he wanted something to eat, so she made some sandwiches and took them to the porch. The Indian ate lunch, bowed, and went on his way, hopefully dispelling some of the young woman's fears.

Walter recalls later years when his family joined the Salish at Pow Wows held at the Medicine Tree:

"Days were spent story telling and dancing. Sid Morton lived up there then, and he was raised by the Salish so he acted as interpreter. We packed up a big picnic lunch and went to the Pow Wow. I was just a kid then and didn't care that much about Indian stories. How I wish now that I had taken more interest! They talked about old times, and my parents listened to every word. The Indians danced in circle dances and had their drums. They had beautiful costumes; it was a big event in those days and everybody had a fine time. I think we stayed the entire afternoon, after we had our picnic lunch. Then some of the people would go to Medicine Hot Springs for a swim".

Walter was born in the Romney house, located between Canyon Creek and Blodgett. The house belonged to Miles Romney, Sr., publisher of the local newspaper, and longtime friend of the Nelsens. Walter, like all of his brothers and sisters, was born at home with his dad assisting in the delivery. He attended school at Canyon Creek School during his first four years of school, then the school district got a team and wagon and consolidated with the Hamilton school. Walter worked on the family farm until World War II, when he joined the military. After the war, he returned to the Bitter Root where he worked on construction of the Ford building in Hamilton. He then went to work for the State Water Conservation Board, building dams and ditches — a job which took him all over Montana.

It was while working on a project in Winnett, that Walter met his wife to be, as she was teaching school there. The couple met at a country dance, and in 1953, were married. Walter and Kay moved around the country working on various projects, until they came back to visit family in the Bitter Root Valley. Kay picked up a newspaper and discovered help wanted ads for both a teacher (her profession) and someone to work at Bitter Root Valley Irrigation. Kay went to work for the Grantsdale School, and Walt got on with BVI, and that put an end to their nomadic life.

The Nelsens became parents of a son, whom they named Miles — after Miles Romney, Sr., Walt later worked for the Conner Mill, but retired in 1973. He dedicated his retirement funds to putting Miles through college. Kay retired from the Grantsdale School.

AUNT TISH NEVINS

The headlines and article in the Western News read **"Death Claims Long Time Resident: Tish Nevins' Funeral Was Today (Sept. 24, 1942) widely known"**

Survivors were members of the Smithey family, who mourn Aunt Tish as one of their own.

Aunt Tish was born June 2, 1862. A minister in Missouri gave her his family name, as she lived with and worked for his family.

The saga of Aunt Tish began in Paris, Missouri, when Nell Smithey was 3 years old, "Pete" was 5, Herb was 7, and Tom was 8 years old. The Smithey children's mother died after the birth of her 10th child, "Mattie", and Tish (a 28-year-old, mulatto housekeeper) took these five youngest children to raise. She took over the management of the children and the family home, tending them with the same care and devotion as if they had been her own.

When the father, Robert L. Smithey, moved his family to the Bitter Root Valley, Aunt Tish naturally went along. While raising the Smithey children, Tish had a reputation as a fine cook, but it wasn't until Mattie (whom she always referred to as "My baby") married Wesley Walls, that

Tish at age 46, started her own dining room and boarding house.

Aunt Tish's first boarding house was located at the intersection of Main and North Sixth Streets. Later it was located just North of the Ravalli (Howe) Creamery. Tish converted two large rooms downstairs into dining rooms. She needed young help, and there were different individuals who needed her help so that high school might be possible. Their spare time from school counted up to save many steps for Aunt Tish and the other women who came in to help with the cooking and serving in the two dining rooms. She maintained these in spotless, homelike order, for her regular boarders and for the many guests from other towns who came to partake of the southern style feasts of fried chicken, apple pie, and all the extras in between.

All of their spare time, as wards of Aunt Tish, wasn't spent on chores however, for Aunt Tish exacted school homework and lesson preparing. No mother could have been more faithful to the job of helping her charges to study and learn their lessons in the after-supper hours, than Aunt Tish who had no formal schooling whatever. She would often remind her working after school children **"that she had never had a chance to learn from schoolbooks, and you ought to be glad to get to that homework, and learn something!"** B. K. Monroe wrote a tribute to Aunt Tish, saying "Tish gave plenty of love to the boys and girls she knew in her home and neighborhood, and she gave counsel too; even to my own sons and daughters who were among these children she knew and helped."

Bill Jellison boarded with Tish one summer and later he and his bride, Gretchen, lived with Aunt Tish for a short while. Aunt Tish would request that after dinner Gretchen read Shakespeare to her. The Jellisons said that when they stayed there, Aunt Tish was cooking two meals a day for the public. A meal never included less than three kinds of meat, several vegetables, white and sweet potatoes, salads, and desserts. They said she always wore a white dress.

In Aunt Tish's zeal for education enlightment, Tish supported the Chataugua tours that brought cultural programs to small towns. She would buy tickets for the whole Smithey family, and spend the whole week at the big tents.

During one tour, William Jennings Bryan came to Hamilton and delivered his famous "Cross of Gold" speech in favor of sterling silver for monetary use, instead of gold. He ate at Tish's table, and later wrote her a note saying, "It was one of the delights of my life". She kept the note pinned to the dining room wall. Although statesmen and politicians ate at her table, talk never reverted to politics. Her table was one of merriment, with talk of families and joys. Tish took an interest in people. Problems of the world didn't concern her, it was friends that mattered! Tish was poised and dignified. "She was royalty", said Bill Jellison, "A very special lady".

About June 3rd, 1939, Aunt Tish's doctor insisted she retire from this chosen vocation of feeding the public, as her health was failing. During retirement, she lived with Aunt Nell Smithey Reimel who hosted an open house for Tish's 80th birthday in 1942. Aunt Tish died on September 24, 1942.

NEWELL FAMILY

by Harry "Bud" Newell

My dad, Harry Newell, was born in 1880 in a cottage in Carthage, Missouri. Dad was the oldest of nine children. Jake, Bill, Joe, Charley, and Bob were his brothers and his sisters were Addie, Faith, and Gladys. One child died. My mother's maiden name was Hertz. Her father came from Pennsylvania. She called them the Holland Dutch. My mother was born in Philipsburg, Granite County, and her parents moved to Deer Lodge shortly so she was raised and went to school in Deer Lodge.

Helen, my sister, was born in 1910 in Deer Lodge. After my folks moved to the Bitter Root Valley, they lived on Skalkaho Road on the Frank Cash place. They drove a horse and buggy to Hamilton, until Dad bought this lot. The house was in the back on the alley. It was only a three room house at the time and they had it moved up here. Katherine, Jack, and I were born in the Bitter Root Valley. I was born in 1914, Katherine was born in 1916, and Jack was born in 1934. Later on about the time WWII broke out, my sister, Katherine, was working for John Peterson, a valley contractor, and they remodeled the house while she worked for them.

I never saw my dad's father. He was living on a ranch east of Drummond and he dropped over dead one morning. I was only a year old when he died.

Helen married Clare Patterson, Dale Patterson's brother. Dale will be 91 soon and is still going pretty strong. He does his own cooking and shopping. The only thing he is losing is his eyesight. He can't see too good. Jack married Betty Willey, Dan Willey's daughter. I married Eleanor Waldy from Boulder. We had two daughters, one lives in Butte and the other in California.

My dad worked for Spaulding at one time. He got so he couldn't work. He had Parkinsons. It came on him before he was 40 years old. He didn't die until he was 80. He was in the Stevensville Rest Home for 14 years. I use to take care of him, that's why I stayed home. Didn't know what to do to feed him. After he entered the rest home, I was able to work in Butte. They paid quite a bit more money there at the time with the union. Dad laid in bed for several years and had to be lifted and carried all over.

I worked for Safeway in Butte and also for an independent over there. I worked for Doug Galbraith and Herb Kent at the Hamilton IGA store. Herb bought the store in 1971.

FROM NEBRASKA TO MONTANA BY WAGON TRAIN

by Mabel Ellen Newell Patterson in 1958

On May 15, 1896, when I was 11 years old, my father, mother, five brothers and sisters, and I left Springview, Nebraska, in a covered wagon. Our family had two wagons so my uncle, Tom Newell, drove one of our wagons. He had no family and carried part of our supplies in the wagon he drove. Mr. and Mrs. Adolph Clear and their two year old daughter, Bertha, also left with us.

We bought some of our supplies on the way and we also killed grouse, prairie chickens and rabbits. We didn't see much big game. We cured most of our meat by drying it and by smoking it. Before we started out, Dad bought a case of crackers which came in handy when we ran out of bread. The only boughten cookies at that time were ginger snaps, which we purchased in bulk. Mother packed a big tub, called a firkin, of butter that lasted us all the way. She packed a layer of butter, then a layer of salt which helped to keep it better — but it did get a little strong by the time we got out here. We also had flour with which to make bread. Mother would mix the bread early in the morning before we started out, then at noon she kneaded it down, and in the evening would bake it in the Dutch Oven.

When we got to Valentine, Nebraska, I saw a train. I had seen one when I was very tiny, but this was the first train I remembered. Also, in Valentine, Nebraska, my uncle bought me a doll. This was my first doll with hair. I had this doll until after I was married and I gave it to my first child. She broke it.

We didn't travel very far in South Dakota. We must have traveled north and then turned up in North Dakota. In Edgemond, ND, we met two more wagons. One was driven by a man whose name I don't remember and a man by the name of Brown drove the other wagon. Mr. Brown and his wife and five children were with them. I don't remember meeting anyone else traveling in wagons. Most people were traveling by train by this time, but we had all our household articles and horses to bring and Dad wanted to look at the country. We had no definite destination, but we had to leave Nebraska because of a three-year drought.

We did meet quite a few people on horse back, and Mom used to say she never heard so many liars! They couldn't estimate distance very well, or else they just didn't care because every time we asked someone how far it was to a water hole or to the next town — we got a different answer.

We had an old washing machine in one of the wagons and we took one day a week off to do the washing. We had to heat water and we dried the clothes by hanging them on the bushes. When there were no bushes, Dad strung up a wire.

We carried our drinking water in a barrel churn in the back of the wagon. Usually we found a place to water the horses, but sometimes we had to drive fast or reach camp late to get to water. We had a bed in the wagon. The sides of the wagon were extended out so that the bed springs would fit. Mother, Dad, and baby Vernon, slept on this while the rest of us pitched tents on the ground. We usually camped near a creek if possible.

My dad played the fiddle. He used to play for dances in Nebraska. Mr. Brown and my uncle Tom were good singers and Mr. Brown played the mouth organ. They used to sing when we camped at night. We used to sing with my uncle Tom in the wagon. We usually sang hymns, but my brother Vernon would make up songs as we went along. I remember one song he made up, "Were it to rain out, we would get all wet, we would get all wet." One time we were going through a town and Mother heard someone say, "That must be the Salvation Army!"

One time we got stuck in the mud. I can't remember just where we were but it was kind of a dry place. The road went down through this mud hole, and we got stuck, and we liked not to get out of there. The men had to unhitch the teams from the back wagons and used them to help pull the front wagons out. We worked half a day getting out and to make it worse, we had to go right up a hill coming out of the mud hole!

I can't remember anyone being sick on the way. The alkali water wasn't too good for us so Dad mixed vinegar, sugar, and ginger, in the water. We liked it this way, and it kept us from getting sick.

We wore ordinary clothes and usually went barefoot. Our dresses were made of cotton and we never dreamed of wearing overalls. Some girls wore denim dresses, but Mother never put them on us. We didn't have much money, but Mom always kept us neat and clean.

We used to get out and walk a lot because the wagons didn't go very fast. One time in Wyoming, we were walking along the railroad tracks. The rest of the children went back to the wagons after awhile, but I kept on walking and I became separated from the wagons! While I was running along the track trying to catch up, I came to a railroad bridge and not seeing it, I fell in and skinned both arms and one knee! I had those scars for years. I ran until I came to a place where I could get to the wagons, and by that time the wagons were coming to a place where the road was under water. I jumped on the last wagon and rode across the water. My folks didn't miss me because I often rode in other wagons, especially my uncle Tom's wagon. When we got out of the water I ran and caught my parents wagon!

According to a diary my brother kept, we were in Wyoming on July 1, 1896. We had been on the road a month and a half by then. We laid over in Sheridan on July 13, 14, and 15th.

The only time we saw Indians was when we went through the Crow reservation. They were all friendly, but they frightened my little sister, Ada, who was only five years old. She wouldn't get out of the wagon because of them and she said to our Mother, "Mommy, they look like their faces are made of leather, don't they?" A young Indian buck traded horses with my brother, Leonard. My brother got the better horse so Dad gave the Indian a six shooter to boot. Sometimes the Indians came out to eat with us. If there was any food left over, they would wrap it up in the corner of their blankets and take it with them.

We followed the present highway and reached Billings, Montana, on July 22, 1896. Sometimes the roads were very rough, as a lot of them were just trails. We reached Helena, MT, the 6th of August and the Four Paws Circus was going on. It was one of the most famous circuses in that day. We didn't get to go to the circus, but we did see the parade. I saw my first elephant, and also a baby elephant. We got to ride on a merry-go-round which was right near our camp. We also got to ride on a street car, but Dad didn't want to take time to see the circus.

I also remember the weather was dreadfully hot.

Sometimes my uncle would let me drive the wagon. I remember driving over a high grade which must have been McDonald Pass. We came through Avon, Elliston, and Bonner, to Missoula. The only graded road was between Bonner and Missoula — and it was a toll road. Dad asked someone if this was the road to Missoula, and the man said, "Yes, this is the toll road." My Dad thought he said coal road. There was another road we could have taken, but when we got to the toll road we couldn't turn around. So, we had to pay $1.00 for each wagon, which was quite a lot of money to us, because money was pretty scarce!

When we got to Missoula, the Clear family went on to Plains, MT, and the Browns went to Idaho. By then we had decided to go to Plains also, but Mother and Dad had relatives in the Bitter Root and we came up here to visit them first. I remember coming over the Lolo grade and I was so scared. We weren't used to mountains. The first night here we stayed with my aunt. I remember my three year old brother, Vernon, cried because he wanted to sleep under the trees. We didn't stay with relatives for very long. My Mother's uncle, Simon Kuhn, had a vacant house, and we moved into it. We decided to stay in the Bitter Root Valley. Dad thought it was the best place he had ever seen! He always liked to irrigate, and this was the ideal place for him. It had taken us nine weeks to come from Springview, Nebraska to the Bitter Root Valley by wagon train. My folks bought some property at Victor, MT, and we lived there until 1900. Some years after I was married, my folks also lived on the Flathead, at Arlee.

Statistics:

Father was Andrew Jackson Newell, born in Correctionville, Iowa on December 18, 1856, and died January 31, 1939, buried at Victor Cemetery. Mother was Lucinda Isabel Kuhn Newell born April 27, 1863, at

Cook County, IL, and died August 29, 1954, buried at Victor Cemetery. Andrew and Lucinda were parents of: Elsie (1881 died as infant). David Leonard (1883-1900) not married, Mabel Ellen (1885-?) married A. B. Patterson, Flossie Adele (1886-1927) married Arthur McMahan, Winona Ida (1889-?) married Ralph Hollibaugh, Ada Eliza (1890-1957) married H. C. McLean, John Vernon (1893-?) married Nellie Sutherlin, Floyd Arthur (1898 -1953) married Peggy DuCharme, Donita Leone (1904-?) married Leonard Greenup.

NOUSANEN FAMILY

by Arne Nousanen

During the period between 1880 and 1915, about one-third of the population of Finland, Norway, and Sweden migrated to the United States of America. Most of the emigrants came to areas where climate and natural resources were similar to their homelands, and provided familiar working opportunities. They often found employment in the mines and timbered areas such as in Michigan, Minnesota, the West Coast, and in western Montana. The section of Hamilton, Montana, just west of the Washington school on North 5th, and on North 6th and 7th, became known as "Fin Town". Descendants of many of the families still live in the Bitter Root Valley and carry names such as Maki, Manti, Kolppa, Halonen, Ajo, Joki (Yoki), Hangas, Hendrickson, Gustafson, Hill, and Kattleus.

My grandfather, Herman Hannila (name changed to Hendrickson upon entry to the U.S.), came to Hamilton about 1880, and was employed at the Daly Mill. He married Mary Kolppa who came from Finland in 1882, to Granite (near Philipsburg) where she worked as a waitress for some time before coming to Hamilton. My mother, Hilda, was born in 1894. My grandfather Herman died of typhoid fever in 1895, and a year later grandmother Mary married Henry Gustafson, another sawmill worker. They had four children: Henry, Anna, Olga (Pat), and Saima (Bud).

My Mother, being the oldest of the Gustafson children, was forced to leave school after the sixth grade and do domestic type work to help feed the family. She worked for the Edwards and Nichols families for several years.

Ollie Nousiainen (name changed to Ole Nousianen after entering the U.S.) left Finland in 1907, and like so many others came to make a stake and return to his homeland in five years. After two or three years, he had no desire to go back. He came first to Milltown where a cousin had previously migrated. One of his first jobs was as a laborer in construction of a Milwaukee Railroad tunnel west of Missoula. Later he came to Hamilton to work in the sawmill. He boarded and roomed with one of the Finnish families and met my mother Hilda. She helped him and many other Finns to speak, read, and write English. They were married in 1911, moved to the Bass Creek area where he worked for George Brooks who owned a large cattle ranch (later owned by Mario Feronato and now George Ruffato). My sister Helen was born there in 1912, and I in 1913.

We moved to Milltown and Dad worked in W.A. Clark's and Anaconda Copper Mining mills until 1921, when Dad bought a thirty (30) acre farm on Sweeney Creek. Two more children joined our family, Loretta in 1929, and Doris in 1938. Helen eventually married Frank Harrington and taught at the Curlew school. I courted a Florence-Carlton schoolteacher, Mary Ethel Scalf, who was from North Dakota, and later married her. At that time, I was appointed Assistant Ranger with the U.S. Forest Service at Philipsburg, and went on in later years to finish a career with the Forest Service. My father worked for the Bonner Mill until his retirement.

I remember a cannery in operation in 1919 and 1920, just south of Bass Creek, near the Three Mile bridge. Farmers in the vicinity of the present Metcalf Refuge raised peas for the cannery and also sour cherries.

OERTLI

by Minnie Lucille Oertli

Casper Oertli was born in Chicago in a log cabin in 1867 and traveled at the age of four with his parents in a covered wagon from Iowa to the plains of Nebraska where they broke the ground and farmed the new soil of that state. He married Lucy Turnell in 1891 in Nebraska and that same year they came west to Montana.

While residing in Missoula, Casper became interested in locating a homesite in the Hamilton area and to find a suitable property, he walked from Missoula to Hamilton. Along the way, near Stevensville, he stopped at an eating place and bought a sandwich for 15¢. To pay for the food, he offered the only cash he had, a $10 bill. At that time, there was an extreme shortage of coins in the Bitterroot and the owner had no change so he didn't charge Casper anything. Casper was greatly impressed by the generosity.

A farm was acquired in 1894 on Sleeping Child Creek where he and Lucy raised a family of six children. He owned and operated one of the early steam threshing outfits going from farm to farm in the fall, threshing grain. At one time, he was foreman of the Bitter Root Stock Farm.

After working the farm for a number of years, Casper, Lucy, and the family moved to Hamilton in 1916 where they built a number of buildings. Casper continued to thresh grain and run the steam engine, a work he greatly enjoyed. Lucy who had a talent for building and business, designed and managed an apartment house and kept track of the growing number of grandchildren. They were a very talented musical family who played various instruments at local dances.

Casper was an active member of the Masonic Lodge for more than 30 years. He and Lucy were well known and active members of the community and contributed significantly to its growth and stability during both easy and difficult times.

ROBERT O'HARA
Hamilton's first Mayor
AND FRANCES ANN HUGHES
Wife

Robert A. O'Hara was born on June 10, 1867, at Plymouth, Indiana. He received his education at St. Thomas College in St. Paul, MN, and at Notre Dame University in South Bend, Indiana, where he studied law. He was admitted to the Minnesota Bar in Filmore County, MN, then his home locality November 13, 1889. He came to Great Falls, Missoula, and Riverside, Montana in 1890. In Riverside, he began acting as an agent for the Bitter Root Development Company which was the owner of the Hamilton Townsite, then being laid out by the late mining magnate, Marcus Daly. When Hamilton was incorporated in 1894, Mr. O'Hara was selected as the first mayor of the town.

He was married to Frances Ann Hughes, (born at Chicago, Illinois, on June 15, 1875, the daughter of Mr. and Mrs. Thomas Hughes) on July 5, 1893, and they established their home in Hamilton. Educated in the Hamilton schools and at St. Vincent Academy in Helena, Frances was graduated there in 1893, and her marriage to Robert produced three daughters. They are: Mary Frances O'Hara Butzerin of Spokane, WA; Geraldine O'Hara McDonald of Hamilton, MT; and Roberta O'Hara Hart of Metuchen, New Jersey. She was an active member of St. Francis Catholic Church and the Hamilton Women's Club.

In 1905, Mr. O'Hara was one of a number of local men who joined to establish the Citizen's State Bank in Hamilton. An ardent Republican, "Bob" as he was familiarly known throughout the Bitter Root, was elected to the Montana House of Representatives. He was a strong supporter of the late Governor Joseph M. Dixon and for years was active in Republican Party affairs in Ravalli County and many times attended state GOP conventions. He was known as a "tenacious opponent in and out of court, a successful business man, an omnivorous reader, a devoted husband, and father." His daughter, Geraldine O'Hara-McDonald, was associated with her father in the practice of law after 1930, and a memorial session of the Ravalli County Bar Association paid respects to Mr. O'Hara at his death in December of 1954. At the time of his death, Mr. O'Hara had practiced law in Montana longer than any other living attorney.

His death followed just by two months the death of his life partner, Frances Hughes O'Hara. She loved to recall the creation of Ravalli County in 1893, and was among the students who witnessed the legislation that made the Bitter Root Valley a county in its own right. A nephew of Robert, Rev. Robert O'Hara, from Sublimity, Oregon, officiated at both funerals. Both Robert and Frances were known as "good neighbors, and loyal friends" throughout their years in Hamilton.

FRED T. PARKER

Veteran of the Spanish-American War under Teddy Roosevelt Pioneer Orchardist and Businessman in the Bitter Root

Fred T. Parker was born near Fulton, Callaway County, Missouri, on October 23, 1880. He was the youngest of eleven children born to John and Ann Lenox Parker. His father, John Thomas Parker, was a native of England, coming to this country in 1840, and living in Chicago except for a short time in Missouri. He had a business as a general contractor and builder in Chicago.

Bitter Root Cannery, Hamilton, Montana. (Photo courtesy Montana Historical Society)

Fred received his education in Chicago, and at 15, left school to become a stock boy in one of the oldest wholesale dry goods houses of Chicago, The John V. Farwell Company. He later became a traveling salesman and was with the company until enlisting in the First Volunteer Infantry, in 1896, to serve in the Spanish-American War. He was mustered in at Springfield, sent to camp at Ckamanza, and then to Tampa, Florida, and from there to Santiago, Cuba. He participated in the great battle, El Caney, and also the engagement at San Juan Hill where all units were under the command of Colonel Theodore Roosevelt. Back home with an honorable discharge, in 1898, he resumed his job as salesman for the Farwell Company.

In 1903, Fred came to Missoula and bought a tract of land in the Orchard Homes, planting it in apple trees and part into truck gardening. In 1905, Miss Bijou Babb came to Missoula accompanied by her father, to join Fred. On April 4, 1905, Fred and Bijou were married in the Hammond building in Missoula. Fred and Bijou were active in the Orchard Homes Country Life Club, both being charter members. Fred was elected the first Secretary, and Bijou, a Trustee. Bijou also played the piano for club activities.

Two years after they were married, Fred's mother died, and they returned to Chicago to be with his father. Returning to the Orchard Homes, they continued raising apples and potatoes. Fred made and sold apple cider vinegar commercially and also made his own spray dope for his fruit trees. He sold this spray dope commercially also, until the barn burned and all the spray material burned with it.

Five children were born to Fred and Bijou: Virginia (Grube) on June 2, 1913, John Thomas on September 23, 1914, Margaret (Lay) on October 3, 1915, Fred T., Jr., on May 27, 1918, and Ruth (Applebury) on February 28, 1920.

After the barn burned, Fred and his young family moved to Hamilton where he purchased a cannery and a Conoco bulk gas business from the Bozeman Canning Company. In 1922, the Parker family moved into a home at 518 S. 8th Street, purchased from a Mr. Thompson. The cannery, which had been canning string beans, was run by Mr. Cline, who later worked for Fred. Fred made the spray dope he sold on the top floor of the cannery. Orchard supplies as well as the spray dope were sold to orchards throughout the valley.

Fred was active in the Horticultural Society and was President of the State Board of Horticulture for four years.

In 1924, the Bitter Root had a hard freeze, damaging many crops. Because of this, Fred was forced to lay off much of his help. In 1926, the cannery began canning Montmorency sour pie cherries, as well as pumpkin, applesauce, and apple butter, and even experimented with cherry preserves.

During the Depression years of 1929-1930's, the cannery processed apple sauce for the Anaconda Company which they used for food supplies for their employees in Butte and Anaconda. The product was similar to applesauce, without the sugar.

Fred died on December 16, 1937, of a heart attack. Son John, who had graduated from the Montana State University, with a degree in Horticulture, operated the business with the help of his sister, Virginia, and his younger brother, Fred, until the war years. With the wartime need for military food supplies, John, with the help of his two brother-in laws, Ned Applebury and Raymond Grube, built and operated a potato dehydrating plant. The plant operated for the duration of the war, dehydrating beets, carrots, and potatoes.

After the war, the plant was dismantled and the building used for expansion of the canning and farm supply business. The business expanded to include the sale of sprinkler irrigation equipment and commercial fertilizers. The Bitter Root Cannery, as it was known by then, was one of the first agricultural sprinkler dealers in the state.

As the business expanded farther, Fred T. Parker, Jr., returned to Hamilton to join the business as a partner in 1958. Fred Jr. had graduated in Electrical Engineering from Montana State University and spent several years with General Electric Company in Erie, PA, as an engineer working on electrical train engines. During the war, he was an inspector of the electrical equipment on the airplanes being built by Boeing Company in Seattle.

In 1959, the first bulk fertilizer plant in Montana was constructed by the Parkers, and the use of bulk fertilizer spreaders was introduced in the valley. The business continued to expand with stores in Stevensville, Ronan, and Salmon, Idaho. By 1975, the outlying stores were sold and the agricultural part of the business was closed.

In 1997, the Bitter Root Cannery still operates, but limits itself to the processing of pie cherries only. The canning process has been converted to processing cherries for freezing.

PETE PARPOLIA

Pete Parpolia was born in Pesaro, Italy, in 1889. He came to the United States as a young man. He married Winifred Leibel on June 24, 1915. Winifred was born in Little Falls, MN, in 1895.

They had five children: Helen, Kathryn, Louise, Margaret, and Carl.

PAULSEN FAMILY

Compiled by Linda Bieber in 1998

Georgiana Paulsen, who prefers to be called **George,** came to Montana from South Dakota in 1913, when she was just six years old. George, her mother, and five of her sisters arrived in Missoula on the Milwaukee train. Her father, James Carnahan, who had come to the Bitter Root ahead of the rest of the family and had purchased land in the Charlos Heights area, met them there. Then they all rode together on the Burlington Northern train to Hamilton.

At that time, there were two passenger trains per day coming into the Bitter Root. During the day, one came as far as Hamilton and then returned to Missoula. Later, another came down and went all the way to Darby; then returned to Missoula the next morning.

George's first memory of the Valley is funny to recall today, but was pretty traumatic for a little six year old girl at that time. It seems that when the family arrived in Hamilton, they were all feeling very hungry, so Mr. Carnahan took them to eat at a Chinese restaurant. George had never been around Chinese people and could not understand what this man with the white coat and long pigtail was saying, so she asked her sister what she thought he meant. Her sister thought it sounded like he was saying, "roast cat". Well, with that thought in mind, George could not eat a thing! She was unable to even drink a glass of milk. She just could not stand the idea of eating cat, whether or not it actually was. Everyone else had a good meal, but she went all day with nothing to eat.

Later on that day, the family rode the afternoon train to Charlos Heights, where her father had rented a house for the family to live in until he could build a home for them.

George's father, known as "Carnie", was a blacksmith by trade. He also ran their one hundred-acre ranch where they raised apples, huge potatoes, and grain. The land had never been farmed before, so they were all kept busy picking rocks, moving tree roots, and all sorts of other things. George still has a collection of arrowheads that were picked right on the family ranch. Her father and another man, Jim Brush, built an apple warehouse where George worked as a teenager packing apples which then were shipped east. They also shipped a lot of potatoes to various locations out of the Valley.

George attended school in the building, which is now occupied by the Charlos Heights Community Church. She was in the second grade when she started school there. She remembers that there was an enormous heater in the back of the room with some sort of fence around it, and it seemed pretty scary to a little girl. The school had double seats; she had to sit with one of her older sisters, and all the grades were in the same room. Next door to the school was a store. Eventually it went out of business and the school took over that building also. There was then extra space for classes in the lower part, and church and school programs were held upstairs. At some point in time, that second building burned down.

George attended social functions in the old clubhouse at the top of Charlos Heights Hill, and says that they really had a lot of good times there. During the summer, the Indians would come and camp in the area to pick strawberries for the local farmers. They also attended some of these social gatherings. Chief Charlo and his sister were among those who attended dances at the clubhouse. George says that he was a "very handsome young man."

In the 1920's, George's parents sold the ranch to the Hackney family and retired in Hamilton, where they lived for the rest of their lives.

The same year (1913) that George's family came to the Bitter Root, nineteen-year-old Larry (Laurids) Paulsen and his younger brother, Jens, immigrated to the United States from Denmark. People today often find it difficult when their children grow up and leave their families in order to pursue their own lives in another place; but how much more difficult it had to have been for the countless families who lived in all the ages before modern travel made the world so much more accessible. Larry and Jens would never see their parents and childhood home again. They and their family must have realized that this was a possibility when the boys came to America. Larry and Jens first settled in Washington, then moved to Alaska, and eventually came to the Bitter Root. George met Larry in 1928. She says, "He looked at me and I looked at him and that was that!" Within three months, they were married. Larry had a farm up in the Golf Course area, and there he and George raised sugar beets, wheat, and sheep. They had three children; Larry, Bob, and Karen. All three live in western Montana, which is nice for George since Larry died in 1967, and she is the only one of her family left. Her last remaining sister died early in 1998, at the age of ninety-nine.

After their children left home, George and Larry found living on the ranch to be unbearably lonesome. In about 1953, they moved to the Helmville area and George went to work as a cook on the Pauley Ranch, where she was responsible for feeding roughly one hundred men. They were there for ten or twelve years, until Mr. Pauley died and the ranch was sold. Moving back to Hamilton, they worked at the Bitter Root Stock Farm. George cooked for a varying number of people there, depending on the time of year and what was happening on the ranch. Sometimes Mrs. Margit Bessenyey would be at George's table. She liked to be involved in work that included riding in the hills.

During the time that George and Larry were at the Stock Farm, they bought a couple of houses in Hamilton. Larry remodeled both of those houses. When he became ill, George retired from her job to take care of him. She did not want to put her dear husband in a nursing home, and those last three years of his life were a special time for them. After Larry died, she sold the larger of the two houses and moved into the smaller one.

Today, George is a very young ninety-three year old. She lives alone in the same small house in Hamilton. After years of sewing, knitting, and crocheting to clothe her family, she now has time to do handwork for pleasure. She makes beautiful crocheted dolls and afghans, many of which are displayed in her home.

George was born in South Dakota, but she has lived in the Bitter Root for eighty-five years. Charlos Heights has changed dramatically over the years, and it makes her sad to see her old haunts disappearing. Her memories of the Valley, as it was, are a real treasure for anyone interested in how things used to be in the Bitter Root.

ERNIE PETERSON

Ernie was interested in photography as a hobby prior to World War II, as evidenced by some photographs dated 1940. However, from the records he left, his professional interest in photography did not begin until 1946, shortly after discharge from the Army.

Ernie was born in 1912. His mother was Anna Swanson Peterson and his father was Carl J. Peterson, known as John. John was one of five brothers and a sister who came here from Sweden. John's brothers were Olaf, Nils, Swan, and twins Andy and Louie. The sister married a Broman in Missoula. The twins came over first in the 1880s and John and Olaf came in 1902. They bought a painting business from the Magni's in 1904, and Olaf's sons, Arnold (Arnie) and Everett, ran it until the 1980s. Everett sold his share in 1980 and Arnie in 1982. They are still residents of Hamilton.

Ernie had a brother, J. Roland, three years older who was an accountant here for many years. He in turn had three offspring, Roland R., an accountant presently practicing; Tom, a financial advisor, also presently practicing; and Sue, a nurse presently at Marcus Daly Memorial Hospital.

Ernie graduated in about 1934 from Whitman, and went to work as a chemist in southern California for the Fuller Company a paint manufacturer. In April 1943, he entered the Army. Eventually, he went to the China Burma Theater, assigned to an Aviation Engineering Battalion, and remained there until ordered stateside for discharge in February 1946. It was then he decided to earn his living in photography.

Ernie married Lillian Fullerton Franke shortly thereafter. They never had any children of their own, but Lillian had a daughter, Gail Franke, by a previous marriage. Lillian's mother was Ivy Fullerton, who ran an early rest home here in Hamilton.

One of his photos was of a Ponderosa Pine, the Montana State Tree, that adorned the Montana Highway Map for a long time. This tree is on the south rim of Blodgett Canyon, and is identified by an aluminum sign. A big break came when National Geographic used many of his photos in an article about Montana that occurred in the June 1950 issue. This issue is in the Bitterroot Public Library's reference section. He also had his pictures appear in other national magazines such as Field and Stream, Sports Illustrated, Saturday Evening Post and Colliers. Some corporations, such as Montana

Ernie Peterson, well-known valley photographer.

Power, Dow Chemical, Chevron and the Anaconda Company, used his photos for annual reports to stockholders as well as publicity promotions.

He took some color transparencies, even a few motion pictures, but worked primarily in black and white, and used oil paints to color his pictures. They have retained their color over the years as you can see in some large mural type pictures that are presently in the old courtroom of the Ravalli County Museum. Most of these are on loan from valley banks where they hung for many years.

He collaborated with a Bitter Rooter by the name of Glen Chaffin to produce two small booklets of photos and verse, the first, about outdoor privies called "Sittin' and Thinkin', and the second, about dog houses, entitled "I'm In The Dog House".

Some of his pictures sold locally in stores. The two that come to mind were a famous one of Lake Como, and another a field of shocks with Blodgett Canyon in the background.

By far the vast majority of his pictures have never been exhibited or sold. He would go alone or with friends on pack trips into the back country looking for subjects to photograph. These might be: mountains, game animals, wildflowers, lakes, streams or anything he thought might make a good composition. His beat was primarily western Montana, Bitter Root Selway, Anaconda Pintlar Wilderness, Flathead Lake, Glacier, Mission Valley. He also included the Salmon River, Redfish Lake and the Sawtooth Range of Idaho. On some vacations, he took pictures in New York City, Washington D.C., and Arizona.

He went to great lengths to get some of his pictures. Sometimes he stayed out for days to get some animal such as a mountain goat. He even used airplanes and one time a hot air balloon, the latter so he would not spook some cows he wanted to photograph. He took many shots of the same subject, using different exposures and filters to get the effect he wanted

He died at the age of 79 in 1991.

PETERSON

Living in the Bitter Root in the '80s and '90s, the name Per Jonason probably would not mean anything to you, but the name Peterson would bring to mind a paint store, an accountant, a nurse at Marcus Daly Hospital, a financial advisor or a famous photographer. These people were all descendants of Mr. and Mrs. Per Jonason.

This couple lived in Stangby, Sweden, and had ten children. Six brothers and one daughter eventually came to the Bitterroot. The first was Andrew who came in 1881 via Canada, Helena, Montana, as a cook for railroad construction crews and Chehalis, Washington, as a homesteader. He traded his land with Tom Beavers for a livery stable that stood on the corner of State Street and Highway 93 where a photo shop is now located. Somewhere along the line his name changed to Peterson.

His twin brothers, Louis and Nels, came in 1888, Swan in 1892, sister Anna in 1896, became Mrs. Andrew Bowman of Missoula, finally in 1903 Carl J. (John) and Olaf.

Louis, Nels and Swan worked a short time in Missoula for the Northern Pacific, but then came to the Bitter Root. At first, Swan and Andrew ran a livery stable, but Andrew left the business to join Louis in building the European and Peterson Blocks on Main Street. Swan later farmed south of Hamilton and died in 1937.

Louis acquired the Hamilton Hotel, a two-story structure and in 1910 built a three-story addition located on the southwest corner of Main and Highway 93, now a parking lot. He also built a number of rental houses and also operated a ranch in the Gilchrist district, which is east of the Hamilton Golf Course. He also served on the city council. He was born in 1862 and died in 1937. His wife, Sophia, died in 1944. A son, Arthur, was an auto dealer and mechanic. A daughter, Nina Roberts of Portland, Oregon, was the mother of Robert Roberts (deceased) who had Roberts Book Store.

Nels and his wife lived in a house on South Fourth that eventually became the home of Lawrence and Irene (Haigh) Applebury. He was in the livery stable business at first with Andrew, later alone until the automobile put a stop to that, so he converted it to rental garages which eventually became a Texaco station and now a photo shop on the corner of State and Highway 93. He passed away in 1948 and Tilda in 1937. They had a son Ralph of Missoula, another son, Carl, an accountant in Seattle now deceased, and two daughters Hazel, deceased, and Inez (Mrs. Rowland Butler of Los Angeles).

John (Carl J.) and Olaf worked as painters in Stockholm, Sweden, then Copenhagen, Denmark finally Berlin, Germany for several years before coming to the United States and working in various places including the Worlds Fair in St. Louis in 1903. In 1906, they arrived in Hamilton and bought a paint shop from Emil Magni located on the southwest corner of Third and Bedford. Soon they outgrew their shop and, with Erick Erickson, built in 1909 a cement block building on the 100 block of South Third where Roland J. Peterson's accounting office now stands. They later acquired the north half from Erick and their paint shop was in the south ground floor, and the north half rented to Arthur Peterson and Harold A. (Pix) Nicol as a garage.

Upstairs, Carl Winthers had a photograph studio, which later became the studio of John and Anna's (Swanson) son, Ernst, the famous local freelance photographer. Later, downstairs, their other son, J. Roland Peterson, had his accounting office. After Anna died in 1919, the two brothers split the property so John had the cement block building and Olaf the duplex which had been built in 1912 where the original paint shop had been. John retired in 1935 and the paint store was operated by Olaf and his two sons Everett and Arnold.

Olaf married Mabel Hartley in 1909 and they lived in a residence behind the duplex after they sold it. He eventually partially retired and Everett and Arnold moved the business in 1945 to the European building, on Main, which their uncles Andrew and Louis had built. They retired and sold the business around 1980. Olaf and Mabel were also the parents of Muriel, who became a registered nurse and eventually superintendent of Marcus Daly Hospital.

J. Roland Peterson had three children, Roland J., an accountant like his father, Tom, a financial advisor; and Sue, a nurse at Marcus Daly Hospital; all still living in Hamilton.

THE PEIRCE FAMILY

by Alberta Richardson Peirce

I believe Grandpa Richardson was born in Connecticut. Grandma was born in Illinois, I think it was Galesburg.

Grandpa was on of those who went to California along with other 49'ers. When he returned from there, he met grandma someway or other and they were married. They had a farm near Darlington, Wisconsin. All of the twelve children were born there. Nine of the twelve lived to maturity and Mother was the third of the family.

Dad's parents were from the East, Rhode Island. Grandmother's family came from Scotland and must have settled in the area. Eventually, they moved to Wisconsin and settled in the town of Mineral Point. Dad was one of seven children born to this union.

Mother and Dad's towns weren't very far apart so they knew each other from High School times. They were married in 1895. They lived in Wisconsin for a little over two years when they moved to Hamilton, where Dad ran the creamery, which Mr. Daly had built. After about four years there, he built a store and creamery at Woodside, where we lived until going to Camas Prairie, in 1911. Ruth and I finished high school in Camas Prairie in 1917.

On June 27, 1917, Wilber Kilpatrick and I were married. Wilber had found a number for a homestead on the Colville Reservation in Washington, so that is where we made our home until Wilber decided to go to Pullman, where he went to school, receiving his degree in Veterinary Medicine in 1929.

I got a little ahead of myself, for our daughter, Jean, was born in Okanogan, on April 28, 1918, and our son, Franklin (Bud), was born April

30, 1920. Jean is married and lives in Seattle and Bud is living in Columbus, Ohio, where he is with the Ohio State University.

Now, I'll get back to us. After Wilber graduated from WSU, he worked for the state of Washington, in some capacity until his retirement ten years ago. We are living in Renton, Washington, and find it a real nice place to be.

Alberto Manning Richardson and Nancy Curtis Rockwell have children: Marvin, Jerome, Jane, Albert and Eliza.

Albert Anson Richardson and Philurs Ingersol have children: Caribel, Minervo, Flora, Charles, Marvin, Adele, Roy and Rex.

Flora Richardson and William H. Peirce have children: Ruth, Alberta and Ansley.

Alberta Richardson Peirce and Wilber C. Kilpatrick have children: Jean Elizabeth and Franklin Peirce (Bud).

ROY AND MARIE PIERSON FAMILY

by May Pierson Dull Vallance and Helen Pierson Haigh

Marie Bemis's great-grandparents, the Cogwells and the Bemis' came to Ipswich, Massachusetts, in 1635, from England. The Bemis family went on to Spencer, MS, and were the second settlers there. The Cogswell home was taken apart about thirty years ago, and rebuilt in the Smithsonian Institute where it stood for many years. Nathaniel and Judith Cogswell had 19 children. The six girls tended the farm, while the 13 boys served in the Revolutionary War.

Marie Bemis married Roy Pierson in Janesville, Wisconsin, on September 20, 1900. Roy operated a bicycle shop, and later a garage which was the first car garage in southern Wisconsin. The first Parker Pen Company was above his garage. A poor telegraphy student, Parker sold his patent for the Lucky Curve Fountain Pen to W. F. Palmer for $100.00. Palmer sold the Parker Pen Company in 1929, for four million dollars and a directorship for his son, Bernard.

In 1910, Roy and Marie came west with their children, May, age nine, and Helen, age five. Roy had visited with Henry Ford before leaving and had told Ford that "his car was too cheaply made, and wouldn't run, and that it would be a cold day in hell before he would sell one!" Needless to say, Roy was never offered a dealership! Roy sold his garage and put some of the money into the forty acres he bought from O. L. Kenny up on what is now called Alta Vista Loop. This was, of course, apple boom time and Roy wanted to have a big apple orchard. He did plant the orchard, but the water promised from Blodgett Creek didn't come through in time to grow a good orchard. All the land Roy purchased was uncleared mountain and

1910. Mill Creek Canyon home of Roy and Marie Pierson.

canyon, with little flat ground. Kenny had told him there was a vein of gold on Tamarack Creek.

As they were moving west by train, they discovered Marie's cousin, Della McElhiney, and her son, Bemis, on the same train in Missoula. Bert and a daughter, Hazel, had gone out a week earlier. The Piersons had no idea the McElhineys were coming west. A good partnership began that day, as the McElhineys decided to buy land with the Piersons. They moved the two families into three large tents on this land while they built one small cabin having two bedrooms and a large kitchen-living room. The McElhineys lived for one delightful year with the Piersons. In the two sleeping tents, they had the two pianos and a lace tablecloth on the large table in the cook tent. Many singing parties were held here.

Soon after they moved, with the Kennys, they went on a picnic up the canyon past the Laura Elliot timber claim house. They returned about 4:00 PM, and were having a drink of water at the Kenny's when great three and four inch sized black cinders began to fall from the sky. They hurried the quarter-mile home, but it was so dark while traveling that they couldn't see the big pine by the roadside. Their chickens couldn't find the chicken house that night, and roosted all over the yard. **This was the fire of 1910.** The darkness lasted for several days.

Mr. W. F. Palmer wrote to Roy in the spring of 1912, saying that his son, Bernard, had tuberculosis. Bernard needed to be outdoors, and he asked if Roy would look after him and find a farm where he might live. Bernard and Marie had attended high school together. So, Roy arranged for

Bernard to come to Montana and buy the Sid Parke place, on what is now called Bowman Road.

How they survived those years on the hill, the girls will never know! Roy had never been on a farm, except to visit relatives for a family meal. Roy's father had raised three boys, and his brother's three boys after a bad epidemic of diphtheria had taken Roy's mother, brother, and sister when Roy was only eight. Roy's father, Frank, had a hardware store in the city. He gave the boys guns and fishing gear, and they camped out often. So, of course, Roy loved the out of doors, but Marie had to milk the cow with Roy keeping her company and carrying the bucket. The farm included chickens, pigs, apple and cherry trees. The one Leghorn rooster lasted only until he chased May into the outhouse one day. Roy came out and shot him and they had chicken for supper. Roy supplemented their income by working many days as a car mechanic for the new car dealer in Hamilton, being the only person in town with experience in this area.

Roy hunted with Earl Malone many times. They had bear, goat, deer, and he got an elk on the eastside the first year they opened the season on the imported elk. But, often times when the old Roan cow was dry, they had "poor man's gravy" made from bacon, and some potatoes. Of course, they had fruit and vegetables they had canned and dried. Jam and jellies were stored in the root cellar, and sometimes they ate sausage which they had canned in its own fat.

May and Helen rode old Buck to the Fairplay School on Dutch Hill. May rode bareback with Helen bouncing along on the oat sack behind. Buck had to be fed and watered at noon. In the winter, Roy built them a bobsled with metal runners and old Buck pulled them along through the snow. May would stick her leg over the side and drag her foot as a brake. Sometimes going down the Mill Creek Hill, Buck just sat down and slid on the ice! After riding bareback for a couple years, May earned part of the money to purchase a saddle. She worked all summer at babysitting, picking gooseberries, and washing millions of dishes for Mrs. Palmer. Total wages were $8.00 for the whole summer.

May remembers her mother finding as many as seven or eight ticks under her braids at night after picking wildflowers on Tamarack Creek. Helen remembers taking the first tick over to Corvallis School, after Fairplay had consolidated with Corvallis. The principal was just going to pull it out of her head. Helen said, "No, ask May." May laughed and said for them to get some turpentine from the drug store, and put some in front of the tick so that it would back out of Helen' s head. This was accomplished, the tick backed out, and it was put on display at the school for a long time.

Roy poisoned gophers one spring and summer for Dr. Frick, who had a shack laboratory in Victor. It was thought that if they killed the gophers it would help to eradicate the ticks. This was partly correct, but the girls don't remember that Roy ever picked any ticks off the gophers. Roy also herded a band of sheep on his place for one summer for Mr. Hawker. Before they sent the sheep back across the Bitterroot River, they had to go to the dipping vat and be dipped to remove any ticks.

The gold bug hit Roy hard in those early days. One Sunday afternoon while returning from a picnic, the family came past old Mr. Evans sitting on a stump by the poor house on Blodgett Creek Road. He told them about an old Indian telling him about a lost gold mine up in the Clearwater Forest. Roy looked for that gold mine all his life. He and Marie worked at the big mine up on Hughes Creek after they returned from two years in Puyallup, Washington, during the war years.

The family never went back to the cabin as they lived one year in Hamilton and May graduated from Hamilton High School. Next, they moved to the Palmer Ranch and Roy farmed the ranch for the Palmers for seventeen years. Then they built their retirement home on Lincoln Lane near Hamilton. In 1925, Roy purchased the Lucerene placer claim and cabin on Robb Gulch from Joe Hubscher. They staked several claims that have been worked by Marie and Roy and their girls and spouses, grandchildren and great-grandchildren. They still had that adventurers twinkle in the eye when Roy died at age ninety-two, and Marie died just short of 100 years old.

Helen married Kenneth (Cub) Vallance and set about raising their four children: Gene, Bob, Holly (Mrs. Ed Patzer), and Shirley (Mrs. Zack Bugli). Cub worked for the Bitter Root Cheese Factory on Three Mile, and lived in the Frank Lloyd Wright designed Bitter Root Inn. Everyone cooked together in the community kitchen. Somewhere, about that time, John Howe taught Cub the art of butter making. The family moved to Missoula where Cub worked for several years at Garden City Dairies. Moving back to the Bitter Root Valley about 1936, they farmed and ranched just south of Hamilton. Cub drove truck, and also worked for "Pop" Wells at his creamery in Hamilton. When the sons went off to war, Cub and Helen, with partners Claire and Merna Knowles, purchased the Wells Creamery, and started Sno Cap Dairies. Sno Cap also had a soda fountain and a short order café, and was the local hangout for the kids in town. Helen, Cub, and all the kids worked in the business. The sons also, when they returned from the war.

Helen later married Herb Haigh. She taught many ceramic and china painting lessons through the years. She won awards for her china painting as well as for her teaching. She also taught knitting, tole painting, and leather working. At the age of 92, she still helps 4-H'ers with leathercraft. She also acted as a judge at the Ravalli County Fair. Helen's mother, Marie, told Helen of knitting mittens and socks for the Red Cross during World War I. Then only about nine years old, Marie knitted while she roller-skated down to exchange the finished mittens and socks for more yarn. After Herb's death, Helen spent many summers working in gift shops in the National Parks in Montana. In 1998, Helen lived on her own on Lincoln Lane, watched over closely by family and friends.

May graduated from high school, and after only a summer of training at Dillon Normal, she began teaching at Sleeping Child School. She also taught in Avon, Shane Ridge, Kemmerer (WY), Heart Butte, and Browning, most of the time with her husband, Ervin (Jerry) Dull, whom she had married in 1924. She remained in teaching even after their son, Donald, was born. In 1932, Jerry died from pneumonia at Heart Butte. His body was taken by bobsled from Alta to the cabin on Robb Gulch by his brother-in-law, Kenneth Vallance, with the aide of five others. It was early spring, with the last of winter snow, when they buried him in the spot he loved — and where he had worked the claim. He and May spent one whole year working that claim.

May later married Bill Vallance, and their three daughters are Sharen (Mrs. Richard Evans), Phyllis, and Judy (Mrs. Waven Schlepp). May continued teaching after the girls were born. She taught at Charlos Heights, Jefferson and Daly in Hamilton. She received her Bachelors Degree from the University of Montana in 1959, the same year her daughter Sharen got hers from Montana State College in Bozeman. May graciously gave up her own graduation exercises to attend Sharen's as they were set for the same day. In 1992, Lillian Sperry nominated May as Citizen of the Year. She wrote, "If you want to learn more about the beautiful Bitter Root Valley and Montana, May Vallance is a wealth of knowledge. Her love of teaching and sharing is a gift she still gives to anyone who wants to learn."

PILE—MORGAN—KEAYS FAMILY HISTORY

by Delbert Pile, submitted 4-7-97

IN 1910, a number of families that were related, and several friends, all living in a small community called Meadow Vale — near Elk River, Minnesota, decided to move to the Bitterroot Valley in Montana. The major reason for leaving Minnesota was the very cold and severe winters, while Corvallis, Montana, offered relatively mild winters.

Among the families were my grandfather, Erastus Morgan (a civil war veteran), and my grandmother, Emma Eaton Morgan, who was a descendant of seven Mayflower passengers who arrived in Plymouth, MA, in 1620. Along with my grandparents were their children (my aunts and uncles) and their spouses and children; all except for my father and mother, David and Edith Pile, and my sister, Clarice, who came two years later in 1912.

My Grandmother Emma, established and managed a millinery store from 1911 to 1915, in Corvallis, in the building that since has been used as a variety store by the Frogges,and for many subsequent years as a barber shop and beauty parlor, located just north of the hardware store owned by Vance Bay.

My Grandfather and Grandmother built a home in 1910, just south of the old Ed Bay residence. This home has been substantially remodeled since then. About 1913, they purchased two acres, one and one-half miles south of Corvallis, on the east side of the road, and built another home. This home was sold to Mr. and Mrs. W. O. Smith about 1921. The house still stands, but is empty and in need of extensive repairs. My grandparents moved to Southgate, California, in 1921.

AUNTS AND UNCLES COMING TO CORVALLIS WERE:

Arthur Morgan (a Spanish-American War veteran) and his wife, Mable (a sister of Ralph Keays who will be discussed later), three sons and two daughters. Arthur was one of the founders of the Masonic Lodge in Hamilton. He built a home, slightly north and across the street from my grandparents, which burned down. Many Corvallis neighbors pitched in and within six weeks a new home had been built. This home later sold to Mr. Boyer, who sold it to Mr. L. M. Goodman about 1927, and was owned and occupied by the late Johnny and Jack Hawker. Arthur then built a home and a barn about two and one-half miles south of Corvallis, on what is now known as the Hamilton Heights Road. He was a rural mail carrier out of the Corvallis Post Office and helped lay the slate roof on the Daly Mansion.

Charles Morgan, his wife Jessie (Sandusky) and his son, Harvey, and his daughter, Blanch lived in a home near the old Corvallis Cheese Factory. This home is no longer there. He then built a home slightly north of the west end of Christopherson's lane and later sold it to Peter Bosket. Charles operated a garage and a gasoline pump in Corvallis until about 1921. The family then moved to the state of Washington.

Frank Morgan and his wife, Grace (Aldrich), built their home one mile north of Corvallis on the westside of what is now known as the Eastside Highway. This home is still occupied and is the second north of Quast Lane. He and my father, David Pile, began the first commercial beekeeping businesses in the Bitterroot Valley. Frank and his wife had three children while in Corvallis; two daughters and one son. The family moved to the state of Washington in 1921.

My Aunt, Mae Morgan Keays, her husband, Ralph, and their son, Vernon, built their home on property bought from Mr. Jacob Marti. The house still stands just north of the Corvallis LDS Church. Ralph Keays' parents, Mr. and Mrs. Alonzo Watts Keays, and their three sons; Ray, Robert (Bob), and Lester, and two daughters, Ruth and Mabel (wife of Arthur Morgan), also moved to Corvallis. Their home still stands and is just south of the Otto Quast home. Ray Keays played on the Corvallis Baseball Team with Buz Hay. In 1921, all of the Keays' family moved to Southgate, California, except for Bob Keays, who had homesteaded up in the Camas

Prairie Valley, where he met his wife, Carrie. They were there a short time and then moved to Corvallis.

My Father, David Pile, was born in 1880, in the small town of Buras, Kentucky. He was one of eleven children and raised on a farm where his father raised tobacco, corn, and grain, as well as having the usual cattle, hogs, chicken and geese. My father went to school in a one room schoolhouse and completed only the eighth grade. About 1902, he went to Elk River, Minnesota, where he managed a farm for his cousin, Henry Hays, for a period of seven years.

It was there, in this community called Meadow Vale, that he met my mother, Edith Morgan. She was born there in 1894, and also went to school in a one-room schoolhouse and completed only the eighth grade. They were married on June 1, 1910, and my sister, Clarice, was born on July 25, 1911. My father, mother and sister moved to Corvallis in 1912.

My Father built a small home just north of that of Frank Morgan (my mother's brother). That home has since been replaced by another house. There are two Poplar trees still alive that Father planted in 1912. His first job after arriving in the Bitterroot was milking cows for Otto Quast's father. He hand milked 20 cows morning and evening. I recall him telling me how very tired his hands were at that job. In 1912, he planted two Spruce (fir) trees that are still growing in front of the old Quast home.

He then built a building on the west side of the Corvallis Main Street, and established and operated the first feed mill in Corvallis. This building is now the main part of the beer parlor, just south of the old Corvallis (Walker) Hotel.

Father's first automobile was a two cylinder Maxwell. He then bought the second Chevrolet ever sold in the Bitter Root Valley.

My Mother and Father bought an acre of ground from my grandparents, one and one-half miles south of Corvallis. It was on the eastside of the road. Here, my Father built a new home for his family. This was in 1914. He had also begun his beekeeping business, which is described in greater detail in a separate chapter entitled "The Beekeeping Industry in the Bitterroot Valley", written by my Mother, Mrs. David (Edith) Pile. During the part of the year when he was not busy with the beekeeping business, he built a number of homes for individuals, specifically they included: a two story home for Mr. Otto Bolen (the top story of which burned in the late 1940's); a home for Mr. Bolen's father and mother-in-law, Mr. and Mrs. Quackenbush; and Mr. and Mr. Bay (grandparents of Vance Bay); the home that Vance and Delores Bay presently live in; and several other homes and outbuildings.

David Pile was elected to the Corvallis School Board and served from 1924 until 1932. It was during this period that the Corvallis main school building that was built in 1914, burned down. He helped select the architect and the design of the present high school building, and was a school board member during its construction.

My parents lived in their home south of Corvallis until 1947, at which time they moved to Hamilton and my father retired.

My sister, Clarice, went to school in Corvallis and was on the Corvallis Women's Basketball Team. She then married W. Ray Goodman, and continued to live in the Corvallis area until World War II. They now reside in Hamilton.

I was born in the home that my parents and sister lived in, on November 11, 1918. I started school at mid-year in January of 1925, in the old wooden school house that was torn down during World War II. I remember how all three grades in that building shared a common drinking cup and pail of water. Often, when a student became ill, many others became ill also! The outdoor toilets were very unsanitary. When I was in the fourth grade, I went to school in the old school building that burned on that very cold, January day. I was in the sixth grade, and Mrs. Capious was my teacher. She said "This is a real one!" The halls were full of smoke. Fortunately all the students marched out of the building safely, just moments before the entire building was engulfed in flames. We had practiced fire drills many times.

I attended all of my public school education at Corvallis. In 1947, I married my wife, Mildred A. Clarke, and we have a son and a daughter. We retired in 1978, and moved back to the Bitter Root Valley and reside in the Hamilton area.

Other persons moving from Minnesota to the Bitterroot Valley and the Corvallis area about 1910-1914 were: Carl, and his brother, Haner Hobblitt, whose home still stands just west of the railroad track on Hawker Lane; Jacob Marti, his wife, two sons and his daughter, Pearl, who married Parson Pile (a brother of David Pile, the Marti home was located where the LDS church is, just south of Corvallis); and Albert Heath, who settled in Stevensville and married and raised his family there.

POPHAM'S,

They helped to Build the Bitter Root

by Clarence Popham

John William Popham was born at Culpepper, Virginia, on October 22, 1835. He was a descendant of the Pophams who formed the "Southern Company", the first English colony in Virginia, established in 1607. John was the son of Hiram Popham and Lucy Brown. They moved from Virginia to Kentucky where he spent his childhood, finally moving on to Monroe County, Missouri. It was there that John married Mary Elizabeth Smithey, on Feb. 1, 1858, and where all the Popham children were born. Mary

Elizabeth Smithey was born in Monroe County, Missouri, May 26, 1836.

After the Civil War, in which Granddad Popham served in the Confederate Army, the family began to feel the urge to migrate westward. In the fall of 1881, the men folks headed west, ostensibly on their way to Oregon Territory, but really just looking for a place they liked.

On their way west, they decided to visit some friends who had settled in the Bitter Root Valley. While visiting around the Valley, Uncle Jack (as Granddad was known) found a place he could buy "the rights and cabin" or house that a man had started to homestead. This made it possible to "prove up" on the land in a much shorter time. After making the deal to purchase the preemption rights on the land, the Popham men made their way back to Missouri, to prepare their possessions for the trip west.

John William and Mary Elizabeth Popham arrived in the Bitter Root in 1882, with their family of two boys — James Thomas and Robert Edward Lee, and two girls — Patsy Victoria and Lucy Frances. The oldest son, Hiram, had died four years before the move.

They traveled by immigrant train and wagons from Paris, Missouri, bringing with them "all their worldly goods", including horses, cattle, turkeys, geese, chickens, seeds and cuttings.

Although the boys were living at home, they both started acquiring land and goods of their own. Robert Edward Lee, known as Ed Popham, was my father. He was born in Missouri, August 20, 1864, and was 18 years of age when he arrived in the Bitter Root and homesteaded land adjacent to the home ranch. James T., known as Jim Popham, farmed with Ed and his father, growing a crop of oats on a portion of the new land the first year. Later, he established a blacksmith shop at Woodside, and ran some of the first threshing machines in the valley. One of the outcomes of this first crop that Uncle Jim grew was the necessity of building a granary to store the oats in. At that time, lumber for this type of building was "whip sawed" by hand. (A whip saw mill is where there is a scaffold for one man to stand on and a pit for a second man, with the saw being pulled up and down.) The sawdust was then bucked out of the pit with a horse and a pole that pulled it up into a pile. The mill, or the stand, for this particular one, was the Birch Creek drainage just east of the home place. The granary built for this first crop is still standing on the Popham Ranch.

The first grain that was threshed in the Bitter Root by the early settlers was done by tromping it out on a canvas and then pouring it from a platform during a breeze, to winnow out the chaff. This wasn't a normal way to thresh when my folks arrived because they did have a thresher that would thresh and separate the grain from the straw. This machine was used on larger crops and was powered by horses and a capstan. However, the way the crop was a reaped still entered into the picture. Small acreages were reaped with a hand scythe and cradle, then tied by hand with a band made from the grain. This was also true of the first reapers. The grain was run into a windrow, then picked up and tied by hand. The whole operation was a very skilled performance.

Matt Vaughn, husband of Patsy Popham, was one of the most skilled men with a scythe, having a reputation that had been established in Missouri and followed him to the Bitter Root.

The fact that the grain was bound into bundles made it necessary to have a band cutter at the thresher. This would be an individual with a long, extremely sharp knife. It was necessary that he cut the band of straw and spread the grain evenly over the feeder all in one motion. Many band cutters carried the scars of severe slashes from their own knives.

Another specialized skill was the "straw bucker". The trade-mark of a good one was the straw pile that he built with his straw-pole or "buck-pole". Of course, each man in the crew was skilled in his duty — the man who sacked the grain and tied it with a "miller's knot" — bucking the sacks

R. H. Smithey and his three sisters, Jane Smithey, Fannie Burton and aunt Mary Popham at the Popham Ranch east of Corvallis.

into piles higher than his head or onto wagons to be hauled away to market or storage, and the man that placed the bundles head toward the machine, for the band cutter to start through the machine.

I suppose that many of these things determined the occupation or way of life that these homesteaders developed. Uncle Jim Popham and his sons, Thomas, David, Arthur, and Charles, probably did as much as anyone in the development of the big steam-driven threshing rigs in the Bitter Root Valley.

The advent of the steam thresher changed harvest greatly, although there were some places that had their own crews who threshed for weeks, for the most part the crews were made up of neighbors trading work. Usually, if you ran a bundle wagon you could expect to do it for up to six weeks in the fall. The same was true for the grain haulers and the spike pitchers. It was a real thrill as a small child to see the steam rig puffing up the road pulling the water wagon and separator with a line of bundle wagons, etc., coming along behind or sometimes already in the fields loading. Of course, the biggest thrill was when a blast of the whistle just as they were right in front of you usually caused you to land on the ground!

Although most of this writer's knowledge is of the Ed Popham family, and comes from his reminiscing, the Jim Popham family, (Col. Jack Popham of Hamilton being the most direct descendant of this branch still living in the Bitter Root), the Patsy Popham Vaughn family, (with Thomas Murphy of Corvallis being a direct descendant of this branch and still farming a portion of the land "proved up" by John William Popham) and the fourth member of the family, Lucy Frances Popham Cole has one descendant left in the area, Lucille Cole Walker, who lives in Missoula. All were part of the early history of the Valley. The Popham's, Vaughn's, and Cole's names show up on many early abstracts and land transfers.

The Popham family worked together quite closely in the development of their farming endeavors and the community. Uncle Jack Popham and the boys helped build the Corvallis Canal, known as the Surprise Ditch. The Old Independent Ditch, which had the oldest right in the river and irrigated part of the homestead, was eventually replaced by the Surprise Ditch. The family helped organize and build the Presbyterian Church at Corvallis. The church, which has been modernized is still being used by the Corvallis Community Church, which welcomes all denominations.

Grandad Popham passed away on January 24, 1908. Grandmother passed away at the age of 95, March 2, 1936. She was still in possession of all of her faculties and smoked her pipe almost until the day of death.

MY FATHER, Ed Popham, homesteaded 160 acres adjacent to his father's place. He established residence on the property in 1882, and it still carries the name Popham Ranch, having remained in the ownership of the family continuously since that time. Ed Popham fenced the land, gradually developing and clearing the sagebrush, growing more and more crops as the fields were expanded. One of the trade-marks of the Popham ranches or farms was their rail fences, Missouri style. These rail fences were made of rails split from cottonwood and aspen trees. These rails were about ten feet long and had a four to five-inch face, usually in a triangular shape. These were laid in a zig-zag manner, with crossed uprights on each corner, with "riders" to help tie the fence together. These fences were about 8 rails or 4 to 5 feet high, and because of the way they were built they were a real snow trap, causing the roads to be almost completely impassible if the wind started snow moving. There were a good many miles of these fences in the Bitter Root, and some of them lasted into the 1930's. They were built without posts or nails or staples, but they certainly were not labor savers!

Maybe things haven't changed that much, but 40 degrees below zero was not uncommon each winter for sometimes as long as a week; drifted roads that made it impossible to get in or out except on horseback. In fact, one of Dad's stories was of taking in the 4th of July celebration at Hamilton. It was quite cold and of course horse-drawn vehicles were cold riding, so Dad decided to wear his buffalo skin coat as many of the events took place in a snow storm! Bobsleds and cutters were as common as buggies, surreys, and wagons in those days.

Many of the incidents which will be related in the remainder of the narrative of the Pophams, will not be concerned with the continuity of

Ed and Naomi Popham in front of their house, 1931.

events, but will be related to paint a picture of pioneer life during the 1880's.

In the early days, most of the crops in excess of what was used by the family, had to be freighted or driven to Missoula. They would load up their wagons with grain or other produce, then with a four-horse team start for Missoula. They would make it as far as "Travellers Rest" on Lolo Creek the first day. The second day, they would go into Missoula, unload their crops, reload with freight for the stores or themselves and return to Traveller's Rest for the night. They could make it home the third day. If they drove cattle to Missoula, it was about the same, but the trip home on horseback was faster. When they had hogs for market, it took them three days to drive them to Missoula and a fourth day to get home.

Much of their living was taken from the streams and the game in the area. Dad spoke of going fishing at Lake Como and bringing home a couple of gunny sacks full of fish to be salted and canned, also of the deer and other game they would get.

They always butchered their own meat, living on salt pork, hams and bacon, canned beef, chickens, grouse, and rabbit. They did not try to preserve beef too much, other than canning, so that was a winter delicacy, along with tongue, heart, brains scrambled with eggs, pig's feet, head cheese, and anything else that could be saved.

During the fall and winter months, they hauled their wheat to Grantsdale and had six or eight hundred pounds of wheat made into flour. They hauled in their year's supply of wood from the hills or the river bottom. They rendered their lard, made sausage, made soap with grease and wood ashes, plucked and saved the feathers from ducks or geese for pillows and down quilts. Turkeys were also a domesticated fowl that many pioneers raised, however, coyotes were many times very competitive in what happened to the turkeys. Not only was the meat relished, but turkey quills were popular as pipe stems, pens, bird calls, and the feathers used for decorations.

As previously mentioned, the Ed Popham ranch was adjacent to his father's, but was without ditches or water. To correct this, it was necessary for Dad to survey and build his ditches. Not having the sophisticated instruments used by surveyors, Dad used a plumb bob and straight edge. He was able to survey a ditch coming out of the uphill side of the Corvallis Canal and running for about three miles on a perfect one-fourth-inch-to-the-rod grade. After surveying the ditch, Dad shoveled and built most of it by hand. Part of the ditch was built around steep gravely hillside where it was necessary to "over-dig" the ditch, then get clay and carry it in sacks on his back to seal the leaks. This same ditch survey is still in use and is known as the Upper Ditch or Popham-Bailey ditch of the Corvallis Canal.

Of course, when the family first homesteaded there were no fences. The town of Corvallis was established, but there were no roads to and from town. When Dad went to town, he would strike off straight across country. The only thing that would bother him would be the sagebrush and other brush. This could be a nuisance and a danger, as the sagebrush was so tall that anyone walking could not be seen on the flat west and south of the present farm. Quite often they would happen onto Indians travelling through the sagebrush, looking for Bitter Roots, rabbits and birds.

In March of 1896, Edward Lee Popham and Naomi Romney were united in matrimony at the Presbyterian Church in Corvallis. They moved into a small house on the homestead that stood where the large house is still standing. Edward Wilder Popham, their first son, was born there on April 4, 1897. He graduated from Corvallis High School in 1916, and from Montana State University Law School in 1925, after two years in France during World War I. He practiced law in Glendive, Montana, until his retirement in 1975. He now lives in the suburbs of Seattle, Washington.

William Lee Popham was born on the ranch on February 26, 1901. He graduated from Corvallis High School in 1917, and from Montana State College in 1926. He went to work for the USDA, retiring as Chief of the Bureau of Plant Entomology, USDA, in Washington, D. C., in 1963. At that time, he started a firm named Senior Consultants, Inc. He still lives in Arlington, Virginia.

Kenneth R. Popham was born August 2, 1905. Although most of his schooling was at Corvallis, he also attended High School in Spokane, WA. He attended and graduated from George Washington University Law School in Washington, D.C. After an active life in manufacturing and as a manufacturers' representative, he has pretty much retired, living in Winter Haven, Florida.

Ruth Marie Popham was born May 2, 1908. She graduated from Corvallis High School in 1926, and then attended the University of Montana. There she met and married Oliver F. Ziebarth. Oliver is now retired as City Planner for Santa Barbara, California, and they are still living there.

Clarence Popham, like the rest of the children, was born on the ranch at Corvallis, on January 12, 1911. After graduation from High School in 1927, he attended and graduated from Montana State College at Bozeman, MT, in 1933. Clarence returned to the ranch and operated it until 1968, at which time he went into the First State Bank of Stevensville, leasing the land to adjacent farmers, but maintaining his residence and management of the ranch two miles north and one mile east of Corvallis, on Popham Lane. Married to Mable Swanson, whose father was one of the first to settle under the "Big Ditch", they have raised four children on the ranch — which still encompasses the original homestead.

MARCUS DALY AND THE "BIG DITCH" changed the pattern of things more than anything else in the Valley. The advent of Marcus Daly in the Bitter Root did not make as great an impact on the Pophams as it did on the people from Corvallis, south. However, the irrigation projects of the Department of Natural Resources, and the Big Ditch, along with the apple boom, forced the open range further away from the homesteaders. The final blow to the open range as known to the homesteaders, was the final influx to the dry land by the people still wanting to homestead, and the establishing of the Forest Reserve.

The building of the "Big Ditch" and the subdividing into orchard tracts made a very unstable period. Beginning as early as 1908, the influx of workers, machines, buyers and investors began to change the peaceful rural atmosphere even more than the Copper Kings.

Other than hand and horse drawn equipment and carpenters to build flumes, real steam shovels were used to build the "Big Ditch". These shovels traveled on rails. The rails were laid on ties ahead of the machine. The operator of the shovel would pick up the rails and ties behind the machine, swinging them around in front where the crew would lay them again. Being on one of the main access routes from the railroad to the construction area, one of these shovels crossed the valley and the river to the railroad on a line running east and west past our place. A large steel cable, a pile of coal and cinders and a few ties remained as a reminder of this passage for a number of years.

One of Dad's achievements after getting settled was to dig a well. At that time, there was no problem with surface water. In fact, Dad went down more than 30 feet to get a good well. Much of this was done by himself, using a large container which was filled with dirt and gravel, then pulled to the surface where he dumped it. It was necessary to crib the well as it was dug — that is boards were fastened in a square and gradually worked down as the well was dug deeper, adding cribs on top as it worked down. After the water had been developed then the well was "rocked up" or lined with a rock wall. This well was so well built and had such good water that many new settlers used the well for years. (The well is still in use, although now a casing is inside the rocked up well.)

By this time, Granddad (J. W. Popham) had passed on, and all of his family had married and had families of their own. As mentioned before, Dad's place was at the foot of the hill on one of the main supply lines to the construction area of the Big Ditch. Having a good well and pump where good water was available for human consumption, hay and grain for the horses, and the fact that the place was easily accessible for the workers, the settlers and the equipment, it made quite a supply depot of the ranch. Many of the people who bought land under the ditch, used the well for their drinking water for quite a few years. Another side-effect of the coming of the Big Ditch, was the increase in water available for the land on the "bench", making an even more productive farm.

Land prices jumped from $50.00 per acre for the best farm land, to

$1,000.00 per acre for rough hill land! In many places, the buyer was convinced that the rougher and rockier the land, and the steeper it was, the better fruit it would grow.

This brings the saga of the Popham family up to the time of the gang plows, shoe drills, and even horse-drawn combines. From that time on, the machine revolution took over even more rapidly. The World Wars, etc, that were so completely overwhelming, causing the rapid changes in the way of living, make it surprising to see anything that resembles the days of their coming to the Bitter Root.

The large barn that is still one of the land marks of the Bitter Root was built in 1916-1917. It was built to store hay and grain and to house the horses to work the land. Actually it served well from 1917 until about 1940, but it certainly was not meant for the machine age.

Ed Popham and Naomi Romney Popham remained on their homestead as long as they lived without ever putting a lien or mortgage on their land. Mother Popham passed away October 29, 1970.

Edward Lee Popham passed away July 31, 1950. He lived at a time when the greatest revolution of agriculture exploded, but he was well endowed to cope with it, traveling all over the area to help other farmers "time" the knotters on their binders, repairing anything mechanical. He was a master farmer in a changing age.

PRINTZ

by Mrs. Royal Printz

Jay's great-grandfather, John Franklin Printz, and great grandmother, Henrietta (Etta Shafer), came from Iowa in 1881 on an immigrant train to Butte, then by stage to Deer Lodge. They were accompanied by his brother Harry, wife and children Frank, Fred and Charles as well as their own children as follows: Willie (William Charles), born in Iowa, 1868;
Maggie (Mary Margaret), born in Iowa, 1871; Julia (later Mrs. Walker), born in Kansas, 1873; Frank, born in Iowa, 1875; Elmer Leander, born in Iowa, 1877; John Clark, born in Iowa, 1879.

Brother Mike Printz, who had been in the Bitter Root since before the Big Hole Battle in 1977, brought them by team and wagon via Missoula to his place now part of the Hawker place.

John was a Civil War veteran farmed on what was the Lester Robinson place and did custom Threshing. The following children were born in the valley: Rebecca, born in 1881; Grace, born in 1884; Charity (Aunt Chat, married Carly Carls), born in 1886; Alta, born in 1889; Louis, born in 1892.

Harry Printz settled in Darby and worked in the sawmills. His daughter married a Robertson. His son Fred's children were Earl and Bob and they settled across the river from the Ford and Hollister Ranch (now Chief Joseph). He had a stepdaughter, Arlene Jones, who married George Baer. Also see story on page 203 in previous Bitterroot Trails.

Mike's children were Annie (married Ollie Jones), Jeff, Bill, John and Ella (married Grant McKinney).

Julia (Mrs. Will Walker) went to school in a one-room schoolhouse in Corvallis on the Charles Johnson land. The teacher was Carl Jones and sometimes his daughter-in-law Sue. Students were Jimmy Jones, William Printz, Julia, Romeo Jones and Fred Jones. She also had the original Walker Hotel, now gas station and convenience store. Her husband carried the mail from Woodside to Corvallis.

Frank worked in woods and had a sawmill up little Willow Creek. He married Maude Hall and they had three children. Cossette, who had polio as a young woman, Carl and Willie.

John Clark Printz worked on sheep ranches, migrated to Livingston where, in 1914, he married his first wife and had one son, John. His wife died a couple of years later. He then married Ethel Binkerd Stiner of Missoula, in 1918, and eventually settled in the Skalkaho area. They had two sons, Royal in 1919, and Robert in 1925.

Royal started work at 16 in the local flour mill and continued for 23 years until it changed hands. He then became sexton at Riverview Cemetery for 32 years. During that time, he also entered the school transportation business and finally supplied all nine busses for the district. He worked for a short time as millwright at the flurspar mine and also supplied busses to the Forest Service during fire season.

Royal married Eva Mayer from North Dakota in 1939. They had six children: Douglas Clark, born 1941; Merrill Albert, born 1942; Paul Royal, born 1945; Peter Jay, born 1946; Sandra Lee, born 1948; Kenneth, born 1949.

Douglas and Paul migrated to Sacramento to work for the state (Doug) and federal (Paul) in an aircraft plant.

Merrill started with AT&T after his stint with the Air Force and lives in Denver.

Ken is a long haul trucker having learned it in the Army during Vietnam.

Paul and Jay served in the Marines during Vietnam.

Sandra and Ken still live in Montana and Jay of course is currently (1998) serving as Ravalli County Sheriff.

JOE PUTMAN & JOE PARDEE

by a niece, Belle Smith, in March 1956

My uncle, Joe Putman, made his home in the Bitter Root Valley from Thursday, August 5, 1875, until the spring before his death on May 9, 1928. The last year of his life was spent in the hospital at the Montana Soldiers' Home, near Columbia Falls, Montana. Before his death, he requested his burial be in his beloved Bitter Root Valley, in the Corvallis Cemetery, where he now lies at rest beside his uncle, the late Joseph Pardee.

The notes that follow he gave to me in March, previous to his death.

His uncle, Joseph Pardee, had been home to visit from the Bitter Root to the home of the Putman's in Taylor Township, Wayne County, Michigan, not far from Dearborn. My Uncle Joe, who was then twenty years old, decided to go back to the Bitter Root with his uncle, Joseph Pardee.

They left Michigan on July 18, 1875, for Chicago, over the Michigan Central Station Railroad, and from there to Omaha, by Chicago, Burlington and Quincy road, and from Omaha to Utah by the Union Pacific. The two men stayed over in Ogden from July 25 to Monday, July 27. On Sunday, the 26th, they took a trip to Salt Lake City returning to Ogden the same evening. From Ogden, they took the Utah Northern Railroad, a narrow gauge road, to Franklin, Idaho, a distance of 80 miles. The balance of the trip was made by stagecoach. The first stop from Franklin was made at Ryan Station near the present location of Dillon, Montana. The stagecoach, by name the Gilmore and Salisbury, was drawn by four and six horses due to the bad condition of the roads. The next stop was Deer Lodge on the evening of July 29th. The next stage was a two horse one and the stage stayed overnight at the mouth of Bear Creek. On July 31, the two men arrived at Missoula, Montana. At that time, the only transportation service to the Valley was a weekly stage. The following day, Joseph Pardee had a chance to go home with a neighbor who was in Missoula on business, but Uncle Joe waited for the stage, and on Thursday, August 5th, arrived at his uncle's ranch on Girds Creek, about three miles south of Corvallis.

The next four years, the two men lived on the ranch and raised cattle. In 1879, Joseph Pardee took a road building contract to build roads in the upper end of the valley, and over the divide at the upper end of Ross' Hole. When the road work was completed, Joseph Pardee sold the cattle and purchased a sawmill, the first steam powered one in the valley, according to Uncle Joe's account. After running just the one summer of 1880, the mill burned to the ground but was replaced and Joseph Pardee also bought a threshing machine with the same steam engine operating either the mill or the threshing outfit. In the fall of 1882, the engine was back in the sawmill and on November 15, Joseph Pardee was injured in an accident from which he died on November 19, of that year. Uncle Joe Putman had been with his uncle or looking after the ranch during the seven years since the two had come from Michigan together, and was the administrator of his uncle's estate.

In July 1883, Uncle Joe went home to Michigan and returned to the Bitter Root in September and my father, Horace Putman, came to the Valley with him at that time. A short time later, the two brothers took up adjoining homesteads about two miles west of Hamilton, and operated their ranches together for twenty years.

After the ranch was sold, the two brothers had their homes by one another in Hamilton where they both lived until near the end of their lives.

One story concerning early days that Uncle Joe told me follows:

The Nez Perce Indians went on the warpath near Lewiston, Idaho, in June of 1877, and fought there until in July. The folks in the Bitter Root Valley felt they might head for the valley and organized militia companies for self protection, the latter part of June. Uncle Joe enlisted in Capt. John B. Catlin's Skalkaho Company of Montana Volunteers and the Company furnished arms and ammunition by the U. S. Government. Volunteers were organized from Corvallis, Stevensville, and Sage Brush (which was near the present town of Victor and east of the river in Etna District). The fighting Indians, driven from Idaho by General Howard's soldiers, did head for the Bitter Root and entered the valley through Lolo Pass, went up the west side of the river and out through Ross' Hole. General Howard, with 800 infantry and 200 cavalry men were following them, "staying a safe distance behind" (Uncle Joe's comment on the distance, I never wrote down, but I remember it well)! Before General Howard entered the Valley, General Gibbons came from Fort Shaw, down the Blackfoot to Missoula and up the Valley. While passing through the Valley, 35 or 40 of the Montana Volunteers joined his command. The Indians were overtaken and surprised near the junction of Ruby and Trail Creek in the Big Hole. The Indian camp was attacked just before daybreak and their warriors were scattered, but soon rallied and recaptured their camp. The soldiers were forced to retreat to point of timber north of Trail Creek where they entrenched themselves by digging rifle pits. They were surrounded by the Indians, and fought all day on August 9th. Twenty-three soldiers and five volunteers were killed and quite a number badly wounded. Later, the Indians admitted a loss of one hundred fifty from battle and wounds. This was the only trouble with the Indians which Uncle Joe ever recounted to me. He was not in the battle, but was one of those who stayed at home to protect homes in the Valley.

MEMORIES

by Emma Parker Puyear

I was born December 25, 1877, in Philipsburg, Deer Lodge County, Territory of Montana, in the south part of town, which a few years later became Parkersville, named for my parents William R. and Mary Etta Kibbee Parker.

My parents were married in Doniphan, Kansas in 1872, and two years later, in the summer of 1874, they came to Montana to make their home. They came by train as far as Corrine, Utah, then by stage to Deer Lodge, Montana. They first came to the Bitter Root Valley in 1875, and they both liked it here. My father was very much in love with this valley, but my mother wished to live in Philipsburg, where money was plentiful (the Bitter Root had almost no money in circulation at this time). One old pioneer lady told me that she only saw one dime, in four years! After the railroad terminal reached Butte, my father hauled freight to Philipsburg, and later to Drummond. The first train in Butte was December 1881. Freighters of those pioneer days saw lots of hardships, especially through the winter months.

I lived in a territory, a state, and two counties, without ever having to move. The territory became the state of Montana, the 41st state, admitted to the union on November 8, 1889. Deer Lodge County was divided and Philipsburg became the county seat of Granite County in 1893. I lived in Philipsburg in the Boom Days of Granite, Rumsey, and Black Pine, and saw them all become ghost towns.

My parents came to the valley again in 1883, and spent the winter near Corvallis, but again returned to Philipsburg in the spring. This was my first trip to the valley. It was while we lived in Corvallis that Mr. Andrew Vogt came to visit my parents and told them he was going to the upper end of the valley to settle, although there would be lots of hardships and loneliness as neighbors were few and Corvallis would be his nearest trading center. That was several years before there was a Hamilton or Darby. This he did and continued to make his home there until old age forced him to retire. This place, now called Sula, is a prosperous community. With the automobile of today it is far different from the covered wagon of yesterday.

I visited the valley in the summer of 1888, with my mother and sisters coming by train to Victor and by stage to about what is now Darby. At that time, all the Bitter Root Valley was in Missoula County. This county divided in 1893, Stevensville becoming the county seat of Ravalli County.

My mother died on June 22, 1892, leaving a family of small children. We continued to live in Philipsburg until the fall of 1897, when my father decided to move to the Bitter Root. He died here in 1928.

My husband, Steve Puyear, came here from Highland, Kansas, in April of 1897, and worked on the Supply Ditch which was being constructed that year. We were married on April 22, 1899. We had four children; Marvin Wesley (married Gertrude Schaffer); Calvin Elmo (married Laura Howard); Muriel Marie (married Wilbur Robinson); and Doris Ester (married Arthur M. Patton). We spent most of our married life on the farm but when Steve had to retire in 1943, we moved to Stevensville. Steve died February 7, 1950.

QUAST FAMILY

The Quast family roots lie in Germany. Otto Quast, Sr., was born in Hamburg in 1869, and came with his parents in 1879 to Red Wing, Minnesota. At the age of 15, he started west with a pack on his back. While he was walking, two Indians on horseback approached him. The Indians talked with one another, then rode off. The lad decided they had not bothered him because they may have thought he was a decoy, being alone. On the way west, he worked on the railroad and first came to Montana in 1887, bringing a load of hay from North Dakota to Fort Buford, MT, during the construction of the Great Northern Railroad.

Otto Quast Sr. arrived in Missoula in 1889, and located in the Rattlesnake area. He first worked for a dairyman, Pete Fedderson, and then began building his own dairy farm.

In 1891, Otto married Helena Ziesing in Missoula. Helena was born in Brooklyn, N.Y., to parents who were also of German heritage. **Otto and Helena had 8 children: Harry,** who died in 1959, after a long illness, **Della** (Gilleland), **Cora** (married W. J. McCormick and taught school for many years in this area), **Helen**, a nurse who married F.O. Burrell, **Emma** a teacher, **Alice** who died when young, **Lillian** who married Ray Morris and raised her family in Corvallis, **and Otto Jr.** who also remained in the Corvallis area.

In 1915, Otto Quast Sr. and wife Helena purchased the John Summers home in the Bitter Root, about one mile north of Corvallis. They moved their Missoula dairy operation to this farm. Helena was an enthusiastic and knowledgeable flower gardener, and was active in state and local garden clubs, until her death in 1941.

OTTO QUAST, JR. AND RUTH BAILEY QUAST

Otto Quast Jr. married Ruth Bailey (daughter of W.S. Bailey), and following his father's death in 1931, they took over the family operation. They raised cattle and sheep, and later grew sugar beets. The Quast Ranch was a very efficient operation. They were the largest sugar beet growers in Western Montana. They planted, irrigated, and harvested in excess of 300 acres of beets. They also rotated hay and grain crops, and raised beef cattle.

Before the development of modern, large, efficient farm equipment, they employed about five or six men steadily, and required additional manpower during harvesting. During this era, there were seven houses between the main ranch buildings and the foot of the hill just to the east on Quast Lane. Two of these houses were for the itinerant Mexican workers who came in to thin, hoe, and top the beets. The full-time help lived in the other houses. In addition, there was a bunkhouse that at certain times had two or three men bunking there. Ruth Quast did the cooking for them.

Stories have been told about Otto Quast, Jr., and his enjoyment in playing practical jokes. He is also remembered for his incentive messages to his employees "to make good use of their time". Otto was a prominent member of the Corvallis community and a participant in community affairs, serving a number of years on the Corvallis School Board. He also was a member of the Ravalli County Fair Board.

Ruth Bailey Quast was an accomplished pianist and gave music lessons in the Corvallis community. She often played the piano for her church, and frequently accompanied other musicians. She and Otto became the parents of two daughters, Karolyn Simpson, who, in 1997, with her husband has returned to the Bitter Root to retire, and Rosemary Quast of Saudi Arabia.

Otto and Ruth sold the original ranch, and built a new home a little to the south. The former home located at the corner of Quast Lane and Eastside Highway has been accepted to the Historical Registry of Homes, and is run as a Bed and Breakfast.

RANDOLPH FAMILY

by Lorna Randolph in 1997

Thomas and Flora Randolph came to the Bitterroot from Wright County, Missouri, with their seven children, James, Jess, Thomas, A. Frances, Mary, Martha, and Henry, who died young.

They settled in the Willow Creek area. After their children were married and gone, they moved to Doran Addition in Hamilton. They also raised Peg King-Simpson whose mother died when she was a baby. Stella Morris, a sister of Peg, lived with her father and other brothers and sisters, (the King family) in Florence.

Thomas A. Randolph married Annie Elizabeth Caples on July 3, 1889. Thomas and Annie spent their entire lives around Corvallis. To them were born four children, Earl, William, Ernie, and Bessie. They all attended Corvallis School and stayed in the valley. Tom was a butcher most of his life. He worked for Sid Wheeler, and eventually owned his own shop. He also worked a few summers for the U.S. Forest Service and later was a stock inspector. Tom was very fond of horses and did a lot of riding when he was younger. He was a happy man and was usually whistling his favorite tunes and hymns. The Randolphs also owned a restaurant and rooming house on Main Street. There was a barber shop owned by E.F. Kempter in the same building and a saloon run by Wes Walls. Thomas died April 15, 1952 of a heart attack and asthma.

Annie Elizabeth Randolph was a wonderful, happy, and caring person and a favorite Aunt to her many nieces and nephews on both sides of the family. Annie was 88 years old when she succumbed to cancer in 1968.

Earl married Ethel Sage Thomas. She had four children and together they had Mary Ann, who is living in a group home in Missoula. Ethel and Earl are both deceased.

William married Lorna Randolph in 1925. Lorna lives in Hamilton in 1998. They had one son, Richard, who was born on March 24, 1928, and passed away in December 1973. He married Jerry Strub and they had three children, Carol, Richard "Rick", and Tom. Carol married Philip Fulbright and they have two children, J.D. and Stephanie.

Ernie married Vina Sage. Vina lives in Kalispell in 1997. They had two children, Bobby and Jerry. Bobby died of a ruptured appendix at age three. Jerry lives in Kalispell. Ernie has passed away.

Bessie married Ray Severns on June 6, 1925 and they had two children — Gene who lives in Missoula and Gail, who lives in Pleasanton, California. Bessie is the only one of Tom and Annie's children who is still living.

To my knowledge, there are seven grandchildren, 6 great grandchildren, 1 great-great grandchild and 2 great-great-great grandchildren as of October, 1997.

RASMUSSEN

Christian H. Rasmussen was a native of Denmark. He came to Wisconsin at an early age with his parents.

Mamie Catherine Guthrie was born in Ireland in 1868, and came to the United States at the age of 12.

Christian and Mamie were married in Eau Claire, Wisconsin where he was in the timber industry. They came to the Bitter Root Valley in 1908. They became parents of five boys and two girls; **Neil**, who migrated to California, **Merton (Mert)**, had a tire shop in Missoula, **Bill**, married Sarah and lived near his brother Hector (Squib) and they farmed together. Bill's wife got Spotted Fever and died. **Chester** who died rather young, and **Hector (Squib)**, who married Gladys Brooks. **Daughter Ruth** married W. H. Christoffersen and daughter **Mary** did not get married.

Christian Rasmussen was Manager of the Land and Tract Department of the Bitter Root Irrigation Development Company and figured prominently in orchard development for several years.

He was highly interested in athletics. He died in 1935. **Mrs. Rasmussen** loved her home and her life interests were centered there. She died in 1922. Some of their neighbors on the Willow Creek were Charles Reeder, Ossie Beck and Bill Neaves. Louis Brooks, Glady's father, helped build the barn, and the place had a two-story house.

Squib was born on August 24, 1908, not long after the family moved here. He was Valedictorian of the 1926 graduating class of Corvallis. He farmed east of Corvallis on the Willow Creek Road. He married Gladys Brooks on September 1, 1942,and they lived at the Brooks Hotel in Corvallis, where Gladys and her sister operated it for guests. Bill and Squib ran the farm. Many years later, Squib had the original two-story home burned by the Corvallis Fire Department. When a young person, Squib put up a swing for one of his brothers in a tree just on the West Side of this home. In 1990, while cutting down this tree, present owner Bret Allen found the old metal swing inside the tree.

Squib and Gladys had no children but Squib was so interested in Corvallis school athletics that many of the young athletes there looked to him for inspiration and encouragement. He often accompanied the teams on their road trips, acting as guardian, scorekeeper, and many times providing the vehicle of transportation. He was very generous with his time where young people were concerned.

Squib and Gladys owned race horses, and raced all over Montana, Idaho and Washington. They won many races and could be counted upon for support of the racing industry. Squib also was an inspector for the State Scales for several years.

When Squib died in 1990, he had been preceded by all of his brothers and sisters. In 1997, Gladys resides at the Discovery Care complex.

JAMES R. RAWLINS FAMILY

by Ruth Rawlins Johnson, in 1997

My maiden name was Ruth Rawlins. I was born in 1903, in Hamilton to **James R. Rawlins and Nellie Ashly Rawlins.** James R. Rawlins was born in Nebraska in 1860, and came to Montana in 1890, at the age of 30. His first stop was in Helena, where he met Nellie Ashly, who was born in Jefferson City, MT, in 1874. **James and Nellie moved to the Bitter Root that same year (1890).**

The year I was born, my father, James R. Rawlins, was a Ravalli County Commissioner. He also served on the Fair Board, and later was a stock inspector and traveled the whole valley. Dad was the second elected Mayor of Hamilton. After he started the livery stable in Hamilton, where the present Post Office is, he took the mail clear to Alta and Sula by horse and buggy, staying over night at the hotel in Darby. He was gone four days with each delivery. In the winter, he often wore his big fur overcoat. The only mortuary in town, at that time, was above the livery stable. A horse drawn hearse was housed at the livery stable. In 1906, Dad sold his livery business to Wesley Swayze, brother in law of Barney Smyth, and moved his family to his ranch two miles East of Corvallis. I was three at that time.

I attended school in Corvallis. Our building was where the present primary building is, and my teacher was Annie Daly. We walked to school until I was in the 5th grade, and after the school consolidated they started putting the children on wagons. Sig Chaffin's daughter, Helen, and I went everyplace together. We were the same age. When her dad was elected as Sheriff, Helen went to Stevensville to stay with her aunt, and went to school there.

To the north of our ranch was the McCarty place. Mrs. McCarty and Mrs. Albert Wood were sisters. The McCartys started a store down by the Albert Wood farm. It became "Casey's Store" after the Caseys bought it.

My father bought that place down there (near Black Lane) because little Fannie Cummins Glass was a music teacher. She rode a bicycle from Hamilton to Stevensville and gave music lessons. One day she was giving a lesson and she said, "I've heard there are 160 acres for sale, down there in Corvallis, for $1.50 per acre. And, you know what Mr. Rawlins, if you would buy 80, I will buy 80!" They did! I can't tell you who from. It was just sagebrush.

When I was real young I can remember all those "Daly" trees. They had Bulgarians come in, and they lived in those "red barns" at the Daly Ranch. They planted all those apple trees. They planted acres and acres of them, and they sold that land for a big price by telling people that the trees would bear fruit in two or three years. It rained and hailed and most of the people lost out. You had to have a lot of money to stay with it! They bought eggs from us because it was fairly close.

When I was going to school, right on the corner there were the big Daly sheep sheds and Dutch Charlie was the boss of the sheep for the Dalys. When we came home from school, he would give us all the orphan lambs to take home and raise. Momma wasn't too pleased with us taking the sheep home, they ate everything!

There were five girls in our family: Momma had one boy, but he died. I was the little one. My oldest sister is 10 years older than I. My youngest sister is 10 years younger.

Since the walk to school was almost two miles, in the winter, Dad would take us on the bobsled. He took all of us kids, the Shelden kids, the Fleming kids and the Taylor kids. We were always glad to see that old sled! We would get under the blankets to keep warm.

The Brooks Hotel was a landmark. As a little girl, the people I can remember were the Hatley's. Dougherty owned it first. Dougherty's had a store where the Masonic Hall is now, and then Slacks had a store in there. The two Slack boys, Charley and Herb, went to school with Joe.

Next, I remember the old school house. Those old stairs were steep, and it was black as pitch because there were no lights. I was scared to death of those old stairs. We always had assembly upstairs. Some students would go dashing past you. They had the contract to build a new school and they used timbers from the old school that were 30 and 40 foot long — with not even one knot in them. This school was built by Mr. Barr. When I was six and in school, Helen Chaffin and I would go over to Bay's Store with a nickel each, and we would get candy or something.

Dan Hoblitt's mother boarded many of the teachers. The Ellis boys rode to school and would unhook their horses from the buggy, and let them drink from the Surprise Ditch. It is now called the Corvallis Canal.

There were two saloons in town then. Bourne's saloon is where the Walker Hotel is now. There was a music store, barbershop, and Tom Smithey had a pool hall in there too. After his first pool hall burned, he moved across the street. When I was in sixth grade, Aldous Thrailkill was the depot agent. There was a big old store in town that Tilton bought. It used to be the old Woodside Store.

I went to high school in 1918. I married Edward Johnson in 1922. We had a daughter and we named her Jean. When she was a little baby, we came from Missoula on the railroad. That was over 70 years ago. It was several years later in 1928, that they moved the railroad from the Westside of the Bitter Root River, to the east side.

I worked for 31 years at Bay's Store. I also worked a couple years at a dehydrating plant.

We were really glad when we got our place paid for, and we could quit raising beets. When we lived up on Willow Creek, it seemed we had to sell everything to pay the taxes. We had men that worked for us, and they would come in and eat meals with us. I was fixing potatoes and gravy. One man said, "You know, you are feeding your dogs better than I am feeding my children". We always had plenty to eat.

We had the prettiest Holstein heifers, and I said, "Oh Ed, couldn't we just keep one of them?" He said, "No, I don't like the taxes to go unpaid." So, we sold them and paid the taxes! We had a couple of real good milk cows which Clyde Wood bought. He bought everything for $150.00, and the next year they would have brought $300.00!

In Corvallis, next to my house, was an old gas station which was closed. In the middle of the night people would kick on the door of it, wanting gas. They were often in a drunken state, which scared me. The building is on Jack Filcher's place now.

Ed died in 1954. Ruth Rawlins Johnson, author of this family history, died in 1998.

Children born to James R. and Nellie Ashly Rawlins were: Mary, born in 1893, and never married; **Katherine M.,** born in 1895, married Lloyd Terry; **Ruth J.,** born in 1903 and married Edward Johnson; **Josephine A.,** born in 1908, married Max Stanley; **Clara E.,** born in 1913 and married Donald Daly.

ROCKAFELLOW FAMILY

by Amy Lee Rockafellow Felix in 1998

The Rockafellow family can be traced back to 1590. The spelling has changed at least six times, and I simply explain that our spelling differs from the John D. family because we are the "poor relatives". Most likely someone in government service changed the spelling by writing it as it sounded to him.

My Great Grandparents:

Samuel Arthur Rockafellow was born March 28, 1841, and met **Mary Elizabeth Andrews**, who was born on March 10,1843, and they were married in 1860. When their son, Joseph William, and his family, moved to the Bitter Root in the early 1900's, Samuel and Mary followed. They settled just south of Woodside, and began raising onions for a living.

My Grandparents:

Joseph William Rockafellow was born December 9, 1867, in Orangeville, Illinois. **Mary Clarinda Linder** was born in Osceola, Iowa, on December 1, 1866. No information concerning my grandmother's family is available. They were married on June 10, 1890, in Weston, Nebraska. Their first seven children were born in Nebraska. **They arrived in the Bitter Root Valley in 1903**, and the last two children were born here. The Rockafellows moved here hoping Joseph's health would improve. He lived for 86 years, passing on April 4, 1953. Mary died October 10, 1939.

Their children: Vera Bell (b.1891) married Ed Albertson, **Ethel Clare** (b.1892) married Earl Rexford White, **Richard S.** (b.1884) married Ruth Moore, **Fredrick** (b.1896-d.1896, died in Nebraska as an infant), **Elsie Marie** (b.1897-d.1905, buried in Riverview Cemetery), **Loyd Milford** (b.1899) married Amy Smithey, **Arthur W.** (b.1903) married Enid Tallent, **Delbert Ray** (b.1905) married Alice Sullivan, **Estella May** (b.1908) married Ingward Nordheim.

My memories of grandmother are lacking as she died when I was still quite young and didn't live near enough for me to get into the habit of dropping in to see her. I do remember her as a small person. She talked very fast and I recall her helping me to put together jigsaw puzzles that she kept for all the grandchildren. She made an apple pudding layered with Graham crackers, which I thought was heaven sent!

Granddad was a fiddler and played for the local dances. My fondest memory was after he was widowed. He had moved into a small house along the Woodside road, but still in town. When it was warm he would leave his door open, and play his fiddle. Cars would soon be lined up on the edge of the road as people sat listening to him. He was good. It was a musical family where most either played an instrument or sang.

Will was a paperhanger and painter. My father, Rocky, used to help him and every once in awhile they would get into a house that had bedbugs! Not so common today, but when this happened they found themselves changing their clothes out in the shed before being allowed into their own homes. Will also had a buzz saw with which he sawed wood into stove lengths for other people. My uncle tangled with this saw and lost three and one-half fingers.

When the family first moved here, they lived in Hamilton, and Will worked in the Northern Pacific Depot. When his parents arrived, he helped his father to raise the onions. He would later purchase and move his family onto the farm at Woodside. The children went to school at Dutch Hill, later going to Corvallis in a horse drawn wagon school bus. My grandparents sold the farm and moved to Corvallis, and this is where my memories began. They belonged to the Odd Fellow Lodge. In his later years, Granddad did quite a bit of traveling, visiting his children that had moved from this area.

Will and Clarinda are buried in the Riverview Cemetery near his parents, a daughter, and a son.

My Parents:

Loyd Milford Rockafellow was born on December 22, 1899, the third son and sixth child of Joseph William and Mary Clarinda Rockafellow. **Amy Laura Smithey** was born on August 19, 1906 and was the third and youngest child of R. Russell and Laura Elbert Smithey. **Loyd and Amy were married on April 14, 1927, and were privileged to celebrate their sixty-five years of marriage just six months before "Rocky" died.**

Amy and Rocky lived in an old three-room shack the first years of their marriage. Dad joked about insulating it with chicken wire. I can remember taking a bath in the washtub and dressing as close to the stove as possible. In 1943, they moved the "Dud Bowden house" onto the same lots. It caused quite a stir about town. As it was wartime and materials for a new house were unavailable. They lived their entire married life in this same location, which was just across the street (East) from the house Amy had been born in.

Rocky was injured early in their marriage and was totally paralyzed for six weeks, and unable to work for more than three years. Amy took odd jobs until 1932; when she was able get full-time work at the Corvallis Post Office. She spent the next forty-three years there, and was Acting Postmaster for one year. Rocky drove truck on a milk route, and a school bus. He worked in a sawmill, a garage, and several years at the cheese factory and decided to open a small café on Main Street in Corvallis. This café was known as "Rocky's", and was a popular establishment. I helped in this endeavor while still in high school.

Rocky was instrumental in getting street lights for Corvallis, and it was a proud night when he threw the switch to turn them on. He was among the organizers of the volunteer fire department, and a charter member of the Corvallis Sportsman's Club. The Sportsman's Club earned money from a raffle and a carnival held in the high school gymnasium. They built the high school track, and for many years sponsored and put on the largest invitational track meet in the State of Montana. At Christmas each year, they placed a large Christmas tree in the center of Main Street, decorated it with lights, and organized a program of special music, singing by the crowd, and lastly — the arrival of Santa, by sleigh, bringing treats for everyone.

Amy and Rocky had just one child, a daughter, and this writer. I was named Amy Lee, and I married Everett Charles Felix. We had two children, a son, Curtis, and a daughter Dalene.

THE ROMNEY'S IN THE BITTER ROOT

written by Clarence Popham

IN THE SPRING OF 1881, after having become disenchanted with the Mormon religion and the political associations of his family and associates in Utah, possibly partly because of the death of his father some three or four years earlier, Thomas Romney decided to take his own family away from Utah. They loaded their possessions in a covered wagon, bringing with them all their household goods, livestock and tools. Whether this migration was a family choice or whether a mutual agreement was arrived at between the Thomas Romney family and the family that remained in Utah, is somewhat of a mystery. Whatever it was, the Thomas Romneys started for Oregon, arriving in Missoula, Montana, at the peak of the flood waters of the spring runoff. This stopped them for a considerable time — in fact, long enough for Thomas Romney to get acquainted with a Mr. Hammond, who convinced them that the Bitter Root Valley had everything that Oregon had and was much closer. Becoming convinced, they made their way up the Bitter Root, finally coming to the Gird's Creek flat just east of Hamilton, where the Hamilton Airport is now situated. Feeling that this was probably a good area, they engaged in negotiations with the squatter presently occupying the property. They finally purchased the 160 acres (the legal amount of ground that could be homesteaded) for $200.00 and a team of mules.

Thomas Romney, the 7th child of 9 children of Miles Romney and Elizabeth Gaskell Romney, was born in 1845, at Nauvoo, Illinois. Miles

Romney and Elizabeth Romney were early converts to the Church of the Latter Day Saints, having become acquainted with a Mormon Elder from America, at a religious gathering on a street corner in Dalton, in Furness, Lancaster, England. In September, 1843, they were baptized into the church. They left England two years later for America, where they settled in Nauvoo, Illinois, until 1846. Upon leaving Nauvoo, on their way West, they stopped at Burlington, Iowa; St. Joseph, Missouri; and St. Louis, Missouri for varying periods. Leaving St. Louis, in the spring of 1850, for Salt Lake City, Utah, they arrived there in October of the same year.

After arriving in Utah, the Miles Romney family was active in the "Public Work Shop" on the Temple Block. It wasn't until 1862, that the family moved to Saint George, Utah, where Miles Romney planned and supervised the building of the Tabernacle, and later the Temple at Saint George.

It was during this time that Thomas Romney was educated, learned the trade of carpenter and cabinet maker, and was married to Annie Wood. Annie was born in England, leaving there with her parents when she was two years old. Annie's mother died aboard ship on her way to America, and was buried at sea, but the family proceeded on west to Utah. Other members of the Wood family besides Grandmother Romney moved to Montana, but are not part of this epistle.

After their marriage at St. George, Utah, Thomas and Annie Romney moved to Beaver City, Utah, where Thomas assisted in the design and supervised the building of the Temple at Beaver City. The four oldest of the eight children were born either at St. George, or Beaver City, Utah. Naomi Romney, mother of this writer, was 5 years old when they arrived in the Bitter Root. She and the other children, Jane, Miles, Thomas, Vernon, Annie, Kenneth, and Winifred, attended school at the Gird's Creek School until they were more or less forced off of their farm by Marcus Daly. Grantsdale was their post office and trade center at that time. Thomas Romney and his family developed the ranch on Gird's Creek, bringing water onto the land from the creek and ditches that had already been developed. This became their home and a feeling of bitterness towards Marcus Daly developed because, by his acquiring land completely surrounding the ranch and cutting off the irrigation, the Romney's were forced to sell their land to him. This feeling of bitterness described before was a feeling that was instilled in me by my mother who told of seemingly unscrupulous ways in which Marcus Daly acquired land, bypassing the town of Grantsdale (because he could not buy it outright) and starting the town of Hamilton.

Marcus Daly purchased many thousands of acres of land, many water rights and where he couldn't purchase the land, surrounded it by cutting off roads, ditches and open range, forcing many farmers to sell their land and give up their rights. It is true that he helped the valley develop much faster by putting the big mill at Hamilton to process the timber for his mines and by his other investments. But, you wonder when you realize how he did it, farms that were already developed, towns like Corvallis, Riverside, and Grantsdale, that were already established, found themselves engulfed, or bypassed because Marcus Daly wanted them for his own. Many people have sung his praises. Many have basked in his reflected glory and many slaved for him and were thankful for their jobs. However, many suffered because of his ruthlessness and because of it waged a never ending battle to keep his kind from over-running the entire country, engulfing the land, the town, and the state. These very differences have been a constant conflict in the politics of Montana and the Romneys have always espoused the part of the true homesteader.

I am not sure of all the facts, but my Mother's impressions as a child carried through to where it was impressed on me as a child that the move by the Romney family to Corvallis, was not a willing move and even may have been a factor in Grandma Romney's early demise. She died at the age of 58, in 1904. Soon after her death, Grandpa Romney left the Bitter Root to do some traveling and relieve his loneliness. He was never heard from again by the family.

My mother, Naomi Romney and my Father, Edward Lee Popham were married at Corvallis, Montana, in March of 1896, and settled on the Popham homestead. The story of the Pophams is told in another portion of this publication, so the balance of this epistle will concern the other members of the Romney family. I would like to note here that Naomi Romney Popham was the surviving member of the Thomas Romney family living until October 29, 1970, passing away at the age of 95.

Thomas Romney was a brilliant man and was always trying to be completely informed in every way possible. He was unique as a man subscribing to the New York Times, and reading it completely, (many weeks after it was printed) so that he might know and understand more, the better to cope with the encroachments of those who would impose their will on the common man.

These same characteristics carried through in all of the Romney's, but it probably showed up the most in Thomas Romney's sons, Miles, the oldest, and Kenneth Romney, the youngest, because of their ability to express themselves so well in print and the fact they had the means to do it through the "Western News" Miles Romney, Sr., after receiving all the education he could here in Montana, went east to Ohio where he was trained to be a teacher and writer. After returning to the Bitter Root, he taught for a time, but in 1893, he purchased a half-interest in the Western News, a local newspaper. By using his education, his knowledge and ability to express himself, he was able to do much for the common people. At all times he was accused of preventing the proper development of the state because he fought the ACM and the power companies. As Mayor of Hamilton, and as a State Senator, where he was the one who instigated and got into law, compensation and assistance for the "black lung" disease of the miners, he carried the case for the common man. He was also a candidate for Secretary of State, Governor of Montana, and was the organizer of the People's Power League. With all of this activity he still had time to marry Elizabeth Robbins, who mothered his son — Miles Romney, Jr., born December 6, 1900. Miles, Sr., also enlisted in the Army during World War I, serving as a Captain in the Quartermaster Corps. He passed away on February 29, 1946.

Aunt Bess, as I remember her, passed away on October 2, 1925. It was at this time that Miles Romney, Sr. began to turn over to their son, Miles, the publishing of the Western News. Miles, Sr., moved to other things, first in participating in the sub-development of a great deal of land in Florida, then participating in many of the programs instigated under the Roosevelt administration.

Miles, Jr., had an excellent background for assuming his position in the community, county, and state. Miles, Jr., attended Hamilton public high school and the University of Montana, majoring in Journalism. Miles had attended West Point for a short time before returning to the University. After graduation, he spent some time as a Ship's Purser traveling the Pacific to the Orient and other places. Later, Miles married his childhood sweetheart, Ruth Gray, in 1925. She was his constant companion and his most loyal supporter all of his life. Miles and Ruth spent considerable time in Washington, D.C., and traveling over the state of Montana while he was employed by the Internal Revenue Service. Miles left the IRS to manage his father's unsuccessful campaign for the office of Governor. However, this turned out to be a welcome break for Miles, because when he left the campaign rather than going back to a job, he purchased the Western News from his father, and became a legend with his unique, but brilliant presentation of news and views. His editorials, though very partisan, were brilliantly written essays unequalled by any of his contemporaries.

Miles was always available to anyone that asked for his help, whether they were friends or just acquaintances. He did his best to assist anyone who asked. He continued with the People's Power League, was a member of the Constitutional Convention, the Montana Legislature from Ravalli County for two terms, and was in his second term as State Senator when he passed away February 19, 1976.

Although the latter part of this epistle carried well into the last half of the 20th century, I believe the full cycle of the Romneys in America and Montana should be told in any history of the Bitter Root Valley.

RUMMEL

by Ruth Lamoreux, George Rummel, and Elsie Rummel Dean

John Rummel was born October 16, 1855, to Henry and Annie (Begattsi) Rummel, in Scales Mound, Illinois. Annie Begattsi was born in Switzerland and Henry was born in Germany. John had five brothers and four sisters. John's father died about 1865 and the family began to drift apart.

In the 1870s, John moved west and in 1883, he homesteaded in the Bitter Root. After the Indians were moved to the Flathead, John pre-preempted 160 acres Southwest of Woodside ($2.25 an acre). The 160 acres were wooded and rocky but there was ample water in the creeks close by. A cabin was built with logs from the land. Later, another home was built slightly west of the original cabin.

In 1884, John married Annie Mary Schiffman. Annie was born in Germany, September 25, 1855, and came to America at age 11. A few years later, they came to the Bitter Root Valley and Grandfather Schiffman homesteaded a large portion of land on a creek a bit northwest of Woodside — it was then called Schiffman's Creek. At some point, the name was changed to "Sheafman Creek", as it is called today.

John and Annie's first child, Emmaline, born July 17, 1887, died just three months later. Next came Elsie, Frank, Mary, Carrie, George, and Emily. On July 12, 1896, giving birth to Emily, Annie died. The labor had been difficult and the doctor was called. Little Emily was born and the doctor left, a few hours later, another child was born. Mother and second child both died. It was not possible for John to care for five small toddlers and a baby. Thus, Emily was cared for by a neighbor. She only lived a few months.

About the time Annie Rummel died, John's mother was living with the family. She decided to spend a few years with her other son, William. William Rummel homesteaded 160 acres farther West (where Pinesdale is now).

It was hard for John to care for and feed five children. John cut wood and hauled it to town, getting $5.00 a cord. In 1898, John Rummel took the family back to Illinois. In 1899, he remarried and returned to the Bitter Root with his new wife and her one son. The marriage was not a success and in about a year, the step-mother and son left and returned to Illinois. John and Annie's youngest son, George, age 19, was thrown from a horse and died April 22, 1915. John Rummel died August 3, 1934 from a stroke.

John Rummel's oldest daughter, Elsie, was born in 1889. She lived on the ranch until 1917 when she married John Dean. John and Elsie Dean lived south of Woodside on a chicken ranch. John was never well, had dreadful asthma attacks and it was a hard life for Elsie. They had a daughter, Mary born in 1922. John died in 1945. Mary then married Merlyn Schram in

1950. Elsie's health began to fail and she moved in with Mary in 1953. Elsie lost her eyesight but was always cheerful about life. She died in 1981 on Schiffman Creek at Mary and Merlyn's home. The Schrams had two children, Maribeth, born in 1950 and David, born in 1952. The family remained and farmed on Schiffman Creek. David moved onto the original Rummel homestead in 1995 and continues to live there.

Frank Rummel lived almost straight east about 1 1/2 miles away. Nina Malone, grew up in the west foothills. Frank says when he and Nina were courting, she would sometimes light a lamp and put it in the upstairs window. When Frank went out to do chores, he then would know Nina was thinking of him.

Frank Rummel married Nina Malone in March 1919. John had bought acreage from George Blodgett and deeded it to Frank. Later, Frank bought more acreage from Mrs. Blodgett-Shetren. A small 4 room house was on the acreage on the edge of Churn Creek. He also purchased 28 acres from Charlie McCrea. The three parcels amounted to 84 acres. Frank farmed that 84 acres and worked with his father, John, on his 160 acres. In 1926, the house was enlarged to 4 bedrooms, a bathroom, and later barns and other buildings.

Four children were born to Frank and Nina: George, December 1919; Ruth, November, 1920; John Clyde, January, 1924; and Donald, in May, 1927. When George and Ruth were three and four years of age, Nina would occasionally put them on "old Bessie" a slow, gentle horse. Nina opened the pasture gate, Bessie would slowly meander across the meadow to Grandpa Rummel's place (about 1/2 mile). The children would call out to Aunt Mary to open the gate. Mary and Grandpa John would spend a couple of hours with the children and then the procedure would be reversed and the old horse would take the children safely home.

Nina Rummel was raised on a fruit and berry ranch. They shipped fancy pack apples to many cities. Every fall for many years, Nina worked for two to three weeks packing apples for Malcom Sizer. Nina had a brisk, gentle horse and small "cutter". Many late falls, she encountered deep snow and drifts but could safely travel to and fro the two miles to Sizer's apple house. The Rummel children were always glad to have the apple packing finished as they didn't like to come home from school to a cold house.

Frank and Nina quit the dairy business and bought feeder cattle (about 1943 to 1945). They continued ranching until 1970. Nina loved her flowers and was a marvelous cook. Nina loved the ranch on the west side and it was a hard choice to sell. When the sale was made, the buyer asked for keys to the front and back door. In the 51+ years, the Rummels lived on Churn Creek, the back door had never been locked. After selling the ranch, they bought land in Corvallis, 3/4 acre, and lived there until their deaths. Frank died in October, 1986, at age 96 and Nina died in July, 1990, also at age 96.

Mill Creek Dam, 1895, west of Woodside. Bottom row is Oscar Garrard and unknown. Top row, unkown, Frank Rummel, Sid Parks, Bill Miller. Photo by A.M. Moore, Hamilton photographer.

John Rummel refused to let his daughter, Mary, get married. She remained unmarried until John died. She and Jess Smith were married in late 1934. Mary and Jess lived on the Rummel ranch until Jess' health failed and they sold the ranch and moved to Hamilton. Jess died in 1957 and Mary remarried in 1958 to Will Reynolds. He died in 1979 and Mary died in February of 1990.

Carrie Rummel, 3rd daughter of John Rummel, was always a frail child. She missed her mother dreadfully. As a young girl, her health failed and her mind became unclear. She could no longer live at home and was moved to Lewistown, Montana, where she lived until her death in October, 1990. Mary sent a monthly "CARE" package of candy, apples, handkerchiefs, and pictures to Carrie for years. As small girls, Mary and Carrie were very close and Mary always watched out for Carrie.

The Rummel clan got together for many holidays and picnics. One July 4th, a big group drove to Lost Horse Lake for a day's outing. After a picnic lunch, the small children (Clyde, age 4 and Ruth Lamoreux, age 4) put on bathing suits and played in the water. Later, they gathered up dish pans and boxes so they could slide down the icy hill west of the lake.

ST. JOHN FAMILIES IN THE BITTER ROOT

Henry St. John came to the Bitter Root Valley from Sparta, Missouri, to visit his sister, Mary St. John Humble and her husband, M. Humble, in the early 1890's. Mary lived north of Victor, and she never had a family. Henry became very much a part of the Victor community. In 1898-1899, he taught school in the Etna and Burnt Fork school districts. He was also one of the organizers of the Farmers State Bank in 1907. Henry operated a drug store in Victor. He married Glen Rose Morris when living in Victor. Glen Rose died in 1904, at the age of 20, when her twin sons, Floyd and Morris, were born.

While still living in Victor, Henry married Martha Waddell, and they had four sons born to them. The firstborn died as an infant; Rex, Max, and Leo finished their schooling. Henry and family moved to Stevensville, where they operated a drug store and became a part of the Stevensville community. They later opened a drug store in Hamilton, on the corner of 2nd Street and Main. This business was operated Max, Rex, and Leo until ill health and death forced disposal of the store. (1980's)

Jim St. John, nephew of Henry and Mary Humble St. John, came to visit his uncle and aunt and worked in the Victor Drug until moving to Corvallis. Jim married Mary Garrison of Garrison, Missouri. They had two sons, Warren and Dan. Warren became a pharmacist, while Dan went into real estate.

DR. THORNTON, who lived in Corvallis, built a drug store out of native soft rock and this drug store still stands on the main street of Corvallis. Dan and Lester Morris, brothers of the first Mrs. St. John (Glenn Rose) operated the drug store for a time. Jim St. John bought the store, and Lester continued in it as pharmacist for several years. Earl Hall worked for Jim St. John for several years. Earl purchased the store, and owned it until selling to Clarence Moyle. Mr. Moyle sold to Marshall Holmberg, who now in 1997, owns and operates it as the Corvallis Drug Store.

Jim St. John went to Missoula and worked as a pharmacist until his wife Mary died. Then he went to California to be near his son.

Viola St. John Chaffin, her husband Earl Chaffin, daughter Madge and son Harry moved to Corvallis from Sparta, Missouri, in 1917. Then five more children were born; Eddie, Lucille, Chester, Myrtle and Virginia. Harry and Chester are deceased. Madge Chaffin Buck still lives in the Corvallis community.

All the male St. John's have passed away, and there is no one in Corvallis or in the Bitter Root to carry on the St. John name. There are several St. John men living in Sparta, MO, and Dan, the son of Jim, lives in California.

SCHWAB

Charles's mother, Mary, lived to be ninety one, the last twenty five years in blindness, as she made her home with her son. It was during this period that poems began to flow from the pen, of this pioneer's colorful life, and his varied experiences rich in "old times", and close to nature and the land.

"C.F. breathed his last August 18, 1959, two days before his eighty-sixth birthday. However, his spirit, his humor, his rare gift of telling a story, his faith, his stalwart character, live on in these poems of yesterday! May all loved ones treasure this rare heritage of the past.

TRUE TALES: C. F. REMEMBERS

A transcript of the year 1893, by Charles F. Schwab, Edited for length:

I was a young fellow, 20 years old and an apprentice in a blacksmith shop at Corvallis, Montana. Jim Vance asked me to go with him to the upper Bitterroot mountains on the Salmon side in Idaho, in what is known as Mineral Hill country, to sharpen drills. There were five of us, and Jim's old dog "Old Hi", the truest, smartest dog I have ever known. Many times Old Hi sniffed out deer, elk and bear. On May 19, 1894, on our way home from home camp we got plenty of meat. We were going to stop for dinner at a little creek, when Old Hi startled a big cinnamon bear out of a swampy place. Jim was in the lead with the gun across the saddle in front of him. He jumped off his horse and took three shots at the bear as it ran up a gulch, but did not hit it. Old Hi didn't slacken his pace a bit. He soon caught up to the bear and took his favorite hold, all of one ham or as much as he could get in his mouth. Mister bear couldn't stand for that. Close by, was a big pine tree and he started up it with Hi still hanging on! The dog lost his hold after he had been carried up over 30 feet, and he dropped back onto the slide rocks pretty hard, but didn't break any bones.

In the meantime, I had trouble getting the horses stopped since they tried to put as much territory between themselves and that bear as they could! Horses don't like bear anytime or anywhere, and the older the horse, the quicker he will leave bear country. At last I got them tied up and back to where Jim and the bear were.

He called out, "Hey, I thought we brought a box of shells down with us. I can't find but one shell." I thought where they might have gone, and realized he was right — only one left. Jim said, "It is your shot as I had three. Try to hit him between the eyes!" I sat down by a little tree and took aim with my elbow on my knee. Jim tossed up a little stick to get the bear to look my way, and I let drive.

"Hell's fire, you missed him," Jim shouted. I said, "I did not! I hit him," for I saw him grip the tree and keep his seat on the limb. "There is blood coming out of his nose." I set the gun by the tree, went up another one as high as I could go, and tried to get Jim to do the same. He said he would if the dog wasn't there, but as long as Old Hi was on the job, there wasn't any danger.

Then I warned, "Look out! He's going to fall. Don't you see him swaying? There he comes on his head on that slide rock," Jim responded, "That fall ought to have killed him," I said, "No, it didn't. I can see his sides moving." "Well, they won't move long. I'll stick him!" Jim took a hunting knife from his side sheath, brushed aside the white stomach hair and rammed the knife to the hilt. Then, the bear "woke up," and I called, "Stay away from him, Jim! He will rip you in two. Look out! Run, Jim, run! Sic'em, Hi!! Sic'em, good old dog! Say, Jim, you run good on all fours. But one more swipe and he would have torn the seat of your pants! I call that a close call. That dog worked quick, and a good thing for you he did!" Jim picked up an old rotten chunk of wood, and slammed the bear full length of his back with it. The bear swung ' round and charged him again, but the dog stopped Mister Bear again! I said, "Why use wood when there are so many rocks?" "That's right, wood brings a fellow too close."

Jim peppered him with rock for awhile, then said, " Hey, Bonesetter, better come down and have some fun. I don't seem to be able to hit his head." I answered, "His head isn't on the end you throw at. Better wait 'till he comes towards you." I saw that the dog knew what he was about, and could keep out of the bear's way. He liked to bite his ham better than anything on earth!!

Right away I came out of the tree to see if I could hit his sore head. At first I was like Jim, I hit everyplace but his head, and he was getting madder all the time. "We've got to lay him out some way soon, or he will wear the dog out." Hi was looking down toward the horses and the bear took a swipe at him. I think the dog could feel the wind, because he moved just in time!

The only way we could hit the bear's head was when he was looking our way, and it didn't look good at all. I'd stand my ground for about two throws while he charged my way. Then, if the dog didn't nip him, I moved. The dog was nipping him most of the time. Finally, I found a sharp-cornered rock about the size of a teacup. As the bear made his charge, I let him get pretty close, then threw the rock as hard as I could! It crushed his skull dead center. He dropped in his tracks dead as a door nail!!

We skinned him since his fur was still prime. He was thin, but large. It took the two of us to lift one end off the ground. His hind foot was 11 inches long, with claws 2 1/2 inches long and sharp as a needle!! We skinned his head, there was a bullet between his eyes. The lick I gave him with the rock had broken his skull. The bullet had missed his brain about one inch. After that shot, he still had enough energy to have wiped us out, if it hadn't been for good, old Hi. As it was, the battle lasted about an hour, and I think we took lots of chances with him. Our battle with the bear made us late getting to camp, but we didn't care!!

CHARLES F. SCHWAB FAMILY

by his son, Richard Charles Schwab

Wagon wheels rumbled along the prairie as a 9-year old boy accompanied his parents westward in 1882.

Moving along the old Oregon Trail from Rockport, Missouri, where Charles Frederick Schwab was born to Jonas and Mary Schwab on August 20, 1873, the seventy-wagon "white tops" faced many severe hardships. A vivid memory to Charles was the death of sweet little two year old Effie, in Nebraska, where they stopped only long enough to bury her out on the prairie.

The family stopped at Red Rock, then were proprietors of the first business, a restaurant-bar, in Dillon, Montana. On one occasion there Jonas was held up by two would-be highwaymen. Reaching quickly across the bar, he somehow knocked their two heads together, then with right and left hands, grabbed each by the nape of the neck and marched to the front door where he threw one up the street and one down the street!

Charles then settled with his parents in the Blackfoot Valley in Camas

Prairie north of Missoula, Montana, moving with them two years later to Corvallis. Except for brief periods near Weiser, ID, and Eugene, OR, the beautiful Bitter Root Valley was home to Charles for the rest of his life.

In Corvallis, Charles attended school, though not beyond the fourth grade. When he was twelve, he had an argument with his dad over planting potatoes. Jonas ran after Charles, catching him at the fence line. The boy threw his arms back and his father snatched the jacket, but Charles left home on the spot, and from then on was "on his own".

In his younger years, Mr. Schwab was a jockey for the late Marcus Daly, Anaconda copper magnate. He hired Charles to be his jockey for a string of thoroughbred horses from England, and he won most of his races on the Montana circuits.

He is credited with discovering the Hughes Creek Gold Mine in Salmon River Country, but was too young to hold his claim.

Charles learned the blacksmithing trade from Milburn G. Kern in a shop at Corvallis and he eventually owned the Corvallis Shop, occasionally riding into town on his Saint Bernard dog!! At about 18 years of age he was the blacksmith in the only logging camp in the Lost Horse area.

Charles was married twice, first to Lillian Hull, with daughter, Melda born to that union. A ruptured appendix while on a fishing trip up the McKenzie River near Eugene, Oregon, proved fatal for Lillian on September 2, 1914. On November 11, 1920, he married Mabel Fitch, a teacher in the Corvallis High School. Richard was born at the ranch about a mile and a half north of Corvallis. These unions brought eight grandchildren: To Melda were Lynn, Conrad and Roger; to Richard were Ann, Timothy, Mary, Ronald and Norman.

THE SEVERNS FAMILY

by Lorna Severns Randolph

The Severns family were prominent Westsiders for many years, maybe remembered for their thirteen children, which was a goodly amount even in those days! Benjamin Severns and Callie Fulwider were both born in Taylor County, Iowa. They were married on Christmas day, 1892.

While still living in Iowa, three sons and two daughters were born to them, Jay, Hazel, Ray, Guy, and Esta. They came to Montana in 1902, and resided for awhile at Stevensville, and while there another daughter, Lela, was born. They moved the family up near Hamilton, on the west side, and a son named Charles was born. Every two years, the stork flew over and left a boy, then a girl. Next, Lorna was born (they always told me, "Down next to the river"). Mabel White Thrailkill has told me many times, she remembers going to school and telling my older brothers and sisters, she knew something they didn't. They had been sent off to school early, as I was about to come into this world and as her mother assisted, she knew it before she left for school!

My older brothers or sisters could have told much more about the family than I can, but, as May insists she has to have something on the Severns family, seems it is up to me to give a few details. Next, Bill was born, and we lived on the Elliott place at that time, then we moved down a couple of miles and lived beside the Shults and Ike Sears family, where Ruth, Rex, Florence, and Franklin were born.

I can't remember the first days of going to Fair Play school, but I can remember Dixie Wilson who was my first grade teacher. I guess I was her pet, or got accused of it. She held me on her lap most of the time one day when a bunch of us girls were building a play house, and somehow a plank got dropped on my food and I couldn't wear my shoe for several days. She took me home with her one night to stay all night. It was the biggest thing that ever happened to me! We walked to Woodside, took the train and went to the Ravalli Hotel, where she lived. She took me to the show and I remember leaving my mittens and she got me to bed, and went back looking for them. Next morning, we had to get up early, catch the train again to Woodside and walk up Dutch Hill to the school house.

Next year, Olive Waddell was my teacher. She also took me home with her for a weekend, such a thrill to go downtown and see kids roller skating! Hamilton seemed to me then as big as New York City would now. I was used to going to Woodside, and not too often at that!

An incident that happened that year, has always stood out in my mind. The youngest kids got out early and we always went home before the bigger kids. We always walked through the woods. We were going down the hill by Mill Creek. Quite a ways ahead of us, we saw a BEAR CROSS THE ROAD! Of course, we were scared to death!! There was Ruth and Dorthea (?), who lived on the Win Burrell place, Alice Heavilin and myself. We went running back up the road to where Flayed Muns lived in a tent, near the Charlie Smith place. We told her and she took a gun, put it over her shoulder, and walked clear through the woods with us — but, we never saw it again. We had a grand time growing up. Always enough kids for any kind of game such as "one old cat", "kick the can", "hunt the ole Grey Wolf", and all sorts of games. We played with the Shults kids and had great times. There is nothing like a large family and those who had one or two brothers or sisters don't know what they missed!

My Dad was one of the most industrious and kind hearted men that ever lived, also, my mother. How she ever stood all us kids, I'll never know, but we always had lots to eat, wear, and wonderful times together, and those of us left still get together often. The only relative, besides our immediate family, was the Burrell family and they were just great.

My Father died from a dynamite explosion on January 31, 1933; Chuck died in August of 1933; Esta died from a heart attack in 1949; Guy from a heart attack in 1959; Mother died in the Stevensville rest home (results of a broken hip); Franklin killed in a car wreck in April, 1968; Shorty (or Ray) from a heart attack in January of 1972; and Hazel from a brain hemorrhage in December of 1972. My only son died in December 1973, from a blood clot in the heart, so with a big family you have many sorrows as well as many joys. But, I feel the Severns family has been richly blessed.

Back to Fair Play School, it was a great experience although I only went there for two years. In a small school, such as it was, you had the best teachers and it is too bad all children don't have that experience and class contact with just neighborhood kids. I don't think there are too many kids I started school with that are still living, but it is great whenever I see Helen Pierson Haigh, or Cora Malone. They are about the only ones I ever see, and Cora not too often.

SHULTS FAMILY

by Clara Shults Bohler

Our father, Victor Levi Shults, was born in Medford, Michigan, November 14, 1869 and he came to the Bitter Root Valley in 1890. His father was Levi Shults and his mother was Sarah Larkin. Our mother's name was Clara A. Blodgett and she was born in Corvallis, Montana, on January 20, 1882. They were married April 2, 1897, and had their 70th Wedding Anniversary on April 2, 1967, just ten days before our father passed away on April 12.

Mother's parents were Mary A. Parker from Cardiff, Wales, and her father was Lyman J. Blodgett, born in Bath, New Hampshire. The Lyman J. Blodgetts came to the Bitter Root Valley in 1867 by wagon train from Salt Lake City, Utah. Polly, a daughter died on the way. There were eleven children in their family, our mother being the youngest. Grandmother died on December 24, 1903 and Grandfather on May 12, 1908. Blodgett and Canyon Creeks were named for them. There is also a family cemetery called Blodgett cemetery. Mary Catherine, the oldest child in the family was the first burial, June 6, 1872. There is another creek on the ranch and Grandmother named it Churn Creek.

I started school in 1904 and for three years had Jeanette Walls for a teacher. When I was in the fourth or fifth grade, a new room was added to the school house. We walked about a mile in all kinds of weather. The name of the school was Fair Play. Hazel Severns took me to school my first day. There were five of our family who went to school there. I went through the eighth grade and as there was no high school, I went to Hamilton High

School for two years. After consolidation of Fair Play with Corvallis, we all went to Corvallis and all graduated there.

by Mary Shults Nicol

First of all, how I envied May Louise Pierson because she had a buckskin pony to ride to school, while we kids had to walk — which, of course, didn't hurt us one bit. I also thought May was very talented since she could take pictures and develop and print her own pictures — amateur as they were, we sure had fun printing them.

I recall very clearly how tired my little fat legs got when I had to walk so far to school as a first grader. Especially in the winter, when we wore long underwear, a pair of long black stockings (wool) and leggings over that.

I also remember how mother worried in the spring when Mill Creek was so high, and that old bridge over it was anything but safe. Dad used to take us that far when it was real bad to see that we were safely over it. The trilliums and other wild flowers were so abundant and pretty as we walked thru the woods. In the fall, we would watch the squirrels store their nuts away in the big trees if they had holes in them.

I am sure that everyone can recall the big board fence that separated the boys from the girls on the school grounds. The girls were rather happy about this arrangement but once in a while the boys would get out of bounds and really disturb us in our play until the teacher would catch them and send them back to their side.

I enjoyed all my teachers and remember hating to leave the first room when I graduated from the third grade to the fourth grade and into another room. I can also remember how scared I was whenever we put on programs and I had to speak a piece or take part in a play. I remember one play I was in and I was a butterfly with filmy wings and I loved floating around with all that fluffy stuff.

When I was in the sixth grade, Hazel Herman was our teacher. She taught us girls sewing and embroidery. The one who got first prize on her work was to get a trip for a week to Hazel's home in Missoula, and I won the trip. It was delightful for a little country girl to get to go to the big city, ride on street cars, see the Bonner Dam and take in movies.

There were so many of us kids to walk to school together — from our part of the district were the Heavilin, Allnut, McKillop, Severns, Gunter, Dunbar and Shults kids. And, probably more than this if I could only remember. I do remember in the winter, when the snow was really deep, my dad would go ahead of us to break trail.

My brother, Ed Shults, and Hughie McKillop were the last students to enroll at Fair Play. Ed was 6 years old on March 13, and started school the next day. At the end of May, the teacher promoted both of them to the second grade. When they went to school in Corvallis that fall, the teacher immediately demoted them to the first grade.

I remember how much fun we all had. Especially with Fred Smith and Harvey Knaak. They were both big teasers. They really gave the teachers a bad time. More than once, we had to stay after school.

But good old Fair Play was a good school and we had good teachers and learned a lot. I know I did.

THE SIMMONS HISTORY

by Alfred Simmons

Gilbert Simmons was born in Delaware County, New York, on October 10, 1841, where he lived with his parents, William and Catherine Simmons. At 16 years of age, he crossed the plains and mined at various places in California, Idaho, and Montana, at times when a shovel was worth $30.00 and a sack of flour $50.00

He came to the Bitter Root Valley in 1867, and settled on Willow Creek, where he remained until he purchased some Island property adjoining Newton Chaffin and John McCarty. This he still owned at the time of his death. In 1876, he purchased the W.B. Harlan property between Stevensville and Corvallis, which I think was on Willoughby Lane. Gilbert joined the Methodist Church in 1877.

A double wedding which joined the Simmons and Chaffin families was performed on Sunday, January 6, 1878, at the Elijah and Margaret Chaffin home which is now part of the Teller Wildlife property. **This wedding united my grandmother, Nancy Chaffin to my grandfather, Gilbert Simmons**, and Nancy's sister, Juda, to John A. Summers.

From the union of Gilbert and Nancy, eight children were born; Leila Margaret was born on April 10, 1879, and she married M. J. Kelly, **Alice May** was born on May 15, 1880, and married Levi LeClair, **Walter A.** born November 14, 1881 and never married, **Lee Elijah** born March 29, 1884, married Rea Myers, **Homer Gilbert** born August 14, 1885, and married Montana Million, **William Howard** born March 27, 1887, and never married, **Edith Grace** born November 28, 1889, and married James Barr, **Robert Mason, who was my father,** born June 16, 1891, and married Irene Butler.

Gilbert and Nancy Simmons made a comfortable home to raise their family, and were busy with the dairy, cattle, and horses. **My father, Mason,** told of he and his sister, Edith, herding their mother's turkeys on the foothills, to be sold in the fall for about $2.50 each. Also, Nancy churned butter and it was freighted to Deer Lodge and other towns of the area.

Gilbert, true to his early mining training, was President of the Buena Vista Mining Company of Eight Mile. He was a man of good habits and few words, a kind and generous person to family and friends. At the age of 50, in January 1892, he died of Brights Disease of the kidneys. At that time there was no treatment, such as dialysis, for this disease. For his burial the next day, a large funeral procession formed of 34 carriages and 25 men on horses escorted him to the Corvallis Cemetery.

The task of raising eight children fell to Nancy Simmons, which she did with full cooperation from the children. The years 1911 and 1912, found them living at the John Summers Ranch as caretakers for Otto Quast, Sr., who having purchased the ranch could not move from Missoula until he had disposed of his dairy there.

World War I saw Howard Simmons in France, having enlisted in the Army. He took part in several major engagements and was wounded severely. Mustard gas inhalation damaged his health which caused his death in 1936.

Homer Simmon's son, George, died in the Philippines in 1942, in the Bataan Death March.

From Gilbert and Nancy's eight children's offspring, there remain four still living in the Bitter Root Valley, but only two living in the Bitter Root, my cousin, Loyce Simmons Teller, and myself, Alfred Simmons.

SIZER FAMILY

Information from Dorothy Sizer Roark and Ethel Sizer Champlin

Fred and Ella Knap Sizer came to Denver, Colorado, by covered wagon and **into the Bitter Root Valley** from Denver in **1918.** They moved onto a farm west and north of Hamilton, and raised apples and cherries. They arrived here in a big hard-tired truck, and were, for many years, the only people near Hamilton with such a big truck. Ella's brother, Charlie Knap, was a lawyer in Chicago and had acquired the Grover place in some kind of deal. He called Ella and asked if she and Fred would like to have it. Though they had never even seen the place, they answered yes, and made the plans to move. A Mr. Whitehall purchased many boxes of their apples, and shipped them to Chicago by train.

Grandma Ella liked to tell the story "that when she married Fred, he was on crutches and seemed to be laid up most of the rest of his life". He was a very medium sized man, but Ella was a very generous sized woman, and found it necessary to stoop over to do her chores. A family story relates that one evening when it was raining, Ella told Fred it was just too wet for her to go outdoors to milk the cow. In a few minutes, Fred appeared at the back door. He had brought the cow onto the back porch so that Ella could milk it! When young Malcom had spinal meningitis, she lovingly nursed him back to health. She was a real homebody, yet loved the outdoors. She loved to mow the lawn, and years later when elderly, she lived with a daughter in Missoula. She insisted she could mow the lawn, and would not accept the gas powered mower offered, choosing instead the push style, even at the age of 96! She lived to the age of 102.

Fred and Ella had children, **Orton (Snort), Wales, Malcom, and Lysle.**

Their son Malcom, his wife Augusta, and their two small daughters, Dorothy and Ethel, arrived here by railroad in 1922. Augusta Peterson Sizer's parents had come to this country from Sweden, and she and Malcom had married in Castle Rock, Colorado. Because Fred and Ella's farm was such a labor-intensive endeavor, they needed the help of Malcom and his family.

Settling into a small house on the ranch, Malcom and Augusta carried on with the life of fruit producers, trimming the trees, irrigating, and picking the apples and cherries, then selling them, often in Butte. They also continued to raise their family, adding to it a set of twins, **Malcom and Margaret**, and later a daughter named **Betty.** This only son, nicknamed "Sonny", lived only to the age of five. The children attended Hamilton schools.

Seventeen years later, 1939, Malcom and Augusta purchased the Tyler place and moved onto it, raising apples and cherries here also. Many more boxes of apples were shipped by boxcar to Chicago. Their neighbors were Clark Gray on one side and Ben Kress on the other. This big house had five bedrooms upstairs, and a tin bathtub that stood on legs. The children loved life in the country, and have many pleasant memories. They all worked hard, and were expected to do their share. Ethel tells of an evening when she and Dorothy forgot to bring in the wood for the fire. About 2 AM, her father came into their room, roused them from sleep, and made then go outdoors to get a load of wood! Malcom often placed heated irons in the girl's bed, to make sure it was warm and cozy for them. They relate that he was a wonderful father, doing lots of little extras to make the family comfortable. He often took them fishing or played ball, and always to the hills for their Christmas tree. The Christmas trees usually came from the Poor Farm, which joined the Sizer place and the Tyler place. Mr. and Mrs. Billy Walker lived there for years. Mr. Walker always told them to help themselves. The snow was deep and they took sleds and made a fun day of gathering the tree.

Sunday's were special! They always had a big dinner and often 20-25 people around for the day. Relatives, friends, and last minute guests were fed a sumptuous meal cooked by Augusta and the girls, then played games, went sleighriding, played cards, or just visited the afternoon away.

Neighborhood dances were held in Miller's apple house, which was just across the fence. The neighbors would bring sandwiches, cake and cookies, and beverages for the midnight supper. Jimmy Stevers and Russell Porter would often provide the music on fiddle and guitar, and parents and children would enjoy this lively affair. There were even beds for the children to sleep on as the parents and older children enjoyed the dancing. Such events made this family a very close knit family, as they loved doing things together.

However, life was not always easy. Ethel recalls that more than once, when the apple crop was bad or ruined, her dad had to find income elsewhere, sometimes working for Clark Gray for $1.00 per day. He also went on Saturday nights out the other side of Missoula and worked at packing apples all week, returning in his model T to the farm on weekends. She also tells that when she was 13, a team of horses ran away with her. She had a number of broken bones, contusions and bruises from this scary experience.

Grandma and Grandpa Sizer owned the place up on the top of Dutch Hill with 20 acres of cherries and apples, but in later years also owned a home in Hamilton, on Cooper Lane. They lived in Hamilton most of the year, but would go out to Dutch Hill in the summertime. Having no water in this house, they had to get water from a spring. Hallie Blodgett was their neighbor on one side. The George Aishe family lived down below — where John Parker has his cherry ranch.

In 1936, they went into the grocery business in Hamilton. They had a store on South Second Street, next to the old Well's Creamery and across from "Haigh's". Much later, they owned and operated the "Economy" grocery on North First Street, where Ethel and Dorothy both worked also. They continued farming also, until 1978 when the place was sold.

Dorothy married Vern Roark and they had two daughters, Verna Marie and Mary Lee. Ethel married Albert Champlin (now deceased) and they had one son, Malcom. Both stayed in Hamilton. Margaret married Maynard Hanson and they live in Ramsey, Montana. Betty married Walter "Bud" Hassell, now deceased, and she lives in Utah.

JACK AND POLLY SLACK

by reporter Georgianna Taylor
as told in the Bitterroot View, March 29, 1997

Jack Slack was born in Philadelphia in 1835, and at the age of 16 he took a ship to Panama, crossed the Isthmus on horseback and shipped out for the West Coast, landing in San Francisco in 1852. He went to Oregon and later to Bannack before making his way to the Bitter Root in 1863, and taking up the 160 acre homestead on which the Slack House still stands. He built a 12 by 20 foot cabin and began farming and soon was hauling potatoes over the mountains to Bannack where they sold for 30 cents a pound. It was in Bannack that he met Polly Chaffin. Polly (whose given name was Mary) had come west with her father, Baalam, and they were joined by her brother Elijah and other family members on their way to Oregon. Perhaps Jack

Slack's interest in Polly spurred him to convince the Chaffins to spend the winter in the Bitter Root before continuing their journey. Jack and Polly were married here in February 1865, the first legally recorded marriage ceremony performed in the valley.

Elijah Chaffin and his family returned to the Corvallis area in the summer of 1866, bringing with them a herd of 50 dairy animals. Polly Slack and Margaret Chaffin began making butter and cottage cheese, which was added to the produce the men were hauling to markets in Missoula and Bannack.

The Slack's had six children over a span of fourteen years. In addition, Jack took in his sister, Emma, and a young half-brother. Emma became the first school teacher in the Missoula area, lured from the Corvallis area by the offer of a larger salary — $100.00 per year, compared with the $85.00 Corvallis could offer.

According to information that the Teller Wildlife Refuge educational coordinator, Mary Stone has gleaned, Jack and Polly's daughter, Margaret, met and fell in love with a young man named Sam Burkhart. But for reasons which no one seems to know, Polly refused to allow her daughter to marry him. She never did, but Margaret and Sam were together for the rest of their lives. Sam is present in many of the family photographs.

In about 1878, the children had grown in size and number and the original house was straining at the seams. The cabin was raised onto a foundation and a 26 x 32 foot addition built, giving them a parlor, dining room, two bedrooms, downstairs and four more on the second floor. The addition and the original logs of the cabin were covered with siding.

Unfortunately, Jack had only a few years to enjoy his large new home. He died in 1883, at the age of 45. Polly continued to live in the house until she was 75. After her death, in 1909, Margaret and her oldest brother, William, who also never married, continued to live in the home for some time. Various other members of the family lived in it until Gilbert Chaffin died and it was sold to the Hershberger family. Otto Teller bought the house from them in 1988.

Although some changes have been made, the structure is still basically the same as Jack and Polly planned it. Stone estimates that some of the trees in the yard have been there for about 100 years, speculating that they were planted as saplings by Jack or Polly.

Two of the Slack sons, Herb and Charles, were excellent athletes. Herb later became a member of the Montana State Highway Patrol.

Original charcoal portraits of Jack and Polly Slack now hang in the 130 year old Slack House on the Teller Wildlife Refuge which is approximately one mile east of Corvallis. These portraits were brought to Montana and donated for hanging by Sandra Slack from Ohio. In 1997, the Slack house, and the Chaffin house nearby, have been refurbished and now are used by the refuge as guest houses and for various social and cultural activities.

BARTON SMITH

prepared and submitted by Corvallis High School Students, June 1997
Jonathan Kirpatrick, Katie Miller, Tabatha Erickson & Michael Siphikas

Barton Smith has spent 87 summers at Medicine Hot Springs. Every spring the Indians used to come there. Across from the hot springs was a place called Rattlesnake Flats. The Indians would pick the Bitterroot flowers. Then they would go to Wisdom, and other places, and hunt buffalo. In the fall they would come back and use the baths at the hot springs.

Barton's father, Edward Mason Smith, came to the Bitter Root Valley in 1888. He was in the pharmaceutical business. He had an uncle living here who was a pharmacist and that is the reason he became one himself. At that time there were many Indians in the valley, especially at the Mission in Stevensville. Mr. Edward Smith learned to speak in their language, but first had to communicate through sign language. Chief Charlo was about 80 years old at the time, and said his people had been camping at the hot springs since the time of his grandfather, making it about 150 years that they had been camping at the Medicine Hot Springs.

Barton grew up at Medicine Hot Springs, and had run it himself for 30 years. Barton's father had purchased the springs in 1908. The actual hot springs had 5,000 gallons of water at about 120 degrees. A hotel was also on this 40 acre site. Then, about 30 years ago, a survey was done and it was found that there had been a building there prior to this hotel. Anyway, the state found some discrepancies and managed to shut them down.

Barton's father, Edward (who was originally from Missouri), eventually got tired of the drug business and started to work for the owner of an implement store. They also sold clothes and food, but Edward was made the manager of the implement department.

Edwin M. Smith and Maude Page were married in 1897, in the dining room of the Hotel Hamilton. The hotel had been moved to Hamilton from the town of Riverside by Harlan Page, a civil war veteran. He was the father of Maude Page and the grandfather of Barton Smith and Zean Smith.

The building right next to Hamilton Pharmacy is where the first hospital in the valley was. Barton Smith was born in this hospital in 1908. He attended his first year of school in Sula. His teachers name was Mrs. Lyman, and his second grade teacher was Mrs. Lord.

Barton met his wife while she was a maid at Medicine Hot Springs. They went out together for four years before they got married. She was a teacher at Victor, but got a job teaching at the West Fork. In those days it was against the law for a teacher to ride the bus. In the winter time it would be safer for her to ride the bus than to drive herself, but they did not let her. Barton told them that if they did not let her ride the bus, he would not let her teach anymore. They let her ride the bus.

CHARLES EDSON SMITH

CHARLES EDSON SMITH, his wife Amelia A. Jenkins Smith, and their three oldest children, arrived at Carlton on April 19, 1899. They were not satisfied there, so came on south to settle on a homestead just east of Corvallis, and here they raised all their twelve children.

Mr. Smith had been born on February 14, 1872, near Knoxville, Iowa. He attended public schools in Iowa and Missouri, and the El Dorado Springs Normal and Business College in Missouri. Then he taught school for about eight years in Kansas and Missouri, as well as doing farming.

In March of 1895, at Altoona, Kansas, Charles married Amelia (Millie) A. Jenkins. This marriage lasted for 54 years, until her death on March 19, 1949.

The Smith family farmed and logged in the Bitter Root until February of 1944, when they moved to Missoula. Charles started exhibiting farm products in 1912, at the Ravalli County Fair. He took first prize on hard red winter wheat and on vegetables. He exhibited wheat samples at Madison Square Garden and other fairs throughout the country. In 1916, he exhibited at Montana State Fair, and continued for eight years (excepting once). Taking many prizes on grain and farm products, wheat, potatoes, peas, oats and similar produce. One year he served as President of the Advisory Board of Montana State Fair. During 1925, and 1926, he was in charge of the Ravalli County exhibits and in 1925, he had charge of the exhibits at the Midland Empire Fair held in Billings, Montana.

In 1927, he won first and World Championship Sweepstakes on hard red winter wheat; first on Durham wheat for the third successive year, which gave him possession of the cup offered as a prize. He was also crowned Wheat King of the World. He also won first in six now Tre-bi and any other barley, the sweepstakes and other premiums. In 1928, he once more won the first World's Sweepstakes and World championship on hard red winter wheat. He was the only exhibitor at that time to win the World's Championship for two consecutive years.

One might wonder what led him to produce these quality grains. For years he had been interested in wheat growing and had a firm conviction that "Montana was the greatest wheat growing state in the union", and he set out to prove his contention. In order to raise money to carry on his private experiments, he began exhibiting. He had the warm desire to bring honor to Montana and the Bitter Root Valley. All the while raising other crops and cattle to make a living. Later on, his wheat growing became more of a hobby. In the later years, Mr. Smith took more interest in fruit trees and berries, and did grafting and tried to develop better strawberries. Always a grower, he tried to improve on the quality of what was being grown.

Millie was always his helper,in raising their family and doing the work on the farm. She was a direct descendant of the Boone and Lincoln families. The records show on the Boone side, dating back to 1605, Devonshire, England, her great-grandfather twice removed, William Boone, I, was a first cousin of Daniel Boone, noted early day pioneer. And, on the Lincoln side, family records go back to 1543, Hingham, England. Abraham Lincoln was a nephew of the wife of William Boone. Mrs. Smith's father, W. Y. Jenkins, early pioneer and associate of the Boone's, was a soldier of the Union Republic Army, serving as a fifer.

Mr. Smith passed away in 1958, and both are buried in the Corvallis Cemetery.

One son, Thomas E. Smith, died at the age of 88, on June 24, 1997. He was born on September 25, 1908, on the homestead east of Corvallis. He graduated from Dominic Grade School and Corvallis High School. He married Madelon I. Wilburn on March 26, 1935, in Missoula, and they had one daughter, Donna Smith Braun. At the time of his death, only one brother, Ralph Smith of Cottonwood, AZ, survived him. Thomas also exhibited wheat and won many titles. He exhibited in Chicago in 1931, at the World's Exhibition and Conference held at Regina, Canada, along with exhibitors from major grain-producing nations of the world. He won first prize with his sample of hard red winter (Karkoff) wheat, which carried with it a cash award of $2,000.00, which he used to help in his schooling at North Dakota State College.

JAMES WELBY SMITH FAMILY

by Wilma Carmichael Allen, great-granddaughter in 1997

James Welby Smith (April 20, 1860 - May 31, 1947) was the son of Benjamin F. Smith and Elizabeth Dawson Smith. His parents were one of the pioneer families who had come from Virginia to establish a new home in what was then a new country. They settled in Ellinorah (Gentry County) Missouri. James had brothers; Dr. George W. Smith, Dr. John Smith, Benjamin and Dexter Smith, and sisters; Mattie (McNeese) Smith and Cora Lee (Gillespie) Smith. Dr. John Smith was the physician on duty when Loyd Rockafellow, later a Corvallis resident, was born in 1899.

James married Buena Vista Shelly (June 22, 1862 - June 21, 1934) and they began their life together **on July 2, 1880**, in Ellinorah, Missouri. Her grandparents had raised Buena Vista and little is known of her family life. We do know she had a sister named Ella Hill, a half-sister named Lizzie

Roberts, and an uncle named L.C. Wilson.

James and Buena parented their first four children in Ellinorah, MO, from 1881 to 1888. In 1889, James came to Montana and began building a home for his family, up on the westside of Ravalli County, above Woodside. James was a very small person physically, but an old history account tells of how he carried a roll of barbed wire from Shiffman Creek (now Sheafman Creek) to his property (on what is now Bowman Road), a distance of over 5 miles. His family joined him in 1890, and their 5th child, a son named Paul Franklin, was born at the family home on December 9, 1890. They brought along from Missouri a colored lady to assist with caring for the household. She returned to Missouri after the children were older. Buena seemed to spend most of her time in bed, and a grand-daughter remembers that Buena twisted the blankets with her fingers, in a very nervous way.

James Welby Smith was a man extremely concerned about achieving his own salvation, and encouraging his family and friends to do the same. He wrote a very lengthy account of his experiences regarding this which he requested be read at his funeral. He was originally of the Camellite faith, which we now call Christian. His wife had been raised in the Methodist religion. Before he was saved at a meeting held in someone's home there on Dutch Hill, he gave this account of trying to live a clean and God-like life.

"I had a younger brother take sick in Pason City, Utah. At this time I offered up the first prayer of my life. I promised God that I would serve Him for the remainder of my life if He would spare my brother. As I supported his skeleton frame through the yard, and into my parent's home, I was reminded of my vow. I quit every bad habit — my dancing, pitching horseshoes, croquet, checkers, — **anything my conscience said was wrong!** My wife's uncle, L.C. Wilson, said he was pleased to see my reformation. It was a dry season, and Brother Wilson and I spent much time together digging wells and building ponds while discussing this great subject of salvation. Yes, I thought I was a Christian man. The brother who had been ill, and a cousin of ours, came to visit. After a late evening discussion of salvation, my brother advised me that "he could wait to accept this great salvation". We went outdoors to feed some hay to the horses, and my brother began to whistle a jig common to the day, called "Leather Britches". I began to dance around — OH MY, MY SINS HAD TRIPPED ME UP, AS I HAD VOWED AGAINST THIS SINFUL HABIT!"

James is reported to have preached at the Corvallis Methodist Church on occasion.

James and Buena had a total of nine children. The Smith children attended Playfair School and are pictured in all the early pictures. May Vallance recalls a poem she wrote in 5th grade, which has a line "hush, hush, dear little Freddy", and when she looked at Fred it always made him blush.

Mary Shults Nicol said Fred was so much fun, as he was a big tease.

Grandchildren remember the Smith household as being one where you visited, but were admonished to sit quietly and not talk, and be as well mannered as possible. In their final years Buena and James lived in Hamilton.

Most of the children stayed in the Bitter Root Valley, and many descendants survive them here today. The oldest child, **Edith Gertrude**, married George Thomas Johnson. Their son is Charles Johnson who married Lillian Foss Johnson. They had no children. Next was **Jess Coffee** who married Mary Shiffman Rummel); then **Charles Welby** who married Mamie Stevens; **Lola May known as Lula** married William Morse; **Paul Franklin – the first Bitter Root born** – married Helen Connaughton; **George Welby** married Hattie Gilbert (a son DeWayne lives in Victor and married Betty Sorenson); **Myrtle Lee (my grandmother)** married Jesse Lee (Skinny) White (daughter is Alice Ann (Chub) Carmichael); **Fred** who never married; and **Mamie B.** who died at the Thornton Hospital when 16 years of age.

THE SMITHEY FAMILY

by Denise Black Severns

Robert Hamilton Smithey was born August 15, 1844, in Paris, Missouri, to William and Patsy Martha Cardwell Smithey. In 1832, they moved to Missouri. William and Patsy had 10 children, and two of their daughters lived in the Bitter Root. Mrs. Mary E. Smithey Popham was born on May 26, 1836 near Florida, MO, and died March 21, 1931, at 94 years of age. Martha Jane Smithey was born in Mercer County, KY, in December of 1831, and died at her home in Corvallis on October 24, 1913, at 82 years of age. She moved to the Bitter Root in about 1893.

Robert Hamilton Smithey married Mattie Moss Woods, the daughter of James and Elizabeth Moore Wood, on March 23, 1871. Mattie was born on April 6, 1847, and died August 29, 1890, about 10 days after baby Mattie Smithey was born. They had 10 children between 1872 and 1890. Robert was in the Confederate forces for three years during the Civil War, and was an ardent Democrat. **He and his children moved to the Bitter Root Valley in the spring of 1899**, and located on the Buhl ranch, ¼ mile west of the Riverside silver bridge at Hamilton. From there he moved to Hamilton on North Eighth Street and worked at his trade of blacksmithing, both in town and at the Bitter Root Stock Farm.

The children are:

Nora L. Smithey, born January 7, 1872, died February 2, 1939 at the age of 67 years. She was a graduate of Kirksville, Missouri, Normal School and was one of the first teachers to be employed at Darby School when the change was made from a district school to a graded institution in 1902. Miss Smithey awarded the first eighth grade diplomas for the Darby School. She taught mostly in the Bitter Root Valley for 41 years, and served three terms as Ravalli County Superintendent of Schools.

Jimmy Smithey was born on April 9, 1873, and died September 22, 1879, **Ernest Smithey** was born October 26, 1874 and died October 17, 1894, **Lizza Pat Smithey** was born on August 21, 1878 and died on September 13, 1879, **Bennie Smithey** was born August 29, 1880 and died on November 30, 1883. Several died of diphtheria.

Thomas J. Smithey was born on April 23, 1882, in Strother, Missouri. He came to the valley on a visit to Corvallis in 1891. This led to him to return to the Bitter Root in 1898, and he was followed by his father and other family members in 1899. Tom attended school in the Corvallis District, worked on the family farm and graduated to working in the woods and mills of the Bitter Root Valley. He was an outstanding baseball player on the early teams of Corvallis. He moved to Tacoma and worked as a steamfitter, and later owned an apartment building with **his wife, Effie Inez Metcalf,** who died in 1953. He moved back to the Hamilton area and lived with his brother, "Pete", until he died in 1974, at the age of 92 years.

Clarence A. "Pete" Smithey was born on July 16, 1885, in Strother, Missouri. He attended Hamilton Schools and then worked for five years at the old Flour Mill at the river end of Adirondac Street. He worked in the sawmills and in the woods, and also on the road as a flour salesman. Pete wintered two years in the Anaconda Company's smelter, but as soon as the snow melted, he came back to the Bitter Root. **He married Rose Reindeau,** a French lady. In 1935, Pete went to work for the US Postal Service and retired from there in 1956. He was also a partner in the old Brunswick Billiard Parlor with Blaine "Dewey" Reimel, who was his brother-in-law.

Herbert H. Smithey was born on October 25, 1883. He was employed for many years by the Northern Pacific Railroad at Paradise, MT, and at Spokane, WA. He was 94 years old when he died in April of 1977. **His wife's name was Anna, and his daughter was Jean Jones of Anderson, IN.**

Mary Nell Smithey was born January 13, 1887, near Strother, Missouri. She was 12 years of age when she arrived at Woodside, and attended schools in Hamilton. **She married Blaine W. "Dewey" Reimel on** September 12, 1911. Dewey and Pete Smithey operated several pool tables, one billiard table and a card room at the Brunswick, which was the main gathering place for the local gentry, in those days of 1910. In 1915, they sold the business to W.H. Grimes, and the Reimel's moved to Butte where he was employed by the Hennessy's department store for many years. They returned to the Valley in 1926, and bought the Woodside General Store from

Harry Thrailkill, operating the business until the Northern Pacific Railroad moved its tracks from the west side of the valley to the east side on September 1, 1928. Dewey was employed for a number of years by the Valley Mercantile, which was in the Bower Building.

"I remember when my Aunt Nell lived in Hamilton, in the yellow house on Shady Lane, she won a blue ribbon on her crabapple pickles, her jelly and her jam, and sent them to Mrs. Daly by the Daly's chauffeur (maybe a Mr. Hill). One Monday morning, Mrs. Daly's chauffeur was at Aunt Nell's door to ask if she would want Mrs. Daly to come in. Aunt Nell said "Yes", and then hurried to change to her good shoes. Later, she noticed **she had put on one black shoe, and one brown shoe**!" Aunt Nell was like a grandmother to my sister, brother, and me. My mother, Electa Walls Black, remembers a pretty, big blue Chandler car which Nell and Dewey drove."

Mattie Smithey was born August 19, 1890, in Strother, Missouri. Mattie was just 10 days old when her mother died and Nell was 3, Pete was 5, Herb was 7, Tom was 8, and Nora was 18. Aunt Tish Nevins, who was a housekeeper for the Smithey family, was 28 years of age. She was a Mulatto, and had been taken in by a minister and given his name. In 1899, when Robert, moved his family to the Bitter Root, Aunt Tish moved with them to help raise the family of five small children. In 1908, **Mattie Smithey married Wesley William Walls,** and they lived several places in the Bitter Root and Drummond. She was a midwife, and would cook meals, do washing and cleaning, and take care of the family, for $50.00 for two weeks care. Some of the people she cared for were Lillian Bay, Nell Lairy, and Amoline Boyer. Her aunt, Jan Smithey, died in 1913, and left Mattie some property which she sold so they could buy their first car, a 1918 4-door Ford which had to be started by cranking. Mattie died at an early age of 40 years old and was greatly missed by her family and friends.

SMITHEY FAMILY

by Amy Lee Felix, Granddaughter, in 1998

Robert Russell Smithey was born May 21, 1869, the second son and fourth child of John Thomas Smithey and Mary Cuzzie Alverson Smithey.

Laura Elbert Neafus was born on October 21, 1882, the eighth child and fourth daughter of William H. and Cornelia Woods Neafus. She was born in Townsend, Montana Territory.

"Russell", as he was known, had arrived in the Bitter Root in 1891, and he and Laura were married on April 16, 1901. They became parents of **Nellie Smithey** born October 13, 1902, she married George Lairy, **Abbie Smithey** born May 7, 1905, she married Elton Dye, and **Amy Laura**

Smithey, born August 19, 1906, and she married Loyd M. Rockafellow (my father and mother).

When Russell arrived in the Valley, his bachelor uncle, Bob, (his father's brother) was his closest relative living here. Bob died in 1922 and is buried in the Corvallis Cemetery. Russell was second cousin to Clarence (Pete) and Tom Smithey from Hamilton. Ed Popham was also a second cousin and had settled his family in the Corvallis area prior to Russell's arrival. He was a branch of the Smithey families that stemmed from Kentucky and settled in the Paris, Missouri area. Laura's family traces back to Kentucky and Missouri.

Jim and Abigail Cowen, 1864 arrivals in Corvallis, had a trading post on what is now the northwest corner of West Second and Main Street. Russell first worked for the Cowens. They had lost their son at the age of six years, and treated Russell as their own. Russell and Laura's daughters referred to the Cowans as "Uncle Jim" and "Auntie Cowan." Jim Cowan died in the early 1900's, and Abigail married Ad Wolfe, whom she outlived also. On her death the Smitheys bid on part of her estate, and acquired the house and the defunct trading post combination. Russell and Laura finished raising their family and lived out their lives in this house. Some of the grandchildren, including myself, were born in this house in what they called the "front bedroom".

The part of the house that was the trading post was often used to hold bodies prior to burial. People would keep 24-hour vigil over the bodies at this time, and Laura spent many hours at this chore. This section was later made into an apartment and rented out.

Because the home had a huge dining room, Grandmother insisted on having all the family birthday and holiday dinners there. The grandchildren, of whom there are five, still talk about their memories of those dinners. Grandmother also had cookies and other goodies ready in case the grandchildren dropped by, and we did that as often as possible. Grandmother had chickens and a rooster that chased all the "youngsters" back to the house. A favorite memory was of staying over night and sleeping in the feather bed. This was a special privilege as it was easier to make up the bed in the front bedroom. Russell was fondly known to his grandchildren as "Hey".

Laura helped to nurse several ailing Corvallis people back to health, keeping them in her home. Her most frightening story was the fighting for and losing the life of a child with Spotted Fever.

Laura was active in community affairs. All my life I have heard about her sense of humor. She was a character in several town plays, and her humor shined. She was a charter member of the Corvallis Order of Eastern Star. In her later years, Laura became crippled from rheumatoid arthritis, but died of cancer on January 5, 1952. Their marriage had lasted fifty-two years and Grandpa Hey never ceased to miss her.

Russell was a charter member of the Corvallis Masonic Order. Known as an honest and hard working man, he did county roadwork using his horses to pull the road grader. He hauled rock from Soft Rock Creek to build the building which now (1998) houses Corvallis Drugstore and Bay's Hardware. With the horses they were able to haul only one load per team, per day. There were two teams hauling. Russell also worked on the Riverside smokestack when it was built. He worked for the Hamilton Pea Seed Company for awhile, and one day while irrigating a field of peas he felt a sharp pain in his shoulder. Though it bothered him, he continued working until quitting time. When he got home Laura saw blood on his shirt and his shoulder was getting stiff. A trip to the doctor confirmed that Russell had been shot with, possibly, a .22. Since the removal of the bullet would mean cutting deeply into the large muscle, the doctor decided not to operate. He carried the bullet to his death, sometimes painfully. It was never felt the shooting was deliberate, but there was no confession of the accident.

Russell worked several years as a cheese maker in the local cheese factory, and I can picture him at the vats — stirring the cheese. In his last days, he and I spent time together. He talked about things dear to him and shared his feelings, as I never expected of him. Those were precious hours, and even now I feel close to him. May 19, 1962, he passed away.

Nellie Smithey Lairy died in 1959, and George Lairy in 1952. Abbie Smithey Dye died in 1994, and Elton Dye in 1952. Amy Laura Smithey Rockafellow lived to age 91, passing on in 1998, and Loyd "Rocky" Rockafellow died in 1992.

BERNARD AND BERTHA SMYTH

by Patricia Turner, daughter of Esther Smyth Knowles, July 1992

When asked to write about my grandfather, Bernard (B.J. or Barney) Smyth I thought of his big red barn which still remains on the Lee Erickson place on Popham Lane, the symbol of the farm he built from his hard work. When asked to write about my grandmother, Bertha Swayze Smith, I remember the smell of cinnamon cookies which she always prepared for her grandchildren as a symbol of her love for them.

Grandpa was born June 21, 1867, in Teteagouche, near Bathurst, N.B., Canada. As a youth, he left his home to work as a lumber worker in Michigan and Maine. In 1892, he and his brother, Ben, and an Ellis cousin left Maine in a covered wagon to journey to Montana. As they traveled West, they passed through Yellowstone country, not yet a National Park, and grandpa later recounted the wonders of the place with its gushing geysers, mysterious paint pots, and abundance of wildlife. The men continued on to the Bitter Root Valley, south of Missoula, Montana.

Grandma was born on March 16, 1879, in Camboro, Ontario, Canada. The malaria epidemic, prevalent in the area, forced her family to move to Greenwood, Nebraska, in 1881. They moved to Dwight, Nebraska, in 1889. Her mother died in Ceresco, near Waverly or Saunders, in 1893. In 1895, Gran Smyth's family moved to Hamilton, Montana. There she met and married Bernard in 1896. They were a striking couple. Grandpa, a handsome, broad chested man, dwarfed his sweetheart, Bertha, who stood 4 foot, 11 inches tall. He always called her "his little woman".

Bernard worked at the Curlew Mine out of Victor, then followed the logging industry which he knew best. He topped trees, the most dangerous of logging jobs. They homesteaded near Hamilton and while he was working, Bertha held down their claim. Later, they sold this place and bought a farm between Hamilton and Corvallis, and this farm gave him the stepping stone with which to buy the farm about three miles north of Corvallis (on Cobb Lane, now known as Popham Lane) which he owned upon his death.

Bernard led an active life in his community, serving as an elder of the Corvallis Community Church, an officer of the Odd Fellows Lodge, and as a charter member of the Rocky Mountain Grange, as well as being a Past Master of the Pomona (county). He served as President of the Farmers Mutual Fire Insurance Company for 33 years. This rural insurance company paid no individual dues unless a member suffered a loss.

Grandfather died when I was very young. I remember him as being very stern and strict. His peers knew him as one having a great sense of humor, but I never saw this. He was a generous man to those in need, and my mother tells me of times he helped the Indians who lived in tepees that could be seen in the flat hills above Corvallis. During the long, hard winters they often suffered hunger, so they would come down into the valley at night. They went through the cellar of grandpa's household and loaded up with food. Grandpa never stopped them, for he understood their ways. He did give them additional meat and clothes.

In 1910, the children remember that the greatest forest fire of all time for this area swept over most of Northern Idaho, the ashes from the fire being carried into Montana and dropping over the fields. When all able bodied men were called to fight the fire, the children had to do the haying. They attached lanterns to the wagons for light, as the sky at noon was darker than at midnight on a regular day.

Grandma had almost inhuman strength. During the smallpox epidemic which hit about 1913, only Grandma and Uncle Bernard (age 5) remained well. My grandfather, my mother, and most of the hired hands almost met death. For over a week, Grandma and Bernard had to care for everyone in the house, and those who worked for them. No one in the family was able to work the farm, so kindly neighbors took care of the animals. This neighborliness of the people living nearby continues to this day to be part of the community life of Corvallis.

To B.J. and Bertha Smyth were born five children:

Leila, born in 1898, lived in Washington in her adult life. She learned the trade of beautician, and knew no strangers, opening her home with a feeling of warmth.

Dora, born in 1900, championed floral beauty and her flowers were known throughout all of Montana. If there was a manpower shortage, she drove the tractor and did the work of a man. She was the only daughter to remain in Corvallis. She married Clifford Wallace and they had children, Wesley and Alice Doreen (Mrs. Robert Hackney). A second marriage was to Maurice Holloran in 1925, and they lived out their lives on a farm on Oil Well Road, east of Corvallis.

Emmett W., born in 1903, lived his entire life in Corvallis where he farmed and operated the village barber shop. He was a pillar of the Corvallis Community Church, as has his son (Bob) been. They have both served as Deacons. Emmett married Ruth Amelia Sutherland in 1923, and they had three children: Louise Smyth Conner, Robert E., and Dorothy Mae McLarren.

Esther, born in 1905, is my mother. She came to Seattle as a trained nurse, and she and my father owned bowling lanes. After father's death, she gained nation wide respect as the first woman to be a bowling lane proprietor.

Bernard J., born in 1908, moved to Washington state, and gifted with a genius in carpentry — he became known as a master builder. He was a happy man, with a gift of gab which brought smiles to all around him, always aiding those neighbors who needed his help. In 1997 he is still living in Kingston, WA.

THE ROBERT SNOW FAMILY HISTORY

Mr. Robert Snow first came to the Bitter Root Valley in 1908, during the apple boom. He was so taken with the beautiful valley that he returned to his home in Illinois and made plans to make a permanent move.

He built a house in sections which he loaded on a boxcar with household goods and livestock, and in 1909, he returned to make the Bitter Root his home. This was perhaps the first pre-fabricated house in the valley. He erected this house on acreage he bought in the Mountain View Orchards area, east of Corvallis. He was very active in the fruit industry that was flourishing in the valley at this time. He planted a large apple orchard and remained in the apple business for many years, having his own label and large apple house. He assisted others in planting their orchards.

He was also active in the organization of the Bitter Root Irrigation district, and was one of the first presidents of the Board of Commissioners of this group. He worked hard and long, with his large team of horses helping to build the Big Ditch. To supplement his farm income he also worked as a carpenter, which had been his trade before coming to the Valley.

In 1942, he and his wife, Linetta, moved to Hamilton, where he worked as a carpenter until the time of his death. He was born on February 19, 1877, at Winona, Illinois, and died in Hamilton on May 30th, 1959.

LINETTE SNOW — Linette Snow came to this valley in 1910, to be the bride of Robert Snow. She was born in Aurora, Illinois, in 1874. She and Robert had one son, Donald Benson Snow. She spent her life as a farmer's wife, helping with the harvesting and working in the apples. She raised chickens and also guinea pigs for the Rocky Mountain Lab. Linette was a lifetime member of the Women's Relief Corp., having joined in her original home in Aurora, in 1900. She continued to be an active member of this organization until her death. She died in 1964, at her home in Hamilton.

DONALD SNOW — Donald Snow was born the son of Robert and Linetta Snow, August 17, 1897. He grew up on the family farm east of Corvallis, and attended grade school and high school at Corvallis. After graduating from high school Don joined the army, serving in the First World War. He served overseas in England and in France. Don was wounded just before the end of the war. He was in the Fort Harrison Hospital recovering from his wounds when he met Harriette McNeil. She and other young ladies were visiting the veterans in the hospital to cheer them up.

Don and Harriette were married soon after, and then moved to Corvallis to help his father on the apple farm. He and Harriette had three children, Robert, Virginia and Richard. Eventually, they bought their own land and moved a house, which they had built, onto it. In 1942, Don and Harriette sold the farm and moved to Hamilton. Don then started working for the Rocky Mountain Laboratory as night watchman, and was employed there until he retired in 1960.

Donald Snow spent a great part of his life helping other veterans to get pensions, getting into hospitals, and getting emergency leaves. He spent ten years as Service Officer for the American Legion, many years as Service Officer for the Veterans of Foreign Wars, and also served as Home Service chairman for the Red Cross. Don was a member of the Presbyterian Church, the American Legion, the Veterans of Foreign Wars, and the Masonic Lodge. He died at his home in Hamilton in 1982.

HARRIETTE McNEIL SNOW — Harriette Snow was born Harriette McNeil, in 1898, in Marrinette, Wisconsin. She was the daughter of Luther and Harriette McNeil. The family moved to Helena when Harriette was four years of age. She attended school in Helena, graduating from high school and then going on to business school. She worked as a secretary at the State Nursery, and also at the Montana State Capitol.

In 1918, she married John Barker and they had two children, Harriette Filby (Hornung) and Dorothy Mae (Chaffin). She was later divorced and married Donald Snow.

She and Don, and Harriette and Mae, moved to Corvallis to join Don's parents on their farm, and eventually they purchased their own farm where they farmed until 1942, when they moved to Hamilton.

Harriette and Donald Snow had three children: Robert Snow, now living in Missoula, Virginia, who married Bill Kindzerski and now lives in Fort Benton, MT, and Richard, who passed away in 1993.

Harriette worked for a while at the old Valley Merc as a clerk and bookkeeper, and then took the position as Deputy Clerk of the Court in the Ravalli County Courthouse, working for Marshall Anderson. Upon his death, Harriette was appointed Clerk of the Court. She stayed in this position, being elected to two four-year terms before her retirement in 1961.

Harriette was very active in many organizations and belonged to the Presbyterian Church, where she was an active member until her death on September 10, 1972.

SOLOMON FERDNAND SOLBERGER

taken from the book, Progressive Men of Montana, page 1249

Solomon Ferdnand Solberger. There is scarcely a lot in life more essentially peaceful and blessed than that of the man who has done his duty well and sees growing and thriving around him the wholesale and beneficial fruits of his labor, in an interesting family for which he has well provided, in an advanced state of thought and development in the community to which he had largely contributed, in a vigorous activity of all the moral and social forces of his people, which he has fostered and encouraged. Such as this is the lot of Solomon Ferdnand Solberger, who resides near Hamilton, in Ravalli County, Montana. He was born on June 1, 1839, at Cleveland, OH, son of John and Elizabeth Solberger, both natives of Switzerland. The family consisted of five children, Solomon being the first born. He attended the public school at Mt. Eaton, Ohio, until he was ten years old, then lived with his grandfather on his farm for four years, until his parents removed to St. Genevieve County, Missouri, whither he accompanied them. There he farmed and learned the trade of a machinist under his father, with whom he remained until 1859.

In 1859, Mr. Solberger went to Pike's Peak and mined until 1863, and then came to Montana. For two years he mined at Bannack, Alder Gulch, and Helena, where he worked two and one-half years mining and running a quartz mill until 1871. From that time until 1877, he worked for Keaton & Blacker at Radersburg at mining, when he moved to Butte and built the old Lexington mill for A.J. Davis, then taking charge of it for two years. After that, he mined for himself, worked at his trade and followed other occupations, including running a shop for himself until 1887, when he came to the Bitter Root Valley and located on a ranch two miles northwest of Hamilton, where he has been residing since.

He has a ranch of 160 acres on which he has a fine orchard in bearing condition and raises numbers of superior cattle and abundant crops of farm produce. He has also eighty acres of timber land a mile and a half west of his ranch. In politics, Mr. Solberger is an ardent Republican, always giving its candidates and policies his earnest support. He served as school

In this photograph taken on May 5, 1894, by A. M. Moore are (from left) Ada Solberger, Ike Lay and Ida Solberger Lay.

board trustee for a number of years, and took a lively interest in all local matters. Being among the pioneers of the state, he is an active member of their association. Mr. Solberger is an ornament to the community, has been of great service in every department of its useful activities and he is secure in the cordial regard, the full confidence and the universal esteem of his fellow citizens. Solomon married Sarah Ann Williamson in May, 1872, in St. Genevieve County, Missouri. From this marriage, he and Sarah had four children, John, Ida, Ada, and Ivy. They were all born in Montana. Ivy, the youngest was born on the ranch near Hamilton on June 7, 1890. In later years, she was married to Harvey Edward Fullerton, remained on the ranch where she and Harvey raised their five children, Edward, Lillian, Effie, William, and Isabella. After the children were raised, Ivy sold the ranch and moved into the old Sullinger house on North 5th Street in Hamilton, where she lived out her life. Ivy's daughter, Lillian, lives in Hamilton also and is married to the well known photographer, Ernst Peterson.

THE SQUIRES FAMILY

Bitter Root Pioneers

This family starts with Orlin Whitney Squires, born in Elyria, Ohio, on March 21, 1841. He was raised to manhood in Madison County, Wisconsin. In 1860, he crossed the plains to Denver, Colorado, which at that time contained only a few houses, and for the first two years, was engaged in raising stock.

In May 1863, he purchased 160 acres of the Cold Spring Ranch at Alder Gulch, Montana, where he continued stockraising for two years and also conducted a stage station having become acquainted with all the old pioneers of Montana.

From there, Mr. Squires came to the Bitter Root Valley and purchased land from the government, near Stevensville. But one year later, sold that place and moved to Grantsdale where he engaged in packing to Washington Territory.

On September 13, 1871, he was married to Elizabeth Ann Blodgett and continued to live in Grantsdale. Of this union there were six children.

He next became interested in sawmilling, having built one of the first mills in the Bitter Root Valley, at Corvallis. He subsequently sold that mill and bought and operated two others. He received from $30.00 to $60.00 per thousand for his lumber. In connection with his sawmilling it became necessary for Mr. Squires to open a blacksmith shop and being a natural mechanic, he soon learned that trade, also.

He followed that occupation for about 20 years and became proprietor of a shop in Hamilton. He was one of the first blacksmiths in Missoula County, which encompassed Ravalli County at that time, and at one time he owned a shop in Corvallis. In addition to his other interests, he owned town property in Grantsdale.

One son, Orlin Whitney, Jr., was born April 1, 1874, and died of a childhood complaint on October 14, 1875.

The following is the record of the other children of Mr. and Mrs. O. W. Squires:

Marietta (Metta), the oldest daughter was born in Corvallis on September 9, 1877. At the age of 15 years, she was afflicted with a diphtheria-like condition and in the flower of her youth, a maiden comely and lovable, intelligent and handsome, was rudely torn from the midst of her sorrowing family on August 18, 1892.

Ezra was born October 16, 1872, a young man widely known as a popular, intelligent and industrious lad. In school, he always led his classes and possessed a brilliant mind. He was the pride of his loving parents, whose sea of troubles knew no end. He was stricken with the same malady as his sister, Metta, and succumbed on August 24, 1892.

At the time of his death, two little sisters were also afflicted with the same malady. Odelpha, the older of the two at nine years of age, succumbed on August 25, 1892.

Little three year old, Ada, was the last victim of the dread malady and passed away on August 28, 1892.

There remained only one child, Henry, who was born in Grantsdale on August 6, 1892, an infant only three weeks old when Ada died.

The remaining family moved from the ranch on Sleeping Child Creek to Grantsdale, where Henry grew up, attending school there.

After graduating from Grantsdale school, Henry went to Canton, South Dakota, to attend higher education. While there he met and married Cora Belle Jackson. They had two daughters born to them, Cora Frances, on August 2, 1913, and Bessie Helen on July 31, 1914. The family then moved to Grantsdale where ROSE MAY was born on August 16, 1916. In 1917, Cora Belle gave birth to another baby girl, but both she and the baby died on October 14, 1917. Shortly after Cora Belle's death, Henry left his three little girls in the care of his mother, Elizabeth Squires, and he entered military service. Henry Squires served in France in World War I, until the war ended. Later he returned to the Bitter Root Valley to make his home.

MARRIAGE OF HENRY SQUIRES AND GRACE BURCH MOE

Henry Squires met Grace Burch Moe who was employed at the Daly Mansion northeast of Hamilton. Later, they purchased a marriage license in Missoula, and planned to be married in Stevensville on March 1, 1920. Due to the fact that their license had been issued in Missoula County, it was not valid in Ravalli County, so they took the minister and the wedding party north to the county line — and were married in the middle of the road — and returned to Stevensville!

After starting married life with five children (Henry's youngest, Rosie, was left with her grandmother, who raised her) they had seven more children: Grace Lenora, Ruby Virginia, Violet Valentine, Ida Ann, Charley Vincent, Don Roy, and Alice Louise, making a family of twelve (12) children.

Henry made a living for the family with a variety of jobs and farming and raising raspberries for market. Everyone in the family helped with the many chores required on a farm. Henry died on January 24, 1944, in Hamilton, Montana, of an accidental gunshot which he received in Darby, where they were living and operating a restaurant.

Grace was a wonderful mother to her own children, and to the step-children who regarded her as their own mother. She was a homemaker until Henry died in 1944, then she moved to California where she worked as a seamstress in a hospital to support her two minor children and send them to school, until severe arthritis forced her to retire. She lived for a number of years with her youngest daughter, Alice Gates, in Whittier, California and in Spokane, Washington. After which she moved back to Hamilton, where she died on November 5, 1973. She was buried in Grantsdale Cemetery alongside Henry and Charlie.

MOONLIGHT MARRIAGE ON MONDAY EVENING

contributed by: Violet Squires Nelson and Grace Squires Simmons

By the light of the moon, assisted by the glare from the headlights of the minister's Ford automobile, Mrs. Grace Moe of Hamilton and Henry Squires, formerly of Grantsdale, were married on the public highway near the Missoula-Ravalli county line. Rev. P.D. Hartman performed the ceremony by the light of the moon, but when it came to signing the necessary documents, it was necessary to utilize the lights of the minister's jitney. Mrs. Hartman and Robert Leitch witnessed the ceremony.

The groom secured his marriage license in Missoula county and was unaware of the provision of the law which limited the license to use in that county. He did not discover his predicament until he applied to Rev. Mr. Hartman to be married in Stevensville. The simplest method, and the one which wasted the least time, was adopted — the party simply repaired to a point beyond the county line.

Mr. and Mrs. Squires will make their home in Stevensville. He is an employee of the Jacky Shoe Shop.

THE SUMMERS

Though perhaps not among the earliest pioneers to come to the Bitterroot Valley, the family of Joseph Richard Summers and Anna Louise Payne arrived in 1918, to play a prominent role in the growth and development of the area and in fact many of their descendants are still active in the various communities of the Valley.

Joseph Richard Summers was born in Bountiful, Utah, on April 21, 1874. He was the fourth child and second son in a family of eight children born to George Summers and Sara Ann Green Summers, who were part of the Mormon emigration to the Salt Lake Valley. George and Sara Ann were married crossing the plains to Utah, when George went back to meet a wagon bringing his mother and his future wife to Salt Lake, where they arrived with the Chipman wagon train on September 15, 1866.

Anna Louise Payne was the daughter of William Payne and Fannie Lawrence Payne, who were neighbors of the George Summers family in Utah. In fact, one of Joseph's brothers married one of Anna's sisters, so the families were always close. Anna was born on May 16, 1890.

Joseph and Anna were married in Salt Lake City, Utah. They lived for a time in Bothwell, Utah, where their two oldest daughters, Lola and Alice, were born. However, they could not afford to purchase land in Utah so around 1911, they moved to Montana where they claimed a homestead about 15 miles out of Valier. Three more children were born to them during the years they lived in Valier — Olive, Joseph Richard, and Clara. During the summer, the family stayed on the homestead, but in the winter they moved to town so that the children could attend school. Joseph Sr. worked as janitor in the school during the winter and farmed during the summer.

Farming in Valier must have been hard going, with a short growing season and arduous living conditions. In 1918, Joseph made an exploratory trip to the Bitterroot Valley because he had heard excellent reports of living conditions there. He located a place to live, then returned home to tell his family that they would be moving and that they would love their new home because apples and prunes grew everywhere.

The family packed their belongings and traveled on the train to Grantsdale where Joseph had rented a farm. One of them remembers that they were all upset because no prunes were in evidence when they got off the train!!

They soon purchased the "old Thompson Place", a farm on the old Grantsdale Road, and stayed there for about two years. After they sold this farm they moved into Grantsdale where they eventually purchased a home between Albert and Mabel Patterson and the John Taylor farm. There they stayed for as long as they both lived.

Two more children were born after their move to Grantsdale —

Beula and Gordon — bringing the number of children to seven. For several years, Joseph worked for the Northern Pacific Railroad in Missoula, polishing steam engines and doing the janitorial work. He stayed in a small house in Missoula, but the family continued to live in Grantsdale.

Joseph retired from the railroad sometime in the 1930's, probably when he reached age 60. He was 17 years older than his wife, so several of the children were still living at home when he retired. All of his children and grandchildren remember him as a kindly presence in the home, and looked up to him for guidance in many of their affairs. He raised a big garden in the summer, but in the winter he spent a lot of time knitting socks and listening to the radio. He also enjoyed making quilts. He never quite learned to turn the heels in the socks, so Anna had to do that for him.

Although some of the children moved away from the Bitterroot after their marriages, all of them except Lola eventually returned and lived out their lives in the Grantsdale area. Most of the grandchildren were raised in the area and attended the old three room Grantsdale school.

Joseph Richard Summers died in Grantsdale on October 23, 1953. He was 79 years old. Anna Louise Payne Summers lived until February 15, 1960, dying at the age of 69.

SUTHERLAND FAMILY

Edward Carlyn Sutherland was born October 8, 1866, in Hooverville, Indiana. Known as "E.C.", he had worked as a tool sharpener and barber in Idaho, and was a brakeman on the railroad in Minnesota. He married Louise Hoblitt on July 14, 1897. He was a charming, loud fellow who chewed and had a bad temper. Louise was a deeply religious person and devoted to her family. They came to Stevensville, Montana, in 1903, from Monticello, Minnesota, as her brothers, Alvin Bailey Hoblitt and Carl Hoblitt and her uncle, Tom Bailey, were already living in the Bitterroot.

On March 13, 1908, E.C. was involved in a shooting with Charles Vansickle on a public road in front of the Sutherland home, at 8:30 AM. A bitter feeling had existed between the two men and Vansickle had made threats to the neighbors against E.C., plus one day had chased him into town. On this morning Vansickle had a shotgun and E.C. had a revolver. Vansickle opened the gate that either E.C. had closed or the wind had blown shut. As Vansickle came on the road he began firing his shotgun and E.C. hid behind a post. When Vansickle emptied his gun, E.C. shot and the bullet hit Vansickle two inches above the breastbone and one inch to the right of his lung. Vansickle was in the hospital for over a week, but recovered from his wound. Both men were severely punished for losing their tempers. E.C. and Louise sold the farm and moved to Days Creek, Oregon.

In 1917, E.C., Louise and family arrived at Daniel Hoblitt's in Corvallis, Montana then bought the farm which is now located at 310 Popham Lane.

E.C. raised pigs, chickens and had about 16 milk cows. He broke workhorses then sold the horses so he was always breaking in a team of horses. He raised hay and grain for the animals and a big garden for the family. Meat was provided by hunting deer, elk, pheasants, and by fishing in the river. He smoked hams and had beehives. Louise canned the produce and cooked the meals plus sewed the clothes.

In 1921 Louise did not survive an operation in Seattle which left the family without a mother. Her body was brought back to Corvallis by train and she was buried at the Corvallis cemetery.

E.C. applied for and got the job of ditch rider for the Corvallis Canal and Water Company in 1921. He married Flora Binkerd in 1932. She died in 1939 and E.C. died in 1940.

Surviving children were Bill, Margaret Hall, Ruth Smyth, Marie Huls, Joe and Dan Sutherland. Dan lived on E.C.'s farm until his death and Dan's son Kit lives on the land at this time.

CHILDREN AND THEIR FAMILIES

Bill Sutherland: Bill married Ruth Jane Waddell and they lived at Bellingham, WA. He worked at the chain factory and enjoyed raising strawberries on his farm. His children were John, Molliann, Janet and David.

Margaret Sutherland Hall: Graduated from Corvallis High School in 1918 and married Dr. John Hall, a dentist. They returned to the Corvallis Willow Creek area in 1962 to ranch.

Ruth Sutherland Smyth: Graduated from Corvallis High School in 1920 and married Emmett Smyth. See the Smyth history.

Marie Sutherland Huls: She graduated from Corvallis High School in 1921 and married Spencer Huls. See the Huls history.

Joseph Sutherland: Joe married Ruby Tubbs on April 20, 1929. The daughter of Andrew Peter and Emma Nelson Tubbs, Ruby was born on December 27, 1912, and had attended school in Seattle, WA. Joe and Ruby bought the farm which is located now at 1730 Sutherland Road. They hired Dan Morris, who had an iron wheeled tractor, to plow the fields. They piled the sagebrush in piles and burned it. Water was hauled from a spring. Lumber for the barn came from the old flume being torn down by the Bitter Root Irrigation Company. Joe purchased a big white horse for $100.00 from his uncle in Florence, and led it all the way home to the farm, while Ruby drove the 1929 Chevrolet car. A black horse was added to make a team. Next came a cow, and some chickens. **Two daughters, Donna Lou** born March 19, 1933, **and Paula Jo**, born May 20, 1934, followed. Ruby carried water from the spring and washed clothes by hand, until Joe and Roy Mosio dug a trench and got a Ram pump to bring water into the house. Cooking for 6 men during the haying season, and 18 men during the threshing season, was common for Ruby. Guy Hall had the threshing machine and hired out to all the neighbors. Donna and Paula stood on apple boxes to help do the dishes. Ruby canned all the vegetables and fruits that Joe grew in the garden. Joe built a straw barn for the cows and he and Ruby milked 23 cows by hand, and sold the cream as a cash crop. **Another daughter, Patsy Anne** was born July 25, 1938. During the World War II years Joe bought a tractor, combine and big truck to haul the grain. Joe and Ruby loved picnics, so often Ruby would kill and fry some chickens and the family would go to a designated spot on the Bitter Root River with Otis and Vergie Talbot's family and the Guy Hall family. The ladies brought potluck food and Otis would tell stories or there would be a singing session. One time, Otis volunteered to bring the meat. After everyone ate the meat and noodles he announced that "It was cooked porcupine!" That made everyone gag!

Donna, Paula, and Patsy rode the school bus driven by Joe's brother, Dan. Joe's sister Ruth's husband, Emmett Smyth cut their hair, and Joe's sister Margaret's husband, Dr. John Hall, did their dental work.

In their later years, Joe and Ruby enjoyed the grandchildren; camping, birdwatching, and Ruby loved making driftwood arrangements. Ruby always had a big holiday dinner on Thanksgiving and Christmas for all the family. On April 20, 1979, Joe and Ruby celebrated their 50th wedding anniversary in Corvallis with family and friends, and in 1989, their 60th anniversary. Ruby died on August 7, 1989, and is buried in the Corvallis Cemetery. Joe missed her so much and found it hard to be happy. He passed away on March 14, 1992, and is buried next to Ruby in the Corvallis Cemetery.

Daniel Sutherland: Graduated from Corvallis High School in 1933. He married Dorothy Hefner and they had children Nicholas, Brian, Jonathan, Ladd, Pamela, Christopher (Kit) and Stephen. Dan was ditch rider for the Surprise Ditch and was school bus contractor and driver for the Corvallis school. Dan and Dorothy raised registered black lab dogs. He also drove milk tanker for Western Dairylines for 15 years, retiring in 1976. He is remembered for the excellent produce he raised and sold at his farm on Popham Lane. Dan died November 13, 1988, and is buried in the Corvallis Cemetery.

CHARLIE AND EMMA SWANSON

C. J. "Charlie" Swanson first came to the Bitter Root Valley in 1908, during the "apple orchard boom". "It was the orchard business that brought me here," he said in later years. He liked the Valley so well, he went back to Oregon, Illinois, and made plans to move his family to Montana.

Karl Johan Svensson (Charlie) was born in 1880, in Norra Sandsjo, Jonkoping, Sweden. When he was about 21 years old, he worked for the factory at Bodafors, Sweden. They sold a boatload of furniture to Germany. He and another man escorted the load to a seaport by rail, and then by boat, to Hamburg, Germany. The furniture was all crated. It took time to sell all the furniture, but Charlie stayed until it was all sold. He used oxen to pull the loaded carts to deliver the furniture to the owners.

In the fall of 1903, he and a friend immigrated to America on the ship called "Oscar II". He had a good job at the Rockford Union Furniture Company in Rockford, Illinois, before he arrived, because of his experience in Sweden. Rockford was a Swedish town and he had many good friends there. The factory advertised itself as "manufacturers of high and medium grade dining and living room furniture". He worked at the factory for more than a year, then took a sightseeing boat down the river to Oregon, Illinois. He liked it there and got a job in the Wurlitzer Piano factory, working on a lathe. It was while working in the piano factory that he met Emma.

Emma Kristina Jonasdotter was born in Vaxjo, Smaland, Sweden, in 1885. She was the middle of five children of Frans and Maria Jonasson. Her father was a Forester for the Lutheran Church.

In 1901, Emma immigrated to America with her brother, Carl. Emma was "sweet sixteen" and her brother, Carl, was twenty-one when they crossed the Atlantic. It took them ten days and cost $52.00. On the morning of March 27th, 1901, they sighted the Statue of Liberty on Bedloe's Island, and then landed at Ellis Island. Emma went directly to her aunt's homes, first to Dekalb and then to Oregon, Illinois. Her Aunt Johanna insisted that she go to private teachers' school in Oregon, which she did for six weeks. It was mainly a brush-up course on subjects that she had taken in Sweden. Circumstances at that time were such, that she went to work in a general store, first, as a sales person, and then, as the bookkeeper. She kept this job for four years, and was earning $35.00 a month, working eleven and twelve hours a day. In 1905, Charlie applied and was accepted as one of the boarders at her Aunt Johanna's home. They became acquainted and liked each other immediately. They began to attend the same church, going together. Two years later, in March of 1907, they were married. In May of 1908, their first child, a daughter Helen Elizabeth, was born.

Charlie continued to work at the piano factory, but his health was declining. It was attributed to a bout with pneumonia in Sweden just before he came to America, and the dust created by the lathe in the piano factory. He was very pale, thin and sickly. His doctors told him that he should get out of the piano factory, and get some good, clean, fresh air. There was literature expounding the wealth that was there for the taking in Western Montana, raising fruit — including apples. He liked the sound of the promotion and he came west to check it out. His health immediately improved.

I bought twenty acres from the Bitter Root Valley Irrigation Company at $100.00 an acre, in March of 1909," continues Charlie. "It was the orchard business that brought me here. It was something I knew. I had some experience with orcharding in Sweden. I picked this land to buy because of the slope of the hill. I felt I could avoid some freezing that the other orchards would have."

His reasoning was sound, since the third and fourth generations of Charlie and Emma's family still live on the parcel that he bought in 1909. He and Peter Erickson built a house, 24 ft by 24 ft, with studs showing where there could someday be four rooms. After spending six months here making his improvements and planting half of the apple trees, he went back to Illinois. He purchased the equipment he would need and returned with a boxcar containing livestock, machinery, and household goods. It was a momentous decision, leaving a good job in a town they loved and all their wonderful friends, to come west.

Swanson house built by Charlie Swanson in 1910-11.

On the 21st of April 1910, Emma and the baby arrived at the depot in Victor, Montana. Charlie had not received the letter announcing their arrival, so there was no one there to greet them. Emma, with the help of the stationmaster, hired a livery wagon to take them to their land. There were no roads or bridges, so a mile south of Victor, they took off across country, fording the river, up and down gullies, bouncing along in the dust through sagebrush and dry grass. Finally, the driver could go no farther as he had come to a gully deeper than the rest, with a big wash in the bottom. He helped Emma and the baby get to the house, and Charlie.

The first year, Charlie wanted to plant some grain for feed for their livestock. With their savings gone, Charlie went to John Franklin Wood, a prominent farmer in Corvallis, to procure some seed. He asked John Wood to trust him with the seed and pledged his gun for security. He got the seed, but the next fall there was still no money. True to his word, he sold one of his two guns, and paid John Wood what was owed him. Charlie was a man of his word, as to sell a gun in those days was a sacrifice, but "a promise is a promise".

Gradually, I expanded and extended my operations until I became a full-fledged general farmer. With profits from my farm work, I have increased my holdings until today the twenty-acre original farm of 1909, has grown to include 400 acres, all under the Bitter Root Irrigation District system.

The Swansons maintained a prize apple orchard and produced excellent crops over the years. Apple orchards were in their heyday in the Bitter Root during this time. The original orchard that Charlie planted is still producing apples almost a hundred years later. Gradually Charlie and Emma expanded their efforts and diversified their crops. With additional land, they turned to raising Hereford cattle.

Three more children were born to the Swansons on their farm. They were Annette Mathilda in 1910, Mable Marie in 1916, and Carl John in 1920. They all grew up and graduated from Corvallis High School and on to college. Two daughters became teachers and one daughter became a nurse. Carl took over the family farm. Their spouses were from local prominent pioneer families. They all continue to live in close proximity to the Swanson Orchards with the exception of Annette who died in 1937.

Slowly they got their start. They never went in debt for a purchase; if they didn't have the money, they didn't buy it. That was the philosophy that lasted them all their lives. They never returned to Sweden, but kept in contact with their relatives and friends in Illinois and Sweden. Theirs was a frugal life, but a good one.

Helen married Morris Strange and their children, Georgiann Dayton and Bill Strange, live in the Stevensville area. **Mable** married Clarence Popham and they have four children; Joanne Just, Dianne Huhtanen, Don and Bob Popham. All except Joanne continue to live and work in the Bitter Root Valley. **Carl** married Lois Brooks and their two children; James and Charlie Swanson live close by, with Charlie and his family operating the apple business. Lois passed away in 1983, of acute leukemia, and in 1985, Carl married Carma Hunter.

Emma died in 1971, at the age of 86. Charlie lived another six years, and he was almost 97 when he died. They are both buried in the Corvallis Cemetery, close to the land that brought them so far together.

THE TALBOT AND MOORE FAMILIES

by Robert W. Talbot, March of 1994

Joseph R. Talbot was born in 1864, at Lisle, New York. His family lived in Iowa and Wisconsin during his younger years. He left home in 1879, at age 14, to become a cowhand on a large ranch in Eastern Montana. He spent several years mining and prospecting and at one time was employed as a meat hunter (wild game) to feed the construction crews on the Canadian Pacific Railroad. When he left that job, he came back into Montana from Medicine Hat, Alberta, Canada. For a time, he and a partner had a meat market in Great Falls, Montana. They conducted their business out of a tent

Charles James Moore and Letha Cable Moore, father and mother of Flora Moore Talbot.

selling mostly wild game. His partner managed the store, and he did the hunting.

Mr. Talbot came to the Bitterroot Valley for the first time in 1886. He mined and prospected until 1891, when he married Flora S. Moore. She was the daughter of Charles J. Moore, a former soldier in the United States Army. Charles J. Moore had served a tour of duty in Montana in 1863, and thinking it was one of the most beautiful places in the world, he returned to his home in Missouri, and brought his family back to the Bitterroot. The Moore family arrived in the Bitterroot in about 1885 or 1886. Mr. Moore acquired a ranch called the Old Sunny Side Ranch, located west of Woodside. In addition to working the ranch, Mr. Moore taught school (including the old Fair Play School), held prayer meetings, taught voice lessons, and gave instruction on several musical instruments. His son, A. M. Moore, had a photography shop in Hamilton (which later became the old Haggerman Studio). This is where Flora Moore and Joseph R. Talbot met.

They were married in 1891, and raised their family on a ranch they acquired through a homestead pre-exemption. The ranch was located northwest of Woodside, on the old Shiffman Creek Road. They had one daughter and eight sons. The children attended the old Fair Play School, on Mill Creek road, walking across country from their home on Schiffman Creek road. Their daughter, May Talbot Luderman, (who lives in Greybull, WY and celebrated her 101st birthday in November of 1993) writes that it was hard to hold her own with all those brothers running the foothills of Mill, Schiffman, and Fred Burr Creeks. My father, Otis, said that when he was a boy they killed a lot of game for food. Deer were plentiful and when someone made a kill, it was shared with the neighbors. They also ate a lot of rabbit, grouse, and fish. They killed a bear whenever they could for the lard they rendered from it. Bear lard was considered far superior to other fats for making pastry, and frying donuts.

One summer when brothers David and Charles Talbot were twelve and thirteen years old, they packed a little food, a couple of blankets, some fishline and hooks, and told their Mother they were going to the head of Mill Creek and cross over and come back down Schiffman Creek and they would be home the following day. However, when they got to the head of Mill creek, they didn't realize that Schiffman Creek did not head up that far west. So, instead of crossing over into the Schiffman Creek drainage, they crossed over into the Bitterroot-Selway Wilderness Area. They went merrily on their way thinking that as they were going downhill, they would soon come out. When it got dark the second night, they figured that Fred Burr Canyon was longer than they had thought. They had long since eaten all their food, so the next morning, they caught some fish, using berries for bait, and roasted them over a fire. They didn't much like the fish without salt, but they ate them anyway. Little did they know that unsalted fish and berries would be their

Top row, Flora Moore Talbot, Joseph R. Talbot, Albert Moore (early Hamilton photographer), Ada Moore Burde, Myrtle Moore McDaniel. Second row, Myrtle's son, Charles James Moore, and her other son.

diet for several more days! They did not realize that they were in Idaho until they came to a stream larger than the one they were following and saw fish "Longer than their arms!" After some discussion, they decided that the fish were Salmon, and they had crossed the Divide, and were indeed, in Idaho! The first thing they did was to climb to the top of the highest mountain around, to see where they were. But, when they got to the top, all they saw were higher mountains! It had been cloudy most of the time since they had left home, but the next morning they watched the sun come up and they concluded that the Bitterroot Valley lay in the same direction. They finally crossed back over the Divide and came down Bear Creek several days after they had left on their over-night adventure. One of them had a dime in his pocket, so they stopped at the first cabin they saw at the mouth of Bear Creek and knocked at the door and asked the man (identity unknown) who lived there if they could buy ten cents worth of potatoes. The man asked, "Where have you boys been to be so hungry?" And when they told him their story, he filled them up with ham, eggs, and potatoes! My Uncle Charlie told me sixty years later that it was the best meal he had ever eaten! The man then drove them to Woodside with his horse and buggy, and from that point it was only another two or three miles home. When their father was asked why he never reported them missing, he said "The boys know the mountains and I knew they would be back. It was a good experience for them".

Joseph R. Talbot died in 1925. His wife, Flora Moore Talbot, died in 1932.

Of the nine children born to them, two survive at the time of this writing, May Talbot Luderman, of Greybull, WY, born November 12, 1892, and David C. Talbot of Madison, WI, born February 18, 1900. (Look for the Luderman story, also in this edition).

The other children were: Otis D. Talbot (my Father), born June 23, 1894, and died January 14, 1981, Elmer K. Talbot, born January 31, 1896, and died July 19, 1961, Joseph R. Talbot, born February 12, 1898, died January 8, 1919, Charles C. Talbot, born November 30, 1901, died March 6, 1977, Curtis O. Talbot, born January 25, 1904, died in 1983, Ralph O., born June 2, 1906, died May 3, 1909, and Emmett L., born October 2, 1909, and died August 28, 1949.

THE OTIS TALBOT FAMILY

My father, Otis D. Talbot, started school at Corvallis in 1899, and continued at the old Fair Play School. He told me that when he was a kid the going wage for hoeing and weeding vegetables and general farm work was seventy five cents a day for a ten hour day. "You could always get a job", he said, "because in those years a lot of fruit and vegetables were shipped on the railroad out of Woodside". He also had stories to tell about being a flunky for "Terrible Tom", the logging crew cook!

Otis married Virginia Bagley in 1917. They had five children: Florence Talbot Eddy, Helen Talbot Anderson, Kenneth G. Talbot (deceased), Jack L. Talbot, and Robert W. Talbot (me). They raised their family on a farm one and one half miles north of Corvallis, on the Eastside Highway.

My father used to fish, for the market, in the Bitterroot River. I have his old ledger which states that the most whitefish he caught in one day (on a line with one hook) was 338! He shipped out 5,400 pounds one winter at twelve to eighteen cents a pound. The price per pound was determined by the shipment destination. For ten years, he contracted to furnish 210 tons of cabbage to the Stevensville Cannery for $10.00 per ton delivered. That's a lot of plants to set by hand!

After market fishing was closed, the winters were spent cutting cottonwood in the river bottom. My father had a power drag saw and would cut about 250 cords of wood every winter, and after it was split with a double bitted axe, it sold for $4.00 a cord on the ground, or $5.00 a cord delivered. According to his ledger, he wore out two drag saws, and sold 2,600 cords of wood!

THE FAMILY OF ED TEW

by Lloydeen Raymond Arnold

Five sons of Ole Gulbrandson and his wife, Maret, immigrated to America from Norway (the gaard or form name TUVE or TUFF that had been brought by their father. Some of Ole's sons retained the gaard name but others changed to Tew, and Vesle Ole became Rev. Ole Olsen.)

There are at least three farms name TUV or TUVE in Vestre Slidre, in Valdres, an area about twelve miles NW from Fagernes. Today's maps also show a village named TUV about 25 miles SW from the old TUVE gaard and some four miles west of Hemsedal.

Ole Gulbrandson married Marit Fodness in 1807 in Norway. They had two sons, Erik Olson Tuff in 1831 in Norway. Ole remarried and had another son, Irwin, in 1852. Eric had four children and Irwin had four children. Ed Tew was the second born of the second family. The second family came from Norway to Minnesota when Ed Tew was in his teens. He came from Minnesota to Corvallis in the early 1900's. That is when he married Estelle Barbara Ward and they homesteaded in the Dominic area. They moved from the Homestead east of Corvallis to Hamilton in the early 1940s where they farmed again on River Road until ill health forced them to sell and move to a nursing home. Ed Tew passed away in December, 1956; Estelle passed away in January, 1957. They are buried in the Corvallis cemetery at Corvallis, Montana.

Ed and Estelle had seven children while living east of Corvallis. Their names were Addie, Louise, Clara, Alice, Alma, Edward Jr., and Barbara.

There are three survivors from Ed and Estelle Tew's family — Ed in Windsor, California and Alma and Alice in Hamilton at a local nursing home.

JOHN STEVENS TREECE

by Beulah Treece Wutzke

John Stevens Treece was born at Bridgeport, Texas, on November 13, 1859, and arrived at Stevensville, Montana, on August 14, 1884. He came to Montana as a hunter for a covered wagon train. Only Treece and his cousin, Mose Anderson, and family arrived here as the others dropped out in Colorado and Wyoming.

At that time, Stevensville consisted of a small store with a Post Office owned by the Missoula Mercantile, the Mission, a store owned by Amos and George Buck, and a blacksmith shop. After they rested a day, they continued up the valley and spent the winter on the old Jack Sheperd place, which is just north of Tucker Road at Eastside Highway. In the spring of 1886, Treece went to the Big Hole where he supervised the building of a ditch for the old Morman Mining Company. He returned to the valley and married Grazilda Frances Alford, who had come here to keep house for her brother, William Alford. She was born at Rogersville, Missouri, on March 24, 1859. Frances and John were married at the John F. Wood ranch which is 5 1/2 miles north of Corvallis. Mrs. Wood was a sister of Frances. They had several sisters in the valley, and the brother, William.

Mr. Treece was active in all matters of a public nature. He was a life-long Democrat, and was elected to the office of Ravalli County Commissioner in 1906, to serve the first term of any man in Ravalli County after the tenure of commissioner was increased from four to six years. He also served as Deputy Assessor on several occasions, and as Chairman of the Ravalli County Democratic Central Committee. He organized the first baseball team in Ravalli County about 1885. George and William Baggs of Stevensville and Homer Babbitt of Victor were members of that team. Mr. Treece served on school board, election boards, and served as a Deputy Sheriff as needed. He was a longtime member of the Masonic fraternity, and a past Master of Victor Lodge # 42.

There were six sons and three daughters in this family. All were born in the Valley, at various homes.

Arthur, the oldest, was born when they lived on what was later known as "the Albert Wood Ranch". He married Ethel Smith Tyson, who had a son, and they had one son, Lester. Arthur would be remembered as running a road grader for the county for many years.

Henry, the second son, was born when they lived east of Stevensville. He served in France in World War I, and after his return to the Valley, he married Orpha Adams, a school teacher. They raised one son and one daughter.

John, also born east of Stevensville, worked for the ACM Company in the woods and also in the mill at Bonner, until retiring. He married Beatrice Atherton, and they had a son and a daughter. His last wife was Sadie Spencer.

Laud was also born east of Stevensville. He worked for the City of Missoula for many years. He drove a street-car and much later was elected City Street Commissioner. He was married to Pearl Collins and they had a daughter and a son. After she died, he married Cora Cook Emerson, and lived in Stevensville until he died.

Bland, was born on the Etna Ranch, south of Stevensville. He worked many years for the Stevensville Creamery and later became a Certified Public Accountant, keeping books for several different businesses. He also did income taxes in his home office. He was married to Blanch Jones Albee, who had two children.

Charles (Dick) was born on the "old John Wood place" on Burnt Fork. He married Zola Smith and ranched on the home place on Tucker

Crossing and Eastside Highway for most of his life. They were parents of three children: Henry married Mary Lou Fleishmann and together they raised five children in the Valley. Katherine was first married to M. O. Haugen, later married to Arthur Slocum, and raised three girls in the Missoula area. Buelah married Daly Loesch and lived in California many years. After retiring, they returned to the Bitter Root where he died. Later, she married Edgar Wutzke.

Della May was born on the 160 acre homestead on what is known as "Treece Gulch", south and east of Stevensville. She married Lloyd Dobbins and they raised one daughter. They lived mostly in the Big Hole and Deer Lodge.

Elizabeth Anne was born on Treece Gulch, and died about six months later of chicken pox.

In the spring of 1905, John and Frances Treece bought the 120 acres just 41/2 miles north of Corvallis, and lived there until their deaths.

TUCKER FAMILY

Twin brothers, Edward Martin Tucker and William Perry Tucker were born on November 8, 1877, in Joplin, Missouri. They were the children of John Tucker and Matilda Evaline Franks Tucker. John died when the boys were just two years of age. When the boys were seven years old, in 1884, their mother and grandmother brought them to the Bitter Root Valley and they located on land in the Tucker Crossing area.

Both boys attended school at the old Fairplay School on the westside, and at the Corvallis School. Edward Martin then attended and graduated from the University of Montana in Missoula, and subsequently from the University of Virginia Law School at Charlotteville, Virginia. He passed the Montana bar examination and began the practice of law in Hamilton. Along with his law practice, he farmed extensively with his twin brother, William Perry, on a 640-acre ranch south of Victor near Tucker Crossing. William's son, Ferd, and his family later owned this ranch.

William was active throughout the years in most civic affairs of the city and county as well as taking part in numerous legal battles. He was a leader in western Montana Townsend Recovery and Pension Plan, and in the Ravalli County Taxpayers League. He was an ardent Democrat and several times ran for the legislature and for County Attorney, as his party's nominee. He was elected Ravalli County Attorney in 1926, defeating George H. Boldt. He served as the City Attorney in Hamilton for a number of years. For 17 years, he was secretary of the Hamilton National Farm Loan Association. Brother Edward was also a staunch Democrat.

Edwin Martin Tucker wed Lucy H. Taylor who had come to the valley, as a child, from her native Illinois. Her father, Joseph Noah Taylor, operated a feed store in Hamilton. Edwin and Lucy made their home at 807 South Third Street, in the former Endley-Hoffman residence, which was built by Frank Lloyd Wright. They had three children; Eleanor (Mrs. Robert Tibbs) of Hamilton, Joseph Martin Tucker of Renton, Washington, and John Randolph Tucker of Corvallis, Oregon. Edward Martin Tucker died in Hamilton on August 6, 1967.

William married Sarah Johnson and they had a son named Ferd W. Tucker. Ferd attended schools in Victor and Missoula. He graduated from Missoula High School and attended the University of Montana in Missoula. He was Postmaster at Victor for several years and engaged in both farming and ranching. He married June Gibson.

THE JOHN AND EMMA EASTMAN VALLANCE FAMILY

by Helen Vallance Haigh and May Valance

The Sarah and Roger Eastman family arrived in America in 1638, from England, and were the first settlers in Salisbury, Massachusetts. The story handed down by word of mouth of the Vallance family's trip to America is very interesting! The family of John were French Huguenot in Vallance, France. Because of the persecution of the French Huguenots, the Johns were afraid of being killed and fled to England. The name then changed to John de Vallance. John's sister, Lucy, married a Language, in London, who was a very rich man. John worked on his farm, stole his pigs, and kept the money for the family. Language was going to have John de Vallance hung, so, good at fleeing, John stowed away on a ship to America.

John Bernard Vallance was born to Frederick John and Persus Jane Irish in Ligonier, Indiana, in 1862. The family moved to Coral, MI, where young John learned the art of wagon making. The family then moved to Breckenridge, MN, then on to Wahpeton, ND, where the family had a farm among the Sioux and Cheyennes. Young John learned to speak the Sioux language, keeping the family safe there and on the covered wagon trip to Magda, KS, in 1877. They helped build the first school in Magda. The family farmed and John was Magda Postmaster for several years, until they moved to Montana in 1910.

Emma and Ella, twins, were born to Ofezra and Emmaline Weeks Eastman in Lazonia, NH in 1862. The family moved to Emporia, KS, where **Emma married John Bernard Vallance in 1884.** John, in those days, was a "handsome young blade" playing his fiddle for all the country dances. One night, returning from a dance, he was caught by a tornado as he was driving his horse and wagon down a barren road. His horse and wagon and the contents were swept away, but, John was left safe! He knew this was a calling from the Lord, and from that day on, he would strive to serve the Lord. He became ordained as a Presbyterian elder in 1888, and became a Bible teacher in every church he attended throughout his life. **Emma and John had seven children before moving to Montana.**

In the summer of 1909, John and his son, Fred, came to check out the Bitter Root. They bought five acres on the north corner of what is now Grantsdale Road and Lincoln Lane. They stayed with the Kligles and Waxelbaums in a little shed behind the house, and proceeded to build the big two-story house that still stands today, just as they built it. They then returned to Kansas where Fred continued his studies at the college in Topeka. The rest of the family moved to the Bitter Root, cows included, on the train.

John was well known for his farming. He planted a small garden of many varieties of apples, cherries, and berries. When Fred returned to the Bitterroot, they leased many acres of land near their home, and became well known for their potatoes, as well as the other vegetables and fruit produce. They had a large potato field up on the flat that was known in those days as "Hungry Hill", and today is known as Bonanza Land, where many homes have sprouted instead of potatoes! John won many honors at fairs, even at the Chicago World's Fair. He many times hired neighborhood women and children to help with harvest and boxing, getting the potatoes ready to send in Glen Thompson's truck to Anaconda and Butte. Sometimes, he filled a whole truck by himself.

John and Emma Vallance home, built in 1909, on the corner of Grantsdale Road and Lincoln Lane.

John and Emma were always very involved in their church. Known in later years by their many friends, as Daddy and Mother Vallance, they hosted many church picnics and very often had Sunday dinners for the pastor and family, and other friends. John believing they should not work on the Sabbath, put lots of work on Emma on Saturdays as well as on Sunday. Sunday dinner, and then visiting in the parlor, were rituals. When you see the parlor today, it is hard to believe that it would hold as many as 20 people. The home on Lincoln Lane is in wonderful condition, thanks to Mr. Dale Jorgensen who restored it, a few years ago, to its original beauty.

Emma took care of the house, and raising the children. Grandchildren still trade her recipes, especially for creamed macaroni and tomato and corn relish.

There are many stories of how strict John was in the discipline of children, purchasing the fabric for all the girls' dresses in brown and black colors. But, there are more stories of holding grandchildren on his knees, and skipping with adolescents, and helping married children who often lived with them while Emma was ill with "dropsy", and later when he was alone. He was a great and helpful neighbor, and had his touring car full of neighbors as he went to church each Sunday. He also served several terms on the Hamilton School Board.

John and Emma had seven children:

Fred married Hazel Shank and they had DeLoss, Lois and Persus Evelyn. Fred was postman in Hamilton for thirty-one years.

Robert married Maud Skelton and they had Dorothy, Florence, and Robert. "Bob" worked in the creamery business in Missoula, making ice cream, for many years until he died at age forty-eight, of a heart attack.

Val was a butcher and had shops in Deer Lodge and Missoula.

Ruth married Claud Waugh and they had Betty Jean and Donald.

Claud worked in the mines in Mullan, ID, for many years, and then they moved to Spokane where he worked as a handy man until his death. "Waugh Gulch" in the south Bitterroot is named for Claud's father, who died very young. His mother then married Than Wilkerson, who raised Claud and his sisters. Than was the first U. S. Forest Service Ranger, working at Alta, the first U. S. Forest Service Ranger Station.

Mildred married Jewel Harris and they had Bill, Bonnie, and Elaine. Jewel died young of Tuberculosis. Mildred worked as a secretary in Kansas City, raising the children alone.

Wilbur (Bill) married **May Pierson Dull and** raised her son, Don Dull, and their three girls, Sharen, Phyllis, and Judy. Bill served in France during WWI, at age 16, and returned to graduate from Hamilton High School with his class of 1920. He farmed with his father until he married, at age 35, and then he bought property on Grant Lane and dairy farmed, while May taught school.

Kenneth (Cub) married **Helen Pierson** and they had Gene, Bob, Holly, and Shirley. Cub served in the Navy, on the Arizona, after graduating from high school. After marriage to Helen, he worked in creameries in Three Mile, Missoula, and Hamilton. They purchased Wells Creamery in Hamilton, and ran it as "Sno Capped Dairies" for many years. They spent many years ranching in-between.

Emma, a much loved, very gentle and kind lady, died at age seventy-eight. **John**, much revered by the community, and delighted by his grandchildren, lived on — farming and growing pansies for Emma's grave, until at the age of 85 he sold the farm. At age 89, he went to be with his Lord.

THE MATTHEW VAUGHN FAMILY

by Ina Murphy, wife of grandson—Tom Murphy

In the 1870's and the 1880's, a large number of people came to the Bitter Root Valley. Matthew Vaughn was one of these. He came, liked it here, and stayed. He worked for Marcus Daly and while employed there, helped plant the Carolina Poplars which still stand on the mansion grounds. He was a "master" with a scythe, whether cutting grain with a cradle or at de-mossing the ditches to keep water flowing. He was an expert at sharpening a scythe and kept his own in "A-1" shape. He also sharpened for other people. In his time here, he farmed his own land, as well as that of others.

In 1872, he married a local lady, Patsy. From this union four children were born: Alfred, Myrtle, Lucy, and Harold. They all attended school in Corvallis and also attended the churches here.

They visited family in Missouri and on one of these trips, Alfred met and married Leta. They had one son, Harold Tom. In the 1930's, they returned to Corvallis and Alfred (known as "Al") worked for the Sugar Company and was the ditch rider for the Willow Creek ditch.

Lucy met a man from Iowa, where they lived out their lives with their three children.

Harold went into the military service and when released, came home to Corvallis and started a greenhouse. He died of a heart-attack.

Myrtle met and married Ray Murphy, Leta's brother, in Missouri. They visited twice before coming here to farm on Myrtle's grandparents farm in 1932. By this time, their only son, Tom, was in first grade. They later bought more land and continued to farm. Their son, Tom, graduated from Corvallis High School and then attended Montana State College in Bozeman. He worked for the Rocky Mountain Laboratory in research before entering the U. S. Navy. Upon his return, he too went into agriculture. He had met a college girl, Ina, and they married and had three children, Louise, Shirley, and Don. Louise resides in Spokane, Shirley in Ohio and Don in Stevensville. They all are college graduates and each have two children.

Before Matthew Vaughn's death, at the age of 96, he wrote a history of the Corvallis Canal and Water Company. It is included in these stories.

Matthew Vaughn was a Mason and an Eastern Star. He served as Worthy Patron for Eastern Star for 21 different Worthy Matrons, during which time he was Worthy Patron with his wife, his daughter, and his grandson's wife. He always knew his ritualistic work letter perfect.

At the age of 95, he still watched baseball games on television. Hard work apparently didn't hurt him.

WILLIAM H. WADDELL FAMILY

William Henry Waddell, the third child of Sarah Ann Lowe Waddell and Alfred Waddell, was born in Sagging County, Illinois on January 26, 1863. The family moved from Illinois to Kansas, and from there William Henry came west in 1881. He worked as a teamster in the vicinity of Helena and Bannock before he came to the Bitter Root. In 1883, he met Mary Bell Ward, and they were married on December 21, 1888, by the Reverend William Lewis.

William Henry Waddell worked on the building of the "old Red Bridge" that crossed the river at the west end of Adirondac. The names of the men who worked on the bridge were inscribed on the under side of the structure, including William Henry's. William and Mary continued to live in the valley until 1892, when they moved to Idaho where Mr. Waddell worked in the mines at Murray for about 15 years. They then returned to the Bitter Root, and resided on the west side until William Henry's death in 1913. Mary and the family continued to live in Hamilton after his death.

Mary and the family moved to their home at 707 North Third. While living there, Mary Bell Waddell, who had Cevero Von Boyer for a neighbor, and who, every Fourth of July curled his long white hair and put red, white, and blue ribbons in it. Grandpa Boyer, as he was known to everyone, was a veteran of the Civil War. Grandpa Boyer was Mrs. Vern Elmore's Grandfather on her Mother's side of the family.

William and Mary had five children: Olive, Charles, Delbert, Hazel, and Thelma Ruth.

Olive Adeline was born in Hamilton on September 7, 1889. Olive graduated from college at Cheney, Washington, with a degree in teaching. She spent her life in the teaching profession mostly in the valley. She taught at the Baker Creek School, and also at Hamilton, Dominic, Ward, and Charlos Heights, and for many years in Darby. She lived with her mother, Mary, at 707 N. 3rd St. until her mother's death, and continued living in

Delbert Waddell at winter camp with U.S. Forest Service.

their home until her death on March 4, 1972.

Charles married Hettie Millis. They had one son, Robert. They continued to live in the Valley. Charles was the assistant Postmaster up to the time of his death.

Delbert served with the A.E.F., in France, and was a veteran of St. Mihiel and the Chateau Thierry conflicts of World War I. Except for the time he spent in the service, Delbert spent most of his life in the valley, working for the Forest Service.

Hazel became a teacher, and also taught in the valley. Her teaching mostly was at the Sleeping Child School. Hazel married Leo McMahon. With good Irish humor, his friends and family changed the letters of his name around and called him "Ole" because he was so blonde and fair complected. Their family consisted of two boys, Leo Joseph (Pat), and Charles Francis (Chuck). Dr. Pat McMahon and his wife, Jan, and daughter Shauna moved to Arizona where Dr. McMahon did much research on cancer before his untimely death. Dr. Charles McMahon and wife Mary Ann, live in Lander, Wyoming, where they have a medical practice in neurosurgery.

Ruth, Mary Bell and William's youngest daughter, married Earl Philips, son of Jesse Edwin Philips and Edith Hoover Philips who although they ranched in the Glasgow area spent the winters at their home in Hamilton. The Philips son, Ed, at one time owned the Trail Garage on North second. Their son, John, was at one time the police chief and fire chief. Earl and Ruth moved to Anaconda where Earl worked for the Intermountain Bus Lines. At the time they were rebuilding Pierce Arrow cars into larger units so as to take passengers between Anaconda and Hamilton by way of Skalkaho. Earl and Ruth's son, Earle, rode the buses many times as a youngster under the watchful eye of the driver, Ray Bell, who saw that he arrived in Hamilton to visit his Grandmother Mary Waddell. Earl and Ruth continued to live in Anaconda until Earl's death in 1946, after which Ruth and the youngsters moved to Hamilton, Ruth and daughters, Norma and Carol, and her son Don, lived at 207 N. Fourth Street. Ruth remained in her home until she passed away.

William Henry Waddell had three brothers who also came to the valley. Edwin and Jess Waddell came in the late 1800's, and Charles Waddell in the early 1900's. Edwin and his second wife, Emma Jane Withers Waddell, owned the brick yard at the base of Canyon Creek. Jesse Waddell owned land west of the river on what is now Ricketts Road. Charlie and his wife, Inez Grover Waddell, and her father (Leland Grover) owned the hardware store on Main Street in Hamilton.

CALVIN WALLS FAMILY

by Denise Black Severns in 1997

Calvin Walls was born in Pike County, Ohio, on January 13, 1848. Apparently, four children were born to him and his first wife (name unavailable). The names of these children are: **Saralli Jane** born in 1869, in Waverly, OH, **Janette** born in 1871, **George** born in 1873, and **Mary** born in Morten Town, Putman County, Missouri in 1875.

Then on April 9, 1876, Calvin Walls married Nancy Jane Current. (Nancy was born on July 3, 1860, in Pike County, Ohio). **Children born to Calvin and Nancy were: Melissa** in 1879, **Clara** in 1880, **Electa** in 1877, **Wesley** on March 26, 1883, at Victor, MT, and **Earl** in 1890, probably at Victor, MT.

Saralli Jane Walls had moved with her parents to Virginia City by covered wagon in 1878, at the age of nine years. In April of 1882, the family moved to Victor, Montana. She married **B. Sig Chaffin** May 12, 1889. They had four children: **Geneve, Lloyd, Dean and Helen**. Dying at the young age of 38, Saralli Jane's funeral on January 7, 1907, was held at the Sig Chaffin family residence on the Bitter Root Stock Farm. Her sister, Janette had lived in Hamilton for a time, and was a friend of Jeanette Rankin. Her brother George was living in California at the time of Rilla's death, as were her parents. Her sister, Mary, lived in Stevensville and had married Louis May. They had two children, Mildred May Griffin and George May.

Wesley William Walls moved from Victor, MT, to California about 1900. At a young age, perhaps 15, he came back to the valley and lived with his half-sister, Rilla, and her husband, Sig Chaffin. He married **Mattie Smithey in** 1908, in Hamilton, and **Geneve Electa Walls Black** was born on November 26, 1909. They moved to Stevensville where he had a butcher shop and a movie picture house (still pictures or slides). **Mabel Lena** was born October 18, 1911, in Stevensville. About 1914, they moved to Darby where Wesley had a butcher shop. Next, they came back to Corvallis and lived north of the Moses Chaffin place on the Westside of the road. Then, a move to Drummond for six years, where he had a pool hall. In about 1920, Wesley and family moved back to Corvallis and he operated a pool hall that was located in a frame structure on the corner afterward occupied by Dick's Service Station. The pool hall building contained a restaurant as well. This structure caught fire and burned one night. There was talk that the fire was intentionally set, as another pool hall also burned about the same time.

Wesley opened a grocery store in the space below the old Masonic Hall, but that didn't last long as the farmers couldn't pay cash, so he moved back to Hamilton to barber. He moved to Missoula in about 1935, and became associated with the late Robert (Mutt) Hay and others in the tombstone business. He was a good carpenter, and had several rentals which kept him busy. Wesley built the house that Electa Walls Black lived in as a bride. It was just to the east of the present Quentin Brown Elementary School.

After Mattie passed away in 1931, Mable and her first husband, Lyle Lesburg, stayed with her dad at the little house across from the Bill Severns place in Corvallis until Wesley married Martha Hayes who had two children. They were later divorced. Wesley William Walls passed away on March 15, 1962.

"I remember going with Grampa and Martha to sell monuments and learning to drink coffee with cream and sugar. They would take a lunch and we would picnic along the way. Also, it seems they would come up the Bitter Root every Memorial Day to have dinner with us, and to decorate the graves of family in the Hamilton Riverview Cemetery. Then, we would always go to Missoula for Thanksgiving and dinner at their house. I especially remember the shrimp cocktail, among the other goodies. They lived at 1538 Sherwood which had a steep lawn reaching down to the street. It seems my brother, Jim, and I would roll down it! What fun! I also remember the "blackouts" in Missoula during World War II. "

Geneve Electa Walls, her sister, and her parents, lived with Sig Chaffin and his young family after Rilla (Sig's wife) died. They all lived on the old Fierce place that is 1½ miles north of Corvallis. During this period, she was called Geneve, but Sig's daughter was also Geneve — and there was confusion, so, everyone began calling her Electa. Electa started school in Hamilton because it was too far to walk to Corvallis School, and lived with her Aunt Nell (Smithey) and Uncle Dewey Reimel and attended Washington School with a Miss Healy as her teacher. Electa's parents and family then moved to Drummond, making the move by train. After six years, they moved back to Hamilton, and Electa finished the 5th grade there. They bought a home in Corvallis, across from Bill Severns. By the time Electa was a senior in high school, the family moved again, so Electa stayed with the Marti family and graduated from Corvallis. Following high school, she went to Normal School at Dillon, MT, and graduated from there. She also attended Nursing School in Missoula for a short time.

Electa's first teaching job was at Beavertail School in Ravalli County, near the Fox Mill in the West Fork. This school had all eight grades. The Jim Brickley family housed her. Evelyn Adams Steinmetz was the other teacher. They each had 9 or 10 students. Electa remembers that Mr. Donica came to school with his two sons, Dave and Ed, and told her, "If there is ever a problem, you just let me know and I will take care of it!" There never was a problem with his boys. Some of the rules in this school were that if a teacher raised one finger it meant for the students to sit in position, hands folded and desk cleared; two fingers raised meant for the student to stand;

and three fingers raised meant for them to march out. Electa also taught for two years in Florence, MT, where she stayed with the Will Gleason family.

On June 4, 1932, Electa Walls and James Black were married at her Aunt Nell's home in Hamilton. The young couple moved into an apartment at the James and Eliza Barr home in Corvallis, and stayed for 1½ years. Then they moved to a pink stucco home which her father had built in Corvallis. This home is just east of the Quentin Brown Elementary School. Their first child, a daughter they named **Joan Denise,** arrived in 1935, and a son, **James William,** followed in 1937 at the Elmore Hospital in Missoula, MT. In the spring of 1938, they moved to a remodeled home that had formerly been located just west of the Verne Black home, on part of the Daly property, and which had been moved to its present location, on the Eastside highway two miles south of Corvallis. On March 9, 1943, Sandra Nell was born. In 1998, Electa still resides on this property and has stayed busy caring for her family. Electa stayed busy after the children graduated, baby sitting grandchildren, and working with the Crisis center and the Red Cross in Missoula. She has a strong faith in God and loves to help in her church.

James Henderson Black had been born to Nellie and Verne Black on June 20th, 1910, in their home on Black Lane. His mother, who was a teacher, taught him first grade at home because the school was too far away. In second grade, he rode his pony "Pomp" to school in Corvallis. After his graduation from Corvallis High School in 1928, he attended Montana State College in Bozeman. He enjoyed playing baseball on the Corvallis team as a young man and continued to follow the national leagues — with the Chicago Cubs as his favorite. He farmed his parent's land of approximately 200 acres and his own. He grew peas for awhile. There was a pea viner on the top of the hill on the Stiner property. He also grew sugar beets for a short time, but for most of his years he was involved in the growing, sorting, and shipping of potatoes. The shipping was by truck or in railroad boxcars. During World War II, German war prisoners were housed just north of Corvallis on the Bailey farm and Jim hired these men to weed the potatoes.

Jim helped his daughter, Denise (Denny), plant a two thousand plant strawberry patch. He helped his son, Jim, get his own acreage for the growing of potatoes. Jim Black, Sr., passed away on February 28, 1981, at 71 years of age.

W. C. WAN AND FAMILY — J. W. MORRIS FAMILY
Early Corvallis Residents

Among the early residents of the Bitterroot were William Clayton Wan, and his wife, Caroline Tennessee Wan. They came to live here in 1883. Both were natives of Tennessee, but had moved with their families to Lawrence county, MO, where they were married in 1850. While in the service of the Confederated Army, he was wounded and shortly after left home for three years. He had been to Oregon and Washington and apparently had seen the Bitterroot sometime in his travels. His impression of the Valley inspired his son-in-law, George W. Ward, to move from Missouri to Montana in 1881. The Ward story is in Vol. 2 of the Bitterroot Trails.

Mrs. Ward was the eldest of the eight Wan daughters who were all born in Missouri but left that state to become pioneers in Washington, Idaho, and Montana. Six of the daughters are buried in the Corvallis Cemetery along with the father, W. C. Wan, who died in 1905, and the mother, Caroline, who died in 1914. These daughters include: Hannah Ward, 1851-1939, Mary E. Watts (John) 1855-1935, Sarah C. Butler (H. M.) 1860-1941, Flora Morris (J. W.) 1863-1952, Tennessee Flugstad (Pete) 1869-1938, Crate L. Stanley (R. Dean) 1876-1942.

John Watts and wife, Mary (daughter of William Wan).

The other daughters, Martha Hunt and Nancy Nicholson were residents of Idaho and Washington when all eight daughters were present for their mother's funeral in 1914.

The Wan property was a mile south of Corvallis and has been farmed continuously by Wan's descendants, thus Shayne Morris is the fifth generation to live on and farm this property.

Flora Wan and John Wesley Morris were married in Halltown, Missouri, in 1882. Their first child, Glenrose, was born there in 1884. She grew up here and married Henry St. John. She died in 1904, when her twin sons, Morris and Floyd were born.

Flora and J. W. Morris came to Montana in 1885, and were met in Missoula by her brother-in-law, G. W. Ward. The homestead was on the Gird's bench. Wes Morris, George Ward and Ben Matthews built the Ward Ditch which was later sold to Marcus Daly, along with the family homestead.

Mr. Morris purchased a farm north of Corvallis from R. Parkhurst and the youngest son, Ray Morris, was born there in 1900.

John Wesley Morris died on July 19, 1906, and in 1910, his widow moved to the Wan home south of Corvallis to care for her mother. She lived there until her death in 1952.

Ray Morris and Lillian Quast were married in 1922, and were the parents of Mrs. William Bean, Bakersfield, CA, and Jack O. Morris. The Morris family farmed the properties north and south of Corvallis.

Ray Morris died in 1966 and Lillian in 1958. Jack remained on the farm until his death in 1995. He and Astrid Wetzsteon of Sula were married in 1951. Their children are: Lark Hanson of Musselshell, MT, Shayne Morris of Corvallis, MT, Tracy T. Morris, Canyon, TX, and Tenley Whittle of Peachtree City, GA.

THE FAMILY OF GEORGE MARION WARD

In the spring of 1883, George Marion Ward and his wife, Rhoda Ann Cooper Ward and their children ranging in age from three years to nineteen, loaded their belongings they planned to take with them to the Bitterroot Valley in Montana, into a wagon — hitched up the mules — and left Missouri. They traveled part of the way by wagon but along the way George Marion sold the wagon and the mules, and they continued on their journey by immigrant train (believe this meant by railroad) to Deer Lodge where a man was hired to bring the family by wagon to the Gird Creek area, arriving at the home of George Washington Ward, the nephew of George Marion Ward, on May 18th, 1883. From there they rented a log cabin in an area that later became the townsite of Hamilton. The children had a playhouse, under some pine trees, near where the old Ravalli Hotel was later built. Mr. Ward then homesteaded 160 acres about 4 1/2 miles east of the

Bitterroot River, and due East of where they were living. It was on this homestead while working in the grainfield in August of 1884, that George Marion Ward passed away. Rhoda and her children stayed in the valley, and those of school age attended school in the Skalkaho school house, before there was any start of the town of Hamilton. Rhoda sold the homestead to George Washington Ward for $800.00, on the 20th of January, 1888.

George and Rhoda's daughter, Mary Bell, played on the grounds of Fort Skalkaho and she often babysat Bobby Nicols while his mother Mrs. Robert Nicols, sorted the mail in the Skalkaho Post Office. (Mary Bell Ward married William H. Waddell).

Hiram Reese Ward stayed with his mother, Rhoda, after her husband George died and helped her in the raising of the younger children. At one time, Reese rode for the pony express in the valley.

The second son, Charles, left Rhoda's home for Seattle, Washington, and has never been heard from. The family feels he met with some sort of accident and his life was lost.

Daughter Margaret Ann, married Willard Mace, and they lived out of the valley.

George Matthew Ward, the youngest son, married Rose Lillick, and they farmed on the Little Sleeping Child. Their children were Fred and Marie.

Fred worked for the telephone company in the valley.

Marie married Sid Evans, and Sid worked for the Asgrow Seed Company, later called the Associated Seed company, until retirement. They were transferred from place to place with the company, but upon retirement returned to the valley. They had two children. Their son, Robert, works for the Rocky Mountain Lab as their photographer. Their daughter, Shirley, married Don Dowling and they reside in Hamilton. Two of their four children reside with their families in Hamilton.

RHODA AND GEORGE MARION WARD also had two younger daughters, Letha, and Laura. Laura, the youngest, had to be born in the valley as her birthdate was October 2, 1883. Both of them left the valley as young women, but upon their death were returned to the valley for burial in Riverview Cemetery, alongside their Mother.

THE WARD AND OHL FAMILIES

by Cecelia Ohl

George and Sarah Ebright, their daughters and sons-in-law, Lincoln and Estella Kennedy, Volney and Jessie Muzzey, Thomas and Addie Ward, and Ella Ebright, came to the Bitter Root Valley in 1882, from Missouri and Kansas. They settled in the Corvallis and Victor areas.

George Ebright was a carpenter, building several barns on the West

Side of the Valley. Lincoln Kennedy was a bookkeeper, working for Joe Bowden in Corvallis. Tom Ward worked cutting timbers for the Curlew Mine, and he later had a forty-acre homestead on South Birch Creek.

The Kennedys and Muzzeys moved to Walla Walla, Washington.

The Wards had eight children: four sons, **Wes, Will, Jim, and Tommy,** and four daughters, **Essie** (Tew), **Cecile** (Ohl), **Francis** (Billings) and **Grace.** Tommy and Grace passed away during a diphtheria epidemic. Will passed away from pneumonia while working on the construction of the Big Ditch.

Wes and family moved to California.

Jim Ward married Alma Rennaker. He worked in the timber industry in Darby and Thompson Falls. Alma, his widow now lives in Hamilton.

Essie Tew lived her life in the Corvallis and Hamilton areas. She and Ed Tew had seven children. They are now: Clara Tingley, Addie Lemire, Louise Raymond, Alma Martin, Alice Roberts, Barbara Taylor and Edward Tew.

Cecile Ohl spent her life in the Bitter Root, living for several years on the Ohl homestead in the East Fork, several years on Charlos Heights, and the remainder on Hamilton Heights. She and Joe Ohl had four children: Mary Pendergraft, Lewis Ohl, Glenn Ohl, and Ruth Miller. Lewis and Glenn live in Hamilton, while Mary lives in California.

Francis Billings returned to the Corvallis area in 1954, and lived there until her death in 1992.

JAMES AND NELLIE WEBER

Information gathered by Marilyn Weber Frost

James Weber was born August 13, 1879, in Grampian, Pennsylvania. **He married Nellie Arbuckle** at Elmira, New York on December 21, 1899.

They came to the Bitterroot, traveling by train, along with their first five children: **Kathryn, Fred, Scott, Winifred,** and six week old **Milton,** arriving in **March of 1907.**

They joined James' brothers, Charles and John, in the Stevensville area around Bell Crossing, farming there until 1914. Charles later settled in the St. Ignatius area and John in the Hamilton Heights area.

Sometime in 1910, or 1911, Mr. Weber bought a new Minneapolis Molene tractor. It was delivered by train, and supposedly one of the first gas tractors in the Valley. Iron wheels and even a factory cab. This tractor served in several capacities over the years. As a working tractor tilling fields, then in the 1940's or 50's many of the grand children played on this tractor, grinding it's gears and pretend driving. It now sits on top of a hill as a landmark, on the Brien Weber ranch.

In 1914, the family moved to the Humble ranch, northeast of Corvallis, and in 1916 they purchased the Kern's ranch on Hamilton Heights. By this time, there were six more children: **William, Leland, David, Hallie, Lillian and Jessie.** Lillian living only a couple of days.

In the spring of 1919, tragedy struck and 16-year-old Scott died of Typhoid Fever. Two sisters, Kathryn and Winifred were too ill to be told of Scott's death and did not attend the funeral. Four younger children were also ill, and Mrs. Weber and baby Jessie were recovering. Two weeks later, 13 year old Winifred also died. Mrs. Weber had a serious relapse and there were still five members of the family sick. There were other cases in the Valley that spring, the source thought to be an employee at Sleeping Child Hot Springs who was a carrier.

Later, Kathryn told the story of knowing when Scott had died. They were being cared for in adjoining rooms and she and Winifred and Scott knocked back and forth on the wall between them, until the day Scott no longer returned their knocks.

In 1921, they purchased the ranch and home where they spent their remaining years. This ranch had formerly been a part of the "Hamilton Orchard, Inc." property, and had been owned by Hamilton Thatcher and associates.

Three more children were added, **John** in 1921, **Joseph** in 1923, and **Robert** in 1925, who was stillborn. Ten living children now. A very busy and organized household they farmed, milked cows, raised chickens, pigs, and a large garden. It seems they always had plenty to eat. The kids went to the Hamilton Heights country school, where for many years, Mr. Weber served on the school board. Mr. Weber also served on the first Board of Directors of the Farmers Union.

Everyone worked hard but there was time for fun. Picnics, a quick dip in the Big Ditch, sledding and skiing with homemade skis, kick the can with neighborhood kids, dances at the McCormick dance hall, and family get togethers. Later, in the 1940's and early 1950's, Sunday dinner at Grandma and Grandpa Weber's was a tradition, with often 25-35 adults and grandchildren there for the day. Always lots of good food and fun! Christmas Eve at Grandpa and Grandma Weber's was a tradition too. Santa Claus always made an appearance, and sitting on Santa's lap (if you weren't afraid!) and getting a little bag of goodies, was the main event of the evening for the grandchildren. Santa didn't wear a pretty red suit though. As I remember, it was a long dark grey wool coat, a weird red pointed hat, and a scruffy, scraggly beard!

There was time for mischief too. One story was told of setting the tail feathers of the chickens on fire, then dunking them in the water trough to put the fire out. The rest of the story is that there were a few little butts spanked that day!

Mrs. Weber passed away on January 4, 1958. Kathryn and Milton stayed on the family farm. Kathryn was a 2nd grade teacher in the Corvallis School District for 38½ years, retiring in 1967.

Mr. Weber passed away April 11, 1973, continuing to farm up to the last. Crippled as he was, he loved to be on a tractor out in the field.

FRANK AND DORA PURDY WHITE

Stories related to Wilma Carmichael Allen

Frank Leslie White was born on January 28, 1859, in Springfield, Illinois, the son of James and Ann Whitney White. **Dora Octavia Purdy** was born on October 6, 1861, in Cedar Rapids, Iowa, the daughter of George R. and Aletha L. Benson Purdy. **They married on Christmas Day in 1880,** in Alma, NB. **Their first 10 children were born in Alma, NB,** and near there. Then, **in 1900, they moved to Hamilton, Montana.** By June of **1901,** their 11th child, **Lela Hazel** was born in Hamilton, and in **1903, the 12th and final child, Jack, arrived.**

Seven boys and five girls! Not so unusual in the period of time we are looking at here. Many families had a goodly number of children and the children provided much of the labor. Farming and working hard was the norm and feeding this large family was a challenge in itself.

Frank and Dora first came into Hamilton, then moved out north and east of Corvallis. Their children attended the Dominic School, above Bailey Lane. They worked hard and managed to eke out a living. Next, they moved over on River Road, west and north from Hamilton. And finally, in their aged years, they lived on Hamilton Heights, near to their son, Jesse (aka Skinny) White and his family. It was at this location that Frank died. He had been poorly for sometime, so Skinny arranged with his mother, Dora, that she was to place a light colored cloth on the clothesline if she needed him in a hurry. One day while out working in the field, Skinny and his son, Lloyd, saw the "sign". They hurried right over, only to find that Frank had passed on, and that Dora had totally taken care of the washing, dressing, and "laying out" of his body.

One granddaughter recalls that her grandma Dora always had hard candy that she sucked on. The children were never invited to "have a piece of candy," but always aware that Dora had more in her apron pocket!

Frank and Dora had saved $900.00 in the Corvallis Bank. When the bank closed its doors in 1924, they lost all their savings. Later, they were given back $75.00. George Smith, Skinny's brother-in-law, had sold something and was on his way to put the money in the Corvallis Bank, when he met up with Clay Groff. Mr. Groff was then a Cashier at Farmers State Bank, and informed George that just that day he had purchased all the furniture from the Corvallis Bank, and that it was going to close. Corvallis

Bank was located on the West Side of the street in Corvallis; about where Nancy's Beauty Shop is now.

Children of Frank and Dora White are: **George Elmus** married Martha Ingabor Tincher, **Fred Elmo** married Edna Ruth Haynes, **Maud Violet** married Arthur A. Adair, **Clyde Eugene** married Brennice Alcinda Griggs, **James Raymon** died when very young, **Earl Rexford** married Claire (Ethel) Rockafellow in 1910, **Jesse Lee married to Myrtle Lee Smith** (daughter of Charles Welby Smith) **Ruby Ethel and Pearl Edith, (twins),** Ruby married Eli Branscom Jones and Pearl married Ned Frederick Wood, (their sons William, Floyd, and Gordon still live in the Bitter Root), **Mabel Lin Emily** married Byron Thrailkill (son Raymond lives in Hamilton), **Lela Hazel** married Clarence Logan, and **Jack,** who married Stella Monk.

JESSE LEE WHITE AND MYRTLE SMITH WHITE FAMILY

Myrtle Smith had been born in 1886 at Woodside, MT, attended Fairplay School, and at the age of 18 (July 1915) married Jesse Lee White. They raised their children on a farm out on Hamilton Heights. This farm, on Wilcox Road to the North, was owned by a Mr. Sacket, and was just rented by the White's. When Skinny wanted to buy the property, Myrtle resisted. He refused to buy her a house after that, and they rented all their life. Some of their neighbors were the Bass, Velvick, Wilcox, Yadon and Grimes families. **Four children were born to Myrtle and Jesse** (aka Skinny). They are **Helen, Alice** (Chub), **Lloyd, and Bobby.**

The children all attended Corvallis Schools, and some wonderful stories are told. One of my favorites is about the time that Bobby White and Bob Talbot put the beet pulp behind the steam heaters in the study hall. The odor permeated throughout the whole school, and school had to be shut down for the day! Halloween was a favorite time of year. Lloyd remembers that he and brother, Bobby, went out to tip over outhouses. They didn't want to be suspected, so they even tipped their own over! Once a group of kids put an outhouse up on the roof of Corvallis High School, and once a wagon on the roof of Bowden's Store. Bud Printz had a model A car, and everyone brought rope. They worked like beavers to raise that wagon to the roof of the store!

Alice Ann White, known to her friends and relatives as "Chub", **married Robert Downs Carmichael** in August of 1937. They lived in Corvallis all their lives, except for a few years when first married. Alice became the Postmaster at Corvallis, and retired from this position in 1980. They became parents of two daughters. **Wilma** married Jerry Allen, and **Janice (Judy)** married Terry Park. Their children and grandchildren make five generations of Whites and Smiths born in the Bitter Root Valley.

Helen, Lloyd, and Bobby White all moved out of state.

ALBERT NEWTON WHITESITT FAMILY

Albert Newton Whitesitt was born in Kansas in 1861. He first arrived in the Bitter Root Valley in 1882. He homesteaded in the Willow Creek area in 1884. He returned to Kansas in 1887, where **he married Mary F. Wagy**. They returned to the Bitter Root homestead and as the years passed, four children were born to this marriage. **Inez E.** on December 4, 1887 (married Calvin Hull), **Alvin H.** on November 25, 1891 (married Lyle L. Hawker), **Mabel L.** on December 16, 1894 (married Charles Allan, who was the Corvallis Postmaster) and **Hazel M.** born August 19, 1897 (married Walter Mack).

Daughter Inez and son, Alvin H., stayed in Montana and in the Bitter Root for the rest of their lives.

Alvin Whitesitt farmed the original homestead until his death on July 3, 1938. His wife, Mary, preceded him in death in June of 1933.

After Albert "Newt" Whitesitt's death, his son and daughter-in-law, **Alvin and Lyle Hawker Whitesitt** took over the ranch, which consisted of 440 acres. Alvin and Lyle farmed, and also owned and operated the old Coughenor Store on Bailey Lane and Eastside Highway. They later owned and operated the Corvallis Tavern. They had two daughters and one son: **Mary Virginia Whitesitt Southmayd, Wilma M. Whitesitt Rasmussen** (married Williard "Bill" Rasmussen, parents of LeeAnn and Jay, all of whom continue to live in the Bitterroot), and **John Albert Whitesitt** (living in California until his death on December 7, 1997).

THE WING AND HALL FAMILIES

by Lola Wing Hall in 1979

Walter and Sally Mowrey Wing and their children, Lola, Burl, and Mae, arrived at Victor, in the Bitter Root, in April of 1902, from Luray, Kansas.

I went to school one year at Victor, and one year at Canyon Creek School. Then my dad, Walter, bought a small acreage on Dutch Hill and I finished grade school at the Dutch Hill School. I went to Hamilton High School for two years. Then Dutch Hill consolidated with the Corvallis School, and I finished High School there in May of 1916.

Willard Hall and Lola Wing were married at the home of the bride on March 30, 1919. We moved to a home he had built on the East Bench, northeast of Corvallis, in which we lived for fifty-three years.

To us was born one son, Roscoe. He attended Corvallis School and finished High School there. Roscoe was called to serve his country and while in the service he married Jane Berland of Conrad, MT. And to them were born two sons, Donald and Terry Hall. They also attended the Corvallis schools finishing High School there. They both went to Bozeman to school. Donald quit after two years and went to doing carpenter work. Donald married Nancy Baker of Whitehall, and they have three sons, Gary, Craig, and Brian. Terry transferred from Bozeman to Washington State College at Pullman to be a Veterinarian and he graduated June 1, 1974, with honors. Terry married Elaine Woodhouse and they live in Wibaux, MT.

Willard and I celebrated our fiftieth wedding anniversary on March 30, 1969, with a reception at the Masonic Temple in Corvallis. We sold our ranch in 1972, and bought a mobile home in Hamilton. Willard passed away on Aug. 3, 1973, at the age of 81. I still live in the mobile village.

THE ELIHUE HALL FAMILY HISTORY

by Paul Roscoe Hall, son of Lola Wing Hall

Elihue "Hue" Hall was born in Mexico, Missouri, in 1855. He was one of four children born to Robert Henry Hall and Elizabeth Lockridge Hall. The others were William, Robert, and Becky.

In 1880, Elihue and John Cobb, a close friend, and possible his brother William, came to Montana on one of the paddle wheel boats. They spent most of the summer around Fort Benton, working on a sheep ranch. That winter, they cut wood in Butte. In the spring, Elihue went back to

Elihue and Eliza Hall.

Missouri. I don't know about the others.

Nothing is known about Elihue until 1887, when he married Eliza Herring, possibly in Fulton, Missouri. They had four children, Rocena, Willard, Guy, and Paul. The family moved to the Bitter Root in February of 1902, and worked for a year or so for John Hay. The Hay place is the limestone house across the road and east of the Corvallis High School. In 1905, they purchased a farm northeast of Corvallis, where they lived for many years. Elihue and Eliza's children grew up and married. Rocena married Bill James, who fired the boiler at the steam laundry, located on the corner where the Citizens State Bank is now located and they had one daughter, Cecil. Willard married Lola Wing, daughter of Walter and Sarah Wing, on March 29, 1919, and they had one child, Paul Roscoe. Guy married Ella Knaak on May 22, 1919, and they had one child, Lewis. Paul moved to California in 1919, and married Alyce Roberts about 1925. They did not have any children.

Elihue's brother, William, married Margaret Cobb. Margaret is the sister of John Milton Cobb. William died in 1904, and Margaret in 1916. They are buried in the Corvallis Cemetery. William and Margaret had two children, Mark and Maude. Mark had four children; Milton, Yvonne, Georgia and Mark, Jr. Maude married Frank Printz and they have three children; Cozette, Carl, and Willie.

Elihue's brother, Bob, married Lilly Sherrill. They went back to

The wedding party, March 31, 1919. Standing, left to right, are Walter Wing, Sarah Wing, Eliza Hall, Elihue Hall and Bill James. Seated, left to right, are Cecil James, Lola Wing Hall, Willard Hall and Guy Hall.

Kansas City, and he was killed in an industrial accident. I do not know what became of her. There were no children.

Elihue's sister, Becky, married Frank Farthing. They were only in the Bitter Root a short time and returned to Missouri.

April 4, 1919, Corvallis, Montana
Newspaper account of the pretty wedding of
MISS LOLA WING TO WILLARD HALL

One of the prettiest weddings of the year occurred Sunday, March 30, 1919, at the home of Mr. and Mrs. Walter Wing, when their daughter, Miss Lola Wing, was given in marriage to Willard Hall. At noon, Mrs. Paul Klise softly played the Lohengrin Wedding March and the bridal party, led by Rev. W. D. Lear, came before the company of twenty relatives and stood beneath a lovely wedding bell, while the ring service was said. Miss Mae Wing acted as bridesmaid and Paul Hall was groomsman. A sumptuous wedding dinner followed the ceremony and soon after the happy pair left by automobile for a destination unannounced. After a few days, they will be at home in the bungalow cottage recently erected and furnished by the groom on his father's ranch, four miles northeast of town.

The bride is a 1917 graduate of Corvallis High School, and she has had a special course in domestic science at a scientist academy in this state. The groom but recently returned from Vancouver, having been honorably discharged from service with the Spruce Division of the Engineers. Before entering the service he had been one of the Valley's most enterprising young ranchers, and he will be employed with his brothers on his father's ranch.

YERIAN FAMILY

as told to Marilynn Frost by family members

Asa Ishem Yerian was born August 12, 1869 in Topeka, Kansas. He married Amanda Catherine White on August 27, 1900 at Carthage, Missouri.

They came to the Bitter Root by train in 1909, along with their first four children, John, Burney, Ray and Nona.

Asa and his family settled in the Hamilton area where Asa started a delivery business. When the train would arrive in Hamilton, Asa would hurry to the train depot, back the dray wagon down to the train and throw the weight out. This was a 20# weight that snapped onto the bit and dropped to the ground. As there was no hitching post, this was his method of holding the team while he loaded the wagon. He loaded merchandise to be delivered to the businesses and also loaded the possessions of families arriving in the Bitterroot. His wagon was a 5th wheel wagon, 14' long and 4' to 5' wide. It had removable stakes on the sides, so he could slide heavy stuff onto the wagon, then replace the stakes. He delivered as far South as the West Fork and the Big Hole, stopping at the Halfway House to spend the night, then traveling on the next day. This halfway house was just above the present Sula Ranger Station. Of course, this was on the old road, not the Lost Trail Highway that we travel today.

Mrs. Yerian took in laundry, doing the wash on the old wash board. She also made barrels of pickles which the kids sold and delivered. A story was told of someone asking Ray where he got the money to buy a new jacket for his eighth grade graduation. He told them he got it from selling pickles!

While living in Hamilton, three more children Nellie, Harry and Margaret were born. Shortly, thereafter, the family moved to a place southeast of Corvallis on a lane, which has since been named Harvey Lane. Over the next eight years, four more children were born: Ethel, Charles, Asa Jr., and Robert. A total of 11 children. Like most families during this period of time, life was a struggle and everyone worked hard, often 16 to 17 hours a day. They did not have many material things, but always food on the table. They used lard bucket lids for plates. They grew a large garden and canned hundreds of ½ gallon jars of fruits and vegetables. They always raised pigs, butchering and salt curing the meat. Each year, sharing part of their harvest, Mr. Yerian donated a pig to the Red Cross.

In 1933, they bought 30 acres in the Hamilton Heights area for back taxes, and over a period of years they added to this acreage and spent most of their remaining life on this farm.

Asa always enjoyed horses. All the farming was done with teams of horses and his only transportation was by his horse and buggy. Over the years he maintained a stable of racehorses, buying, trading, training and racing them. Whenever there was a race card staged in the valley or somewhere nearby, Mr. Yerian was there running his horses or watching the events with a keen and knowing interest. Sons Burney, Charles, Asa Jr., Robert, several grandchildren and even great grandchildren share this interest in horses today. An interesting tidbit recalled by some of the family was that Mrs. Yerian was always afraid and uncomfortable around horses!

Asa Yerian passed away in Hamilton in 1957, and his wife, Amanda, died in 1967.

P. R. YOUNG

From History of Montana 1885, compiled by M. A. Leeson
Warner, Beers & Co., Chicago, Publisher
"Personal History and Reminiscences" (p.1320)

P. R. Young, Corvallis, born December 2, 1817, in Vermont, was the son of Phinias and Sarah Young, being the youngest of five children. In youth he clerked in a store and learned something of carpentering, and in April of 1850 started for California via Panama, stopping for four months at the latter place where he and his brother built a house for the agent of the steamship company.

Mr. Young arrived in San Francisco on September 2, 1850, and he remained in California until 1860, when he went to Portland, OR, and thence to Lewiston, ID. On October 6, 1863, he left Elk City, Idaho in company with Daniel Kinney, Matthew Adams and John Murphy, packers; a cook named Bill; and a train of thirteen animals; intending to go to Virginia City, Montana. Before reaching the Clearwater they met the men who had murdered Magruder, and consulted with them in reference to a camping place. After they traveled about three weeks a violent snowstorm set in and they lost the trail and were obliged to cache their goods. On October 17, Adams, Murphy, and Bill started out to find grain, leaving Young and Kinney behind with the animals where they had agreed to wait for ten days.

Young and Kinney waited until after the expiration of the time agreed upon, and having in the meantime found the trail, took four animals and started on their journey. After a day or two they lost the trail and in going around a point of rocks, one horse went over the precipice and two days were spent in trying to get their remaining animals out of this place. They were compelled to abandon them, and taking just their guns, axes, provisions and blankets, pushed on.

The snow by this time was waist deep, it having snowed for fifteen days. At night they would dig a hole in the snow and in this build a fire which was kept burning all night. On November 15, they cooked their last cake and ate a portion of it. Kinney went out to procure game, and they did not leave camp until nearly noon; soon after which they came across the newly-made trail of two men which they recognized as that of Adams and Murphy, and at once started after them, but after having traveled about a quarter of a mile with so little progress, it became evident it would be impossible to overtake them. Several shots were fired but they received no reply.

After camping for the night, Young and Kinney could hear the others chopping wood, and guns were fired again, but to no purpose. A note was written and placed on a stick and planted in the snow as a last hope of catching their attention. They then pushed forward, without food for five days, then the flour sack was scraped and from nine spoonfuls of lumps thus obtained, pots of porridge were made at intervals of five days to December 1, 1863. During this time they made but a few hundred yards per day.

One night the snow fell so fast they were unable to keep a fire, and both were badly frozen, Kinney being so badly frozen that he had no use of his hands, became so weak they could go no further, and Kinney being unable to rise, begged Young to push on and leave him behind. This Young refused to do, and for two days was barely able to collect firewood enough to keep the fire alive, but felt that he could not do so another day — his hands being so badly swollen that he could hardly hold the ax.

P. R. Young tied up a diary with his own and his companion's names written plainly on the fly leaf and the date and their condition, together with a small Bible in a handkerchief, and hung this on the limb of a tree overhanging the trail. While meditating on their condition, Young heard voices, and by almost superhuman exertion, managed to rise up far enough to see out of the hole, and a glad surprise met his gaze. Murphy and Adams were coming down the trail, a moment more and Murphy jumped into the hole with them and was greeted with "God bless you, John, have you anything to eat?" A little coffee and a spoonful of boiled wheat were given them. Adams hurried down the mountains to where they had flour and returned with this by sundown, and as soon as the moon rose Adams started for the Bitter Root Valley, sixty or seventy miles away, for assistance.

On arriving he was so exhausted he could not return, but Joe Blodgett and Fred Loveland started back with provisions. A sled was constructed with poles and a blanket and Kinney was drawn on this. When Mr. Young's boots were taken off, the bones of his big toes protruded through the flesh half an inch, and his legs to his knees were badly frozen and raw, and covered with blood; his feet were tied up in rags, and in this condition he hobbled along for two days. The party followed the trail and then abandoned it and went down into the canyon, thinking the horses could be gotten, but the sick men could go no further. Blodgett leaving Loveland to take care of them, went on to find help — for five days they waited for help, and were three days again without anything to eat, when they were taken to the Bitter Root Valley by A. Talman, Loveland and Brown.

It had been forty days since they had lain down to sleep. Kinney lived but ten weeks. Mr. Young recovered and still lives to tell the tale. He is now engaged in the mercantile business at Corvallis.

Index

M

N